Variation across speech and writing

Variation across speech and writing

Douglas Biber

Department of Linguistics, University of Southern California

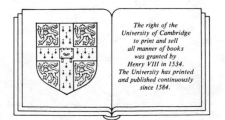

The right of the
University of Cambridge
to print and sell
all manner of books
was granted by
Henry VIII in 1534.
The University has printed
and published continuously
since 1584.

CAMBRIDGE UNIVERSITY PRESS

Cambridge
New York   New Rochelle   Melbourne   Sydney

Published by the Press Syndicate of the University of Cambridge
The Pitt Building, Trumpington Street, Cambridge CB2 1RP
32 East 57th Street, New York, NY 10022, USA
10 Stamford Road, Oakleigh, Melbourne, 3166, Australia

First published 1988

Printed in Great Britain at
the University Press, Cambridge

British Library cataloguing in publication data

Biber, Douglas
Variation across speech and writing.
1. spoken language related to written language.
I. Title
001.54

Library of Congress cataloguing in publication data

Biber, Douglas.
Variation across speech and writing / Douglas Biber.
    p.   cm.
Bibliography.
Includes index.
ISBN 0 521 32071 2
1. Language and languages – Variation.   2. Oral communication.
3. Written communication. I. Title.
P120.V37B54 1988
001.54–dc19   87–38213

ISBN 0 521 32071 2

VN

For my parents,
Martha and Herb Biber

Contents

Figures

Tables

Acknowledgments

I first became interested in the relationship between speech and writing during my dissertation research, and several of the methodological tools used in the present study were developed at that time. More recently, my dissertation advisors have become my academic colleagues, so that I owe them thanks for both their earlier guidance and their continuing criticism and support. In particular, Edward Finegan, Elinor Ochs, Edward Purcell, and June Shoup have helped me from the earliest stages of this research. Ed Finegan deserves special thanks, since he has been intimately involved in all stages of the research study presented here. As my dissertation chair, he helped conceptualize the methodological approach used here; for example, Ed was the first to suggest that I use computational tools to analyze spoken and written texts, and he went to considerable effort to help obtain computerized text corpora for analysis. He has worked with me on numerous papers and research studies, and his criticisms have ranged from writing style and rhetorical organization to theoretical interpretation and conceptual presentation of results. Finally, over the last several years Ed and I have collaborated on many related studies of variation in English. It is not possible to isolate individual effects of these contributions; they have all influenced the final form of the present study.

Several other colleagues helped directly with the present book. Pat Clancy and Gunnel Tottie both read the manuscript and made especially detailed and helpful comments. Bill Grabe and Niko Besnier helped me through numerous conversations as well as their comments on the manuscript. Larry Ploetz answered numerous computer-related questions during the development of the linguistic analysis programs used here.

Other colleagues at U.S.C. did not help directly with this book but offered their friendship and support; of these, I want to single out Steve Krashen, Larry Hyman, and Joseph Aoun.

Finally, this book would not have been possible without the continued support and understanding of my wife, Teresa, and my children, David and Martha. Although their contributions are less tangible, they are in many ways greater than any of the others.

Part I: Background concepts and issues

1 Introduction: textual dimensions and relations

1.1 Introduction

A considerable body of research in the humanities and social sciences has dealt with the similarities and differences between speech and writing. Work in history, sociology, anthropology, psychology, education, comparative literature, and linguistics has described ways in which the choice between speech and writing is closely related to developments in other social institutions. For example, the development of widespread alphabetic literacy in ancient Greece was probably a catalyst for other social and intellectual developments there. Widespread literacy enabled a fuller understanding and participation by citizens in the workings of government, which might have promoted a democratic form of government in which citizens play a relatively active role. Literacy enabled a permanent, accurate record of ideas and the possibility of knowledge without a living 'knower'. As such it probably aided in the transition from 'myth' to 'history' and the development of critical attitudes towards knowledge. Prior to literacy and a permanent record of beliefs and knowledge, a society can alter its beliefs and not be faced with the possibility of a contradiction; competing ideas which evolve slowly over generations will be accepted as equally factual when there is no contradictory record of earlier ideas. Written records, however, force us to acknowledge the contradictory ideas of earlier societies and thus to regard knowledge with a critical and somewhat skeptical attitude. For example, we know that earlier societies believed that the earth was flat, because these beliefs are permanently recorded in writing. The permanency of writing thus confronts us with the incorrect 'knowledge' of earlier generations and thereby fosters a generally critical attitude towards knowledge.

The permanency of writing also enables the dissection of texts, so that ideas can be critically examined in the abstract and the logical relations among ideas can be discussed. Literacy enables language itself to be the

3

object of inquiry. These possibilities helped foster the development of philosophy as we know it. Similarly, the use of literacy aided the development of new literary forms. Oral literature tends to be poetic, because poetic forms are more easily memorized and transmitted from one generation to the next. The permanency of written texts enables an accurate transmission of any literary form, enabling experimentation with non-poetic types. Although the transition to literacy did not by itself cause any of these intellectual or social developments, it seems to have been an important catalyst.[1]

The transition to literacy seems to have important consequences for individuals as well as societies. Some researchers have claimed that radically different thought processes are enabled by literacy. In particular, it has been claimed that abstract, 'decontextualized' thought depends on literacy, so that non-literate individuals can think in only concrete, contextualized ways. This claim is difficult to evaluate because literacy in Western culture is always confounded with formal education, and thus intellectual differences between literate and non-literate individuals might be due to either the acquisition of literacy or the educational process itself. Research in West Africa by Scribner and Cole (1981) has helped to isolate the effects of literacy from those of formal schooling. The Vai people, who live in Liberia, have developed an indigenous writing system that is used only for traditional, non-academic purposes. Vai literates are taught how to write on an individual basis apart from any other formal schooling. Other members of this tribe become literate in Arabic to study the Quran, or in English by attendance at government schools. Scribner and Cole found that there are specific intellectual abilities which are enhanced by each type of literacy, depending on the particular functions served. For example, Quranic literacy among the Vai greatly enhances memorization abilities because beginning students learn to 'read' the Quran without understanding, and they use their readings to help memorize large portions of the text. Consequences of this type are minor and quite specific to different types of literacy; Scribner and Cole found no global intellectual consequences of literacy apart from the influence of formal schooling.

Although the primary intellectual consequences of literacy are subsumed under those of formal education, there is obviously a very close relationship between school success and literacy. Children who fail at

---

[1] See Goody and Watt (1963), Goody (1977), Stubbs (1980), Ong (1982), and Street (1984) for further discussion of the social and cultural consequences of literacy.

reading and writing fail at school; children who fail at school don't learn how to read. It is difficult to establish a causal relationship here, but schooling is inextricably bound to literacy in Western culture. Several researchers have investigated the acquisition of literacy, and its relation to school success, in Western societies. Some studies describe the problems caused by reliance on spoken language strategies in the compositions of basic writers. Other researchers, such as Heath and Wells, emphasize that many successful students acquire the language-use strategies associated with literacy long before they can actually read and write, and that these strategies are crucially important to literacy acquisition and the types of language use required for school tasks. These patterns of language use can be conveyed by reading to children in the home, but they are further developed by decontextualized spoken interactions; for example, hypothetical discussion of what a storybook character might have done in a particular situation. Students who begin school 'literate', in the sense that they already realize that language can be used for abstract, decontextualized purposes, are the ones who adapt most easily to the requirements of Western education.

Studies similar to these, which look for social or intellectual correlates of writing as distinct from speaking, are found throughout the humanities and social sciences. Given this wide range of interest, it might be expected that the linguistic characteristics of spoken and written language have been thoroughly analyzed. There have, in fact, been many linguistic studies of speech and writing, but there is little agreement on the salient characteristics of the two modes. The general view is that written language is structurally elaborated, complex, formal, and abstract, while spoken language is concrete, context-dependent, and structurally simple. Some studies, though, have found almost no linguistic differences between speech and writing, while others actually claim that speech is more elaborated and complex than writing.

There has also been considerable disagreement concerning the need for a linguistic comparison of speech and writing. Historically, academics have regarded writing, in particular literary works, as the true form of language, while speech has been considered to be unstable, degenerate and not worthy of study. In the nineteenth century this situation began to change when linguists such as Grimm in Germany began to study speech in its own right. The development of phonetics as a separate discipline in Britain, primarily through the work of Henry Sweet and Daniel Jones, further encouraged linguists to study speech. These research trends, however, did not result in linguistic comparisons of speech and writing. Rather, by the early twentieth century, linguists uniformly regarded speech as primary and writing as a secondary form of language derived from speech; thus only speech was considered worth serious linguistic analysis. This bias can be traced from the time of Sapir up to the present, for example:

Sapir: *writing is 'visual speech symbolism' (1921:19–20)*

Bloomfield: *'writing is not language, but merely a way of recording language by visible marks' (1933:21)*

Hall: *'speech is fundamental and writing . . . only a secondary derivative' (1964:8–9)*

Postal: *'writing is a crude way of representing linguistic structure rather than a sign system with a direct relation to the world' (1966:91, n. 20)*

Fillmore: *written communication is 'derivative of the face-to-face conversational norm' (1981:153)*

Aronoff: *notes 'the undoubtedly correct observation that spoken language is "true" language, while written language is an artifact' (1985:28)*

Assuming this secondary, derivative nature of written language, there was no motivation within structural linguistics for comparison of speech and writing.

Although the bias that speech is primary over writing has been extremely important in guiding research efforts within linguistics, it has not been widely accepted outside of linguistics. In fact, the historical view that written, literary language is true language continues as the dominant lay perception to the present time. Our children need to study English at school, which includes written composition and the prescriptive rules of writing, not speech. We criticize immigrant children for not knowing 'English' when they are relatively fluent in a conversation; the problem is that they are not literate in English. We expect our grammars and dictionaries to present the correct forms of written language; when dictionaries present both literate and colloquial vocabulary, they are severely criticized for destroying the standards of English, as happened to

Webster's Third, which has been described as a 'disappointment', 'a scandal and a disaster' (see discussion in Finegan 1980). In our business, legal, and political systems, written commitments are binding and 'real' while spoken commitments are often ignored. As teachers, we explain to children that words like *know* have a silent [k], and words like *doubt* have a silent [b]. Sometimes we even change our pronunciation to reflect an unusual spelling; for example, *often* is now frequently pronounced with a [t], and *palm* with an [l], although these segments were not pronounced at some earlier stages of English. Thus, although speech is claimed to have linguistic primacy, writing is given social priority by most adults in Western cultures.[2]

Even within structural linguistics, researchers have not been entirely consistent regarding the primacy of speech. In particular, there has been a gap between theory and practice in recent syntactic research. In theory, writing is disregarded as secondary and derivative from speech. In practice, however, speech is also disregarded as unsystematic and not representative of the true linguistic structure of a language. This view is especially prominent within the generative-transformationalist paradigm, where grammatical intuitions are the primary data to be analyzed. Although these intuitions are typically collected by means of verbal elicitation, they are in many respects more like writing than speech. Thus the data for analysis within this paradigm deliberately exclude performance errors of 'actual speech', dialect, and register variation, and any linguistic features that depend on a discourse or situational context for interpretation. Although these data are not taken from actual speech or actual writing, they are much closer to stereotypical writing than speech in their form.

All of these perspectives regard either speech or writing as primary and representative of 'true' language; none grants independent status to both speech and writing. However, given the range of arguments on both sides of this issue, it might well be the case that neither speech nor writing is primary; that they are rather different systems, both deserving careful analysis. This is in fact the view advocated by Hymes and other researchers studying communicative competence. That is, in addition to the knowledge that all speakers have about the grammatical structure of

---

[2] The discussion here owes much to Stubbs (1980). Other works dealing with the primacy of speech or writing include Householder (1971), Vachek (1973), Basso (1974), Schafer (1981), Akinnaso (1982), and Stubbs (1982).

their language, speakers also have extensive knowledge about the use of their language. The former knowledge is grammatical competence, which includes the traditional areas of phonology, syntax, and semantics. The latter knowledge is known as 'communicative competence', and includes formal knowledge of the range of speech-act variation, dialect variation, and register variation, as well as knowledge of when these different linguistic forms are appropriate. Grammatical competence is concerned with the linguistic structure of 'grammatical' utterances; communicative competence is concerned with the form and use of all language – both speech and writing. Within this framework, neither speech nor writing needs to be considered primary to the exclusion of the other. Rather, both require analysis, and the linguistic comparison of the two modes becomes an important question.

Of course, in terms of human development, speech has primary status. Culturally, humans spoke long before they wrote, and individually, children learn to speak before they read or write. All children learn to speak (barring physical disabilities); many children do not learn to read and write. All cultures make use of spoken communication; many languages do not have a written form. From a historical and developmental perspective, speech is clearly primary.

Once a culture has developed written communication, however, there is no reason to regard writing as secondary within that context. It has long been known that cultures exploit variation in linguistic form for functional purposes. For example, variation between lexical items such as *lorry* and *truck* functions to mark geographical differences; variation between pronunciations such as [ka:] versus [kar] and [ðis] versus [dis] functions to mark social differences; variation in address terms, such as *Dr. Jones* versus *Sue*, functions to mark the formality of the situation and the social role relationship between speaker and listener. Similarly, once a culture develops a written form in addition to a spoken form, the two modes come to be exploited for different communicative purposes. Although either speech or writing *can* be used for almost any communicative need, we do not in fact use the two forms interchangeably. Rather, depending on the situational demands of the communicative task, we readily choose one mode over the other. Usually this choice is unconscious, since only one of the modes is suitable or practical. For example, we have no trouble choosing between leaving a note for someone or speaking to the person face-to-face; the situation dictates the mode of communication. Similarly, we have no problem deciding between writing an academic exposition for an audience and addressing the audience by means of a spoken lecture. We could in fact write a lecture or a note to a physically present audience, but this would take more effort and time than required, and it would fail to take advantage of the opportunities for interaction. Conversely, speaking a lecture or note to an addressee who is separated by time or place is usually not possible at all; apart from the use of telephones and tape recorders, the written mode is required in situations of this type. These simple examples illustrate the fact that the two modes of communication have quite different strengths and weaknesses, and they therefore tend to be used in complementary situations. From this perspective, neither can be said to be primary; they are simply different. The linguistic characteristics of each mode deserve careful attention, and the relationship between the two modes must be investigated empirically rather than assumed on an a priori basis.

1.2 Dimensions and relations

In the present book, spoken and written texts are compared along 'dimensions' of linguistic variation. Researchers have considered texts to be related along particular situational or functional parameters, such as formal/informal, interactive/non-interactive, literary/colloquial, restricted/elaborated. These parameters can be considered as dimensions because they define continuums of variation rather than discrete poles. For example, although it is possible to describe a text as simply formal or informal, it is more accurate to describe it as more or less formal; formal/informal can be considered a continuous dimension of variation.

I will illustrate the concept of 'dimension' in this section by analysis of a few linguistic features in four texts. This illustration greatly over-simplifies the linguistic character of the dimensions actually found in English. Chapters 5–8 present a full analysis based on the distribution of 67 linguistic features in 481 texts. The discussion here thus provides a conceptual description of dimensions, rather than actually describing the complex patterns of variation in English speech and writing.

Following are two quite distinct text samples, which differ along several dimensions. Readers should identify some of the differences between them before proceeding to the following discussion.

Text 1.1: Conversation – comparing home-made beer to other brands

A:	*I had a bottle of ordinary Courage's light ale, which I*	1
	always used to like, and still don't dislike, at Simon	2
	Hale's the other day –	3
	simply because I'm, mm, going through a lean period at	4
	the moment waiting for this next five gallons to be ready,	5
	you know.	6
B:	*mm*	7
A:	*It's just in the bottle stage. You saw it the other night.*	8
B:	*yeah*	9
A:	*and, mm I mean, when you get used to that beer, which*	10
	at its best is simply, you know, superb, it really is.	11
B:	*mm*	12
A:	*you know, I've really got it now, really, you know, got*	13
	it to a T.	14
B:	*yeah*	15
A:	*and mm, oh, there's no, there's no comparison. It tasted*	16
	so watery, you know, lifeless.	17
B:	*mm*	18

Text 1.2: Scientific exposition

Evidence has been presented for a supposed randomness in   1
the movement of plankton animals. If valid, this implies that   2
migrations involve kineses rather than taxes (Chapter 10).   3
However, the data cited in support of this idea comprise   4
without exception observations made in the laboratory.   5

Text 1.1 is taken from an ordinary, face-to-face conversation between friends. It represents the type of communication that we all experience every day. Text 1.2 is much more specialized, coming from a scientific exposition. In contrast to the conversation, relatively few speakers of English commonly read texts like 1.2, and an extremely small proportion are expected to write texts of this type. We might thus distinguish texts 1.1 and 1.2 on a dimension of common versus specialized.

These texts might also be contrasted on a dimension of unplanned versus planned. In text 1.1, speaker A talks without careful planning. At one point he switches topic in the middle of a sentence – in line 10, he begins a thought with *when you get used to that beer*, and two utterances later, in line 16, he completes the sentence with *there's no comparison*; in between these two utterances he notes that his homemade beer is superb when made properly (lines 10–11), and that he really knows how to make the brew now (lines 13–14). Text 1.2 is quite different, having a very careful logical progression indicating careful planning. An idea is presented in lines 1–2, implications of the idea are given in line 3, and the idea is qualified in lines 4–5. This logical progression continues in the rest of text 1.2.

There are several other dimensions that these two texts could be compared along. For example, text 1.1 is interactive while text 1.2 is not; in text 1.1, speaker A refers directly to himself and to speaker B (*I* and *you*), and speaker B responds to A. Text 1.1 is dependent on the immediate situation to a greater extent than text 1.2; in text 1.1, speaker A assumes that B can identify *Simon Hale's* (line 3), *the other day* (line 3), *this next five gallons* (line 5), and *the other night* (line 8). The speaker in text 1.1 displays his feelings enthusiastically and emphatically, while the feelings of the writer in text 1.2 are less apparent; speaker A in text 1.1 repeatedly emphasizes his point with *really*, *simply*, and *you know* (lines 4, 6, 11, 13, 17).

When only two texts are compared, these parameters seem to be dichotomies. If we add a third text, however, we begin to see that these parameters define continuous dimensions. Thus, consider text 1.3 below:

Text 1.3: Panel discussion – discussing corporal punishment as a deterrent to crime

W: **But Mr. Nabarro, we know that you believe this.**

L: **quite**

W: **The strange fact is, that you still haven't given us a reason for it. The only reason you've given for us is, if I may spell it out to you once more, is the following:**
the only crime for which this punishment was a punishment, after its abolition, decreased for eleven years.

You base on this the inference that if it had been applied
to crimes it never had been applied to, they wouldn't have
increased.
Now this seems to me totally tortuous.

Text 1.3 is intermediate between texts 1.1 and 1.2 with respect to the
dimensions outlined above. Text 1.3 is certainly not a common everyday
communication like text 1.1, but it is not as specialized as text 1.2; text 1.3
is relatively unplanned, but it is more carefully organized than text 1.1;
text 1.3 is interactive, but not to the extent of text 1.1; text 1.3 shows little
dependence on the immediate situation, but more so than text 1.2; and for
the most part, the main speaker in text 1.3 does not reveal his own
feelings, although they are more apparent than those of the writer in text
1.2. Text 1.3 is more like text 1.1 with respect to some of these
dimensions, and more like text 1.2 with respect to others. However, it has
an intermediate characterization with respect to texts 1.1 and 1.2 on each
dimension, indicating that these are continuous parameters rather than
simple dichotomies.

To this point, we have discussed the notion of dimension from a
situational or functional point of view. It is also possible to discuss this
notion from a strictly linguistic perspective. In the same way that texts
can be described and compared in terms of their situational characterization, there are dimensions that compare texts in terms of their linguistic
characterization, e.g., nominal versus verbal, or structurally complex
versus structurally simple. Thus consider texts 1.1, 1.2, and 1.3 again. A
general impression of text 1.1 is that it is verbal rather than nominal (i.e.,
many verbs, few nouns) and that it is structurally simple (e.g., little
phrasal or clausal elaboration). Text 1.2, on the other hand, seems to be
extremely nominal and structurally complex, while text 1.3 seems to have
a linguistic characterization between these two. Several questions arise,
though: (1) What evidence can we give to support these linguistic
impressions? (2) Do these characterizations represent a single linguistic
dimension, or two dimensions, or more than two? How can a researcher
determine how many linguistic dimensions are required to account for
the variation among a set of texts? (3) Are there other linguistic
dimensions that are not represented by the above linguistic impressions?
If so, how can they be discovered?

I develop an overall empirical approach in the present book that
addresses these questions (cf. Section 1.3, Section 3.5, and Chapter 4).

The raw data of this approach are frequency counts of particular linguistic features. Frequency counts give an exact, quantitative characterization of a text, so that different texts can be compared in very precise terms. By themselves, however, frequency counts cannot identify linguistic dimensions. Rather, a linguistic dimension is determined on the basis of a consistent co-occurrence pattern among features. That is, when a group of features consistently co-occur in texts, those features define a linguistic dimension. It should be noted that the direction of analysis here is opposite from that typically used in studies of language use. Most analyses begin with a situational or functional distinction and identify linguistic features associated with that distinction as a second step. For example, researchers have given priority to functional dimensions such as formal/informal, restricted/elaborated, or involved/detached, and subsequently they have identified the linguistic features associated with each dimension. In this approach, the groupings of features are identified in terms of shared function, but they do not necessarily represent linguistic dimensions in the above sense; that is these groupings of features do not necessarily represent those features that co-occur frequently in texts. The opposite approach is used here: quantitative techniques are used to identify the groups of features that actually co-occur in texts, and afterwards these groupings are interpreted in functional terms. The linguistic dimension rather than functional dimension is given priority.

This approach is based on the assumption that strong co-occurrence patterns of linguistic features mark underlying functional dimensions. Features do not randomly co-occur in texts. If certain features consistently co-occur, then it is reasonable to look for an underlying functional influence that encourages their use. In this way, the functions are not posited on an a priori basis; rather they are required to account for the observed co-occurrence patterns among linguistic features.

In fact, there are several unaddressed issues surrounding dimensions identified on functional bases. Although many functional dimensions have been proposed in recent years, few researchers have attempted to relate them to one another or rank them in importance. Consider the following partial list of functional dimensions: informal/formal, restricted/elaborated, contextualized/decontextualized, involved/detached, integrated/fragmented, abstract/concrete, colloquial/literary. Are these all separate dimensions? Do some of them overlap? Are they all equally important? Are they all well-defined in terms of their linguistic characterization? The approach used here begins to answer these questions. By defining 'dimension' from a strictly linguistic perspective, it is possible to identify the set of dimensions required to account for the linguistic variation within a set of texts. Each dimension comprises an independent group of co-occurring linguistic features, and each co-occurrence pattern can be interpreted in functional terms. The result is an empirical assessment of how many independent dimensions there are; an assessment of which functions are independent and which are associated with the same dimension; and an assessment of the relative importance of different dimensions.

The discussion can be made more concrete by considering some frequency counts in texts 1.1, 1.2, and 1.3. In Table 1.1, I list the frequencies for four linguistic features: passive constructions (including post-nominal modifiers, e.g., *the data [which are] cited*), nominalizations, first and second person pronouns, and contractions. The table includes the raw frequency count and the frequency per 100 words; I use the frequency counts normalized to a text of 100 words to compare the three texts.[3]

The conversational text (1.1) and scientific text (1.2) are quite different with respect to these linguistic features. The scientific text has almost seven passives per 100 words and eleven nominalizations per 100 words; the conversation has no passives and less than one nominalization per 100 words. Assuming that these two texts are representative of their kind, their frequency counts indicate that passives and nominalizations tend to co-occur and thus belong to the same linguistic dimension – when a text has many passives, it also has many nominalizations, as in the scientific text; when a text has few passives, it also has few nominalizations, as in the conversational text. Similarly, these two texts indicate that first and second person pronouns and contractions belong to the same dimension – when a text has many first and second person pronouns, it also has many contractions, as in the conversational text; when a text has few first and

---

[3] Raw frequency counts cannot be used for comparison across texts because they are not all the same length. That is, long texts will tend to have higher frequencies simply because there is more opportunity for a feature to occur; in these cases, the higher count does not indicate a more frequent use of the feature. Comparing the frequency per 100 words eliminates this bias. These normalized frequencies are computed as follows:

(actual frequency count ÷ total words in text) × *100*

For example, the normalized frequency of contractions in text 1.1 is:

(6 ÷ 118) × *100* = *5.1*

Table 1.1 *Frequency counts for texts 1.1, 1.2, and 1.3 (raw frequency count followed by normalized count per 100 words)*

	passives	nominal-izations	1st & 2nd person pronouns	contrac-tions
conversation	0 / 0	1 / .84	12 / 10.2	6 / 5.1
sci. prose	3 / 6.8	5 / 11.4	0 / 0	0 / 0
panel disc.	2 / 2.2	4 / 4.3	10 / 10.8	3 / 3.2

second person pronouns, it also has few contractions, as in the scientific text.

In addition, we might conclude from these two texts that the passive–nominalization dimension and the pronoun–contraction dimension were in fact parts of the same dimension, because there is a consistent co-occurrence pattern between them. That is, when a text has many passives, it has many nominalizations as well as markedly few pronouns and contractions; conversely, when a text has few passives, it has few nominalizations as well as markedly many pronouns and contractions. For these two texts, knowing the frequency of any single feature allows the researcher to predict the frequencies of the other three features, indicating that they comprise a unified dimension. Passives/ nominalizations and pronouns/contractions are not independently related in these two texts – a marked presence of the one set predicts a marked absence of the other. In this sense, dimensions encompass features that consistently occur together and those that consistently complement one another.

Consideration of the panel discussion (text 1.3), however, indicates that passives/nominalizations and pronouns/contractions belong to two separate dimensions. Unlike either the conversation or the scientific text, the panel discussion has high frequencies of all four features. This text confirms the existence of two basic co-occurrence patterns – when a text has many passives, it has many nominalizations; when a text has many first and second person pronouns, it has many contractions. But, the panel discussion shows that these two co-occurrence patterns do not have a consistent relation to one another. It is possible for a text to have many passives/nominalizations and few pronouns/contractions (e.g., the scientific text); it is possible to have many pronouns/contractions and few passives/nominalizations (the conversation); and it is also possible to have many occurrences of both sets of features (the panel discussion). In fact, it is possible for a text to have few passives/nominalizations and few pronouns/contractions, as the following text sample from a novel shows:

Text 1.4: Fiction – K 4

> **She became aware that the pace was slackening; now the coach stopped. The moment had come. Upon the ensuing interview the future would depend. Outwardly she was calm, but her heart was beating fast, and the palms of her hands were damp.**

This text has no passives, no nominalizations, no first or second person pronouns, and no contractions. While this distribution further confirms the two basic co-occurrence patterns identified above – passives co-occurring with nominalizations and pronouns co-occurring with contractions – it also confirms the conclusion that these two patterns belong to two independent dimensions. These two dimensions can be plotted to illustrate their independent status, as in Figures 1.1, 1.2, and 1.3. Figure 1.1 shows that conversation and fiction are alike with respect to the passive/nominalization dimension, as are the scientific text and panel discussion. Figure 1.2 shows a different pattern for the dimension comprising first and second person pronouns and contractions: the conversation and panel discussion are alike, as are the scientific and fictional text. The pattern defined by these two dimensions together is shown in Figure 1.3.

Other linguistic dimensions comprise different sets of co-occurring features. For example, in the above four text samples past tense verbs and third person personal pronouns seem to represent a third co-occurrence pattern. Table 1.2 shows that the scientific text has no past tense verbs and no third person pronouns, that the conversation and panel discussion have a few past tense verbs and no third person pronouns, and that the fiction text has a very frequent number of both past tense verbs and third person pronouns. This co-occurrence pattern is independent from the above two patterns, as shown by Figure 1.4.

Once the linguistic co-occurrence patterns are identified, the resulting dimensions can be interpreted in functional terms. The co-occurrence patterns by themselves are not very interesting. Instead, we want to know why these particular sets of features co-occur in texts; we want to know

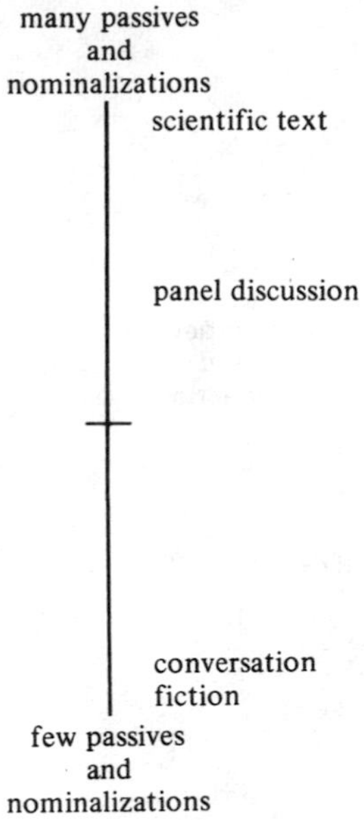

```
many passives
      and
nominalizations
                  scientific text
        │
        │
        │
                  panel discussion
        │
        │
        ┼
        │
        │
        │
        │
                  conversation
        │         fiction
        │
  few passives
      and
nominalizations
```

Figure **1.1** *One-dimensional plot of four genres: nominalizations and passives*

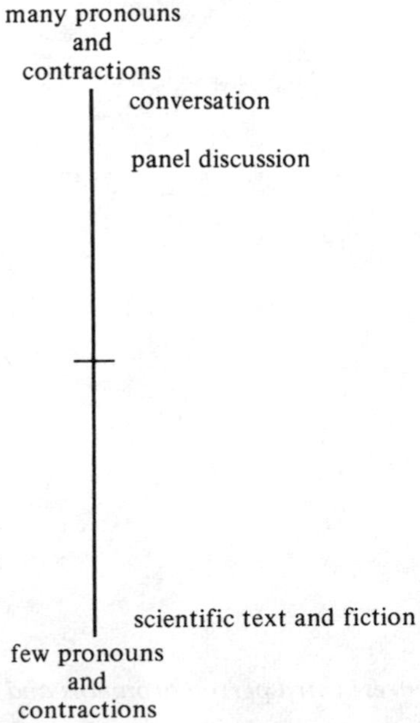

```
many pronouns
      and
  contractions
                  conversation
        │
                  panel discussion
        │
        │
        │
        │
        ┼
        │
        │
        │
        │
        │
        │
        │
                  scientific text and fiction
  few pronouns
      and
  contractions
```

Figure **1.2** *One-dimensional plot of four genres: first and second person pronouns and contractions*

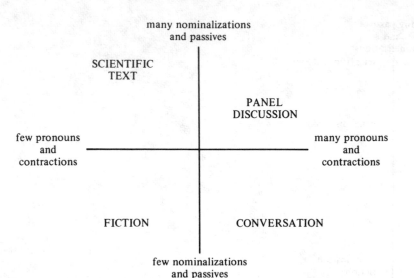

many nominalizations
and passives

SCIENTIFIC
TEXT

PANEL
DISCUSSION

few pronouns
and
contractions

many pronouns
and
contractions

FICTION

CONVERSATION

few nominalizations
and passives

Figure 1.3 *Two-dimensional plot of four genres*

many pronouns
and
past tense verbs

fiction

panel discussion and conversation

scientific text

few pronouns
and
past tense verbs

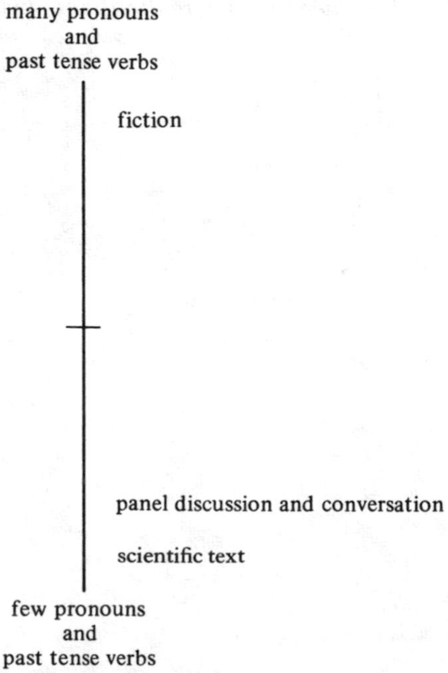

Figure 1.4 *One-dimensional plot of four genres: third person pronouns and past tense verbs*

Table 1.2 *Additional frequency counts for texts 1.1, 1.2, 1.3, and 1.4*
(*raw frequency count followed by normalized count per 100 words*)

	past tense	3rd person pronouns
conv.	2 / 2.1	0 / 0
sci. prose	0 / 0	0 / 0
panel disc.	3 / 2.5	0 / 0
fiction	6 / 14.3	4 / 9.5

what functional or situational parameters relate to the co-occurring sets
of features, influencing their systematic use across a range of texts. For
example, from a functional perspective, contractions and first and second
person pronouns share a colloquial, informal flavor. They are used in
interactive situations that require or permit rapid language production.
In the present case, they are used frequently in the conversation and the
panel discussion, which are both interactive situations. The linguistic
dimension of first and second person pronouns and contractions might
thus be interpreted as the surface manifestation of an underlying
interactive functional dimension.

The other dimensions could be interpreted through a similar process.
The co-occurrence pattern between passives and nominalizations can be
interpreted as representing an underlying abstract or informational
focus. The co-occurrence pattern between past tense verbs and third
person pronouns can be interpreted as representing an underlying
narrative focus. Any interpretations need to be verified and refined by
analysis of the co-occurring features in particular texts. Through this
approach, though, we can proceed from the linguistic features that are in
fact used systematically in texts to an account of the underlying
functional dimensions of English. In this way, we can identify the
functional dimensions that are important enough to be systematically
marked, and we will be able to specify the extent to which different
discourse functions are independent or overlapping.

Once linguistic dimensions are identified and interpreted, they can be
used to specify the 'textual relations' among different kinds of texts in
English. Each text can be given a precise quantitative characterization
with respect to each dimension, in terms of the frequencies of the co-

occurring features that constitute the dimension. This characterization enables a direct comparison of any two texts with respect to each dimension. The textual relations between two texts are defined by a simultaneous comparison of the texts with respect to all dimensions.

Comparison of texts with respect to any single dimension gives an incomplete, and sometimes misleading, picture. For example, consider texts 1.1–1.4 again. If we considered only the passive/nominalization dimension, we would conclude that the fiction text and conversation are linguistically similar and that the scientific text and panel discussion are similar; and that the first two are quite different from the second two. If we considered only the first and second person pronouns/contractions dimension, we would arrive at a quite different set of conclusions: that conversations and panel discussions are quite similar, fiction and academic prose are quite similar, and these two sets of texts are quite different from each other. Finally, considering only the past tense/third person pronouns dimension would lead us to conclude that fiction is very different from the three other texts, which are in turn quite similar to one another. All of these conclusions regarding similarities and differences among texts are inadequate, because the relations among texts cannot be defined unidimensionally. Fiction is not simply similar to or different from scientific prose; rather, it is more or less similar or different with respect to each dimension. Given that the linguistic variation among texts comprises several dimensions, it is no surprise that the relations among texts must be conceptualized in terms of a multi-dimensional space.

The example discussed in this section is extremely simplistic and intended to be illustrative only. To uncover the strong co-occurrence patterns that actually define linguistic dimensions in English, we need to analyze much longer texts, a much larger number of texts taken from many genres, and frequency counts of many linguistic features. Those features that co-occur in different texts across several genres are the ones that define the basic linguistic dimensions of English. A representative selection of texts and linguistic features for analysis is thus a crucial prerequisite to this type of analysis; the range of possible variation must be represented in the texts chosen for analysis, and the range of possible co-occurrence patterns must be represented in the features chosen for analysis. These prerequisites are discussed fully in Chapter 4.

1.3   Theoretical bases for the notion of 'dimension'

The notion that linguistic variation must be analyzed in terms of sets of co-occurring features has been proposed in several places. Ervin-Tripp (1972) and Hymes (1974) discuss co-occurrence relations among linguistic features in terms of 'speech styles,' a variety or register that is characterized by a set of co-occurring linguistic features. Brown and Fraser (1979:38–9) emphasize that:

> it is often difficult, or indeed misleading, to concentrate on specific, isolated [linguistic] markers without taking into account systematic variations which involve the cooccurrence of sets of markers. A reasonable assumption is that socially significant linguistic variations normally occur as varieties or styles, not as individual markers, and it is on those varieties that we should focus.

Although the theoretical importance of co-occurrence patterns among linguistic features has been well established by these researchers, the empirical identification of salient co-occurrence patterns in English discourse has proven to be difficult. One of the few studies to propose specific sets of co-occurring features is Chafe (1982). This study focuses on two fundamental differences between typical speaking and writing – that speaking is faster than writing, and that speakers interact with their audiences to a greater extent than writers – and it proposes an underlying dimension associated with each of these situational differences: integration/fragmentation and detachment/involvement. Along the integration/fragmentation dimension, integration is marked by features that function to pack information into a text, such as nominalizations, participles, attributive adjectives, and series of prepositional phrases; fragmentation is marked by clauses in succession without connectives or joined by coordinating conjunctions. Along the detachment/involvement dimension, detachment is marked by passives and nominalizations; involvement by first person pronouns, emphatic particles, and hedges. Chafe describes conversational texts as fragmented and involved, showing that they have many loosely joined clauses and many involved features such as first person pronouns and emphatics. He describes academic texts as integrated and detached, showing that they have many features like participles, attributive adjectives, nominalizations, and passives. This study is exemplary in that it recognizes the need to discuss linguistic variation among texts in terms of co-occurring features and actually to identify two dimensions of such variation.

Several other researchers have looked at the distribution of linguistic features across social groups and situations: Bernstein (1970) describes restricted versus elaborated codes; Ervin-Tripp (1972) and Irvine (1979) discuss variation between formal and informal registers; Ferguson (1959) describes the differences between high and low varieties (and standard versus non-standard dialects); Ochs (1979) presents differences between planned and unplanned discourse; and several researchers have described linguistic differences between speech and writing. All of these studies describe functional ways in which groups of features co-occur in particular types of texts.

The notion of linguistic co-occurrence patterns is thus well-established in sociolinguistic theory. There are, however, three fundamental differences between earlier conceptualizations and the notion of dimension that I use here. First, most previous studies analyze linguistic variation in terms of a single parameter, while the present study is based on the assumption that linguistic variation in any language is too complex to be analyzed in terms of any single dimension. The simple fact that such a large number of distinctions have been proposed by researchers indicates that no single dimension is adequate in itself. In addition to the distinctions listed above, such as restricted versus elaborated and formal versus informal, linguistic features vary across age, sex, social class, occupation, social role, politeness, purpose, topic, etc. From a theoretical point of view, we thus have every expectation that the description of linguistic variation in a given language will be multi-dimensional, and this expectation forms the basis of the present study.

A second way in which the notion of dimension used here differs from previous conceptualizations relates to their characterization as continuous parameters of variation. Most previous studies have treated linguistic variation in terms of dichotomous distinctions rather than continuous scales. There is no reason, however, to expect that dimensions of variation should be dichotomous. Hymes (1974:41) points out that 'the fact that present taxonomic dimensions consist so largely of dichotomies . . . shows how preliminary is the stage at which we work'. This situation has changed little in the decade since Hymes wrote. In the present study, dimensions are identified as *continuous* quantifiable parameters of variation, i.e., as continuous scales. These scales are labelled in terms of their poles, but a continuous range of texts can be characterized along each dimension. That is, styles, registers, genres, and text types are not related in terms of dichotomous differences; rather they are similar (or different) to differing extents with respect to each dimension. In the approach used in the present study, each text is assigned a precise quantitative characterization with respect to each dimension. The statistical techniques used to compute the dimensions are described in later chapters; the point to note here is that the notion of dimension is quantitative and permits description of a continuous range of variation.

The third difference in the conceptualization of dimension is also a consequence of the quantitative approach adopted here. Previous studies have relied on functional analysis to identify a set of linguistic features that distinguishes among registers. This approach groups together features that are claimed to be functionally similar, but there is no independent check on the extent to which these features actually co-occur in texts. In fact, there are likely to be several overlapping co-occurrence patterns within any set of linguistic features, making it extremely difficult to identify the dimensions of co-occurring features using only functional criteria. In the present analysis, quantitative statistical techniques are used to achieve this goal. Based on the frequencies of features in texts, these techniques provide a precise quantitative specification of the co-occurrence patterns within a set of features. As noted above, these statistical techniques are discussed in later chapters; the point here is that dimensions comprise those features that actually co-occur, rather than a set of features that the researcher expects to co-occur given a particular functional interpretation.

Arguments for or against a parameter of variation that has been proposed on functional grounds are typically presented in terms of the plausibility of the interpretation underlying the grouping of linguistic features. Neither the original analyses nor the criticisms of such studies are based on identification of the actual co-occurrence patterns of linguistic features, because the tools required to identify such patterns have not been readily available to linguists. Thus, for example, Bernstein's distinction between elaborated and restricted codes proposes a group of features that are functionally associated with elaboration and a group of features that are functionally associated with restricted code; and this distinction has been criticized on the grounds that the functional interpretation is not valid. Neither analysts nor critics have determined whether the associated features in fact co-occur in texts.[4] The approach

---

[4] The analyses by Poole (1973) and Poole and Field (1976) analyze the relation between restricted and elaborated codes in terms of continuous dimensions.

adopted here enables a direct consideration of the co-occurrence patterns among features in texts, and thus provides a solid empirical foundation for the identification of underlying dimensions. This approach does not replace functional analysis; it merely changes the order of analysis. Previously, functional analyses were conducted first, in order to identify sets of related linguistic features. In contrast, the present approach first identifies groups of co-occurring features and subsequently interprets them in functional terms.

In summary, the notion of dimension developed here has three distinctive characteristics: (1) no single dimension will be adequate in itself to account for the range of linguistic variation in a language; rather, a multi-dimensional analysis is required; (2) dimensions are continuous scales of variation rather than dichotomous poles; and (3) the co-occurrence patterns underlying dimensions are identified empirically rather than being proposed on an a priori functional basis.

1.4   Is there a spoken/written dimension?

Describing the variation among texts in terms of textual dimensions and relations has important implications for the study of speech and writing. We have seen that situational dimensions such as formality versus informality have no a priori linguistic validity. Similarly, there is no reason to assume that the situational difference between speech and writing constitutes a linguistic dimension in English. This is rather an empirical question: is there a linguistic dimension of co-occurring features that distinguishes between spoken and written texts? That is, if there is a spoken/written dimension, then there will be a set of co-occurring linguistic features that functions to distinguish all written texts from all spoken texts. This question cannot be answered by consideration of a few texts and a few linguistic features. Rather it requires analysis of the distribution of many linguistic features in many different types of speech and writing in English. This book identifies several of the basic linguistic dimensions of variation among spoken and written texts in English, and it specifies the multi-dimensional relations among several different kinds of speech and writing. It shows that the variation among texts within speech and writing is often as great as the variation across the two modes. No absolute spoken/written distinction is identified in the study. Rather, the relations among spoken and written texts are complex and associated with a variety of different situational, functional, and processing considerations. The goal of the study is to specify the multi-dimensional relations among the many different types of speech and writing in English. As a by-product of this analysis, the issue of an absolute spoken/written distinction is addressed and put aside as not central to the relations among spoken and written texts.

1.5 Outline of the book

The remainder of Part I presents other background notions and research. Chapter 2 presents a preliminary typology of 'functions' (communicative purposes served by particular linguistic features in texts) and 'situations' (configurations of cultural, physical, temporal, and psychological features that define the situational context of texts). This typology provides the theoretical foundation required for the interpretation of the quantitative results given in later chapters. Chapter 2 also includes a discussion of the major situational and functional parameters distinguishing among typical spoken and written genres.

In Chapter 3, I present an overview of previous linguistic research on speech and writing in English. I divide studies into quantitative and non-quantitative approaches, and I discuss some of the methodological restrictions that have been shared by both approaches. In a concluding section, I introduce the multi-feature/multi-dimensional approach to textual variation, which is designed to avoid these methodological restrictions, and I summarize the major research findings to date using this approach.

Part II of the book deals with methodological issues. In Chapter 4, I show the necessity of both micro and macro approaches to textual variation, summarize the linguistic features and multivariate statistical analyses used in the study, and describe the particular texts used in some detail. Chapter 5 presents a fairly detailed introduction to factor analysis. It describes the steps involved in doing a factor analysis and presents the particular factor analysis that forms the basis of the present study. Sections 5.2–5.5 are relatively technical; they are not prerequisites to understanding the theoretical results presented in Chapters 6–8.

Part III, which comprises Chapters 6, 7, and 8, constitutes the heart of the study. In Chapter 6, I interpret the factors described in Chapter 5. Six primary factors are identified by the analysis, and the textual dimension underlying each of them is interpreted in functional terms. Then in Chapter 7, the relations among spoken and written genres are identified and interpreted in terms of this six-dimensional space. That is, each of the dimensions identifies a set of similarities and differences among the genres, and consideration of all six dimensions enables a rich assessment of the relations among genres in English. This chapter first considers the relations among genres with respect to each dimension separately, analyzing representative text samples from particular genres in some detail. Then, an overall account of the relations among genres with respect to all six dimensions is given. This chapter addresses the extent to which there is an absolute spoken/written difference in English. It shows that no dimension defines a dichotomous distinction between speech and writing, although several dimensions distinguish among oral and literate genres in different respects.

Chapter 8 extends this description by showing that spoken and written genres differ in their internal coherence; that the texts within some genres differ greatly from one another, while the texts within other genres are highly similar to one another. Some of this variation reflects the extent to which the cultural norms for particular genres are highly constrained. For example, face-to-face conversations can vary considerably in their form and still be considered representative of their genre; official documents, on the other hand, tolerate much less variation in their form. In addition, some genres, such as academic prose and press reportage, permit considerable internal variation because they are composed of several distinct sub-genres, which differ in both their communicative purposes and linguistic form. Relations among sub-genres within academic prose, press reportage, editorials, broadcasts, and telephone conversations are examined with respect to the six textual dimensions.

Finally, Chapter 9 summarizes the major research findings of the book and identifies several applications of the model of textual relations developed here. Applications to dialect, discourse, stylistic, historical, and cross-linguistic comparisons are discussed. In conclusion, the development of a typology of texts is identified as a remaining major research goal. Research conducted towards this goal is described, and it is shown how the description of textual relations among spoken and written genres provides the necessary foundation for a more complete typology.

Four appendices are included in the book. Appendices I, II, and IV support the methodological discussion of Part II, and Appendix III presents descriptive data in support of the analyses in Part III. Appendix I lists the specific texts used in the study. Appendix II gives a detailed description of the linguistic features used in the study, including the algorithms for their automatic identification and their characteristic communicative functions. The appendix begins with an overview of the computational techniques used for the automatic identification of linguistic features. It describes in broad terms the programs used to 'tag' words in texts for their grammatical category and to identify occurrences of particular syntactic constructions. The appendix then discusses, for each feature, the algorithm for automatic identification and the discourse functions associated with the feature in previous studies. Appendix IV presents a correlation matrix of all linguistic features used in the study, which forms the basis of the factor analysis.

Appendix III presents mean frequency counts of all linguistic features for each of the 23 genres used in the study. This appendix is included to support the analyses in Part III and to enable further micro-analyses of particular features (cf. Section 4.5).

2 Situations and functions

This study is based on both macroscopic and microscopic analyses of textual variation (see Section 4.1). Macroscopic analyses identify the dimensions of variation among texts and specify the overall relations among genres with respect to those dimensions. Microscopic analyses describe the functions of linguistic features in relation to the speech situations of individual texts. Linguistic features mark particular components of the situation, in addition to their functions as markers of relations within a text. In this chapter, I describe the salient components of the speech situation and provide a brief overview of the major communicative functions served by linguistic features. I then turn to the situational and functional differences between 'typical' speaking and writing and propose a framework for comparing more or less typical genres in terms of their situational characteristics.

2.1 Components of the speech situation

There are several studies that catalog the components of the speech situation, which provides the situational context for 'speech events'. One of the earliest and most complete descriptions is presented in Hymes's (1974:53ff) components of speech, which include message form, message content, speaker, hearer, purposes, key, channels, and norms of interaction. This description is further elaborated by Duranti (1985). Fishman (1972) identifies three primary components of the situation of language use: (1) the participants and the relationship among them, (2) the topic, and (3) the setting. Halliday (1978) also distinguishes among three components of the communicative situation: (1) the type of social action (the 'field'), (2) the role relationships (the 'tenor'), and (3) the symbolic organization (or 'mode'). Brown and Fraser (1979) present a thorough discussion of the components of situation, distinguishing among the three primary components of purpose, setting, and participants, each of which has several sub-components. The discussion below draws heavily on Brown and Fraser (1979) and Hymes (1974, Chapter 2).

Based on these earlier studies, I distinguish eight components of the speech situation, several of them having sub-components: (1) participant roles and characteristics, (2) relations among the participants, (3) setting, (4) topic, (5) purpose, (6) social evaluation, (7) relations of participants to the text, and (8) channel. These components are summarized in Table 2.1.

'Participant roles and characteristics' refers to the communicative roles of participants plus the individual characteristics of each participant, including their own personal characteristics and those characteristics determined by group membership. It is necessary to distinguish at least three groups of participants: addressor(s), addressee(s), and audience. The addressor produces the message (Hymes further distinguishes a sender, who conveys the message); the addressee is the intended recipient of the message; and the audience are participants who hear or overhear the message but are not usually the intended recipients. Although 'speaker' refers strictly to speech, I will use the terms 'speaker' and 'addressor' interchangeably throughout this study.

Participants also have personal characteristics that influence their language use. These characteristics can be stable (e.g., personality, interests, beliefs) or temporary (e.g., mood, emotions). These personal characteristics are presumably the primary influence on a person's personal style, but this is an area that has not been much studied from a linguistic point of view. In addition to personal characteristics, participants can be characterized by their group membership, i.e., a characterization in terms of social class, ethnic group, sex, age, occupation, etc. There has been considerable research relating linguistic use to these group characteristics.

'Relations among the participants' has several facets. First of all, it refers to the social role relations among participants, that is, their relations in terms of relative social power, status, etc. It also refers to the more exclusively personal relationship between participants, that is, whether they like each other, respect each other, etc. The relationship between the addressor(s) and addressee(s) can differ in terms of the amount of specific and cultural/world knowledge they share. Intimate friends will share considerable specific knowledge about one another; business associates will share little specific personal knowledge but much cultural knowledge; participants from different cultures might share little

Table 2.1 *Components of the speech situation*

I. Participant roles and characteristics

   A. Communicative roles of participants

      1. addressor(s)
      2. addressee(s)
      3. audience

   B. Personal characteristics

      1. stable: personality, interests, beliefs, etc.
      2. temporary: mood, emotions, etc.

   C. Group characteristics

      1. social class, ethnic group, gender, age, occupation,
         education, etc.

II. Relations among participants

   A. Social role relations: relative social power, status, etc.

   B. Personal relations: like, respect, etc.

   C. Extent of shared knowledge

      1. cultural world knowledge
      2. specific personal knowledge

   D. 'Plurality' of participants

III - IV - V. Scene: the interaction of components III, IV, and V

III. Setting

   A. Physical context

   B. Temporal context

   C. Superordinate activity type

   D. Extent to which space and time are shared by participants

IV. Topic

V. Purpose

   A. Conventional goals

   B. Personal goals

Table 2.1 (*cont.*)

VI. Social evaluation

    A. Evaluation of the communicative event

        1. values shared by whole culture

        2. values held by sub-cultures or individuals

    B. Speaker's attitudes towards content

        1. feelings, judgements, attitudinal 'stance'

        2. key: tone or manner of speech

        3. degree of commitment towards the content,
           epistemological 'stance'

VII. Relations of participants to the text

VIII. Channel

    A. Primary channel: speech, writing, drums, signs, etc.

    B. Number of sub-channels available

---

specific or cultural knowledge. The relations among participants will differ depending on the plurality of speaker and addressee. Addressing a large class of people is very different from addressing an individual; similarly, a group production of a message is very different from the more typical individual production. Finally, relations among participants can differ in the extent of interaction possible or appropriate, although this factor will be influenced by the physical/temporal setting and the purpose of communication.

'Setting' refers to the different aspects of the physical and temporal context. Where the communication takes place, when it takes place, and what larger activity it is part of are all components of the setting. The extent to which participants share time and space is an important component of the setting. In addition, the presence or absence of an audience might be considered part of the setting.

The 'topic' is simply what the message is about. This component is closely related to the fifth component, the 'purpose', which refers to the

outcomes that participants hope for, expect, or intend from the communicative event. Hymes distinguishes between conventionally recognized outcomes (e.g., participants expect a bargaining session to result in
a business agreement) and the specific goals of each participant (e.g., to
make a friend, further one's own interests). The setting, topic, and
purpose combine to determine the 'scene', which is the psychological
setting of communication. That is, as purpose and topic shift within a
given setting, the perception of the speech activity also shifts. Similarly, a
move to a new setting, holding topic and purpose the same, might cause a
shift in the perception of scene. For example, an instructor and students
can sit in a classroom before class having an informal conversation. As the
time for class passes, the instructor can begin to teach, causing the
perception of communicative activity to shift from an informal conversation to a more formal lecture or class discussion. The participants and
the physical and temporal setting remain constant, but the perception of
the scene changes. Because it is derivative from the components of
setting, topic, and purpose, I have not included scene as a separate
component in the scheme presented here. The notion of scene, however,
is crucial to understanding the differences among communicative
situations.

'Social evaluation' refers to the attitudes of the participants, and of the
culture at large, to the communicative event and the specific content of
the message. In different cultures, some types of language are valued
more highly than others. For example, in Western culture schooled
language tends to be valued more highly than nonschooled language, and
writing tends to be valued more highly than speech. In traditional Somali
culture, oral poetry is valued more highly than either schooled language
or writing. Values of this type can be shared within a culture or they can
be restricted to sub-groups. For example, some groups in American
culture frequently use an argumentative style and place high value on
argumentative speech events, while other groups avoid an argumentative
style at all costs, having a quite negative attitude towards this type of
discourse (see Kochman 1981; Schiffrin 1984b). The participants'
attitudes towards the content should also be considered here. These
attitudes involve expression of the speaker's feelings, judgments, or
attitudinal stance. Hymes uses the term 'key' to refer to the tone or
manner of speech, for instance serious or sarcastic. Finally, the degree of
commitment towards the content, or epistemological stance, can also be
considered as part of this component; that is, to what extent is the speaker
certain of the truthfulness of the message.

'Relations of participants to the text' is a component of the situation that has not been much discussed. Chafe (1982) notes that one of the key differences between typical speaking and writing relates to the ability of the communicative participants to interact with the text: the writer can write as slowly and carefully as (s)he wishes; the reader can read as quickly or as slowly as (s)he wishes; but speakers and listeners must produce and comprehend language 'on-line', with little opportunity for interaction with the text. Thus, relation to the text is an additional important component of the situation.

Finally, 'channel' refers to the medium of the message. Two aspects need to be distinguished here. The first concerns the primary channel of communication. This is typically either speech or writing, but might also be drums, sign language, telegraph, etc. In addition, the number of sub-channels available for communication must be considered. For example, in typical speaking three sub-channels are available: (1) the lexical/syntactic, (2) prosodic, and (3) paralinguistic (gestures, etc.). In contrast, writing is typically restricted to the lexical/syntactic sub-channel.

All of these components are important in the specification of the situational context of communication. Describing the situation is a precursor to functional descriptions of language use. That is, identification of the salient components of the situation enables an interpretation of the roles played by particular linguistic features within that context. To these functions we turn next.

2.2 Linguistic functions

The notion of function is closely associated with the notion of situation. A primary motivation for analysis of the components of situation is the desire to link the functions of particular linguistic features to variation in the communicative situation. Much work of this type has been undertaken with respect to the phonological markers that distinguish among speakers of different social dialects in different situations (e.g., Labov 1972). This research shows that linguistic form varies systematically with the social category of the speaker and the formality of the situation, so that different linguistic forms function as markers of social category and formality. There has been less research on the ways in which linguistic form varies with other differences in the situation. Such work has typically been done as part of the analysis of 'register', linguistic variation associated with differences in use rather than group differences associated with the user (e.g. Halliday 1968; Ferguson 1977, 1983). Brown and Fraser (1979) discuss the functions of linguistic features as markers of situation, that is, the ways in which linguistic features function to distinguish different aspects of the communicative situation (see also Hymes 1974:22ff; Halliday 1978).

I distinguish here among seven major functions that can be served by linguistic features. Each of these functions identifies a type of information that is marked in discourse. The seven functional categories are: (1) ideational, (2) textual, (3) personal, (4) interpersonal, (5) contextual, (6) processing, and (7) aesthetic. These functions are summarized in Table 2.2.

Ideational functions refer to the ways in which linguistic form is used to convey propositional or referential content. Although most linguists have regarded this as the primary function of language, researchers such as Halliday and Hymes claim instead that this is merely one of several important functions. Certain types of language (e.g., typical face-to-face conversation) have a very low focus on informational content, and, as is shown in Chapter 7, these same types of language have few of the linguistic features that are functionally important for conveying pro-positional content (such as frequent nouns and prepositional phrases, or a highly varied vocabulary). The ideational function of linguistic features is important, but the present analysis shows that it is only one of several functions determining the linguistic structure of texts.

Textual functions are of two types: to mark information structure or to mark cohesion. Information structure refers to the way in which a text is packaged, including the marking of focus, topic–comment constructions, and theme, by features such as clefts, pseudo-clefts, extraposed clauses, and passives. Cohesion, on the other hand, refers to surface features that mark the ways in which the sentences of a text are referentially related, for example, through the use of pronominal reference, demonstratives, lexical substitution (e.g., 'do' for a verb phrase), and ellipsis (Halliday and Hasan 1976).

The ideational and textual functions are strictly linguistic; they deal respectively with clause structure and text-internal structure. The remaining functions are ways in which linguistic form can serve to mark information outside of the text itself. Personal functions include markers of group membership, personal style, and attitudes towards the com-municative event or towards the content of the message. In contrast, interpersonal functions are those that depend on some aspect of the

Table 2.2 *Functions of linguistic features*

I.   Ideational functions

A. Presentation of propositional meaning
B. Informational density

II.   Textual functions

A. Different ways of marking informational structure and prominence
B. Different ways of marking cohesion
C. The extent to which informational structure, prominence, and cohesion are marked

III. Personal functions

A. To mark group membership of addressor
B. To mark idiosyncratic characteristics of addressor
C. To express attitudes towards the communicative event or content

IV.   Interpersonal functions

A. To mark role relations
B. To express attitudes towards particular participants

V.   Contextual functions

A. To mark physical or temporal setting
B. To mark purpose
C. To mark the psychological 'scene'

VI.   Processing functions: caused by or in consideration of the production and comprehension demands of the communicative event

VII. Aesthetic functions: personal and cultural attitudes towards form

A. To conform to grammatical prescriptions
B. To conform to "good style"

relationship between participants: role relationships, overtly expressed attitudes towards participants, the extent of shared knowledge, and the interactional possibilities of the communicative event.

Contextual functions are those relating to the physical and temporal setting of communication (actual space and time, and the extent to which place and time are shared), the purposes of communication, and the perception of the scene. Processing functions are those relating to the production and comprehension demands of the communicative event. These can reflect differences in production constraints, or they can reflect the addressor's concern for producing text that is readily understood. Finally, aesthetic functions are those relating to personal or cultural attitudes about the preferred forms of language. These include grammatical prescriptions established by language academies and other linguistic 'guardians' as well as individual notions about 'good' style and rhetorical effect.

Although there are probably other functions served by linguistic features, these seven seem to be the most important. In Appendix II, I describe the specific communicative functions that have been associated with each of the linguistic features used in the present study. In Chapters 6–7, I show that a group of features can share a common, underlying function; that texts are systematically related by their exploitations of those functions; and that textual dimensions can be interpreted by determining the most widely shared functions underlying a group of co-occurring features. As background to the analysis in those chapters, the remainder of the present chapter describes the salient situational and functional distinctions between 'typical' speaking and writing.

2.3   Situational and functional differences between 'typical' speaking and writing

2.3.1   The notion of typical speech and writing

One of the central findings of the present study is that there is no linguistic or situational characterization of speech and writing that is true of all spoken and written genres. On the one hand, some spoken and written genres are very similar to one another (e.g., public speeches and written exposition). On the other hand, some spoken genres are quite different from one another (e.g., conversation and public speeches), as are some written genres (e.g., personal letters and academic exposition). The relations among these genres are systematic but must be specified in a multi-dimensional space.

Despite the fact that speech and writing are not homogeneous types, I find it useful to use the notion of typical speech and writing to refer to the unmarked genre in each mode. From one perspective, this notion refers to the most frequent or common type of speech and writing. From another perspective, this notion refers to the types of speech and writing that have the stereotypical characteristics of their mode. In terms of its situational characteristics, stereotypical speech is interactive, and dependent on shared space, time, and background knowledge; stereotypical writing has the opposite characteristics (see Section 2.3.4). In terms of its linguistic characteristics, stereotypical speech is structurally simple, fragmented, concrete, and dependent on exophoric (situation-dependent) reference; again, stereotypical writing has the opposite characteristics (see Section 3.1). These stereotypical descriptions are based on consideration of the most frequent or common types of speech and writing, so that these two perspectives dovetail into one. Both perspectives indicate face-to-face conversation as typical speech and informational exposition as typical writing. I adopt the notions of typical speech and writing here to make sense out of previous research. In later chapters, I return to this notion to examine the extent to which conversation and exposition are in fact typical of their mode when considered from a multi-dimensional perspective.

2.3.2 Situational differences

Analysis of the situational differences between typical speaking and writing has been undertaken in several places. Rubin (1980) provides an overall taxonomy of these differences, but useful discussions can also be found in Kay (1977), Olson (1977), Olson and Torrance (1981), Green and Morgan (1981), Akinnaso (1982), Stubbs (1982), Heath (1982a,b), Lakoff (1982a,b), Rader (1982), Gumperz *et al.* (1984), and Tannen (1985). These studies are concerned with the particular components of the situational context that are important in distinguishing between speech and writing. Other studies, and the discussion in the first part of this chapter, attempt to identify the full range of components defining the situational context of a discourse. Many components that are important to a full specification of situational context are not highly relevant to the contextual differences between typical speech and writing. These other components include social categories (e.g., class, ethnic group, sex, and age), individual personality characteristics of the speaker and addressee, and the social role relationship (e.g., power and status) between speaker and addressee. The present section does not include discussion of these components; it is limited to the situational components that are central to the distinctions between speaking and writing.

Table 2.3 outlines six situational components identified from previous research as major distinctions between typical speaking and writing; I have divided these components into sixteen situational parameters. Although these parameters might be considered as dichotomies, the poles do not characterize all speaking and writing situations. Rather, these dichotomies describe typical speaking and writing, commonly represented by face-to-face conversation and expository prose. Certain situational characteristics are commonly associated with speaking and others with writing, but none of these characteristics (except the physical mode distinction) is associated exclusively with speaking or writing situations. This point is illustrated in Section 2.3.4.

1.   Physical channel
     refers to the choice of the spoken or written mode as the primary channel, and the total number of sub-channels available for communication.
         a. 'spoken or written channel' merely marks the fact that speaking uses the auditory channel and writing the visual channel. Even an obvious statement like this must be qualified: writing can be produced to be spoken (a speech or dramatic play); speech can be produced to be written (dictating a letter).
         b. 'prosodic and paralinguistic sub-channels available or not' refers to the restriction of writing to the lexical/syntactic channel (i.e., morphemes and their arrangement), as opposed to the multi-channel nature of speech (including prosody, gestures, etc.). It has been claimed that this difference causes writing to be more linearly explicit than speech, since the information structure of written texts must be marked entirely in the grammatical channel, whereas spoken texts can utilize several channels. Sometimes writing uses channels other than the strictly grammatical channel. For example, printed writing can use underlining, bold face, italics, and other fonts (Vachek 1979; Lakoff 1982a). Notes left on the kitchen table can use arrows to point to the immediate context, almost as a paralinguistic gesture. Speaking, on the other hand, can be restricted in the number of available channels; for example, neither a conversation in a dark room nor a tape-recorded speech can use paralinguistic gestures.
2.   Cultural use
     refers to differences between speaking and writing due to the attitudes

Table 2.3 *List of major situational parameters distinguishing between typical speaking and writing*

1. Physical channel

    a. spoken or written channel
    b. prosodic and paralinguistic sub-channels available or not

2. Cultural use

    a. home-acquisition or school-acquisition
    b. high or low social evaluation
    c. maintenance of social status

3. Relation of communicative participants to each other

    a. extent of interaction
    b. extent of shared knowledge about each other
    c. degree of goal negotiability
    d. effort expended to maintain relationship
    e. extent of shared cultural world-knowledge

4. Relation of communicative participants to the external context

    a. extent of shared time
    b. extent of shared space

5. Relation of communicative participants to the text

    a. degree of permanence of the text; opportunity for
       interaction with the text in production (planning or
       revising) and in comprehension
    b. speed of production
    c. speed of comprehension

6. Primary purpose of communication

    a. ideational or interactional

towards and use of each within a given society. These differences change from one cultural group to the next (see Stubbs 1982; Heath 1982a,b).

a. 'home-acquisition versus school-acquisition' refers to the fact that in Western society, literacy is explicitly taught and learned in the schools, while speech is naturally acquired in the home. This results in literacy taking on the decontextualized and formal aspects of educational institutions.

b. 'social evaluation' refers to the attitude that writing is more valuable than speech. This evaluation is by no means a cultural universal (e.g., Philips 1983). In Western societies, however, where writing is considered to represent the 'correct' form of the language, this factor will exert an important influence on the amount of attention paid to speech versus writing.

c. 'maintenance of social status' refers to the tendency of speakers from the upper socio-economic classes, speakers in formal situations, and writers to resist phonological and syntactic reductions as a means of maintaining social distance from other social classes or speech situations (Kroch 1978; Kroch and Small 1978; Finegan and Biber 1986a; and Finegan 1987). This tendency is claimed to result in a closer form–meaning correspondence, and can perhaps be seen as a source of the prescriptive rules common in composition textbooks, which generally advocate a one-to-one correspondence between form and meaning.[1]

3.   Relation of communicative participants to each other

refers to the differences related to the addressee as an active, individual listener in typical speaking versus addressee as a passive group of readers in writing (where 'active' and 'passive' refer to interaction with the speaker, not interaction with the text). I have divided this component into five categories:

a. 'extent of interaction' refers to the listener's unique opportunities to respond directly in speaking situations. These responses can present additional information or opinions, can request clarification of earlier statements, or can simply indicate understanding and continued interest. Readers cannot provide direct feedback of this type, and typically they do not have opportunity to provide any response at all.

b. 'extent of shared knowledge about each other' refers to the speaker/writer's knowledge of the addressees' backgrounds, e.g., their personalities, beliefs, knowledge, interests, etc. In speech, such knowledge is variable, although often intimate, while in writing it is often minimal or

---

[1] It is interesting to note that these distinctions can be in conflict with one another. For example, teachers of composition in Western schools normally advocate the use of an active style. Society in general, however, attaches a more 'learned' value to a nominal/passive style. Thus, schools and society at large have different expectations concerning good literate style. Williams (1980) describes an experiment in which composition teachers rated essays written in a nominal style more highly than similar essays written in an active style, despite their professed preference for the latter. In actual practice, the values of society at large seem to dominate in this case.

irrelevant. This dimension is influential because a speaker (as opposed to a writer) can reduce the informational content of an utterance on the basis of shared personal knowledge and still expect to be understood.

c. 'negotiability of communicative goal and topic' refers to the on-going negotiation of purpose and topic in typical speech, versus the impossibility of such negotiation in writing. Recently several authors have pointed out that the reading process must also be viewed as an interactive one. For example, Widdowson (1979:174) writes: 'In this view, reading is regarded not as reaction to a text but as interaction between writer and reader mediated through the text' (see also Dillon 1981). Reading is necessarily an interactive process in this sense; readers approach a text with different communicative goals, and come away with different understandings of the meaning. But this interaction takes place between the reader and the text, and it does not influence the form of the text in any way. The writer of a text is concerned only with the general interests of the intended audience, not with the specific interests of individual potential readers. Thus, individual readers must simply decide if the stated goal is agreeable or not – with no recourse to negotiation.

d. 'effort required to maintain relationship' refers to the fact that, in speech, communication crucially depends on the establishment and subsequent maintenance of a focused social relationship between participants, while in writing this necessity does not exist (Olson and Torrance 1981). If a social rapport is not established at the start of a spoken encounter, the encounter is likely to end prematurely (e.g., when the listener leaves, turns to address a third party, or simply stops paying attention). Further, once a relationship has been established between speaker and listener, there must be a continual monitoring of the other party to ensure its maintenance.

The social relationship between reader and writer is also important. In this case, however, the relationship is established a priori, and the reader must decide to either accept or reject that relationship. This decision will be influenced by the writer's stance towards the intended audience and subject-matter. However, in contrast to speech, once a writer takes a given stance, there is no tendency to modify that stance in order to maintain a relationship with a specific addressee. This factor is important in causing speech to be highly concerned with the metacommunicative functions, and writing to be much less concerned with those functions, so that it is free to focus on the ideational functions.

e. 'extent of shared cultural world-knowledge' refers to the general cultural background that writers and speakers assume in their addressees. Rader (1982) has shown that this type of shared knowledge is important in written imaginative fiction as well as in speech. However, the extent of shared cultural background knowledge is in general greater in speech than in writing. That is, in speech the addressee interacts directly with the speaker, and therefore her/his cultural background is usually known (or readily apparent), whereas writing is typically addressed to a broader range of cultural backgrounds. Despite this claim, it is apparent that cultural background knowledge does not represent an absolute distinction between the modes: nothing inherent in writing causes it to be intended for all cultures, just as nothing inherent in speech automatically overcomes the problems of interethnic communication.

4.   Relation of the communicative participants to the external context
refers to the spatial and temporal contexts of speech and writing.
   a. 'extent of shared space' refers to the fact that speaker and listener normally share a physical context, while writer and reader typically do not and thus do not refer to the physical surroundings.
   b. 'extent of shared time' refers to the fact that speaker and listener typically share a temporal context, while writer and reader are usually separated by a considerable period of time.

5.   Relation of communicative participants to the text
   a. 'degree of permanence' refers to the temporary nature of speech in contrast to the permanence of writing. Especially with respect to the development of written discourse within Western society, this distinction has been crucial. For instance, the permanence of writing enables a prolonged visual inspection of the text, and the associated activities of planning, organizing, and revision, plus the general high attention to form associated with writing. These activities enable the maximally explicit, highly integrated texts which are associated with writing (Chafe 1982).
   b. 'speed of production and comprehension' refers to the fact that the production of speech is much faster than that of writing, while the speed of comprehension is potentially reversed in the two modes. That is, the reader is free to comprehend at his/her leisure, or to skim an entire text in a few seconds; the listener must comprehend language as it is produced.

6.   Purpose
refers to the fact that writing is typically for ideational purposes, to convey propositional information, while speaking is more often for personal, interpersonal, and contextual purposes in addition to, or instead of, ideational purposes. Conversational participants often speak to express their personal feelings, or to establish or reaffirm their interpersonal relationship, rather than to convey propositional information.

2.3.3   Functional differences

There are several functional differences between typical speech and writing, which are associated with the typical situational characteristics of the two modes. For example, linguistic features are used for informational elaboration and explicit, situation-independent reference in typical writing, while other features function to mark interaction, expression of personal feelings, and direct reference to the external situation in typical speech.

Chafe (1982, 1985; Chafe and Danielewicz 1986) proposes four functional notions that are particularly useful in the interpretation of the textual dimensions identified in the present study: 'integration', 'fragmentation', 'involvement', and 'detachment'. Each of these functions relates to a particular aspect of the speech or writing situation, and each is marked by several linguistic features.

Integration refers to the way in which a large amount of information is packed into relatively few words in typical writing, because the writer operates under few time constraints and can therefore construct a carefully packaged text. Similarly, the reader, who can read as quickly or slowly as (s)he pleases, is able to take advantage of a highly integrated text. In contrast, typical speech cannot be highly integrated because it is produced and comprehended on-line. Features that are used to integrate information into a text include attributive adjectives, prepositional phrase series, phrasal coordination, and careful word choice.

Fragmentation refers to the linguistic characteristics of texts produced under severe time constraints, the case for typical speech. Under these conditions, information cannot be carefully incorporated into the text, and the resulting structure is much looser, or fragmented. Linguistic features associated with a fragmented text include clauses strung together with simple conjunctions (e.g., *and*) or with no connectives at all.

Involvement refers to those linguistic features which reflect the fact that speaker and listener typically interact with one another, while writer and reader typically do not. Due to this interaction, speakers often make direct reference to the listener (by use of second person pronouns, questions, imperatives, etc.), and they are typically concerned with the expression of their own thoughts and feelings (e.g., marked by use of first person pronouns, affective forms such as emphatics and amplifiers, and cognitive verbs such as *think* and *feel*). As a result of this concern, speech often has a distinctly non-informational and imprecise character (marked by hedges, pronoun *it*, and other forms of reduced or generalized content). These features can be considered together as the characteristics of involved text. In contrast, detachment refers to the characteristics of typical writing which result from the fact that writer and reader usually do not interact (e.g., marked by agentless passives and nominalizations).

These functional notions are useful in the interpretation of the textual dimensions (Chapters 6 and 7), although no dimension corresponds in a one-to-one fashion to any particular notion. For example, one dimension identified in the present analysis indicates that involved texts are also typically fragmented in certain respects; and that these texts are markedly not integrated. Another dimension indicates that certain types of structural elaboration reflect a type of fragmentation; that is, in informational texts produced under strict time constraints, information seems to be tacked on as additional dependent clauses, in a fragmented manner, rather than being tightly integrated into the text. The actual co-occurrence patterns among linguistic features identified in the present study differ from those proposed on functional grounds in some other studies; but the functional notions developed elsewhere provide an important aid to the interpretation of the textual dimensions and to the explanation of the relations found among spoken and written genres.

2.3.4   A situational comparison of four genres

As noted throughout this discussion, the situational differences described here are characteristic of typical speaking and writing. Only two of these characterizations approach absolute distinctions between speaking and writing: (1) the channel difference (many sub-channels available in speaking; only the lexical–syntactic sub-channel available in writing), and (2) the opportunity for interaction with the text (no real-time constraints in writing; severe real-time constraints in speech). Even these two differences are not absolute. Features such as underlining, bold-face, and certain punctuation marks can be used to represent prosodic or paralinguistic sub-channels in writing. Tape-recorded speech bypasses some of the real-time constraints of speech, more so in comprehension than in production. In-class compositions represent writing under severe real-time constraints, although much less so than in speaking. Thus, although each of the parameters listed on Table 2.3 is useful as a distinction between many speaking and writing situations, none of them is an absolute situational distinction between the two modes of communication.

Although these situational distinctions are true only of typical speaking and writing, they can be used to characterize non-typical situations. Following Tannen (1982a, 1985), I use the term 'oral' to refer to typical speaking and 'literate' to refer to typical writing. The differences listed in Table 2.3 can be taken as characteristics of oral and literate situations. Later chapters will discuss the linguistic characteristics of oral and literate genres, specifying how they are typically spoken or written in their linguistic characteristics. It is also possible to classify the communicative situations of particular genres as oral or literate. As noted in Section 2.3.1, I am using face-to-face conversation to represent typical speaking and expository prose to represent typical writing. In Figure 2.1, I compare the situational characteristics of these two typical genres to the characteristics of academic lectures and personal letters, to illustrate the fact that there is no one-to-one correspondence between speaking and writing on the one hand and oral and literate situational characteristics on the other.

In Figure 2.1, face-to-face conversation is presented as a typical speaking situation: for each of the situational dichotomies presented in Table 2.3, ordinary conversation shows the value typical of the speaking situation. Similarly, academic expository prose is presented as a typical writing situation. The characterization of academic lectures and personal letters is more interesting. Academic lectures are spoken but show literate situational characteristics for school acquisition, social value, shared personal knowledge among participants, and information load. In many respects, therefore, lectures can be classified as a literate situation. The opposite characterization is seen for personal letters. Although they are written, they show oral situational characteristics for shared personal knowledge, effort expended to maintain the relationship, and informational load, and intermediate situational characteristics with respect to most of the other differences. Only with respect to physical channel and opportunity for interaction with the text do they show literate values. Thus, personal letters can be classified as having relatively oral situational characteristics although they are written.

These four genres were singled out because they show widely different situational characteristics. They illustrate the fact that there is no simple correspondence between speaking/writing and oral/literate characteristics. Face-to-face conversation is a spoken genre with highly oral situational characteristics; academic prose is a written genre with highly literate situational characteristics; academic lectures represent a spoken genre with relatively literate situational characteristics; and personal letters represent a written genre with relatively oral situational characteristics. In Chapter 7, a similar disparity between the linguistic characterization of genres as spoken/written and oral/literate is shown.

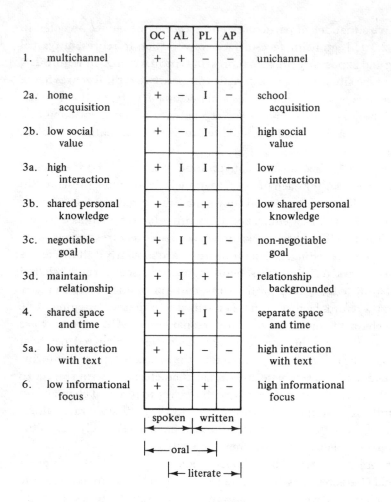

Figure 2.1 *Oral and literate situational characteristics of four genres*
Key: OC = ordinary conversation, AL = academic lectures, PL = personal
letters, AP = academic prose. '+' marks an oral situational value, '−'
marks a literate situational value, 'I' marks an intermediate situational
value.

3 Previous linguistic research on speech and writing

3.1 Overall linguistic generalizations

There is a long history of research on the linguistic characterization of speech and writing. Although a variety of approaches has been adopted, the shared goal of most previous studies has been to identify specific linguistic features that distinguish between the two modes. Many studies also offer overall linguistic characterizations of speech and writing. In general, writing is claimed to be:

1. more structurally complex and elaborate than speech, indicated by features such as longer sentences or T-units and a greater use of subordination (O'Donnell *et al*. 1967; O'Donnell 1974; Kroll 1977; Chafe 1982; Akinnaso 1982; Tannen 1982a, 1985; Gumperz *et al*. 1984);
2. more explicit than speech, in that it has complete idea units with all assumptions and logical relations encoded in the text (DeVito 1966; 1967; Olson 1977);
3. more decontextualized, or autonomous, than speech, so that it is less dependent on shared situation or background knowledge (Kay 1977; Olson 1977);
4. less personally involved than speech and more detached and abstract than speech (Blankenship 1974; Chafe 1982; Chafe and Danielewicz 1986);
5. characterized by a higher concentration of new information than speech (Stubbs 1980; Kroch and Hindle 1982; Brown and Yule 1983); and
6. more deliberately organized and planned than speech (Ochs 1979; Rubin 1980; Akinnaso 1982; Brown and Yule 1983; Gumperz *et al*. 1984).

As is often the case with broad generalizations, the characterizations listed here do not adequately describe the details of the relations between speech and writing. None of these generalizations is true of all spoken and written genres, and while most of them are characterizations of typical speech and typical writing, some do not seem adequate even in that regard.

The generalization that writing is decontextualized, while speech is contextualized, is based on the perception that speech maximally depends on a shared situation and background while writing does not depend on such a shared context. Tannen (1982a, 1985) notes that this characterization is true of the linguistic differences between conversation and expository prose, the two genres most frequently used to represent speech and writing, but it is not true of speech and writing in general. Spoken genres such as academic lectures do not show a high dependence on a shared context, while written genres such as personal letters or office memos do show such a dependence. Rader (1982) shows that imaginative fiction, which might be regarded as highly literate and therefore decontextualized, depends crucially on background information supplied by the reader and an active role on the part of the reader in the creation of an imagined world. Finally, Prince (1981) raises questions concerning the adequacy of this generalization for even academic prose and face-to-face conversation. In a comparison of a written academic article and a spoken narrative, she finds many more evoked entities (previously mentioned or physically present in the situational context) in the spoken text, but many more inferable entities (reference that is dependent on logical or plausible reasoning by the addressee) in the written text. From this perspective, conversation is contextualized in that it refers directly to the physical speech situation and participants; but academic prose is contextualized in that it crucially depends on shared (academic) background knowledge for understanding.

The claims that writing is more complex, elaborate, and explicit than speech are the most widely accepted of the above characterizations. This greater complexity is generally attributed to two distinctive characteristics of writing: the lack of strict time constraints during production, and the need to establish cohesion strictly through the lexical–syntactic channel. Thus, Chafe (1982:37) notes that 'in writing we have time to mold a succession of ideas into a more complex, coherent, integrated whole', whereas speech, because it is produced on-line, is more fragmented. Tannen (1982a:3) notes that 'cohesion is established in spoken discourse through paralinguistic and non-verbal channels (such as intonation, gesture, and eye-gaze), while cohesion is established in writing through lexicalization and complex syntactic structures which make connectives explicit'. Similar characterizations are offered by Akinnaso (1982), and Gumperz *et al.* (1984). This generalization, however, is not universally accepted. In particular, two studies claim that speech is more structurally complex than writing (Poole and Field 1976;

Halliday 1979), and Blankenship (1962) concludes that there are no important linguistic differences between the two modes. The present study investigates the adequacy of this generalization further, showing that elaboration and structural complexity are not homogeneous constructs and that there is no single characterization of speech and writing with respect to them.

The remaining characterizations listed above, concerning personal involvement, concentration of new information, and overall organization, are similarly inadequate as absolute differences between speech and writing. The present study shows that each of these generalizations holds for some spoken and written genres, but they are not adequate as proposals concerning general linguistic differences between the two modes.

3.2 Previous quantitative studies

To support the generalizations listed in the last section, researchers have looked at the distribution of specific linguistic features in spoken and written texts. For example, structural complexity and elaboration have been measured by the frequency of different subordinate constructions, prepositional phrase series, adjectives, etc.; complex texts are claimed to make frequent use of these features. Explicitness has been measured by features such as word length and type/token ratio, which is the ratio of the number of different words to total number of words. Detachment and decontextualization have been measured by the frequency of passives, nominalizations, noun series, etc. Personal involvement has been measured by frequency of personal pronouns, questions, exclamations, and similar features.

I noted in the last section that none of the overall generalizations about speech and writing are uniformly accepted. In the same way, more specific disagreements among studies are common. In a few cases, the cause of the disagreement may simply be definitional. For example, Blankenship (1962, 1974) found sentence length in speech and writing to be nearly the same, while other researchers (e.g., O'Donnell 1974; Poole and Field 1976) have found the mean length of sentences, clauses, or T-units to be considerably longer in writing. A major problem here concerns the definition of 'sentence' in speech (in English), and since most studies do not define their particular use of the term, there is no basis for comparison. A similar example is the description of speech in

Horowitz and Newman (1964) as containing more ideas and subordinate ideas, and being more elaborated, than writing, in contrast to the generally accepted view that writing is more elaborated than speech. The problem with this study concerns the definition of 'idea', which is conceptualized as a cognitive entity rather than a syntactic unit. This study thus does not describe linguistic complexity or elaboration at all; rather, it shows that, given the same amount of time, a speaker can verbalize more 'ideas' than a writer.

Other contradictions are more difficult to explain. The most striking of these relates to the extent of subordination in the two modes. Most studies have found that writing has a much higher degree of subordination than speech, reflecting its greater structural complexity (O'Donnell 1974; Kroll 1977; Kay 1977; Chafe 1982; and Brown and Yule 1983). Other studies, though, do not support these results, finding little difference in the overall number of subordinate clauses between speech and writing (Blass and Siegman 1975; Cayer and Sacks 1979). In fact, some studies have found the opposite. Poole and Field (1976) found a higher index of embedding in speech, Price and Graves (1980) found a higher ratio of dependent clauses in speech, and Halliday (1979) found more 'complex sentence structures' (i.e., more clauses) in speech. Beaman (1984) presents a careful analysis of subordination in spoken and written narratives; she notes that previous studies have been overly simplistic and that different subordinate constructions may have differing communicative functions.

Another striking contradiction involves the frequency of passive constructions in the two modes. Passives have been associated with decontextualization or detachment and therefore claimed to be characteristic of writing to a greater extent than speech (e.g., Chafe 1982; Brown and Yule 1983). In contrast, Blankenship (1962) found only slightly more passives in writing than speech, while Poole and Field (1976) found few passives in either mode.

Other contradictions may be less striking, because the measures involved are less stereotypically associated with one or the other mode, but they are equally confusing. For instance, with respect to degree of elaboration, Cayer and Sacks (1979) and Stubbs (1980) found more adverbs in writing; Blankenship (1974) found no significant difference in the frequencies of adverbs; and Poole and Field (1976) and Tottie (1984) found more adverbs in speech. The findings are more consistent with respect to adjectives, with Poole and Field, Cayer and Sacks, and Chafe

finding more in writing. Blankenship (1974), though, found no significant difference between the modes, but she did find this to be a useful
measure for distinguishing among genres within both speech and
writing.

Beaman (1984) is one of the few researchers using a quantitative
approach who addresses these widespread contradictory findings. She
notes that the failure to control for differences in register, purpose, degree
of formality, and planning contributes to the confusing picture emerging
from previous quantitative studies. Other researchers have abandoned
quantitative approaches altogether for these same reasons. In the next
section, some non-quantitative studies of speech and writing are
discussed.

3.3 Non-quantitative approaches

Researchers like Akinnaso (1982) and Gumperz *et al.* (1984) claim that
quantitative studies have not addressed the important issues relating to
speech and writing, and that they are perhaps unable to do so. Thus,
Akinnaso questions the validity of previous generalizations regarding the
overall relationships between speech and writing:

> comparative studies of spoken and written language have emphasized
> general, rather than specific, consequences of writing on language
> structure, the working assumption being that written language is
> generally more complex than spoken language. Yet contradictions occur
> when different studies are compared on specific findings. (1982:110)

Akinnaso goes on to conclude that the very attempt to quantify the
relations between speech and writing is at the root of these contradictory
findings. He notes, for example, that a central problem of previous
studies is

> their quantitative orientation, each researcher deciding on what and
> how to count. It is commonplace in social science that statistical counts
> usually capture only 'etic' rather than 'emic' categories, thereby
> ignoring the underlying logic behind surface behavior. (1982:110)

In contrast to the quantitative approach of earlier studies, Akinnaso
and Gumperz propose to study speech and writing from the perspective
of thematic cohesion, an analysis of the ways in which surface structure
elements in a text are connected to mark their unified function in
developing a common theme (Halliday and Hasan 1976). By investigating the ways in which thematic cohesion is achieved in each mode, these

researchers attempt to uncover the underlying differences between speech and writing.

Several other researchers have also opted for a non-quantitative approach. Tannen (1982a) analyzes two texts in detail with respect to linguistic features of integration and involvement. Rader (1982) analyzes a written narrative in detail to show that writing as well as speech can rely heavily on context. These and other researchers have chosen a non-quantitative approach for the greater detail and depth of analysis possible when the linguistic characteristics of a text are directly interpreted in terms of their function(s) in the communicative interaction.

In the present study, I use both quantitative and non-quantitative analyses because the two approaches have complementary strengths and weaknesses (see Chapter 4). Quantitative analyses give a solid empirical foundation to the findings; non-quantitative analyses are required for the interpretation. Either type of analysis in isolation gives an incomplete description. The research results of this combined approach argue against the assessment that quantitative analyses are sterile and invalid. Rather, I claim here that other major restrictions in experimental design, found in both quantitative and non-quantitative studies, have been the cause of the inadequate and contradictory conclusions reached in many previous studies. We now turn to these restrictions and the general design requirements of any study intending to reach valid generalizations concerning speech and writing.

3.4   Requirements for global conclusions concerning speech and writing

The research designs of many previous studies have three major restrictions, and it is these restrictions, rather than a quantitative or non-quantitative approach, that limit the extent to which they can provide global conclusions regarding the linguistic relations among spoken and written genres. Studies with restricted research designs can contribute valuable analyses of individual linguistic features in individual texts and genres, but they do not provide an adequate foundation for global conclusions concerning speech and writing. The three restrictions are:

1.   assigning undue weight to individual texts – because most studies have been based on few texts, an unusual or idiosyncratic text can have a major influence on the analysis;

2.   assigning undue weight to the genres chosen for analysis – most studies

have compared only two genres, one spoken and one written, and many of these have not controlled for the communicative task represented by those genres;

3.　assigning undue weight to particular linguistic features – although most studies have considered only a few linguistic features, they have considered a differential distribution in any individual feature to be important evidence.[1]

Schafer (1981:12) notes similar restrictions and finds it 'frustrating' that although previous studies 'are based on texts produced in particular circumstances by only a few subjects . . . speaking and writing in only one situation, this doesn't prevent researchers from offering their results as accurate generalizations of universal differences between speaking and writing'. These restrictions can be found in both quantitative and non-quantitative studies.

First, nearly all previous studies analyze only a few texts. It is very time-consuming to analyze a large number of texts, but the potential influence of idiosyncratic texts on global conclusions must be recognized in studies where it is not possible to analyze a large sample.

The second restriction involves two parts: many studies compare only two genres, and they do not control for the communicative task represented by those genres. The problems resulting from the failure to control for communicative task have been noted by several recent researchers (Akinnaso 1982; Tannen 1982a, 1985; Beaman 1984; Gumperz *et al.* 1984). That is, several earlier studies find striking differences between speech and writing because they compare very different communicative tasks, such as face-to-face conversation and academic prose; other studies find speech and writing to be nearly the same because they compare similar communicative tasks in the two modes, such as expository articles and public speeches. When attempting to reconcile these studies, it is very difficult to determine whether observed dif-

---

[1]　There is actually a fourth restriction, in that previous studies have assigned undue weight to the choice of speaker/writer and the choice of language. That is, most studies have taken the speech and writing of middle-class academics to be representative of the English-speaking community as a whole. This decision has been pragmatic, in that it is relatively easy to collect data in academic contexts, but it represents a serious limitation on our general knowledge of speech and writing in English. Further, although most studies have examined only English, they tend to generalize their findings to 'speech' and 'writing', as if the relations among spoken and written genres were the same in all languages. This is particularly not true in the case of non-Western language and cultures, where both the functions and form of spoken and written genres vary considerably from Western norms (Besnier 1986a).

ferences are due to the mode distinction or to some other difference in communicative purpose or situation. To remedy this problem, researchers like Beaman, Tannen, and Gumperz recommend comparing the same communicative task across the two modes: Beaman and Tannen compare written and spoken narratives, and Gumperz compares a written and spoken exposition. Such a comparison guarantees that any observed difference is indeed attributable to differences in the production channel.

A pair-wise comparison of genres, however, cannot determine the overall relations among texts in speech and writing. That is, the final goal in all of these studies is an overall description of the similarities and differences among the full range of spoken and written genres in English. We would like to know, for all spoken and written genres, the ways in which they are similar, the ways in which they are different, and some measure of the extent of their similarities and differences. Such a goal cannot be achieved by a restricted comparison of a few genres, whether they represent the same task in the two modes or not. Rather, it requires comparison of the full range of genres in a single analysis.

Finally, previous studies have focused on relatively few linguistic features as the crucial discriminators among spoken and written texts. Earlier quantitative studies focused on the number of subordinate clauses, passives, etc.; non-quantitative researchers focus on features like thematic cohesion. The analyses presented in Chapters 6–8 of the present book, however, demonstrate that no single linguistic feature can adequately account for the full range of variation among spoken and written texts. Research in sociolinguistics conducted over the last twenty years has shown natural language variation to be quite complex, giving every reason to expect multiple dimensions of variation among spoken and written genres. Work by Hymes, Labov, Gumperz, and others has described systematic linguistic variation across a wide range of social and situational parameters, including the social class and ethnic group of participants, the social and situational relationship between the participants, the setting, and the purpose of communication (Brown and Fraser 1979). The picture emerging from this research is one of a complex coupling of linguistic features and functions, with single features serving many functions and single functions being marked by many features. Thus, the expectation that multiple linguistic features and multiple dimensions will be required for an adequate description of linguistic variation among genres is supported by our general knowledge of language use in society. It is this expectation which forms the basis of the present study.

The discussion in earlier sections has shown that the relations among spoken and written genres are highly complex and still not well-understood. The present section has shown that this is due, at least in part, to the restricted research designs often adopted in earlier studies. An approach is needed that can combine a much broader perspective with an adequate empirical analysis of the linguistic measures involved.

3.5   A new approach: multi-feature/multi-dimensional analysis

The present study is based on the assumption that there are few, if any, absolute differences between speech and writing, and that there is no single parameter of linguistic variation that distinguishes among spoken and written genres. It seeks to systematically describe the linguistic characteristics of the range of genres in English, whether typically spoken, typically written, or other. For each genre we need to know the particular ways in which it is oral and the ways in which it is literate. Thus the present study attempts to identify the linguistic parameters along which genres vary, so that any individual genre can be located within an 'oral' and 'literate' space, specifying both the nature and the extent of the differences and similarities between that genre and the range of other genres in English.

The two key notions of this framework, textual dimension and textual relation, have been described in Chapter 1. Dimensions are bundles of linguistic features that co-occur in texts because they work together to mark some common underlying function. Relations are defined in terms of the dimensions; they specify the ways in which any two genres are linguistically similar and the extent to which they are similar. Both dimensions and relations can be specified quantitatively using computational tools, while careful microscopic analyses of texts are required to interpret the functions underlying the dimensions and to explain the observed relations among genres. These tools are described in detail in Chapters 4–5; the important point here is that the co-occurrence patterns underlying dimensions are identified empirically and quantitatively, rather than on the basis of informed intuitions about texts.

The multi-feature/multi-dimensional (MF/MD) approach to linguistic variation (Biber 1985, 1986a) has been developed to describe the textual relations among spoken and written genres. This approach uses standardized computer-based text corpora and automatic identification techniques to compute the frequencies of salient lexical and syntactic features. The co-occurrence patterns among these features are analyzed through multivariate statistical techniques to identify the functional dimensions of linguistic variation among texts and to provide an overall description of relations among genres with respect to these dimensions.

Research designs using an MF/MD approach avoid the three restrictions identified in the last section. First, large-scale text corpora are used to provide a data base of several hundred text samples. Secondly, texts representing several major genres, such as conversation, broadcast, public speeches, academic prose, and fiction are included in the analysis. The large number of texts precludes a confounding influence from idiosyncratic variation, and inclusion of several genres insures that the analysis will adequately represent the range of variation among texts in spoken and written English.

Thirdly, an MF/MD approach analyzes the distribution of many lexical and syntactic features representing a broad range of the communicative functions served in speech and writing, such as content elaboration and interaction of communicative participants. The frequency of each feature is counted in each of the texts, and statistical techniques are used to empirically group the linguistic features into clusters that co-occur with a high frequency in texts.

Studies using an MF/MD approach show that quantitative approaches are not inherently narrow or theoretically uninteresting. This approach takes advantage of the strengths of both quantitative and non-quantitative approaches while avoiding the restrictions shared by previous studies. The MF/MD approach adopts the notion that co-occurrence patterns are central to register variation from earlier socio-linguistic theory, and it uses computational tools to identify dimensions quantitatively based on these co-occurrence patterns. For all of the above reasons, an MF/MD analysis is well-suited to the description of the global relations among spoken and written genres in a language.

3.6   Summary of the textual dimensions identified to date

Several previous studies have used an MF/MD approach to identify textual dimensions in speech and writing (Biber 1984, 1986a, 1986b; Finegan and Biber 1986b). To date, this research has identified three primary dimensions of linguistic variation among texts in English (see especially Biber 1986a). To reflect their underlying functions, these dimensions are tentatively labelled as follows:

Dimension I: Interactive versus Edited Text
Dimension II: Abstract versus Situated Content
Dimension III: Reported versus Immediate Style

Each dimension represents a group of linguistic features that co-occur in texts, identified by computational analyses. Dimension I is characterized linguistically by features like questions and first and second person pronouns versus word length and more varied vocabulary. Dimension II is characterized by features like nominalizations and passives versus place and time adverbs. Dimension III is characterized by past tense versus present tense features.

These studies have consistently shown that the relations among genres are complex and that no single dimension adequately captures the similarities and differences among genres; rather, a multi-dimensional model is required. This finding can be illustrated by consideration of the relations among four genres, academic prose, professional letters, broadcast, and conversation, along the first two dimensions listed above. With respect to Dimension I (Interactive versus Edited Text), conversation and academic prose are at opposite extremes; conversation is characterized as highly interactive and not edited; academic prose is highly edited but not interactive. These characterizations are precisely quantifiable in terms of the frequencies of co-occurring linguistic features in the genres. Along this same dimension, professional letters, although written, are more similar to conversation than to academic prose, while broadcast, although spoken, is more similar to academic prose than to conversation.

With respect to Dimension II (Abstract versus Situated Content), the relations among these four genres are quite different. Conversation and academic prose are again at opposite poles: conversation highly situated, academic prose highly abstract. Contrary to their positions with respect to one another along Dimension I, however, broadcast is very similar to conversation with respect to Dimension II: both are highly situated. Similarly, both professional letters and academic prose are highly abstract with respect to this dimension.

While consideration of the distribution of texts along any individual dimension is informative, a fuller picture of the relations among these four genres results from a joint consideration of Dimensions I and II: conversation is interactive and situated; professional letters are interactive and abstract; broadcast is situated but not markedly interactive or markedly edited; academic prose is edited and abstract. In these earlier studies, analysis of the similarities and differences among spoken and written genres with respect to all three dimensions enabled a first approximation of a model of textual relations in English.

Taking these earlier studies as its departure point, the present book greatly extends prior research findings and develops a comprehensive model of textual relations among spoken and written genres in English. Many additional linguistic features are included here, as are some additional genres, enabling identification of additional dimensions. In all, six textual dimensions are identified and interpreted in the present study, and the relations among spoken and written genres are analyzed with respect to this six-dimensional model.

Part II: Methodology

4 Methodological overview of the study

4.1 Macroscopic and microscopic approaches to textual variation

Within the broad framework of investigation into the psychological and sociological underpinnings of linguistic variation, researchers have investigated textual variation through macroscopic and microscopic analyses. Macroscopic analysis attempts to define the overall dimensions of variation in a language. Microscopic analysis, on the other hand, provides a detailed description of the communicative functions of particular linguistic features (e.g., clefts as markers of informational prominence, or first person pronouns as markers of personal involvement).

Much of the previous work analyzing linguistic variation in texts falls into the category of microscopic analysis. For instance, Schiffrin (1981) looks at the different functions of past tense and present tense forms in referring to past events in narrative. Aijmer (1986) and Stenström (1986) study the functions of *actually* and *really* respectively in conversational texts. Thompson (1983) studies the functions of detached participial clauses in descriptive texts. And Tannen (1982a) contrasts the level of imageability in written and spoken narratives to illustrate the use of oral strategies in written discourse. These and other studies are characterized by their detailed attention to the functions of specific features in representative texts.

Macroscopic analyses identify the overall parameters of linguistic variation within a given 'domain', e.g., spoken and written texts in English or the range of expository prose in English; they are based on the notions of textual dimension and textual relation. There are few previous examples of macroscopic analyses using quantitative statistical techniques. One of the earliest studies was by Carroll (1960), who examines written prose in English to uncover six dimensions of style, labelled:

General Stylistic Evaluation, Personal Affect, Ornamentation, Abstractness, Seriousness, and Characterization. In a similar study, Marckworth and Baker (1974) uncover three dimensions of style in non-fictional prose in English; they do not propose labels for their dimensions. Poole (1973) identifies six underlying dimensions of restricted and elaborated code variation. In a series of studies at the University of Southern California, a MF/MD approach to macroscopic variation has been used to examine relations among spoken and written texts in English (Biber 1984, 1986a, 1986b), relations among spoken and written texts in Nukulaelae Tuvaluan (Besnier 1986a), relations among American and British written genres (Biber 1987), dimensions of discourse complexity (Finegan and Biber 1986b), dimensions of sociolinguistic prestige (Finegan and Biber 1986a), dimensions of literary and expository style (Biber and Finegan 1988b, 1988c; Grabe 1984a), styles of 'stance' (Biber and Finegan 1988a, forthcoming), and a typology of English texts (Biber and Finegan 1986; Biber forthcoming). Biber (1985) presents a methodological overview of the multi-feature/multi-dimensional approach to textual variation.

Micro and macro approaches to text analysis have complementary strengths and weaknesses. Microscopic text analysis is necessary to pinpoint the exact communicative functions of individual linguistic features. It complements macroscopic analysis in two ways: (1) it identifies the potentially important linguistic features and genre distinctions to be included in a macro-analysis, and (2) it provides detailed functional analyses of individual linguistic features, which enable interpretation of the textual dimension in functional terms. Microscopic analysis, however, is not able to identify the overall parameters of linguistic variation within a set of texts because it is restricted to analysis of few linguistic features in individual texts.

In contrast, macroscopic analyses are needed to identify the underlying textual dimensions in a set of texts, enabling an overall account of linguistic variation among those texts and providing a framework for discussion of the similarities and differences among particular texts and genres. Macro-analysis is restricted in that it overlooks relatively minor parameters of textual variation and relies on form-to-function correlations established in micro-analyses.

These two approaches to text analysis are mutually dependent. Macro-analysis depends on micro-analysis for the identification and functional interpretation of potentially important linguistic features, while micro-analysis benefits from the overall theoretical framework provided by macro-analysis; that is, the choice of texts and linguistic features deserving detailed micro-analysis will be influenced by knowledge of the underlying textual dimensions within a set of texts. The analysis of speech and writing presented here depends on both approaches: it uses a macroscopic approach to analyze the co-occurrence patterns among 67 linguistic features in 481 texts, identifying seven textual dimensions; and it uses microscopic analyses to interpret these dimensions in functional terms.

4.2   Methodological overview of the study

The distinctive methodological characteristics of the present study are: (1) the use of computer-based text corpora, providing a standardized data base and ready access to a wide range of variation in communicative situations and purposes; (2) the use of computer programs to count the frequency of certain linguistic features in a wide range of texts, enabling analysis of the distribution of many linguistic features across many texts and genres; (3) the use of multivariate statistical techniques, especially factor analysis, to determine co-occurrence relations among the linguistic features; and (4) the use of microscopic analyses to interpret the functional parameters underlying the quantitatively identified co-occurrence patterns.

Table 4.1 summarizes the methodological steps of the analysis, which is based on the MF/MD approach to textual variation (Biber 1985). The initial steps involve the choice of texts and linguistic features for analysis. This is followed by the quantitative steps: computational identification of linguistic features in texts, analysis of co-occurrence patterns using factor analysis, and comparison of texts with respect to the dimensions based on computed factor scores. Functional analyses are used to interpret the dimensions identified by the factor analysis and to interpret the relations among texts specified by the factor scores.

A more complete description of factor analysis and factor scores is given in Chapter 5; here I will only summarize the essential concepts. Factor analysis uses frequency counts of linguistic features to identify sets of features that co-occur in texts. As noted in Chapter 1, the use of this technique to identify underlying textual dimensions is based on the assumption that frequently co-occurring linguistic features have at least one shared communicative function. It is claimed here that there are relatively few primary linguistic functions in English, and that the

Table 4.1   *Steps in the analysis*

```
Preliminary analyses:

        -- review of previous research to identify potentially
              important linguistic features
        -- collection of texts and conversion to machine-readable
              form; review previous research to insure that all
              important situational distinctions are included
              in the text sample
        -- count occurrence of features in the texts (through the
              use of computer programs written in PL/1)



Step 1:  Factor analysis:

        -- clustering of linguistic features into groups of
              features that co-occur with a high frequency in texts
        -- interpretation of the factors as textual dimensions
              through assessment of the communicative function(s)
              most widely shared by the features constituting each
              factor



Step 2:  Factor scores as operational representatives of the
         textual dimensions:

        -- for each factor, compute a factor score for each text
        -- compute an average factor score for the texts within
              each genre
        -- comparison of the average factor scores for each genre
        -- further interpretation of the textual dimensions in
              light of the relations among genres with respect
              to the factor scores
```

---

frequent co-occurrence of a group of linguistic features in texts is indicative of an underlying function shared by those features. Working from this assumption, it is possible to decipher a unified dimension underlying each set of co-occurring linguistic features. In this sense, I am using factor analysis as it is commonly used in other social and behavioral sciences: to summarize the interrelationships among a large group of variables in a concise fashion; to build underlying dimensions (or constructs) that are conceptually clearer than the many linguistic measures considered individually.

Although factor analysis enables quantitative identification of underlying dimensions within a set of texts, it cannot be employed usefully apart from a theoretically-motivated research design. That is, before performing a factor analysis, the range of communicative situations and purposes available in a language must be determined, and texts representing that range of variation must be collected. In the same way, linguistic features that are potentially important indicators of variation within the domain must be identified in advance and measured in each of the texts. Inadequate preparation or skewing in these theoretical prerequisites can invalidate the results of a factor analysis (Gorsuch 1983:336ff). That is, factor analysis provides the primary analytical tool, but is dependent on the theoretical foundation provided by an adequate data base of texts and inclusion of multiple linguistic features.

4.3 Text selection

In selecting the texts to be used in a macroscopic textual analysis, care must be taken to include a broad range of the possible situational, social, and communicative task variation occurring in the language. Factor analysis identifies sets of features that co-vary, but if the texts to be analyzed do not represent the full range of situational variation, then neither will the dimensions. The first step in the analysis, then, is to identify the range of situational variation in English and to collect texts representing that range. As noted in earlier chapters, texts can vary along several situational parameters, including their reliance on context, their processing constraints, their communicative purposes, and their relationships among communicative participants.

In English, the task of collecting texts representing the range of situational possibilities is relatively easy due to the availability of standard computerized text corpora, which provide a large number of texts taken from a wide range of genres. A standard corpus enables the verification of results and the direct comparison of results from one study to the next. The use of a computerized corpus also enables automatic identification of linguistic features in a very large collection of texts. In a factor analysis, the data base should include five times as many texts as linguistic features to be analyzed (Gorsuch 1983:332). In addition, simply representing the range of situational and processing possibilities in English requires a large number of texts. To analyze this number of texts without the aid of computational tools would require several years;

computerized corpora enable storage and analysis of a large number of texts in an efficient manner.

Two major text corpora are used for the present analysis. The first is the Lancaster–Oslo–Bergen Corpus of British English, known as the LOB Corpus (see Johansson *et al.* 1978 and Johansson 1982). This corpus is drawn exclusively from printed sources published in 1961. It comprises 500 text samples of about 2,000 words each, taken from fifteen genres: press reportage, editorials, press reviews, religion, popular lore, skills and hobbies, biographies and essays, official documents, learned writings, fiction (including general, mystery, adventure, science, and romance), and humor. The total corpus contains approximately one million words of running text.

The second corpus is the London–Lund Corpus of Spoken English (Svartvik and Quirk 1980; Johansson 1982). This corpus is a collection of 87 spoken British English texts of about 5,000 words each. The total corpus contains approximately 500,000 words, representing six major speech situations: private conversations, public conversations (including interviews and panel discussions), telephone conversations, radio broadcasts, spontaneous speeches, and prepared speeches.

A third corpus, the Brown University corpus of written American English (see Francis and Kucera 1982), has been used in previous studies but is not used here. This is the oldest of the three corpora, and is probably the first large-scale computer-based corpus to be compiled. The LOB corpus is a direct replication of the Brown corpus, so that parallel text samples exist for British and American written English. To avoid any confounding influences from a comparison of British and American English (Biber 1987), the analyses in the present book do not use the Brown corpus.

Since the standard corpora do not include non-published written texts, I have added a collection of professional and personal letters. The professional letters were written in academic contexts but deal with administrative rather than intellectual matters. They are formal and directed to individuals, but their purposes are both informational and interactional.[1] The personal letters are written to friends or relatives; they range from intimate to friendly. Most of the letters are written by Americans, but some of them are written by Canadian or British writers.

Table 4.2 lists the 23 genres used in the study. These genres represent

---

[1] The professional letters were collected by William Grabe.

Table 4.2 *Distribution of texts across 23 genres*

GENRE	# OF TEXTS
Written -- genres 1-15 from the LOB corpus	
1. Press reportage	44
2. Editorials	27
3. Press reviews	17
4. Religion	17
5. Skills and hobbies	14
6. Popular lore	14
7. Biographies	14
8. Official documents	14
9. Academic prose	80
10. General fiction	29
11. Mystery fiction	13
12. Science fiction	6
13. Adventure fiction	13
14. Romantic fiction	13
15. Humor	9
16. Personal letters	6
17. Professional letters	10
Spoken -- from the London-Lund corpus	
18. Face-to-face conversation	44
19. Telephone conversation	27
20. Public conversations, debates, and interviews	22
21. Broadcast	18
22. Spontaneous speeches	16
23. Planned speeches	14
Total:	481
Approximate number of words:	960,000

the full range of situational possibilities available in the corpora: fifteen written genres from the LOB corpus, six spoken genres from the London–Lund corpus, plus the two types of letters. These texts were analyzed by computer to identify occurrences of the relevant linguistic features. The computational analysis involved two steps: automatic grammatical analysis by computer programs (described in Appendix II), and editing the computer results by hand to check for errors. Because the editing was quite time-consuming, not all of the texts in the corpora were used, although all genres in the corpora are represented. A list of the specific texts from the corpora used in the study is given as Appendix I.

The composition of some of these genres requires elaboration because some of the genre categories comprise several sub-genres. Table 4.3 lists these sub-genre distinctions. Press includes several sub-classes: political, sports, society, spot news, financial, and cultural. Editorials includes institutional and personal editorials as well as letters to the editor. Popular lore contains texts about politics, history, health, etc., taken from popular magazines and books (e.g., *Punch*, *Woman's Mirror*, *Wine and Food*). Official documents are primarily government documents, but also foundation reports, industry reports, and a section from a university catalog. Academic prose combines several sub-classes: natural sciences, medicine, mathematics, social and behavioral sciences, political science/law/education, humanities, and technology/engineering. Public conversations, debates, and interviews represent public, relatively formal interactions (e.g., on radio talk shows). Spontaneous speeches are unprepared public monologues, for example, from a court case, dinner speech, or speeches in the House of Commons. One of these texts (a court case) includes some dialogic exchanges also. Prepared speeches are planned but without a written text, and are taken from sermons, university lectures, court cases, etc. Finally, broadcast is composed of radio sports broadcasting and other radio commentary on non-sports events. The other text categories are self-explanatory. For the LOB corpus, Johansson *et al.* (1978) further describe the kinds of texts in each genre and give bibliographic references for each of the texts. For the London–Lund corpus, some further information about the genre classes and the speakers can be found in Svartvik and Quirk (1980).

I use the term 'genre' to refer to text categorizations made on the basis of external criteria relating to author/speaker purpose. The genre categories in the present study are adopted from the distinctions used in the corpora. Some of these categories are complex and might be considered to be a combination of several genres. For example, prepared speeches comprise sermons, university lectures, final statements in court, and political speeches, all of which can be considered as different genres. In these cases, the general category (e.g., prepared speeches) might be considered as a 'way of speaking' (Hymes 1974), representing a super-ordinate category, while the specific categories might be considered as the 'genres'. Although this more specific use of the term might be theoreti-

Table 4.3 *List of sub-genres used in the study*

Press:
     political
     sports
     society
     spot news
     financial
     cultural

Editorials:
     institutional
     personal
     letters to the editor

Official documents:
     government documents
     foundation reports
     industry reports
     college catalog
     industry house organ

Academic prose:
     natural sciences
     medicine
     mathematics
     social and behavioral sciences
     political science, law, and education
     humanities
     technology and engineering

Broadcasts (radio):
     sports
     non-sports

Spontaneous speeches:
     case in court
     dinner speech
     radio essays
     speeches in House of Commons

Prepared speeches:
     sermons
     university lectures
     cases in court
     political speech
     popular lecture

---

cally preferable, in the present study I use the term 'genre' for the general categories distinguished in the LOB and London–Lund corpora. In Chapter 8, however, I consider the relations among several of the more specific 'sub-genre' categories included in the corpora and listed in Table 4.3.

Texts can differ by subject-matter, purpose, rhetorical structure, and style in addition to situational parameters such as the relation between the communicative participants, the relation of the participants to the external context, and the relation of the participants to the text itself. As noted above, I use the term 'genre' to refer to categorizations assigned on the basis of external criteria. I use the term 'text type', on the other hand, to refer to groupings of texts that are similar with respect to their linguistic form, irrespective of genre categories (similar to the 'speech styles' discussed by Ervin-Tripp 1972 and Hymes 1974). For example, a science fiction text represents a genre of fiction (relating to author's purpose), but it might represent an abstract and technical text type (in terms of its linguistic form), similar to some types of academic exposition and different from most other fictional texts. In a fully developed typology of texts, genres and text types must be distinguished, and the relations among them identified and explained (see Biber and Finegan 1986; Biber forthcoming). The present study deals only with the relations among spoken and written genres, but the model developed here provides the basis for a typology of texts as well.

The makers of the corpora do not provide a great deal of information concerning the writers and speakers. As the written texts have all been published (except for the private collections of letters), it can be assumed that all writers are educated and probably from the middle-class. The speakers in the London–Lund corpus are more diverse. They range in age from 20 to 87 years, and they include academics, students, secretaries, housewives, engineers, doctors, bankers, clerks, electricians, broadcasters, MPs, ministers, and judges.

The genres used in the present study represent a broad range of the situational possibilities of speaking and writing in English, discussed in Chapter 2. Among the written genres, press is directed towards a more general audience than academic prose, involves considerable effort towards maintaining a relationship with its audience, and is concerned with temporal and physical situations in addition to abstract information. Editorial letters are less concerned about offending potential readers, but make greater assumptions concerning specific shared background knowledge (e.g., concerning particular social issues or past articles appearing in the press). Professional letters are structured like academic prose, often stating a thesis with several supporting arguments, but they are directed towards individuals, require concern for the interpersonal relationship, and enable a relatively high degree of interaction between participants and reliance on shared background. Fiction is directed to a very broad audience but requires a considerable amount of shared cultural assumptions and builds its own internal shared physical and temporal context. Finally, personal letters are informal and directed to individuals, they deal with truly personal matters, and they assume a high degree of shared background knowledge between writer and reader.

Among the spoken genres, public speeches are directed towards broad audiences and thus permit little interaction and relatively little dependence on shared knowledge. Spontaneous and planned speeches differ in the amount of time permitted for production, although both allow little time for comprehension in comparison to written genres. Broadcast is directed towards an extremely broad audience, while at the same time being highly dependent on the temporal and physical contexts being reported. In contrast, interviews show little concern for the temporal/physical context but have a high interactional focus, often involving only two direct communicative participants plus a broad audience of passive participants. Finally, in face-to-face and, to a lesser extent, telephone conversation the interactional focus is primary, usually overshadowing the informational focus. Conversation is characterized by a high degree of interaction and goal negotiability, considerable effort at maintaining a relationship, and considerable shared background knowledge. Both face-to-face and telephone conversation share a temporal context, but the shared physical context is more important in face-to-face conversation.

Other genres not included in the present study differ in further ways. Written notes left on the kitchen table, dialogues conducted across a computer network, and tape-recorded 'letters' are three such genres. The genres included in this study, though, represent a broad range of situational possibilities across the written and spoken modes.

4.4 Selection of the linguistic features

Prior to any comparison of texts, a principled decision must be made concerning the linguistic features to be used. For the purposes of this study, previous research was surveyed to identify potentially important linguistic features – those that have been associated with particular communicative functions and therefore might be used to differing extents in different types of texts. No a priori commitment is made concerning the importance of an individual linguistic feature or the validity of a previous functional interpretation during the selection of features. Rather, the goal is to include the widest possible range of *potentially* important linguistic features.

A survey of previous research on spoken/written differences identified the 67 linguistic features used in the present study. Table 4.4 lists these features, organized by their grammatical class; the features fall into sixteen major grammatical categories: (A) tense and aspect markers, (B) place and time adverbials, (C) pronouns and pro-verbs, (D) questions, (E) nominal forms, (F) passives, (G) stative forms, (H) subordination features, (I) prepositional phrases, adjectives, and adverbs, (J) lexical specificity, (K) lexical classes, (L) modals, (M) specialized verb classes, (N) reduced forms and dispreferred structures, (O) coordination, and (P) negation. Although the organization of Table 4.4 reflects the grammatical function of each feature rather than its discourse function, each of these features has been described as a functional marker in texts. The present study is based on the functional aspects of these features, represented by their co-occurrence distributions in texts. These 67 features represent several form–function pairings; features from the same grammatical category can have different functions, and features from different grammatical categories can have a shared function. As such, these features provide a solid basis for determining the underlying functional dimensions in English.

Appendix II gives a detailed description of these features. This appendix provides two types of information. The first concerns the computer programs used for the automatic identification of linguistic features in texts. The appendix sketches the broad outlines of these programs and provides the specific algorithms used for each feature. I have included this information for readers interested in programming applications and for readers who want to know exactly which forms were counted for each feature. The second part of Appendix II presents, for each feature, a summary of the functions proposed in previous research and a list of relevant studies. The functional analyses summarized in this appendix form the basis for the dimension interpretations offered in Chapters 6–8. Further, this information should be useful to readers undertaking microscopic analyses of particular linguistic features.

Table 4.4 *Features used in the analysis*

A. Tense and aspect markers

   1. past tense
   2. perfect aspect
   3. present tense

B. Place and time adverbials

   4. place adverbials (e.g., <u>above</u>, <u>beside</u>, <u>outdoors</u>)
   5. time adverbials (e.g., <u>early</u>, <u>instantly</u>, <u>soon</u>)

C. Pronouns and pro-verbs

   6. first person pronouns
   7. second person pronouns
   8. third person personal pronouns (excluding <u>it</u>)
   9. pronoun <u>it</u>
  10. demonstrative pronouns (<u>that</u>, <u>this</u>, <u>these</u>, <u>those</u> as pronouns)
  11. indefinite pronouns (e.g., <u>anybody</u>, <u>nothing</u>, <u>someone</u>)
  12. pro-verb <u>do</u>

D. Questions

  13. direct WH-questions

E. Nominal forms

  14. nominalizations (ending in <u>-tion</u>, <u>-ment</u>, <u>-ness</u>, <u>-ity</u>)
  15. gerunds (participial forms functioning as nouns)
  16. total other nouns

F. Passives

  17. agentless passives
  18. <u>by</u>-passives

G. Stative forms

  19. <u>be</u> as main verb
  20. existential <u>there</u>

H. Subordination features

  21. <u>that</u> verb complements (e.g., <u>I</u> <u>said that</u> he <u>went</u>.)
  22. <u>that</u> adjective complements (e.g., I'm <u>glad that</u> <u>you</u> <u>like</u> <u>it</u>.)
  23. <u>WH</u> clauses (e.g., <u>I</u> <u>believed</u> <u>what</u> <u>he</u> <u>told</u> <u>me</u>.)
  24. infinitives
  25. present participial clauses (e.g., <u>Stuffing</u> <u>his</u> <u>mouth</u> <u>with</u>
       <u>cookies</u>, <u>Joe</u> <u>ran</u> <u>out</u> <u>the</u> <u>door</u>.)

Table 4.4 (*cont.*)

26. past participial clauses (e.g., Built in a single week, the house would stand for fifty years.)
27. past participial WHIZ deletion relatives (e.g., the solution produced by this process)
28. present participial WHIZ deletion relatives (e.g., the event causing this decline is...)
29. that relative clauses on subject position (e.g., the dog that bit me)
30. that relative clauses on object position (e.g., the dog that I saw)
31. WH relatives on subject position (e.g., the man who likes popcorn)
32. WH relatives on object position (e.g., the man who Sally likes)
33. pied-piping relative clauses (e.g., the manner in which he was told)
34. sentence relatives (e.g., Bob likes fried mangoes, which is the most disgusting thing I've ever heard of)
35. causative adverbial subordinators (because)
36. concessive adverbial subordinators (although, though)
37. conditional adverbial subordinators (if, unless)
38. other adverbial subordinators (e.g., since, while, whereas)

I. Prepositional phrases, adjectives, and adverbs

39. total prepositional phrases
40. attributive adjectives (e.g., the big horse)
41. predicative adjectives (e.g., the horse is big)
42. total adverbs

J. Lexical specificity

43. type/token ratio
44. mean word length

K. Lexical classes

45. conjuncts (e.g., consequently, furthermore, however)
46. downtoners (e.g., barely, nearly, slightly)
47. hedges (e.g., at about, something like, almost)
48. amplifiers (e.g., absolutely, extremely, perfectly)
49. emphatics (e.g., a lot, for sure, really)
50. discourse particles (e.g., sentence initial well, now, anyway)
51. demonstratives

L. Modals

52. possibility modals (can, may, might, could)
53. necessity modals (ought, should, must)
54. predictive modals (will, would, shall)

Table 4.4 (*cont.*)

M. Specialized verb classes

    55. public verbs (e.g., <u>assert</u>, <u>declare</u>, <u>mention</u>, <u>say</u>)
    56. private verbs (e.g., <u>assume</u>, <u>believe</u>, <u>doubt</u>, <u>know</u>)
    57. suasive verbs (e.g., <u>command</u>, <u>insist</u>, <u>propose</u>)
    58. <u>seem</u> and <u>appear</u>

N. Reduced forms and dispreferred structures

    59. contractions
    60. subordinator <u>that</u> deletion (e.g., <u>I think</u> [that] <u>he went</u>)
    61. stranded prepositions (e.g., <u>the candidate that I was</u>
        <u>thinking of</u>)
    62. split infinitives (e.g., <u>he wants to convincingly prove</u>
        <u>that</u> ...)
    63. split auxiliaries (e.g., <u>they are objectively shown to</u> ...)

O. Coordination

    64. phrasal coordination (NOUN <u>and</u> NOUN; ADJ <u>and</u> ADJ; VERB <u>and</u>
        VERB; ADV <u>and</u> ADV)
    65. independent clause coordination (clause initial <u>and</u>)

P. Negation

    66. synthetic negation (e.g., <u>no answer is good enough for</u>
        <u>Jones</u>)
    67. analytic negation (e.g., <u>that's not likely</u>)

4.5 Frequency counts of the linguistic features

The frequency counts of all linguistic features are normalized to a text length of 1,000 words (except for type/token ratio and word length – see discussion in Appendix II). This normalization is crucial for any comparison of frequency counts across texts, because text length can vary widely. A comparison of non-normalized counts will give an inaccurate assessment of the frequency distribution in texts. For example, suppose that there were three texts in a comparison, text A with 1,000 words, text B with 2,000 words, and text C with 1,330 words; and that text A had 20 adjectives, text B had 30, and text C had 20. From the raw frequencies, we would conclude that texts A and C had the same frequency of adjectives, but that text B had a third more adjectives than the other texts, a quite substantial difference. However, the total of 30 adjectives in text B is based on a count of the number of adjectives per 2,000 words of text, which provides twice as many opportunities for adjectives to occur than in the 1,000 words of text A. Similarly, the total of 20 adjectives in text C is based on a count per 1,330 words of text. Thus, these counts are raw *totals*, but they do not represent comparable *frequencies* of occurrence. By normalizing the total counts to a text length of 1,000 words – that is, computing how many adjectives *would* occur if the text had been 1,000 words long – the frequencies can be compared directly. In the present example, the frequency counts would be:

Text A:
(20 (adjs.) ÷ 1,000 (length of text)) × 1,000 = 20 (adjs.)

Text B:
(30 (adjs.) ÷ 2,000 (length of text)) × 1,000 = 15 (adjs.)

Text C:
(20 (adjs.) ÷ 1,330 (length of text)) × 1,000 = 15 (adjs.)

That is, when the counts are normalized so that they represent frequencies per 1,000 words, we see that text B uses adjectives less frequently than text A, and that texts B and C use adjectives with the same frequency, in marked contrast to the relations indicated by the raw counts.

Table 4.5 presents descriptive statistics for the frequencies of the linguistic features in the entire corpus of texts. Included are: (1) the mean frequency, (2) the maximum and minimum frequencies, that is, the maximum and minimum occurrences in any text, (3) the 'range', that is, the difference between the maximum and the minimum values, and (4) the 'standard deviation', a measure of the spread of the distribution – 68% of the texts in the corpus have frequency values within the spread of plus or minus one standard deviation from the mean score. This table does not enable characterization of particular genres, but it provides an assessment of the overall distribution of particular features in English texts. Some features occur very frequently, for example, nouns with a mean of 180 per 1,000 words; other features occur very infrequently, for example, causative adverbial subordinators with a mean of 1 per 1,000 words. The variability in the frequency of features also differs from one feature to the next; some features are rather evenly distributed across the

Table 4.5 *Descriptive statistics for the corpus as a whole*

Linguistic feature	Mean	Minimum value	Maximum value	Range	Standard deviation
past tense	40.1	0.0	119.0	119.0	30.4
perfect aspect verbs	8.6	0.0	40.0	40.0	5.2
present tense	77.7	12.0	182.0	170.0	34.3
place adverbials	3.1	0.0	24.0	24.0	3.4
time adverbials	5.2	0.0	24.0	24.0	3.5
first person pronouns	27.2	0.0	122.0	122.0	26.1
second person pronouns	9.9	0.0	72.0	72.0	13.8
third person pronouns	29.9	0.0	124.0	124.0	22.5
pronoun IT	10.3	0.0	47.0	47.0	7.1
demonstrative pronouns	4.6	0.0	30.0	30.0	4.8
indefinite pronouns	1.4	0.0	13.0	13.0	2.0
DO as pro-verb	3.0	0.0	22.0	22.0	3.5
WH questions	0.2	0.0	4.0	4.0	0.6
nominalizations	19.9	0.0	71.0	71.0	14.4
gerunds	7.0	0.0	23.0	23.0	3.8
nouns	180.5	84.0	298.0	214.0	35.6
agentless passives	9.6	0.0	38.0	38.0	6.6
BY passives	0.8	0.0	8.0	8.0	1.3
BE as main verb	28.3	7.0	72.0	65.0	9.5
existential THERE	2.2	0.0	11.0	11.0	1.8
THAT verb complements	3.3	0.0	20.0	20.0	2.9
THAT adj. complements	0.3	0.0	3.0	3.0	0.6
WH clauses	0.6	0.0	7.0	7.0	1.0
infinitives	14.9	1.0	36.0	35.0	5.6
present participial clauses	1.0	0.0	11.0	11.0	1.7
past participial clauses	0.1	0.0	3.0	3.0	0.4
past prt. WHIZ deletions	2.5	0.0	21.0	21.0	3.1
present prt. WHIZ deletions	1.6	0.0	11.0	11.0	1.8
THAT relatives: subj. position	0.4	0.0	7.0	7.0	0.8
THAT relatives: obj. position	0.8	0.0	7.0	7.0	1.1
WH relatives: subj. position	2.1	0.0	15.0	15.0	2.0
WH relatives: obj. position	1.4	0.0	9.0	9.0	1.7
WH relatives: pied pipes	0.7	0.0	7.0	7.0	1.1
sentence relatives	0.1	0.0	3.0	3.0	0.4
adv. subordinator - cause	1.1	0.0	11.0	11.0	1.7
adv. sub. - concession	0.5	0.0	5.0	5.0	0.8
adv. sub. - condition	2.5	0.0	13.0	13.0	2.2
adv. sub. - other	1.0	0.0	6.0	6.0	1.1
prepositions	110.5	50.0	209.0	159.0	25.4
attributive adjectives	60.7	16.0	115.0	99.0	18.8
predicative adjectives	4.7	0.0	19.0	19.0	2.6
adverbs	65.6	22.0	125.0	103.0	17.6
type/token ratio	51.1	35.0	64.0	29.0	5.2
word length	4.5	3.7	5.3	1.6	0.4
conjuncts	1.2	0.0	12.0	12.0	1.6
downtoners	2.0	0.0	10.0	10.0	1.6
hedges	0.6	0.0	10.0	10.0	1.3
amplifiers	2.7	0.0	14.0	14.0	2.6
emphatics	6.3	0.0	22.0	22.0	4.2
discourse particles	1.2	0.0	15.0	15.0	2.3
demonstratives	9.9	0.0	22.0	22.0	4.2

Table 4.5 (*cont.*)

Linguistic feature	Mean	Minimum value	Maximum value	Range	Standard deviation
possibility modals	5.8	0.0	21.0	21.0	3.5
necessity modals	2.1	0.0	13.0	13.0	2.1
predictive modals	5.6	0.0	30.0	30.0	4.2
public verbs	7.7	0.0	40.0	40.0	5.4
private verbs	18.0	1.0	54.0	53.0	10.4
suasive verbs	2.9	0.0	36.0	36.0	3.1
SEEM/APPEAR	0.8	0.0	6.0	6.0	1.0
contractions	13.5	0.0	89.0	89.0	18.6
THAT deletion	3.1	0.0	24.0	24.0	4.1
stranded prepositions	2.0	0.0	23.0	23.0	2.7
split infinitives	0.0	0.0	1.0	1.0	0.0
split auxiliaries	5.5	0.0	15.0	15.0	2.5
phrasal coordination	3.4	0.0	12.0	12.0	2.7
non-phrasal coordination	4.5	0.0	44.0	44.0	4.8
synthetic negation	1.7	0.0	8.0	8.0	1.6
analytic negation	8.5	0.0	32.0	32.0	6.1

corpus, for example, split infinitives have a maximum frequency of 1 per 1,000 words and a minimum frequency of 0 per 1,000 words; other features show large differences, for example, first person pronouns occur 122 times in some texts but not at all in other texts.

Appendix III provides descriptive statistics of the frequency of each linguistic feature in each genre; it includes a table with the same format as Table 4.5 for each of the genres. This appendix provides a wealth of information concerning the distributions of individual features among the genres. It enables a characterization of each genre and comparison of genres with respect to individual linguistic features. Consideration of the frequencies of individual features, however, cannot provide a comprehensive description of the dimensions of textual variation or the textual relations among genres. For these purposes, multivariate statistical techniques provide an invaluable research tool, and we turn next to a description of these techniques as applied to the analysis of textual variation.

5 Statistical analysis

5.1 Factor analysis: introduction

Factor analysis is the primary statistical tool of the multi-feature/multi-dimensional approach to textual variation. In a factor analysis, a large number of original variables, in this case the frequencies of linguistic features, are reduced to a small set of derived variables, the 'factors'. Each factor represents some area in the original data that can be summarized or generalized. That is, each factor represents an area of high shared variance in the data, a grouping of linguistic features that co-occur with a high frequency. The factors are linear combinations of the original variables, derived from a correlation matrix of all variables. For instance, if the linguistic features in an analysis were first person pronouns, questions, passives, and nominalizations, the correlation matrix for these features might look like this:

	1st pers. pro.	questions	passives	nominal-izations
1st pers. pro.	1.00			
questions	.85	1.00		
passives	−.15	−.21	1.00	
nominal-izations	.08	−.17	.90	1.00

The size of a correlation (whether positive or negative) indicates the extent to which two linguistic features vary together. A large negative correlation indicates that two features covary in a systematic, complementary fashion, i.e., the presence of the one is highly associated with the absence of the other. A large positive correlation indicates that the two features systematically occur together. Squaring the correlation coefficient (R-squared) provides a measure of the percentage of variance shared by any two variables, indicating directly the importance of the relationship between them. For example, in the above hypothetical matrix, first person pronouns and questions have a high correlation of .85, which translates into an R-squared of 72% ; that is, 72% of the variance in the frequency values for first person pronouns and questions is shared. In concrete terms, a correlation of this magnitude shows that when first person pronouns occur in a text, it is highly likely that questions will occur to a similar extent, and when first person pronouns are absent from a text it is likely that questions will be absent also.

Overall, the correlations shown in the above matrix form a clear pattern: first person pronouns and questions are highly correlated, and passives and nominalizations are highly correlated; while the other four correlations (between passives and first person pronouns, passives and questions, nominalizations and first person pronouns, and nominalizations and questions) are all quite low. Intuitively, two distinct factors can be identified from this matrix, Factor A having first person pronouns and questions, and Factor B having passives and nominalizations. The matrix also indicates that these two factors are relatively independent or uncorrelated with one another, since the linguistic features on Factor A show low correlations with the features on Factor B.

This example is simplistic, but indicative of the way in which factors are computed. They are defined by correlations among the frequency counts of linguistic features. When several linguistic features are highly correlated, showing that they frequently co-occur, then a factor is defined. A factor analysis of the above correlation matrix might produce the following two factors:

Factor A =   *.82 (1st pers. pro.) + .82 (questions)*
         + .11 (nominalizations) − .23 (passives)

Factor B = −.16 (1st pers. pro.) − .19 (questions)
         + .91 (passives) + .76 (nominalizations)

The numbers in front of the linguistic features on each factor are referred to as factor 'loadings' or 'weights'. There is no one-to-one correspondence between these loadings and the correlation coefficients, but they both indicate the same pattern: one factor representing a strong co-occurrence relationship between first person pronouns and questions (Factor A), and another factor representing a strong co-occurrence relationship between passives and nominalizations (Factor B). Factor loadings indicate the degree to which one can generalize from a given factor to an individual linguistic feature. The further from 0.0 a factor loading is, the more one can generalize from that factor to the linguistic feature in question. Thus, features with higher loadings on a factor are better representatives of the dimension underlying the factor, and when interpreting the nature of a factor, the features with large loadings are given priority. In the above two fictitious factors, first person pronouns and questions are the important loadings on Factor A (i.e., first person pronouns and questions are features strongly representative of the dimension underlying Factor A) and passives and nominalizations are the important loadings on Factor B.

Multivariate statistical techniques such as factor analysis are not practical without the aid of computers. A factor analysis involves many lengthy computations using matrix algebra. The starting-point for a factor analysis is a simple correlation matrix of all variables, yet a small study of twenty variables would require calculation of nearly 200 correlation coefficients, a task that would take many hours in itself if done by hand. To compute an entire factorial structure by hand might require several weeks of work. Fortunately, factor analysis routines are usually included as part of the standard statistical packages (e.g., SAS, SPSS, SPSSX) available on computers at most academic institutions. This computational tool makes possible a new range of linguistic research, but the proper use of factor analysis requires understanding of several technical points, including a grasp of the theoretical prerequisites, the differences among the various extraction and rotation techniques, the nature of the resulting factors, and the nature of the final interpretations. An overview of these points is presented in the following sections, and fuller details can be found in any standard reference work on factor analysis (e.g., Gorsuch 1983). The discussion in the following sections is relatively technical; the information given here enables a relatively complete understanding of the research methodology used in the study. The research results presented in Chapters 6 and 7, however, can be understood without reading the technical descriptions given here.

5.2 Factor analysis: technical description

The first step in a factor analysis is to choose a method for extracting the factors. Because the use of factor analysis in linguistics is usually exploratory (rather than confirmatory), a principal factor solution should be used (Gorsuch 1983 – Chapter 6). There are several options available, but the most widely used is known as 'common factor analysis' or 'principal factor analysis'.[1] This procedure extracts the maximum amount of shared variance among the variables for each factor. Thus, the first factor extracts the maximum amount of shared variance, i.e., the largest grouping of co-occurrences in the data; the second factor then extracts the maximum amount of shared variance from the tokens left over after the first factor has been extracted, and so on. In this way, each factor is extracted so that it is uncorrelated with the other factors.

Once a method of extraction has been chosen, the best number of factors in a solution must be determined (Gorsuch 1983 – Chapter 8). As noted above, the purpose of factor analysis is to reduce the number of observed variables to a relatively small number of underlying constructs. A factor analysis will continue extracting factors until all of the shared variance among the variables has been accounted for; but only the first few factors are likely to account for a nontrivial amount of shared variance and therefore be worth further consideration. There is no mathematically exact method for determining the number of factors to be extracted. There are, however, several guidelines for this decision. One of the simplest is to examine a plot of the eigenvalues, which are direct indices of the amount of variance accounted for by each factor. Such a plot is called a scree plot, and will normally show a characteristic break indicating the point at which additional factors contribute little to the overall analysis.

The first eleven eigenvalues for the factor analysis used in the present study are given in Table 5.1, and the scree plot corresponding to these values is given in Figure 5.1. As shown in Table 5.1, the eigenvalues can be used to indicate the percentage of shared variance that is accounted for by each factor. Thus, in the present analysis, Factor 1 accounts for 26.8% of the shared variance, Factor 2 for an additional 8%, etc.

Both the table and the scree plot show that the first factor accounts for the greatest proportion of variance by far. As noted above, the scree plot can also be used to indicate the optimal number of factors. The clearest

---

[1] Another commonly used factoring procedure is principal components. The primary difference between principal factor analysis (PFA) and principal components analysis (PCA) is that a PCA attempts to account for *all* of the variance in the data while a PFA attempts to account for only the *shared* variance. In PCA, unique and error variance get treated as if they were shared variance, which can result in factor loadings that are inflated. The solutions produced by PFA are thus more accurate and have been preferred in recent social science research (see Farhady 1983).

Table 5.1 *First 11 eigenvalues of the unrotated factor analysis*

Factor number	Eigenvalue	% of shared variance
1	17.67	26.8%
2	5.33	8.1%
3	3.45	5.2%
4	2.29	3.5%
5	1.92	2.9%
6	1.84	2.8%
7	1.69	2.6%
8	1.43	2.2%
9	1.32	2.0%
10	1.27	1.9%
11	1.23	1.9%

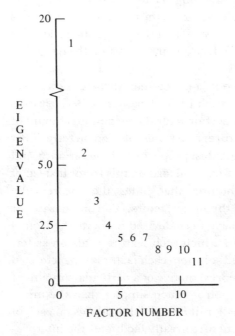

Figure 5.1 *Scree plot of eigenvalues*

Table 5.2 *Inter-factor correlations*

	FACT1	FACT2	FACT3	FACT4	FACT5	FACT6	FACT7
FACTOR1	1.00						
FACTOR2	0.24	1.00					
FACTOR3	-0.49	-0.34	1.00				
FACTOR4	0.17	0.12	0.12	1.00			
FACTOR5	-0.23	-0.21	0.30	0.16	1.00		
FACTOR6	0.16	-0.24	0.01	0.00	0.05	1.00	
FACTOR7	-0.01	-0.01	-0.10	0.24	-0.05	-0.09	1.00

break in the plot occurs between the fourth and fifth factor, but a second break occurs between the seventh and eighth factor. When faced with a choice between a larger or smaller number of factors, the more conservative procedure is to extract the larger number and then discard any unnecessary factors (Gorsuch 1983; Farhady 1983). Extracting too few factors will result in loss of information, because the constructs underlying the excluded factors will be overlooked; it might also distort the factorial structure of the remaining factors, because multiple constructs are collapsed into a single factor. In the present case, solutions for 4, 5, 6, 7, and 8 factors were examined, and the 7-factor solution was settled on as optimal; I discuss this decision and illustrate the danger of under-factoring in Section 5.3.

A final, and very important, step in a factor analysis before interpretation is rotation of the factors (Gorsuch 1983 – Chapter 9). Because each factor in a principal factor analysis accounts for the maximum amount of variance, it is often difficult to interpret a factorial solution directly. That is, the first factor accounts for the greatest proportion of the variance, and thus a majority of the linguistic features will load on this factor instead of subsequent factors – a representation that hides the theoretically interesting constructs underlying the other factors. To compensate for this problem, various techniques have been devised to rotate the factors to a simple structure, a solution in which each feature loads on as few factors as possible. In such a rotated solution, each factor is characterized by the few features that are most representative of a particular amount of shared variance. The rotated solution is much simpler than the initial extraction (which allows many small, but not trivial, loadings on each of the factors), and this simplified structure greatly facilitates the interpretation of the constructs underlying each factor.

There are several different methods of rotation, many of them available as part of the standard statistical packages. Two of these are used commonly: Varimax and Promax. These two rotation methods differ in that Varimax maintains orthogonal structure, requiring the assumption that the factors are uncorrelated, while Promax permits oblique structure, that is, it permits minor correlations among the factors. In the description of textual variation, where the factors represent underlying textual dimensions, there is no reason to assume that the factors are completely uncorrelated, and therefore a Promax rotation is recommended.[2] In the present case, the intercorrelations among the factors are small, shown in Table 5.2: the largest inter-factor correlations are between Factors 1 and 3 ($-.49$), Factors 2 and 3 ($-.34$), and Factors 3 and 5 (.30).

5.3 The factorial structure

The final rotated factor pattern for the present study is given as Table 5.3. This factorial structure is based on analysis of 67 linguistic features counted in 481 spoken and written text samples.[3] In the last section, I pointed out that the factorial structure is derived from a correlation matrix of all variables; the correlation matrix for the present analysis, including a key to the abbreviations, is given as Appendix IV.

In the final factor solution, seven factors were extracted using a principal factors solution, and the factors were subsequently rotated using a Promax rotation. Table 5.3 presents the factor loadings for each of the linguistic features on each of the factors. As noted above, a factor loading indicates the extent to which one can generalize from a factor to a particular linguistic feature, or the extent to which a given feature is representative of the dimension underlying a factor. The loading of a feature on a factor reflects the extent to which the variation in the frequency of that feature correlates with the overall variation of the factor; it indicates the strength of the co-occurrence relationship between

[2] In fact, oblique solutions might be generally preferable in studies of language use and acquisition, since it is unlikely that orthogonal, uncorrelated factors actually occur as components of the communication process. That is, from a theoretical perspective, all aspects of language use appear to be interrelated to at least some extent, and thus there is no reason to expect mathematically uncorrelated factors representing those aspects (see Hinofotis 1983).

[3] Table 3 shows factor loadings for only 66 linguistic features – split infinitives were dropped from the analysis because they occur very infrequently (see p. 78).

Table 5.3　*Rotated factor pattern for the 7 factor solution (Promax rotation)*

LX FEATURE	FACTOR1	FACTOR2	FACTOR3	FACTOR4	FACTOR5	FACTOR6	FACTOR7
PRO1	0.744	0.088	0.025	0.026	-0.089	0.008	-0.098
PRO2	0.860	-0.043	-0.018	0.016	0.007	-0.168	-0.064
PRO3	-0.053	0.727	-0.074	-0.018	-0.167	-0.076	0.138
PANY	0.618	0.046	0.011	0.085	-0.094	-0.085	-0.032
PDEM	0.756	-0.166	-0.001	-0.108	0.004	0.306	-0.077
PERFECTS	0.051	0.480	0.049	-0.016	-0.101	0.146	0.143
PASTTNSE	-0.083	0.895	0.002	-0.249	-0.049	-0.052	0.021
N	-0.799	-0.280	-0.091	-0.045	-0.294	-0.076	-0.213
N_NOM	-0.272	-0.237	0.357	0.179	0.277	0.129	-0.019
N_VBG	-0.252	-0.127	0.216	0.177	0.087	-0.052	0.052
PREP	-0.540	-0.251	0.185	-0.185	0.234	0.145	-0.008
ADVS	0.416	-0.001	-0.458	-0.020	-0.156	0.053	0.314
CONJNCTS	-0.141	-0.160	0.064	0.108	0.481	0.180	0.217
SUB_COS	0.661	-0.080	0.110	0.023	-0.061	0.078	-0.076
SUB_CON	0.006	0.092	0.100	-0.071	0.010	-0.056	0.300
SUB_CND	0.319	-0.076	-0.206	0.466	0.120	0.103	-0.007
SUB_OTHR	-0.109	0.051	-0.018	0.008	0.388	0.102	0.109
INF	-0.071	0.059	0.085	0.760	-0.274	-0.005	-0.074
PRO_DO	0.821	0.004	0.071	0.049	-0.057	-0.077	-0.056
SEEM	0.054	0.128	0.160	-0.010	0.015	0.045	0.348
DOWNTONE	-0.084	-0.008	0.021	-0.080	0.066	0.113	0.325
AMPLIFR	0.563	-0.156	-0.028	-0.124	-0.124	0.225	-0.018
PL_ADV	-0.417	-0.060	-0.492	-0.094	-0.067	-0.018	-0.023
TM_ADV	-0.199	-0.062	-0.604	-0.020	-0.290	0.116	-0.046
TH_CL	0.045	0.228	0.125	0.265	0.053	0.558	-0.122
ADJ_CL	-0.124	0.066	-0.080	0.123	0.171	0.360	0.183
CONTRAC	0.902	-0.100	-0.141	-0.138	-0.002	-0.057	-0.032
TYPETOKN	-0.537	0.058	0.002	-0.005	-0.311	-0.228	0.219
SYNTHNEG	-0.232	0.402	0.046	0.133	-0.057	0.176	0.110
NOT_NEG	0.778	0.149	0.017	0.125	0.019	0.001	0.037
BE_STATE	0.713	0.056	0.075	0.008	0.014	0.292	0.180
POS_MOD	0.501	-0.123	0.044	0.367	0.122	-0.022	0.115
NEC_MOD	-0.007	-0.107	-0.015	0.458	0.102	0.135	0.042
PRD_MOD	0.047	-0.056	-0.054	0.535	-0.072	0.063	-0.184
PUB_VB	0.098	0.431	0.163	0.135	-0.030	0.046	-0.279
PRV_VB	0.962	0.160	0.179	-0.054	0.084	-0.049	0.106
SUA_VB	-0.240	-0.035	-0.017	0.486	0.051	0.016	-0.237
PRTCLE	0.663	-0.218	-0.128	-0.029	-0.096	0.165	-0.140
GEN_HDG	0.582	-0.156	-0.051	-0.087	-0.022	-0.145	0.096
GEN_EMPH	0.739	-0.216	0.015	-0.027	-0.188	-0.087	0.210
SENT_REL	0.550	-0.086	0.152	-0.118	-0.025	0.048	-0.041
WH_QUES	0.523	-0.024	0.117	-0.111	-0.032	0.036	-0.094
P_AND	-0.253	-0.091	0.355	-0.066	-0.046	-0.324	0.126
O_AND	0.476	0.041	-0.052	-0.161	-0.139	0.218	-0.125
WHIZ_VBN	-0.382	-0.336	-0.071	-0.137	0.395	-0.128	-0.103
WHIZ_VBG	-0.325	-0.114	0.080	-0.169	0.212	-0.070	-0.093
CL_VBN	-0.025	-0.154	0.029	-0.050	0.415	-0.142	-0.059
CL_VBG	-0.211	0.392	-0.142	-0.076	0.268	-0.217	0.121
EX_THERE	0.262	0.108	0.113	-0.124	-0.004	0.318	0.017
DEM	0.040	-0.062	0.113	0.010	0.132	0.478	0.153
WRDLNGTH	-0.575	-0.314	0.270	-0.009	0.023	0.028	0.081

Table 5.3 *(cont.)*

LX FEATURE	FACTOR1	FACTOR2	FACTOR3	FACTOR4	FACTOR5	FACTOR6	FACTOR7
REL_SUBJ	-0.087	-0.067	0.453	-0.027	-0.174	0.228	0.047
REL_OBJ	-0.072	0.049	0.627	-0.060	-0.083	0.302	0.165
REL_PIPE	-0.029	0.026	0.606	-0.144	0.046	0.280	0.192
THTREL_S	0.051	-0.036	0.021	0.019	-0.058	0.184	0.033
THTREL_O	-0.047	0.053	0.201	0.223	-0.125	0.457	-0.065
WH_CL	0.467	0.143	0.221	0.032	-0.050	-0.044	-0.027
IT	0.706	-0.021	-0.038	-0.034	-0.038	0.022	0.060
ADJ_PRED	0.187	0.076	-0.089	0.248	0.311	-0.012	0.210
ADJ_ATTR	-0.474	-0.412	0.176	-0.055	-0.038	-0.064	0.299
THAT_DEL	0.909	0.036	0.098	-0.059	-0.005	-0.178	-0.081
SPL_AUX	-0.195	0.040	0.012	0.437	0.043	0.120	0.239
FINLPREP	0.426	0.007	-0.124	-0.210	0.023	0.340	-0.100
PRES	0.864	-0.467	-0.008	0.229	-0.006	0.011	0.011
BY_PASV	-0.256	-0.189	0.065	-0.124	0.413	-0.089	-0.045
AGLS_PSV	-0.388	-0.145	0.109	0.060	0.430	0.063	-0.057

the feature in question and the factor as a whole. There are several techniques for determining the required magnitude of statistically significant loadings, that is, the loadings not due to random patterns of variation. Most of these techniques depend on the number of observations in the analysis (Gorsuch 1983:208ff), but loadings having an absolute value less than .30 are generally excluded as unimportant even if they are statistically significant. Only the important, or 'salient', loadings should be interpreted as part of each factor.

For example, Factor 2 on Table 5.3 shows the following salient loadings having weights larger than .30: past tense (.895), third person personal pronouns (.727), perfect aspect (.480), public verbs (.431), synthetic negation (.402), present participial clauses (.392), present tense (−.467), attributive adjectives (−.412), past participial WHIZ deletions (−.336), and word length (−.314). These loadings are not equally large, and therefore these features are not equally representative of the dimension underlying Factor 2. Past tense and third person pronouns show quite large loadings; present tense, perfect aspect, and public verbs all have large loadings; word length and past participial WHIZ deletions have minimally salient loadings. In the interpretation of each factor, greater attention is given to those features with the largest loadings.

A positive or negative sign does not influence the importance of a loading; for example, present tense (−.467) has a larger loading on Factor 2 than public verbs (.431). Rather than indicating differences in importance, positive and negative loadings show groups of features that are distributed in texts in a complementary pattern. That is, with respect to Factor 2, the features with positive weights (past tense, third person pronouns, perfect aspect, public verbs, etc.) all co-occur with a high frequency in texts; the features with negative weights (present tense, adjectives, etc.) mark a similar group of co-occurring features; and these two groups of linguistic features have a special relationship to each other: they occur in a largely complementary pattern. Thus, when past tense, third person pronouns, and perfect aspect verbs occur with a high frequency in a text, present tense verbs and adjectives are likely to be notably absent from that text, and vice versa. In the interpretations of the factors, both the negative and positive cluster of features must be taken into consideration.

Table 5.4 summarizes the salient positive and negative loadings on each of the factors of the present analysis. The decision to extract seven factors was based on consideration of these salient loadings. It will be remembered from Section 5.2 that a scree plot of the eigenvalues provides a first indication of the optimal number of factors. The scree plot in Figure 5.1 shows a sharp break between Factors 4 and 5, and a lesser break between Factors 7 and 8. The solutions for 4, 5, 6, 7, and 8 factors were therefore examined to determine how well the factors were represented in each case. In the 4 factor solution, each factor was represented by at least eleven salient loadings; in the 5, 6, and 7 factor solutions, each factor was represented by at least five salient loadings; in the 8 factor solution, one of the factors was represented by only two salient loadings. In general, five salient loadings are required for a meaningful interpretation of the construct underlying a factor. Thus, the eight factor solution was excluded as over-factoring. Similarly, since all of the factors in the 5, 6, and 7 factor solutions were sufficiently represented for interpretation, the 4 factor solution was excluded as obviously under-factoring.

I noted in the last section that it is generally preferable to extract too many rather than too few factors, once the choice has been narrowed down to two or three different solutions. If too many factors are extracted, it might be necessary to exclude some of them from interpretation because they are not theoretically well-defined. If too few factors are extracted, however, certain constructs will not be represented in the final factorial structure, and a confused picture of the other constructs might result because factors have been collapsed. In the present analysis,

Table 5.4 *Summary of the factorial structure (features in parentheses were not used in the computation of factor scores – see discussion in Section 5.5)*

FACTOR 1

private verbs	.96
THAT deletion	.91
contractions	.90
present tense verbs	.86
2nd person pronouns	.86
DO as pro-verb	.82
analytic negation	.78
demonstrative pronouns	.76
general emphatics	.74
1st person pronouns	.74
pronoun IT	.71
BE as main verb	.71
causative subordination	.66
discourse particles	.66
indefinite pronouns	.62
general hedges	.58
amplifiers	.56
sentence relatives	.55
WH questions	.52
possibility modals	.50
non-phrasal coordination	.48
WH clauses	.47
final prepositions	.43
(adverbs	.42)
(conditional subordination	.32)

- -

nouns	-.80
word length	-.58
prepositions	-.54
type/token ratio	-.54
attributive adjs.	-.47
(place adverbials	-.42)
(agentless passives	-.39)
(past participial WHIZ deletions	-.38)
(present participial WHIZ deletions	-.32)

FACTOR 2

past tense verbs	.90
third person pronouns	.73
perfect aspect verbs	.48
public verbs	.43
synthetic negation	.40
present participial clauses	.39

- -

(present tense verbs	-.47)
(attributive adjs.	-.41)
(past participial WHIZ deletions	-.34)
(word length	-.31)

FACTOR 3

WH relative clauses on object positions	.63
pied piping constructions	.61
WH relative clauses on subject positions	.45
phrasal coordination	.36
nominalizations	.36

- -

time adverbials	-.60
place adverbials	-.49
adverbs	-.46

Table 5.4 (*cont.*)

FACTOR 4		FACTOR 5	
infinitives	.76	conjuncts	.48
prediction modals	.54	agentless passives	.43
suasive verbs	.49	past participial	
conditional		clauses	.42
subordination	.47	BY-passives	.41
necessity modals	.46	past participial	
split auxiliaries	.44	WHIZ deletions	.40
(possibility modals	.37)	other adverbial	
		subordinators	.39
		(predicative adjs.)	.31

-- no negative features --

                (type/token ratio   -.31)

FACTOR 6		FACTOR 7	
THAT clauses as		SEEM/APPEAR	.35
verb complements	.56	(downtoners	.33)
demonstratives	.55	(adverbs	.31)
THAT relative clauses		(concessive	
on object positions	.46	subordination	.30)
THAT clauses as		(attributive adjs.	.30)
adj. complements	.36		
(final prepositions	.34)		
(existential THERE	.32)		
(demonstrative			
pronouns	.31)		
(WH relative clauses			
on object positions	.30)		

                -- no negative features --

(phrasal coordination -.32)

---

the 7 factor solution was thus chosen over the 5 and 6 factor solutions. It turns out that all seven factors in the final solution seem to be theoretically well-defined, which further supports the decision to extract seven factors.

A brief comparison of the 6 and 7 factor solutions illustrates the danger of under-factoring. The first, second, fourth, and fifth factors in the 7 factor solution correspond directly to factors in the 6 factor solution, having the same features with salient weights. The third and sixth factors from the 7 factor solution, however, have been collapsed in the 6 factor solution. That is, the third factor in the 6 factor solution, shown in Table 5.5, has the following major loadings: *that* clauses as verb complements

Table 5.5　*Factor 3 of the 6 factor solution*

```
    FACTOR 3

THAT clauses as
  verb complements    .57
THAT relative clauses
  on object positions .51
demonstratives        .46
WH relative clauses
  on object positions .39
pied piping
  constructions       .35
(WH relative clauses
  on subject position .33)
(existential THERE    .32)
(THAT clauses as
  adj. complements    .31)
(final prepositions   .30)


-------------------------

-- no negative features --
```

(.57), *that* relative clauses on object position (.51), demonstratives (.46), WH relative clauses on object position (.39), pied piping constructions (.35), WH relative clauses on subject position (.33), and *that* clauses as adjective complements (.31). Comparing Table 5.4 and Table 5.5 shows that this third factor in the 6 factor solution combines the major loadings from Factor 3 and Factor 6 of the 7 factor solution. If we based our final interpretation on the 6 factor solution, we would miss the finding that *that* complements, *that* relative clauses, and demonstratives function as part of a different construct from WH relative clauses and pied-piping constructions.

5.4　Interpretation of the factors

In the interpretation of a factor, an underlying functional dimension is sought to explain the co-occurrence pattern among features identified by the factor. That is, it is claimed that a cluster of features co-occur frequently in texts because they are serving some common function in those texts. At this point, micro-analyses of linguistic features become crucially important. Functional analyses of individual features in texts enable identification of the shared function underlying a group of features in a factor analysis. It must be emphasized, however, that while the co-occurrence patterns are derived quantitatively through factor analysis, interpretation of the dimension underlying a factor is tentative and requires confirmation, similar to any other interpretive analysis.

With this caution in mind, we can proceed to a brief discussion of the considerations involved in factor interpretation. Table 5.4 lists the salient features on each of the seven factors in the present analysis. The linguistic features grouped on each factor can be interpreted as a textual dimension through an assessment of the communicative functions most widely shared by the features. The complementary relationship between positive and negative loadings must also be considered in the interpretation.

For example, consider Factor 2. The features with salient positive loadings are past tense, third person personal pronouns, perfect aspect, public verbs, present participial clauses, and synthetic negation. These features can all be used for narrative purposes: past tense and perfect aspect verbs are used to refer to actions in the past; third person personal pronouns are used to refer to animate, usually human, individuals who are not participating in the immediate communicative interaction; public verbs are used frequently for reported speech; and present participial clauses are used for depictive discourse. The two major features with negative loadings are present tense and attributive adjectives, which are used for more immediate reference. Thus, a preliminary interpretation of the dimension underlying this factor would describe it as distinguishing texts with a primary narrative emphasis, marked by considerable reference to past events and removed situations, from texts with non-narrative emphases (descriptive, expository, or other), marked by little reference to a removed situation but by high reference to a present situation. A full interpretation of each of the factors is presented in Chapter 6.

As noted above, interpretations of the factors are tentative until confirmed by further research. One technique used to confirm a factor interpretation uses scores computed from the factors as operational representatives of the hypothesized dimensions; these scores are known as 'factor scores'. In the present case, the factor scores represent textual dimensions. A factor score, or dimension score, can be computed for each text, and the similarities and differences among genres (the textual 'relations') can be analyzed with respect to these scores to support or refute hypothesized interpretations. I discuss the computation of factor scores in Section 5.5 and analyze the relations among genres with respect to the factor scores in Chapter 7. A second technique used to validate hypothesized factor interpretations is confirmatory factor analysis. In this type of analysis, additional features are included in a subsequent analysis, and predictions are made concerning the factors that these features should load on, if the interpretations in question are correct. To the extent that these additional variables load on factors as hypothesized, the interpretation is confirmed. Many additional variables that were not included in Biber (1986a) have been added to the present analysis; in Chapter 6, I discuss the extent to which the interpretations presented in the 1986 analysis are confirmed by the distribution of these additional features.

5.5 Factor scores

In the same way that the frequency of passives in a text might be called the passive score of that text, factor scores are computed for each text to characterize the text with respect to each factor. A factor score is computed by summing, for each text, the number of occurrences of the features having salient loadings on that factor. Due to the large number of features loading on most of the factors in the present analysis, I use a conservative cut-off of .35 for those features to be included in the computation of factor scores. Seven features did not have a weight larger than .35 on any factor and were therefore dropped from the analysis at this point, viz., predicative adjectives, gerunds, concessive subordination, downtoners, present participial WHIZ deletions, existential *there*, and *that* relativization on subject position.

Some features have salient loadings on more than one of the factors (e.g., present tense on Factors 1 and 2); to assure the experimental independence of the factor scores, each feature was included in the computation of only one factor score (Gorsuch 1983:268). Thus, each linguistic feature is included in the factor score of the factor on which it has the highest loading (in terms of absolute magnitude, ignoring plus or minus sign). Salient loadings not used in the computation of the factor scores are given in parentheses on Table 5.4. For example, present tense has a loading of .86 on Factor 1 and −.47 on Factor 2, and therefore it is included in the factor score for Factor 1.

To illustrate the computation of factor scores, consider Factor 2 on Table 5.4. The factor score representing Factor 2 is computed by adding together the frequencies of past tense forms, perfect aspect forms, third person pronouns, public verbs, present participial clauses, and synthetic negation – the features with positive loadings – for each text. No frequencies are subtracted in this case, because the two features with negative loadings larger than .35 – present tense and attributive adjectives – both have higher loadings on Factor 1. For example, one of the general fiction texts in this study (text K:6 from the LOB corpus) has 113 past tense forms, 124 third person personal pronouns, 30 perfect aspect forms, 14 public verbs, 5 present participial clauses, and 3 occurrences of synthetic negation, resulting in the following factor score for Factor 2:

$$(113+124+30+14+5+3)=289$$

In the present study, all frequencies were standardized to a mean of 0.0 and a standard deviation of 1.0 before the factor scores were computed.[4] The means and standard deviations of each feature are listed in Table 4.5. The mean is a measure of the central frequency of a feature; the standard deviation is a measure of the spread of frequency values of a feature: 68% of the texts in the corpus have frequency values within the range of plus or minus one standard deviation from the mean score. When the frequency values are standardized, they are translated to a new scale. For example, consider past tense verbs. Table 4.5 shows that this feature has a mean value of 40.1 and a standard deviation of 30.4. Thus, if a text had 40 past tense verbs, it would have a standardized score of 0.0 for this feature, because its frequency equals the mean; the standardized score of 0.0 indicates that this text is unmarked with respect to past tense verbs. If, on the other hand, a text had a frequency of 113 past tense verbs, as in the above example, it would have a standardized score of 2.4, that is,

$$113=(2.4\times30.4)+40.1$$

The score of 113 is 2.4 standard deviations more than the mean of 40.1, and the standard score of 2.4 shows that this text is quite marked with respect to past tense verbs.

This procedure prevents those features that occur very frequently from having an inordinate influence on the computed factor score. For example, in the above factor score of 289 for text K:6, the frequencies for past tense and third person pronouns have a much larger influence than those for perfect aspect verbs, public verbs, etc. Frequencies standardized to a standard deviation of 1.0 retain the range of variation for each linguistic feature while standardizing the absolute magnitudes of those

---

[4] This standardization procedure should not be confused with the normalization of frequencies to a text length of 1,000 words (Section 4.5). That is, all frequencies are both normalized to a text length of 1,000 words, so that the frequency values for different *texts* are comparable, and they are standardized to a mean of 0.0 and standard deviation of 1.0, so that the values of *features* are comparable because they are translated to a single scale.

frequencies to a single scale. For comparison, the factor score of the above text (K:6) is computed using standardized frequencies:

$$(2.4+4.2+4.1+1.5+2.3+1.4)=15.9$$

(i.e., 2.4 past tense forms, 4.2 third person personal pronouns, 4.1 perfect aspect forms, 1.5 public verbs, 2.3 present participial clauses, 1.4 occurrences of synthetic negation).

This method of computation shows that the frequencies of all of these features are markedly high in this text, most of them more than 2 standard deviations above the corpus mean. A standardized score can be negative also, if the frequency of a feature in a text is markedly less than the mean frequency for the entire corpus. For example, the standardized score for present tense in the above text is -1.1, reflecting the fact that there are fewer present tense forms in this text than the mean number of present tense forms in the corpus as a whole. The effect of this method of computation is to give each linguistic feature a weight in terms of the range of its *variation* rather than in terms of its absolute frequency in texts. Thus, in the above example, perfect aspect verbs occur only 30 times in this text sample, but this absolute frequency is four standard deviations above the corpus mean for perfects, showing that this is a very frequent use of perfects in relation to their use in the corpus as a whole. This standardized value, reflecting the magnitude of a frequency with respect to the range of possible variation, is a more adequate representation for the purposes of the present study.

The relations among spoken and written genres can be considered through plots of the mean values of the factor scores, representing the underlying textual dimensions, for each genre. That is, a factor score for each factor is computed for each text, as illustrated above. Then, the mean of each factor score for each genre is computed. For example, if there were only three fiction texts, having factor scores for Factor 2 of 16.6, 12.0, and 10.4, the mean score for fiction on Dimension 2 (Factor Score 2) would be:

$$(16.6+12.0+10.4) \div 3=13.0$$

To illustrate, Figure 5.2 presents the mean scores of Factor Score 2 for each genre, showing the relations among the genres along that dimension. A statistical procedure called General Linear Models[5] can be used to test if there are significant differences among the genres with respect to each factor score. In the present case, the F and p values reported at the bottom

---

[5] General Linear Models is an ANOVA/Regression type procedure that does not depend on the presence of balanced cells. It is one of the multivariate procedures available in SAS, a computational package for statistical analysis.

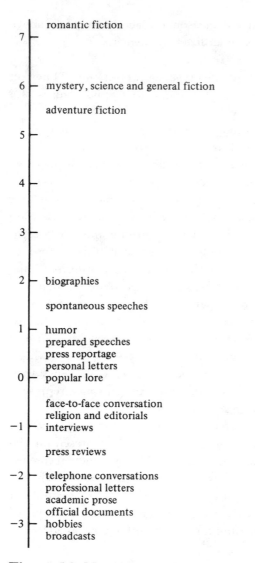

Figure 5.2 *Mean scores of Dimension 2 for each of the genres*
Dimension 2 (F=32.30, p < .0001, R*R = 60.8%)

of Figure 5.2 show that there are significant differences; a p value smaller
than .05 indicates a statistically significant relationship. The R*R value
presented at the bottom of Figure 5.2 gives the squared multiple
correlation coefficient, which indicates the *importance* of the factor score,
that is, the percentage of variance in the factor score accounted for by

knowing the genre distinctions. The R*R value of 60.8% shows that Factor Score 2 is quite important, in addition to being a statistically significant discriminator among genres.

A full interpretation of a textual dimension is made possible by considering: (1) the factor score means of each genre, (2) the situational and processing parameters associated with the distribution of factor scores, and (3) the linguistic features constituting the factor score. Consider briefly the plot of genres along Textual Dimension 2 shown in Figure 5.2. The fictional genres have the highest values, reflecting high frequencies of past tense verbs, third person personal pronouns, etc. Public speeches, biographies, humor, press reportage, and personal letters have intermediate values; and genres like broadcast, academic prose, and official documents have the lowest values, reflecting very low frequencies of past tense verbs, third person pronouns, etc. in these genres. This distribution confirms the interpretation of a dimension that distinguishes among texts according to their focus on narrative concerns versus non-narrative concerns. Fictional texts are largely narrative; public speeches, biographies, humor, press reportage, and personal letters include both narrative and non-narrative portions and thus have intermediate scores on this dimension; broadcasts, academic prose, and official documents are largely non-narrative and so have quite low scores on this dimension. The distribution of genres along the other dimensions can be examined in a similar way, to further refine the factor interpretations and to specify the relations among genres. The distribution of texts along each dimension is discussed fully in Chapter 7.

5.6 Summary of Chapter 5

This chapter has presented a technical overview of factor analysis and a discussion of the factorial structure of the present analysis, including the rationale for the extraction of seven factors, an overview of the factor interpretation process, and a discussion of the computation and use of factor scores. The following two chapters use these methodologies to develop a comprehensive description of textual variation among spoken and written texts in English. Chapter 6 presents the factor interpretations, describing the textual dimensions uncovered in the present study; Chapter 7 presents a comparison of spoken and written genres with respect to their dimension scores and an overall discussion of the textual relations among genres with respect to all seven dimensions.

Part III: Dimensions and relations in English

6 Textual dimensions in speech and writing

6.1 Summary of factor interpretation principles

In this chapter we turn to an interpretation of the factors presented in Chapter 5, to identify the construct or dimension underlying each factor. Recall that the factor analysis identifies groups of linguistic features that co-occur frequently in texts. The interpretation of the factors is based on the theoretical assumption that these co-occurrence patterns indicate an underlying communicative function shared by the features; that is, it is assumed that linguistic features co-occur frequently in texts because they are used for a shared set of communicative functions in those texts. The interpretation of each factor thus involves an assessment of the communicative function(s) most widely shared by the co-occurring features. Functional analyses of individual features in texts are crucially important in the interpretation process, since they provide the foundation for determining the function(s) underlying a set of features. In the present case, functional interpretations from previous research are summarized in Appendix II, and micro-analyses of features in particular texts are further discussed in Chapter 7. The interpretations presented here are based both on the findings of previous research and the analyses given in Chapter 7.

Table 5.4 (in Chapter 5), which summarizes the final factorial structure, is repeated here for convenience as Table 6.1. This table presents the important linguistic features comprising each factor. I pointed out in Chapter 5 that the features with positive and negative weights on a factor have a special relationship to one another: the features with positive weights co-occur in texts; the features with negative weights co-occur in texts; and these two groups of features occur in a largely complementary distribution. That is, when a text has several occurrences of the features with negative weights it will likely have few of the features with positive weights, and vice versa. In assessing the shared function

101

Table 6.1 *Summary of the factorial structure*

FACTOR 1		FACTOR 2	
private verbs	.96	past tense verbs	.90
THAT deletion	.91	third person pronouns	.73
contractions	.90	perfect aspect verbs	.48
present tense verbs	.86	public verbs	.43
2nd person pronouns	.86	synthetic negation	.40
DO as pro-verb	.82	present participial	
analytic negation	.78	clauses	.39
demonstrative			
pronouns	.76	------------------------	
general emphatics	.74		
1st person pronouns	.74	(present tense verbs	-.47)
pronoun IT	.71	(attributive adjs.	-.41)
BE as main verb	.71	(past participial	
causative		WHIZ deletions	-.34)
subordination	.66	(word length	-.31)
discourse particles	.66		
indefinite pronouns	.62		
general hedges	.58		
amplifiers	.56		
sentence relatives	.55		
WH questions	.52		
possibility modals	.50		
non-phrasal			
coordination	.48	FACTOR 3	
WH clauses	.47		
final prepositions	.43	WH relative clauses on	
(adverbs	.42)	object positions	.63
(conditional		pied piping	
subordination	.32)	constructions	.61
		WH relative clauses on	
-------------------------		subject positions	.45
		phrasal coordination	.36
nouns	-.80	nominalizations	.36
word length	-.58		
prepositions	-.54	-------------------------	
type/token ratio	-.54		
attributive adjs.	-.47	time adverbials	-.60
(place adverbials	-.42)	place adverbials	-.49
(agentless passives	-.39)	adverbs	-.46
(past participial			
WHIZ deletions	-.38)		
(present participial			
WHIZ deletions	-.32)		

Table 6.1 (*cont.*)

FACTOR 4		FACTOR 5	
infinitives	.76	conjuncts	.48
prediction modals	.54	agentless passives	.43
suasive verbs	.49	past participial	
conditional		clauses	.42
subordination	.47	BY-passives	.41
necessity modals	.46	past participial	
split auxiliaries	.44	WHIZ deletions	.40
(possibility modals	.37)	other adverbial	
		subordinators	.39
		(predicative adjs.)	.31

-- no negative features --

(type/token ratio   -.31)

FACTOR 6		FACTOR 7	
THAT clauses as		SEEM/APPEAR	.35
verb complements	.56	(downtoners	.33)
demonstratives	.55	(adverbs	.31)
THAT relative clauses		(concessive	
on object positions	.46	subordination	.30)
THAT clauses as		(attributive adjs.	.30)
adj. complements	.36		
(final prepositions	.34)		
(existential THERE	.32)		
(demonstrative			
pronouns	.31)		
(WH relative clauses			
on object positions	.30)		

-- no negative features --

(phrasal coordination   -.32)

underlying a factor, the researcher must consider the reasons for the complementary distribution of these two groups of features as well as the reasons for the co-occurrence patterns of positive and negative features.

6.2   Interpretation of the factors as textual dimensions

6.2.1   Interpretation of Factor 1

Consider Factor 1, on Table 6.1. This is obviously a very powerful factor: 34 linguistic features have weights larger than .30 on this factor; 24 features have weights larger than .50. In an unrotated factor solution, it would not be surprising to find such a powerful first factor (see Section 5.2). In the present case, however, the factors have been rotated, so that each linguistic feature tends to load on only one factor, and each factor is characterized by those relatively few features that are most representative of the underlying construct. Thus, the structure of Factor 1 is not an artifact of the factor extraction technique. This is rather an extremely powerful factor representing a very basic dimension of variation among spoken and written texts in English.

To interpret this dimension, we must assess the functions shared by these co-occurring features. There are relatively few features with negative weights, and their interpretation is relatively straightforward. Nouns, word length, prepositional phrases, type/token ratio, and attributive adjectives all have negative weights larger than .45 and none of these features have larger weights on another factor. High frequencies of all of these features can be associated with a high informational focus and a careful integration of information in a text. Nouns are the primary bearers of referential meaning in a text, and a high frequency of nouns thus indicates great density of information. Prepositional phrases also serve to integrate high amounts of information into a text. Word length and type/token ratio similarly mark high density of information, but they further mark very precise lexical choice resulting in an exact presentation of informational content. A high type/token ratio results from the use of many different lexical items in a text, and this more varied vocabulary reflects extensive use of words that have very specific meanings. Chafe and Danielewicz (1986) find that precise lexical choice is a very difficult production task and is thus rarely accomplished in speech. Longer words also convey more specific, specialized meanings than shorter words; Zipf

(1949) shows that shorter words are more frequently used and correspondingly more general in meaning. Attributive adjectives are used to further elaborate nominal information. They are a more integrated form of nominal elaboration than predicative adjectives or relative clauses, since they pack information into relatively few words and structures. Together, these five features are used to integrate high amounts of information into a text; to present information as concisely and precisely as possible. These features are associated with communicative situations that require a high informational focus and provide ample opportunity for careful integration of information and precise lexical choice.

The other features with negative weights are place adverbials, past participial WHIZ deletions, agentless passives, and present participial WHIZ deletions. These features are less important in the interpretation of Factor 1: they all have weights less than .42, and most of them have larger weights on some other factor. They are all informational in one way or another, often marking highly abstract types of information. WHIZ deletions are used to modify nouns, further elaborating the nominal content. Passives are associated with a static, nominal style. The co-occurrence of place adverbials with these other features is surprising, but might be due to text internal deixis in highly informational texts (e.g., *It is shown here*; *It was shown above*). Thus, these less important features share the same highly informational functions as nouns, prepositional phrases, type/token ratio, word length, and attributive adjectives.

The features with positive weights on Factor 1 are more complex. All of them can be associated in one way or another with an involved, non-informational focus, due to a primarily interactive or affective purpose and/or to highly constrained production circumstances. These features can be characterized as verbal, interactional, affective, fragmented, reduced in form, and generalized in content.

Private verbs and present tense forms are among the features with largest weights on this factor, indicating a verbal, as opposed to nominal, style. These features can also be considered interactive or involved. Present tense refers to actions occurring in the immediate context of interaction; although informational prose can also be written in the present tense, it uses relatively few verbs. Private verbs (e.g., *think, feel*) are used for the overt expression of private attitudes, thoughts, and emotions. First and second person pronouns, which also have large weights on this factor, refer directly to the addressor and addressee and are thus used frequently in highly interactive discourse. Similarly WH-questions, which have a lower weight, are used primarily in interactive discourse where there is a specific addressee present to answer questions. Emphatics and amplifiers both mark heightened feeling, and sentence relatives are used for attitudinal comments by the speaker (e.g., *He went to the store today, which I think is ridiculous*). All of these features are used for involved discourse, marking high interpersonal interaction or high expression of personal feelings.

Other features with positive weights on Factor 1 mark a reduced surface form, a generalized or uncertain presentation of information, and a generally fragmented production of text. Reduced surface form is marked by *that*-deletions (e.g., *I think* [*that*] *I'll go*), contractions, pro-verb *do*, which substitutes for a fuller verb phrase or clause, and the pronominal forms, *it*, demonstrative pronouns, and indefinite pronouns, which substitute for fuller noun phrases. Final (stranded) prepositions mark a surface disruption in form–meaning correspondence (e.g., *that's the person I talked to*). In most of these cases, a reduction in surface form also results in a more generalized, uncertain content. Thus, contractions result in homophonous expressions, for example, [its] can mean *it is*, *it has*, or *it*-possessive; *it*, demonstrative pronouns, and indefinite pronouns all stand for unspecified nominal referents; and *do* stands for an unspecified verbal referent. In addition, hedges and possibility modals are used to flag uncertainty or lack of precision in the presentation of information. Analytic negation, *be* as main verb, and non-phrasal coordination can all be associated with a fragmented presentation of information, resulting in a low informational density. Analytic negation (*not*) is an alternative to the more integrative synthetic negation (*no*, *neither*). Non-phrasal *and* is used to string clauses together in a loose, logically unspecified manner, instead of integrating the information into fewer units through the use of prepositional phrases, relative clauses, adjectives, etc. *Be* as main verb is typically used to modify a noun with a predicative expression, instead of integrating the information into the noun phrase itself; for example, *the house is big* versus *the big house*. Discourse particles (e.g., *well*, *anyway*) are generalized markers of informational relations in a text. They help to maintain textual coherence when a text is fragmented and would otherwise be relatively incoherent.

Four subordination features are included among the features with positive weights on this factor: causative subordination (*because*), sentence relatives, WH-clauses, and conditional subordination. The co-occurrence of these features with a variety of involved and generalized-content features, and in a complementary pattern to highly informational features, is surprising. This distribution disagrees with the expectations of O'Donnell (1974), Kay (1977), and others – that subordination marks greater elaboration and thus should be characteristic of informational discourse – but it agrees with the findings of Poole and Field (1976) and Halliday (1979) that subordination is associated with the production constraints characteristic of speech. In the present study, subordination features are found on all seven factors, showing the theoretical inadequacy of any proposal that attempts to characterize subordination as a functionally unified construct. The subordination features grouped on Factor 1 seem to be associated with the expression of information under real-time production constraints, when there is little opportunity to elaborate through precise lexical choice. These features also seem to have a primary affective function. A major function of sentence relatives is to express attitudinal comments. WH-clauses provide a way to 'talk about' questions (Winter 1982). Causative and conditional subordination can also be considered as markers of affect or stance, that is, as justification for actions or beliefs (*because*) or conditions for actions or beliefs (*if, unless*). These subordination features thus seem to be associated with a relatively loose presentation of information due to real-time production constraints, and they seem to mark a range of affective functions relating to the elaboration of personal attitudes or feelings.

In summary, Factor 1 represents a dimension marking high informational density and exact informational content versus affective, interactional, and generalized content. Two separate communicative parameters seem to be involved here: (1) the primary purpose of the writer/speaker: informational versus interactive, affective, and involved; and (2) the production circumstances: those circumstances characterized by careful editing possibilities, enabling precision in lexical choice and an integrated textual structure, versus circumstances dictated by real-time constraints, resulting in generalized lexical choice and a generally fragmented presentation of information. Reflecting both of these parameters, I propose the interpretive label 'Informational versus Involved Production' for the dimension underlying this factor.

The distribution of features seen on Factor 1 shows that these two parameters are highly related. That is, discourse characterized by strict production constraints typically has an involved, interactive purpose, and vice versa. This is not surprising, since it represents a natural evolution of discourse purposes in accordance with production possibilities. Discourse produced under real-time conditions will be constrained in its lexical precision and informational density; it is therefore not surprising that such discourse is associated with non-informational purposes. Conversely, as society has developed the need for highly informational texts, it is not surprising that we have turned to those production circumstances that enable precise lexical choice and high informational density. In fact, in some cases these two concerns seem to have an immediate influence on one another. For example, personal letters would appear to contradict the above generalization, being produced without time constraints and yet being involved in focus. However, despite the opportunity for careful production, many personal letters are produced under strict self-imposed time constraints, perhaps reflecting an assessment of the amount of attention deserved by involved discourse. That is, in the case of personal letters, the affective and interactive purposes of the writer seem to result in self-imposed constraints on production opportunity.

It was noted above that the large number of features grouped on this factor identify it as a very important, fundamental dimension of linguistic variation among texts. This dimension has many of the features that have been associated previously with basic discourse dichotomies, for example, nominal versus verbal styles (Wells 1960) and oral versus literate discourse (Tannen 1982a, 1985). This dimension combines features from Chafe's (1982) two dimensions of integration–fragmentation and detachment–involvement. Although the overall interpretation given here is not in terms of oral and literate discourse, this dimension indicates that there is a fundamental parameter of variation among texts that marks the extent to which they are oral or literate in terms of their production characteristics and primary communicative purposes.

6.2.2   Interpretation of Factor 2

Factor 2 was used throughout Chapter 5 to illustrate the methodology of factor analysis. The interpretation of this factor is more straightforward than for Factor 1. There are seven features with weights larger than .40 on Factor 2. The features with positive weights – past tense verbs, third person personal pronouns, perfect aspect verbs, public verbs, synthetic negation, and present participial clauses (.39) – can be considered as markers of narrative action. Past tense and perfect aspect verbs describe past events. Third person personal pronouns mark reference to animate, typically human, referents apart from the speaker and addressee. Narrative discourse depends heavily on these two features, presenting a sequential description of past events involving specific animate particip- ants. Public verbs are apparently used frequently with these other forms because they function as markers of indirect, reported speech (e.g., *admit, assert, declare, hint, report, say*). In addition, one subordination feature, present participial clauses, is grouped with these narrative-marking features. Thompson (1983) characterizes these participial clauses as detached in their syntactic form and shows how they are used to create vivid images in depictive discourse. The grouping of features seen on this factor thus indicates that narrative discourse is often depictive; that the narration of past events is often framed by the vivid imagery provided by present participial clauses. The grouping of synthetic negation with these other features needs further analysis, although it might be due to a high frequency of denials and rejections in the reported reasoning processes of narrative participants. Tottie (1983a) further notes that synthetic neg- ation is more literary than analytic negation and so would be preferred in literary narrative; this might be related to the stronger emphatic force of synthetic negation (e.g., *he said nothing* versus *he did not say anything*).

Only two features have large negative weights on Factor 2: present tense and attributive adjectives. Present tense has a very large weight on Factor 1 in addition to its weight on Factor 2, and attributive adjectives have a slightly larger weight on Factor 1 than Factor 2. The com- plementary distribution of present and past tense verbs on Factor 2 is intuitively transparent: a discourse typically reports events in the past or deals with more immediate matters, but does not mix the two. The co- occurrence of attributive adjectives and present tense verbs apparently reflects a more frequent use of elaborated nominal referents in non- narrative types of discourse than in narrative discourse.

Overall, this dimension can be considered as distinguishing narrative discourse from other types of discourse. It might also be considered as distinguishing between active, event-oriented discourse and more static, descriptive or expository types of discourse. This dimension can thus be interpretively labelled 'Narrative versus Non-narrative Concerns': nar- rative concerns marked by considerable reference to past time, third person animate referents, reported speech, and depictive details; non- narrative concerns, whether expository, descriptive, or other, marked by immediate time and attributive nominal elaboration.

6.2.3   Interpretation of Factor 3

Three different forms of relative clauses are grouped as the primary positive features on Factor 3: WH relative clauses on object positions, WH relative clauses on subject positions, and pied piping constructions. In addition, phrasal coordination and nominalizations have smaller positive weights on this factor. The three forms of WH relative clauses can all be considered as devices for the explicit, elaborated identification of referents in a text. Several researchers have noted functional differences among these forms (Kroch and Hindle 1982; Frawley 1982; Beaman 1984), but their grouping on a single factor indicates that these differences are minor in comparison to the shared function of referential explicitness. The co-occurrence of phrasal coordination and nominalizations with these relativization features indicates that referentially explicit discourse also tends to be integrated and informational.

Three features have large negative weights on Factor 3: time adverbials, place adverbials, and other adverbs. Place and time adverbials are used for locative and temporal reference (e.g., *above, behind; earlier, soon*). They can be used for text-internal referents, but they are more commonly used for reference to places and times outside of the text itself. In fact, these forms often serve as deictics that can only be understood by reference to an external physical and temporal situation. The class 'other adverbs' has a much broader range of functions, which includes time and place reference in addition to specification of manner, etc.

Considering both positive and negative features, the dimension underlying Factor 3 seems to distinguish between highly explicit, context-independent reference and nonspecific, situation-dependent reference. WH relative clauses are used to specify the identity of referents within a text in an explicit and elaborated manner, so that the addressee will have no doubt as to the intended referent. Time and place adverbials, on the other hand, crucially depend on referential inferences by the addressee: for text-internal references (e.g., *see above; discussed later*), the addressee must infer where and when in the text *above* and *later* refer to; in the much more common text-external references, the addressee must identify the intended place and time referents in the actual physical context of the discourse. This dimension thus corresponds closely to the distinction between endophoric and exophoric reference (Halliday and Hasan 1976). Overall, the label 'Explicit versus Situation-Dependent Reference' can be suggested for this dimension.

6.2.4 Interpretation of Factor 4

Factor 4 has only features with positive weights: infinitives, prediction modals, suasive verbs, conditional subordination, necessity modals, split auxiliaries, and possibility modals. Looking ahead to the microanalysis of these features in texts, presented in Section 7.2.4, it is possible to suggest here that they function together to mark persuasion: either explicit marking of the speaker's own persuasion (the speaker's own point of view) or argumentative discourse designed to persuade the addressee. Prediction modals are direct pronouncements that certain events *will* occur; necessity modals are pronouncements concerning the obligation or necessity of certain events, that they *should* occur; possibility modals are pronouncements concerning the ability or possibility of certain events occurring, that they *can* or *might* occur. Suasive verbs (e.g., *command, demand, instruct*) imply intentions to bring about certain events in the future, while conditional subordination specifies the conditions that are required in order for certain events to occur. Although infinitives can have other functions, they are most commonly used as adjective and verb complements; in these constructions, the head adjective or verb frequently encodes the speaker's attitude or stance towards the proposition encoded in the infinitival clause (e.g., *happy to do it; hoped to see it*). Split auxiliaries occur when adverbs are placed between auxiliaries and their main verb; the fact that these auxiliaries are often modals probably accounts for the co-occurrence of split auxiliaries with these other features. Considering the function shared by these different features, I propose the interpretive label 'Overt Expression of Persuasion'. That is, this dimension marks the degree to which persuasion is marked overtly, whether overt marking of the speaker's own point of view, or an assessment of the advisability or likelihood of an event presented to persuade the addressee.

6.2.5 Interpretation of Factor 5

The features with positive weights on Factor 5 are conjuncts, agentless passives, adverbial past participial clauses, *by*-passives, past participial WHIZ deletions, other adverbial subordinators, and predicative adjectives with a relatively small weight. The frequency counts of agentless passives, past participial clauses, *by*-passives, and past participial WHIZ deletions are all independent; that is, the counts of *by* and agentless

passives include only those passive forms *not* counted as past participial
WHIZ deletions or clauses. From one point of view, *by* and agentless
passives serve different thematic functions (Thompson 1982; Weiner and
Labov 1983), but the strong co-occurrence of these two passive types on
Factor 5 reflects the importance of a more basic function shared by these
forms. Similarly, the co-occurrence of passive subordinate clauses
(adverbial and WHIZ) with main clause passive forms shows that the
passive function is more important here than any subordinate/main
clause distinction. These forms are all used to present propositions with
reduced emphasis on the agent, either demoting the agent to object
position or eliding the agent altogether. They are used to give prominence
to the patient of the verb, the entity acted upon, which is typically a non-
animate referent and is often an abstract concept rather than a concrete
referent. Passives are frequently used in procedural discourse, where the
same agent is presupposed across several clauses and the specific agent of
a clause is not important to the discourse purpose. Discourse with very
frequent passive constructions is typically abstract and technical in
content, and formal in style. Apparently conjuncts and adverbial
subordinators frequently co-occur with passive forms to mark the
complex logical relations among clauses that characterize this type of
discourse.

No feature has a large negative weight on Factor 5, although the
negative weight for type/token ratio ($-.31$) is interesting. That is, the
distribution of high lexical variety, represented by type/token ratio, in a
complementary pattern to passives, conjuncts, etc. is quite surprising,
since both sets of features have been associated with discourse having a
highly informational focus. This distribution indicates that abstract,
technical discourse, marked by frequent use of passives and conjuncts,
has a relatively low lexical variety when compared to other types of
informational discourse. Apparently technical discourse repeatedly uses
a small set of precise technical vocabulary to refer to the exact concepts
and entities intended (Grabe 1984a). Other texts can be highly informational but not technical in this sense. The high loading of type/token
ratio on Factor 1 indicates that all informational discourse, technical or
not, has a high lexical variety in contrast to interactive, affective types of
discourse; the lesser loading of type/token ratio here on Factor 5 indicates
that non-technical informational discourse has a markedly higher lexical
variety than abstract, technical discourse.

Overall, the dimension underlying this factor seems to mark informational discourse that is abstract, technical, and formal versus other types of discourse, suggesting the label 'Abstract versus Non-Abstract Information'. As with the other factors, this interpretation is further supported by the analysis of these co-occurring features in particular texts, presented in Section 7.2.5.

6.2.6 Interpretation of Factor 6

Three subordination features have high positive weights on Factor 6: *that* complements to verbs, *that* complements to adjectives, and *that* relative clauses on object positions. In addition, demonstratives have a large positive weight on Factor 6, while final prepositions, existential *there*, demonstrative pronouns, and WH relative clauses on object positions have smaller weights. The only feature with a salient negative weight on this factor is phrasal coordination, which is described by Chafe (1982; Chafe and Danielewicz 1986) as a device for idea unit expansion and informational integration.

The distributional pattern shown on Factor 6 runs counter to previous theoretical expectations: several subordination measures that are typically associated with informational elaboration co-occur here with demonstratives, final prepositions, and demonstrative pronouns, which are associated with informal, unplanned types of discourse; while all of these features occur in a largely complementary distribution to phrasal coordination, which is used to integrate information into idea units. The co-occurrence of these subordination features with features such as stranded prepositions suggests that they function to mark informational elaboration in relatively unplanned types of discourse, an interpretation that is supported by Halliday (1979) and Biber (1986a). Halliday's description of the structural complexity associated with speech has been noted previously; that is, because spoken language is produced and comprehended as an on-going process, it is characterized by 'an intricacy of movement [and by] complex sentence structures with low lexical density (more clauses, but fewer high-content words per clause)'. The subordination features grouped on Factor 6 apparently mark informational elaboration that is produced under strict real-time constraints, resulting in a fragmented presentation of information accomplished by tacking on additional dependent clauses, rather than an integrated presentation that packs information into fewer constructions containing more high-content words and phrases (as on Factor 1).

In addition, *that* complements to verbs and adjectives can be used for elaboration of information relative to the personal stance of the speaker, introducing an affective component into this dimension (e.g., *I wish that* . . .; *it is amazing that* . . .; *I am happy that* . . .). The co-occurrence of demonstratives with the other features having positive weights on Factor 6 needs further investigation, because the frequency count of demonstratives does not distinguish among text-internal and text-external functions. It can only be suggested here that cohesion in unplanned informational discourse relies heavily on demonstratives.

Overall, the dimension underlying Factor 6 seems to distinguish discourse that is informational but produced under real-time conditions from other types of discourse. The label 'On-line Informational Elaboration' is suggested here, but the interpretation of this dimension will be considered in greater detail in Section 7.2.6.

6.2.7   Interpretation of Factor 7

Factor 7 has no loadings over .40, it has only five features with weights larger than .30, and most of these features have larger weights on some other factor. Any interpretation of this factor is thus extremely tentative. Despite this caution, the few features grouped on this factor seem to be theoretically coherent, enabling an initial interpretation. That is, the function underlying these features seems to be that of academic hedging, to qualify the extent to which an assertion is 'known' in academic discourse. *Seem* and *appear* mark perception (Quirk *et al.* 1985:1183) rather than bald assertion of fact; downtoners indicate the degree of probability of an assertion, as opposed to hedges which load on Factor 1 and simply mark an assertion as uncertain; concessive subordination indicates that an assertion is true within the bounds of some other, possibly contrasting, assertion (*although* ASSERTION 2, ASSERTION 1). One of the functions of adverbs is to indicate possibility or generalization (e.g., *possibly, generally, approximately*), and it is probably in this function that total *-ly* adverbs co-occur with these other features. Similarly, adjectives can function to mark qualification or possibility (e.g., *a possible explanation*). Thus, the dimension underlying this factor seems to mark academic qualification or hedging. Future research is required to confirm or deny the existence of a dimension with this function; the factorial structure of Factor 7 is not strong enough for a firm interpretation, and this factor will therefore not be considered further in the present study.

6.2.8 Summary of the textual dimensions

The first six factors in this analysis have strong factorial structures, and the features grouped on each factor are functionally coherent and can be readily interpreted on the basis of prior microscopic research. I have suggested interpretive labels for each factor, to describe the underlying functional dimension.

Dimension 1 is labelled 'Informational versus Involved Production'. The poles of this dimension represent discourse with interactional, affective, involved purposes, associated with strict real-time production and comprehension constraints, versus discourse with highly informational purposes, which is carefully crafted and highly edited. This dimension is very strong and represents a fundamental parameter of variation among texts in English.

Dimension 2 is labelled 'Narrative versus Non-Narrative Concerns'. It distinguishes discourse with primary narrative purposes from discourse with non-narrative purposes (expository, descriptive, or other). Dimension 3 is labelled 'Explicit versus Situation-Dependent Reference' and distinguishes between discourse that identifies referents fully and explicitly through relativization, and discourse that relies on nonspecific deictics and reference to an external situation for identification purposes. Dimension 4 is labelled 'Overt Expression of Persuasion'; the features on this dimension are associated with the speaker's expression of own point of view or with argumentative styles intended to persuade the addressee.

Dimension 5 is labelled 'Abstract Non-Abstract Information' and distinguishes between texts with a highly abstract and technical informational focus and those with non-abstract focuses. Dimension 6 is labelled 'On-line Informational Elaboration'. It distinguishes between informational discourse produced under highly constrained conditions, in which the information is presented in a relatively loose, fragmented manner, and other types of discourse, whether informational discourse that is highly integrated or discourse that is not informational. Factor 7 seems to mark academic hedging or qualification but is not sufficiently represented for a full interpretation.

6.3 Comparison to the 1986 analysis

In my 1986 analysis of spoken and written textual dimensions (Biber 1986a), three primary dimensions are identified and interpreted. These dimensions are labelled 'Interactive versus Edited Text', 'Abstract versus Situated Content', and 'Reported versus Immediate Style'. In this section, I will discuss the extent to which the 1986 factorial structure is replicated by the present analysis and the extent to which the interpretations proposed in that earlier analysis are confirmed here.

The factorial structure of the 1986 analysis is summarized in Table 6.2. There are striking similarities between the first three factors of the 1986 analysis, which were the only factors interpreted, and Factors 1, 2, and 5 of the present analysis. Factor 1 of the present analysis corresponds directly to Factor 1.1986; Factor 2 corresponds to Factor 3.1986; and Factor 5 corresponds to Factor 2.1986. All five of the features with large weights on Factor 3.1986 load on Factor 2 in the present analysis (past tense, third person personal pronouns, and perfect aspect with positive weights; present tense and adjectives with negative weights). A majority of the features with large weights on Factor 1.1986 load on Factor 1 in the present analysis (pro-verb *do*, contractions, first and second person pronouns, hedges, WH clauses, WH questions, pronoun *it*, emphatics, and present tense with positive weights; word length and type/token ratio with negative weights). Two other features on Factor 1.1986 have split off to group with additional features as Factor 6 in the present analysis (*that* verb complements and final prepositions). Finally, three of the most important features on Factor 2.1986 load on Factor 5 of the present analysis (conjuncts, agentless passives, and *by*-passives). In addition, nominalizations and prepositions, which have high weights on Factor 2.1986, have notable weights on Factor 5 of the present analysis (.28 and .23 respectively), although they both have higher weights on other factors. Place and time adverbials, which grouped as two of the primary features with negative weights on Factor 2.1986, have split off with nominalizations (one of the primary features with a positive weight) to group with other features forming Factor 3 of the present analysis.

Overall, the factorial structure of the 1986 analysis is closely replicated by the present analysis. The major differences between the two analyses are due to the addition of several linguistic features in the present analysis, which enables identification of additional dimensions that were collapsed in the earlier analysis; thus, two features from Factor 1.1986 have split off to group with additional features as part of Factor 6 in the present analysis, and two features have split off from Factor 2.1986 to group with additional features as part of Factor 3 in the present analysis.

Given this replication of the factorial structure, it is reasonable to consider the extent to which the interpretations proposed in the 1986

Table 6.2 *Summary of the factorial structure of 41 linguistic features, taken from Biber (1986a)*

FACTOR 1		FACTOR 2	
questions	.79	nominalizations	.74
THAT-clauses	.76	prepositions	.61
final prepositions	.68	specific conjuncts	.61
pro-verb DO	.67	agentless passives	.60
contractions	.67	BY-passives	.47
first and second		IT-clefts	.45
person pronouns	.62	split auxiliaries	.42
general hedges	.61	word length	.40
IF-clauses	.56	attitudinal disjuncts	.35
WH-questions	.52		
pronoun IT	.49	-------------------------	
other subordinators	.48		
specific emphatics	.46	place adverbs	-.57
demonstrative BE	.42	time adverbs	-.55
present tense	.42	relative pronoun	
WH-clauses	.41	deletion	-.50
general emphatics	.41	THAT deletion	-.42
infinitives	.35	third person	
		pronouns	-.35
-------------------------			
word length	-.71		
type / token ratio	-.65		

FACTOR 3	
past tense	.89
third person pronouns	.61
perfect aspect	.47
-------------------------	
present tense	-.62
adjectives	-.40

analysis have been confirmed by the present analysis. In a confirmatory factor analysis (see Section 5.4), additional linguistic features are included in the analysis to see if they load as hypothesized. To the extent that features with certain functions load on the factors hypothesized to have the same functions, those functional interpretations of the factors are confirmed. To greater or lesser extents, the interpretations for the first five factors of the present analysis represent confirmations of the hypothesized interpretations in the 1986 analysis.

The easiest case to consider is Factor 3.1986, labelled 'Reported versus Immediate Style'. This factor is completely replicated by Factor 2 in the present analysis. In addition, three new features added to the present analysis are grouped with the previous features. One of these, public verbs, has a primary function of marking reported speech, which agrees fully with the interpretation of a dimension marking reported, narrative discourse. The second new feature, present participial clauses, extends the earlier interpretation to include depictive details as part of this reported style. The third additional feature, synthetic negation, in no way disconfirms the hypothesized interpretation, but it is not obvious how it fits into this dimension. Together, these features confirm the interpretation of a dimension marking a 'removed' or narrative style.

Factor 1 in the 1986 analysis was hypothesized to differentiate between texts 'produced under conditions of high personal involvement and real-time constraints (marked by low explicitness in the expression of meaning, high subordination, and interactive features) as opposed to texts produced under conditions permitting considerable editing and high explicitness in the lexical content, but little interaction or personal involvement' (1986a:395). Several additional features in the present analysis group on Factor 1 in a way that confirms the basic outlines of the above interpretation. Three of these features, demonstrative pronouns, indefinite pronouns, and discourse particles, mark reduced lexical content and interpersonal involvement, confirming that aspect of the interpretation. Three other features, private verbs, sentence relatives, and possibility modals, emphasize the affective aspect of personal involvement. Finally, a count of all nouns (excluding nominalizations) was added to the present analysis, and this feature groups with word length and type/token ratio (marking lexical content elaboration and specificity) as expected.

Other aspects of the interpretation of Factor 1.1986 are extended by the present analysis, being identified as belonging to a separate dimension (Factor 6). Thus, it was hypothesized in the 1986 interpretation of Factor 1 that discourse produced under real-time constraints has its own complexities, marked by *that* clauses, *if* clauses, and other adverbial clauses. The addition of *that* adjectival complements and *that* relative clauses to the present analysis confirmed the existence of this complexity, but showed that it functions as part of a separate dimension: one marking informational (rather than interactional) discourse produced under real-time constraints, viz. the dimension underlying Factor 6.

Finally, Dimension 2.1986 was labelled 'Abstract versus Situated Content' and was interpreted as distinguishing discourse with highly abstract, formal content (marked by passives, conjuncts, nominalizations, etc.) from discourse with concrete, situation-dependent content (marked by place and time adverbials, etc.). The existence of a hypothesized dimension marking abstract, formal content is confirmed by the features with positive weights on Factor 5 in the present analysis. These features include the new features of adverbial past participle clauses and past participial WHIZ deletions, which mark abstract information and have large weights on this factor. The existence of a dimension marking situation-dependent content is also confirmed by the present analysis, but not as part of the same dimension. That is, the addition of relative clause features in the present analysis shows that abstract and situated content are not best analyzed as opposite poles of the same dimension. Rather, the features associated with situated content (primarily place and time adverbials) are shown to be part of a referential dimension in the present analysis, marking explicit versus situation-dependent reference (Factor 3). This extended interpretation is enabled by the three WH relative clause features added to the present analysis, which are found to occur in a complementary pattern to the situated content features from the 1986 analysis.

In summary, the major aspects of the 1986 dimensions are replicated and confirmed by the present analysis. Specifically, in both analyses there are three major dimensions that mark (1) interactive, involved discourse versus edited, informational discourse; (2) formal, abstract information versus non-abstract types of information; and (3) reported, narrative discourse versus non-narrative types of discourse. In addition, the present analysis extends the 1986 interpretation, identifying additional aspects of the earlier dimensions or showing that some aspects actually function as part of additional dimensions. These extensions include: (1) the importance of affect as part of interpersonal involvement on Factor 1; (2) the importance of depictive details in narrative discourse (Factor 2); (3) the fact that abstract, technical discourse is relatively low in lexical diversity (Factor 5); (4) the separation of informational discourse produced under real-time constraints (Factor 6) from involved discourse produced under real-time constraints (Factor 1); and (5) the separation of a dimension marking situation-dependent reference versus highly explicit reference (Factor 3) from a dimension marking non-abstract information versus abstract information (Factor 5).

Comparison of these two analyses provides a relatively solid foundation to the interpretations of Dimensions 1–3 and 5–6 in the present analysis. Dimension 4 is not a confirmation of any earlier study and thus is more speculative. As noted above, the dimension underlying Factor 7 is not sufficiently well-represented to warrant further interpretation. The remaining analyses in this book will use the first six dimensions described here to compare the relations among spoken and written genres.

7 Textual relations in speech and writing

7.1 Factor scores and textual relations

The primary goal of this study is specification of the textual relations in English speech and writing, that is, the linguistic similarities and differences among English texts. To this point, six parameters of variation have been identified through a factor analysis and interpreted as underlying textual dimensions. In the present chapter, the similarities and differences among genres are considered with respect to each of these dimensions, and the overall relations among genres in speech and writing are specified by consideration of all dimensions simultaneously. Genres can be similar with respect to some dimensions but quite different with respect to others; the textual relations among genres are determined by the joint assessment of similarities and differences with respect to all dimensions.

Genres can be compared along each dimension by computing factor scores (see Section 5.5). To recapitulate, factor scores are computed by summing the frequency of each of the features on a factor, for each text; for example, the factor score of a text for Factor 2 might equal 23 past tense + 50 third person pronouns + 10 perfect aspect verbs + etc. The factor scores for each text can be averaged across all texts in a genre to compute a mean dimension score for the genre, and these mean dimension scores can be compared to specify the relations among genres.

Table 7.1 presents the dimension scores of each genre. This table presents, for each of the dimensions, the mean score for each genre, the minimum and maximum dimension scores within the genre, the range, which is the difference between the minimum and maximum scores, and the standard deviation, which measures the spread of the distribution – 68% of the texts in a genre have dimension scores that are plus or minus one standard deviation from the mean dimension score for the genre. Large standard deviations show that the texts in a genre are widely

Table 7.1 *Descriptive dimension statistics for all genres*

Dimension 1:   'Involved versus Informational Production'
Dimension 2:   'Narrative versus Non-Narrative Concerns'
Dimension 3:   'Explicit versus Situation-Dependent Reference'
Dimension 4:   'Overt Expression of Persuasion'
Dimension 5:   'Abstract versus Non-Abstract Information'
Dimension 6:   'On-Line Informational Elaboration'

Dimension	Mean	Minimum value	Maximum value	Range	Standard deviation
--- Press Reportage ---					
Dimension 1	-15.1	-24.1	-3.1	21.0	4.5
Dimension 2	0.4	-3.2	7.7	10.9	2.1
Dimension 3	-0.3	-6.2	6.5	12.7	2.9
Dimension 4	-0.7	-6.0	5.7	11.7	2.6
Dimension 5	0.6	-4.4	5.5	9.9	2.4
Dimension 6	-0.9	-4.0	3.9	8.0	1.8
--- Press Editorials ---					
Dimension 1	-10.0	-18.0	1.6	19.5	3.8
Dimension 2	-0.8	-3.5	1.8	5.3	1.4
Dimension 3	1.9	-2.9	5.4	8.3	2.0
Dimension 4	3.1	-1.8	9.3	11.2	3.2
Dimension 5	0.3	-2.4	4.5	6.9	2.0
Dimension 6	1.5	-1.8	5.7	7.5	1.6
--- Press Reviews ---					
Dimension 1	-13.9	-20.5	-8.6	11.8	3.9
Dimension 2	-1.6	-4.3	2.7	7.0	1.9
Dimension 3	4.3	-1.8	10.3	12.2	3.7
Dimension 4	-2.8	-6.5	1.5	8.1	2.0
Dimension 5	0.8	-3.1	5.8	9.0	2.1
Dimension 6	-1.0	-3.7	3.9	7.6	1.9
--- Religion ---					
Dimension 1	-7.0	-17.2	16.5	33.7	8.3
Dimension 2	-0.7	-4.4	5.5	9.9	2.7
Dimension 3	3.7	-0.6	9.8	10.4	3.3
Dimension 4	0.2	-2.9	6.2	9.1	2.7
Dimension 5	1.4	-2.4	5.2	7.6	2.4
Dimension 6	1.0	-2.0	6.5	8.4	2.4
--- Hobbies ---					
Dimension 1	-10.1	-18.8	-2.0	16.9	5.0
Dimension 2	-2.9	-4.8	1.6	6.4	1.9
Dimension 3	0.3	-5.7	10.0	15.7	3.6
Dimension 4	1.7	-5.8	11.0	16.8	4.6
Dimension 5	1.2	-3.6	13.0	16.6	4.2
Dimension 6	-0.7	-3.0	2.5	5.5	1.8

Table 7.1 (*cont.*)

Dimension	Mean	Minimum value	Maximum value	Range	Standard deviation
--------------------------- Popular Lore ---------------------------					
Dimension 1	-9.3	-24.7	9.9	34.5	11.3
Dimension 2	-0.1	-4.7	9.2	13.9	3.7
Dimension 3	2.3	-2.1	11.5	13.6	3.5
Dimension 4	-0.3	-4.4	13.3	17.8	4.8
Dimension 5	0.1	-3.9	3.0	6.9	2.3
Dimension 6	-0.8	-3.8	3.8	7.6	1.8
--------------------------- Biographies ---------------------------					
Dimension 1	-12.4	-21.4	7.5	28.9	7.5
Dimension 2	2.1	-1.5	8.0	9.5	2.5
Dimension 3	1.7	-2.4	8.8	11.2	3.5
Dimension 4	-0.7	-3.9	1.8	5.7	1.6
Dimension 5	-0.5	-3.5	6.0	9.5	2.5
Dimension 6	-0.3	-3.3	3.6	6.9	2.2
--------------------------- Official Documents ---------------------------					
Dimension 1	-18.1	-26.3	-9.1	17.2	4.8
Dimension 2	-2.9	-5.4	-1.5	3.9	1.2
Dimension 3	7.3	2.1	13.4	11.3	3.6
Dimension 4	-0.2	-8.4	8.7	17.1	4.1
Dimension 5	4.7	0.6	9.4	8.8	2.4
Dimension 6	-0.9	-3.8	2.7	6.5	2.0
--------------------------- Academic Prose ---------------------------					
Dimension 1	-14.9	-26.5	7.1	33.6	6.0
Dimension 2	-2.6	-6.2	5.3	11.5	2.3
Dimension 3	4.2	-5.8	18.6	24.3	3.6
Dimension 4	-0.5	-7.1	17.5	24.6	4.7
Dimension 5	5.5	-2.4	16.8	19.2	4.8
Dimension 6	0.5	-3.3	9.2	12.5	2.7
--------------------------- General Fiction ---------------------------					
Dimension 1	-0.8	-19.6	22.3	41.9	9.2
Dimension 2	5.9	1.2	15.6	14.3	3.2
Dimension 3	-3.1	-8.2	1.0	9.2	2.3
Dimension 4	0.9	-3.2	7.2	10.3	2.6
Dimension 5	-2.5	-4.8	1.5	6.3	1.6
Dimension 6	-1.6	-4.3	2.7	6.9	1.9
--------------------------- Mystery Fiction ---------------------------					
Dimension 1	-0.2	-15.4	12.6	28.0	8.5
Dimension 2	6.0	0.7	10.3	9.7	3.0
Dimension 3	-3.6	-7.2	4.8	12.0	3.4
Dimension 4	-0.7	-5.6	4.2	9.7	3.3
Dimension 5	-2.8	-4.5	-0.4	4.1	1.2
Dimension 6	-1.9	-4.3	-0.2	4.1	1.3

Table 7.1 (*cont.*)

Dimension	Mean	Minimum value	Maximum value	Range	Standard deviation
------------------------- Science Fiction -------------------------					
Dimension 1	-6.1	-12.1	-1.7	10.4	4.6
Dimension 2	5.9	2.4	8.7	6.3	2.5
Dimension 3	-1.4	-6.0	3.8	9.8	3.7
Dimension 4	-0.7	-3.0	1.8	4.8	1.7
Dimension 5	-2.5	-3.6	-1.7	1.8	0.8
Dimension 6	-1.6	-3.5	0.4	3.9	1.6
------------------------- Adventure Fiction ----------------------					
Dimension 1	-0.0	-11.9	11.1	23.1	6.3
Dimension 2	5.5	2.2	10.5	8.3	2.7
Dimension 3	-3.8	-7.8	-1.6	6.2	1.7
Dimension 4	-1.2	-5.0	5.6	10.6	2.8
Dimension 5	-2.5	-4.5	-0.8	3.7	1.2
Dimension 6	-1.9	-4.0	1.8	5.8	1.7
------------------------- Romantic Fiction ----------------------					
Dimension 1	4.3	-6.5	15.3	21.9	5.6
Dimension 2	7.2	1.4	11.7	10.3	2.8
Dimension 3	-4.1	-6.4	-1.2	5.2	1.6
Dimension 4	1.8	-1.1	7.2	8.2	2.7
Dimension 5	-3.1	-4.2	-1.5	2.7	0.9
Dimension 6	-1.2	-3.8	2.1	5.9	2.2
------------------------- Humor ------------------------------------					
Dimension 1	-7.8	-13.7	7.6	21.3	6.7
Dimension 2	0.9	-2.0	3.0	5.0	1.8
Dimension 3	-0.8	-3.5	4.2	7.7	2.6
Dimension 4	-0.3	-4.8	3.8	8.6	2.7
Dimension 5	-0.4	-3.0	1.2	4.2	1.4
Dimension 6	-1.5	-3.6	1.3	4.8	1.7
------------------------- Personal Letters ----------------------					
Dimension 1	19.5	13.8	27.0	13.2	5.4
Dimension 2	0.3	-0.9	1.7	2.6	1.0
Dimension 3	-3.6	-6.6	-1.3	5.3	1.8
Dimension 4	1.5	-1.6	6.4	8.0	2.6
Dimension 5	-2.8	-4.8	0.5	5.4	1.9
Dimension 6	-1.4	-3.7	0.3	4.0	1.6
------------------------- Professional Letters ---------------------					
Dimension 1	-3.9	-17.1	24.8	41.9	13.7
Dimension 2	-2.2	-6.9	4.6	11.5	3.5
Dimension 3	6.5	1.4	12.4	11.0	4.2
Dimension 4	3.5	-5.3	11.0	16.3	4.7
Dimension 5	0.4	-3.5	4.4	7.9	2.4
Dimension 6	1.5	-3.6	9.6	13.2	3.6

Table 7.1 (*cont.*)

Dimension	Mean	Minimum value	Maximum value	Range	Standard deviation
-------------------------	Face-to-face Conversations		--------------		
Dimension 1	35.3	17.7	54.1	36.4	9.1
Dimension 2	-0.6	-4.4	4.0	8.4	2.0
Dimension 3	-3.9	-10.5	1.6	12.1	2.1
Dimension 4	-0.3	-5.2	6.5	11.7	2.4
Dimension 5	-3.2	-4.5	0.1	4.6	1.1
Dimension 6	0.3	-3.6	6.5	10.1	2.2
-------------------------	Telephone Conversations		------------------		
Dimension 1	37.2	7.2	52.9	45.8	9.9
Dimension 2	-2.1	-4.2	4.7	8.9	2.2
Dimension 3	-5.2	-10.1	2.3	12.5	2.9
Dimension 4	0.6	-4.9	8.4	13.3	3.6
Dimension 5	-3.7	-4.8	0.1	4.9	1.2
Dimension 6	-0.9	-4.8	3.3	8.1	2.1
-------------------------	Interviews	------------------------------			
Dimension 1	17.1	3.5	36.0	32.5	10.7
Dimension 2	-1.1	-5.0	2.7	7.8	2.1
Dimension 3	-0.4	-6.3	8.3	14.7	4.0
Dimension 4	1.0	-3.4	6.1	9.5	2.4
Dimension 5	-2.0	-4.1	0.4	4.5	1.3
Dimension 6	3.1	-1.4	10.5	11.9	2.6
-------------------------	Broadcasts	------------------------------			
Dimension 1	-4.3	-19.6	16.9	36.6	10.7
Dimension 2	-3.3	-5.2	-0.6	4.6	1.2
Dimension 3	-9.0	-15.8	-2.2	13.6	4.4
Dimension 4	-4.4	-6.9	-0.3	6.5	2.0
Dimension 5	-1.7	-4.7	5.4	10.0	2.8
Dimension 6	-1.3	-3.6	1.7	5.3	1.6
-------------------------	Spontaneous Speeches		---------------------		
Dimension 1	18.2	-2.6	33.1	35.7	12.3
Dimension 2	1.3	-3.8	9.4	13.2	3.6
Dimension 3	1.2	-5.4	9.7	15.1	4.3
Dimension 4	0.3	-5.5	7.4	12.9	4.4
Dimension 5	-2.6	-4.5	0.7	5.1	1.7
Dimension 6	2.6	-2.4	10.6	13.0	4.2
-------------------------	Prepared Speeches	-----------------------			
Dimension 1	2.2	-7.3	14.8	22.1	6.7
Dimension 2	0.7	-4.9	6.1	11.0	3.3
Dimension 3	0.3	-5.6	6.1	11.6	3.6
Dimension 4	0.4	-4.4	11.2	15.5	4.1
Dimension 5	-1.9	-3.9	1.0	5.0	1.4
Dimension 6	3.4	-0.8	7.5	8.3	2.8

scattered around the mean score; small standard deviations show that the texts are tightly grouped around the mean score.

For example, the first set of dimension scores on Table 7.1 are for the genre press reportage. The mean dimension score for Dimension 1 is −15.1, reflecting the fact that the texts in this genre have high frequencies of nouns and prepositions, long words, and high type/token ratios (the features with negative weights on Factor 1) combined with low frequencies of private verbs, present tense verbs, contractions, first and second person pronouns, emphatics, etc. (the features with positive weights on Factor 1). Press reportage texts are not tightly grouped around this mean score, however. Table 7.1 shows that the lowest dimension score for a press text on Dimension 1 is −24.1, while the highest is −3.1, giving a spread, or range, of 21.0. The standard deviation of 4.5 shows that 68% of the press reportage texts have dimension scores between −19.6 and −10.6; i.e., the mean score (−15.1) plus or minus one standard deviation. This spread is not overly large, but it indicates that there is diversity within the genre press reportage (see further discussion in Chapter 8).

Table 7.2 presents overall F and correlation values for each dimension. These values were computed using a General Linear Models procedure. The F value is a test of statistical significance, indicating whether a dimension can distinguish among genres to a significant extent. The p value shows the probability that the F value is significant, based on the size of the F score and the number of texts being considered; values of p smaller than .05 indicate that there is a statistically significant relationship. Because statistical significance is tied closely to the number of texts in a study, it is possible in very large studies to have significant relationships that are not very important and therefore not very interesting from a theoretical point of view. In contrast, the values of R*R, the squared multiple correlation coefficient, indicate the *importance* of each dimension in distinguishing among the genres, and thus they are more useful in evaluating the overall predictive power of a dimension. R*R values directly indicate the percentage of variance in the dimension scores that can be predicted by knowing the genre distinctions; that is, the R*R value indicates the percentage of variation in the dimension scores of texts that can be accounted for by knowing the genre category of the texts.

For example, Table 7.2 shows that Dimension 1 ('Informational versus Involved Production') has an F score of 111.9, which is significant at

Table 7.2 *F and correlation scores for the six textual dimensions*

Dimension 1:   'Involved versus Informational Production'
Dimension 2:   'Narrative versus Non-Narrative Concerns'
Dimension 3:   'Explicit versus Situation-Dependent Reference'
Dimension 4:   'Overt Expression of Persuasion'
Dimension 5:   'Abstract versus Non-Abstract Information'
Dimension 6:   'On-Line Informational Elaboration'

Dimension	F value	Probability (p)	R*R
1	111.9	p < .0001	84.3%
2	32.3	p < .0001	60.8%
3	31.9	p < .0001	60.5%
4	4.2	p < .0001	16.9%
5	28.8	p < .0001	58.0%
6	8.3	p < .0001	28.5%

$p < .0001$; that is, Dimension 1 is a significant predictor of genre differences. More interestingly, the R*R value of Dimension 1 is 84.3%; that is, 84% of the variation in values for Dimension Score 1 can be accounted for by knowing the genre categories of texts. There is thus an extremely strong correlation between the genre distinctions and the values of Dimension Score 1.

In fact, Table 7.2 shows that all of the dimensions have strong relationships with the genre distinctions, although there are large differences in their predictive power. The distinctions among genres with respect to each dimension are significant at $p < .0001$. Four of the six dimensions have R*R values greater than 50%, while a fifth (Dimension 6) has an R*R of 29%. Only Dimension 4 shows a relatively small R*R of 17%, which is still large enough to be noteworthy. Overall, these values show that the dimensions identified in the present study are very powerful predictors of the differences among spoken and written genres.

The textual relations among genres can be further considered by plotting the mean dimension score for each genre, as in Figures 7.1–7.6. These plots are graphic presentations of the mean dimension scores given in Table 7.1. For example, Figure 7.1 presents the mean dimension score

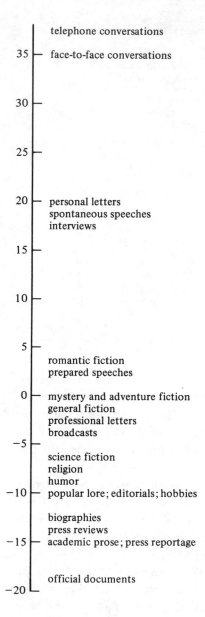

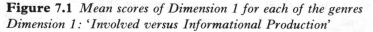

Figure 7.1 *Mean scores of Dimension 1 for each of the genres*
Dimension 1: 'Involved versus Informational Production'

of each genre for Dimension 1, situating the genres with respect to one another along a continuous parameter of variation that has been labelled 'Informational versus Involved Production'. To more fully interpret each dimension, it is necessary to consider: (1) the similarities and differences among genres with respect to their mean dimension scores, summarized in Figures 7.1–7.6; (2) the linguistic features constituting the dimension, summarized in Table 6.1; and (3) the underlying functional parameter(s) (situational, processing, or other) associated with the dimension. As noted elsewhere, the interplay between micro- and macro-analyses is crucial for an overall description of the relations among genres. In Chapter 6, micro-analyses of individual features provided the foundation for the initial interpretations of the factors as dimensions. In the present chapter, macro-analysis determines the overall relations of genres relative to one another, while micro-analyses of text samples from particular genres are used to seek fuller functional interpretations of the dimensions. I first discuss the similarities and differences among genres with respect to each dimension in turn, and then I assess the overall relations among genres with respect to this six-dimensional model.

7.2   Relations along Dimensions

7.2.1   Relations along Dimension 1

The relations among genres with respect to Dimension 1 are summarized in Figure 7.1: a plot of the mean of Dimension Score 1 for each genre. This figure shows that face-to-face and telephone conversation have very high mean scores on Dimension 1, while biographies, press reviews, academic prose, press reportage, and official documents have very low scores. Personal letters, spontaneous speeches, and interviews have moderately high scores, while science fiction, religion, humor, popular lore, editorials, and hobbies all have moderately low scores. From Chapter 6, we know that the genres with high mean scores on Dimension 1 are characterized by frequent occurrences of private verbs, *that*-deletions, present tense, contractions, second person pronouns, etc. (the features with positive weights on Factor 1), together with markedly infrequent occurrences of nouns, prepositions, long words, more varied vocabulary, and attributive adjectives (the features with negative weights on Factor 1). Genres with low scores on this dimension have the opposite characteristics. These characteristics can be illustrated by the following two text samples – one from a telephone conversation, with a very high score on this dimension, and the other from an official document, with a low dimension score.[1]

Text 7.1: Telephone conversation (LL:7,3,f)

B: *anyway #*
         how did you get on [pause] skiing #

A: *skiing # [pause]*
         skiing was good fun actually #

B: *oh #*

A: *mm # [pause]*
         I I I enjoyed actually skiing #
         and it was [pause] really quite funny #
         being with [short pause] thrust together with #
         sort of sixteen other people for a fortnight and # [pause]
         and

B: *oh #*
         I'd love a fortnight's holiday where you can relax #

A: *well it's it's fantastic #*
         because it's [pause] so completely different from anything
            that you [short pause] you know #
         would ever get yourself to do otherwise #

B: *yes #*
         yes #

A: *I think #*

B: *yes*

[1] Texts are labelled as follows:
CORPUS:GENRE,TEXT-NUMBER,SUBTEXT
For example, text 7.1 is labelled LL:7,3,f, because it is from the London–Lund Corpus, genre 7 (telephone conversation), text no. 3 within that genre, and subtext f within that text – see Appendix I for details.

Text 7.2: Official document (LOB:H,26 – Royal College of Surgeons of England, Annual Report for 1960–1)

The restoration of a further volume of the collection of Hunterian drawings has been completed at the British Museum. A selection from the collection of Pharmacy Jars was lent to The Times Book Shop in connexion with their Royal Society Tercentenary Exhibition. Two coloured engravings of the College in the early nineteenth century were presented to the Royal Australasian College of Surgeons by the President when he visited Melbourne.

Text 7.1 illustrates many of the linguistic characteristics of texts having high scores on Dimension 1: a high level of interaction and personal affect, shown by many references to *I* and *you*, private verbs (e.g., *think, love*), emphatics (e.g., *really, so completely different*), WH questions (e.g., *how did . . .*), and causative subordination (e.g., *because*); and a generalized and fragmented presentation of content, shown by hedges (e.g., *sort of*), discourse particles (e.g., *anyway, well*), contractions (e.g., *I'd, it's*), non-phrasal *and*, *be* as main verb, pro-verb *do*, and pronoun *it*. Even though the topic deals with past events, much of the text is in the present tense, emphasizing the immediacy of the interaction (e.g., *it's fantastic, it's so completely different*). In addition to frequent occurrences of the features listed above, text 7.1 is characterized by the relative absence of the features with negative weights on Dimension 1: markedly few nouns and prepositions, relatively short words, and much repetition of vocabulary (a low type/token ratio). Thus, text 7.1 is highly involved, interactive, and affective. It packages information in general rather than specific terms, and it focuses on interpersonal and affective content rather than strictly informational content.

In contrast, text 7.2 is highly informational and shows almost no concern for interpersonal or affective content. This text shows a very high frequency of nouns and prepositions (e.g., *of a further volume of the collection of Hunterian drawings*), while it has only four verbs in the entire passage. There are many quite long words and a careful selection of vocabulary, resulting in a high type/token ratio (e.g., *restoration, collection, engravings, century*). None of the involved or generalized types of features that characterize text 7.1 are found in text 7.2.

In Chapter 6, Dimension 1 was interpreted as distinguishing between texts having an informational focus and texts having an involved focus.

The dimension was further interpreted as distinguishing between texts produced under conditions permitting careful word choice and high informational density versus texts produced under strict real-time constraints resulting in generalized lexical content and lower informational densities. Official documents, illustrated by text 7.2, and conversations, illustrated by text 7.1, clearly represent these two opposite communicative concerns and production circumstances.

A cursory examination of Dimension 1 on Figure 7.1 might suggest that this parameter identifies a dichotomy between spoken and written texts: spoken genres like face-to-face and telephone conversation have very high scores, and written genres like biographies, press reviews, academic prose, press reportage, and official documents all have very low scores. A closer examination shows that this interpretation is not adequate; personal letters have a score higher than all non-conversational spoken genres, romantic fiction has an intermediate score which is higher than the scores for prepared speeches and broadcasts, while broadcasts have a score in the lower half of this scale, directly among the majority of written genres. This distribution of texts in no way corresponds to a spoken–written distinction. It can be understood, however, in terms of the interpretation of involved real-time production versus informational, edited production.

Personal letters, for example, are written but have an involved focus. In addition, they are typically produced under self-imposed time constraints, and thus do not show careful word choice or a high informational density. These characteristics are illustrated by text 7.3:

Text 7.3: Personal letter (private corpus, no. 2)

> **How you doing? I'm here at work waiting for my appointment to get here, it's Friday. Thank goodness, but I still have tomorrow, but this week has flown by, I guess because I've been staying busy, getting ready for Christmas and stuff. Have you done your Christmas shopping yet? I'm pretty proud of myself. I'm almost finished. Me and L went shopping at Sharpstown last Monday and I got a lot done, I just have a few little things to get. Thanks for the poster, I loved it, I hung it in my room last night, sometimes I feel like that's about right.**

This written passage shows many of the same interactive and affective characteristics as conversation. There is a high frequency of the pronouns

I and *you*, WH questions, contractions, and private verbs (e.g., *feel*, *love*). The letter is written primarily in the present tense, although writer and reader do not share time. It shows little lexical variety, few long words, and few nouns or prepositions; rather, it relies heavily on forms that are not at all precise in their informational content, for example, pronoun *it*, demonstrative pronouns (e.g., *that's about right*), pro-verb *do*, and hedges. The fact that personal letters are written has little bearing on their characterization with respect to Dimension 1; rather, their affective, interactional purpose and the relatively little attention given to production are the important functional parameters to be considered here.

Professional letters, although similar to personal letters in that they are written from one individual to another, differ with respect to the functions underlying Dimension 1. They are written for informational purposes and only acknowledge interpersonal relations in a secondary manner. Further, they are written with considerable care, sometimes even being revised and rewritten, and thus they can show considerable lexical variety and informational density. Thus consider text 7.4:

Text 7.4: Professional letter (private corpus, no. 8)

> *We felt that we needed a financial base on which to work, but the goals which we indicated for I. are also included in the goals of L., including of course the occasional papers . . . In the meantime, we are going ahead with plans to establish three language resource institutes resource centers in ESL, which will have three functions: (1) to be a resource center with a reading library of ESL materials and directors who are competent ESL professionals, (2) as a funnel for consultant activities both outward using local expertise needed in other areas where we have L and inward bringing into the area needed expertise and including workshops, mini-conferences, and seminars, and finally (3) to offer educational programs.*

This text portion shows that interpersonal communication can be highly informational. There are few features that refer directly to personal emotions or the interaction between reader and writer, while there are frequent nouns and prepositions, and a relatively varied vocabulary. Letters of this type are interactive (shown, e.g., by the use of first and second person pronouns), but their primary focus is informational rather than involved.

Finally, the dimension score of broadcasts is noteworthy with respect to Dimension 1. Broadcasts are not typically reckoned among the literate genres: they directly report events in progress rather than conceptual information. It is thus surprising that broadcasts have a low mean score and appear to be quite similar to the majority of written genres with respect to Dimension 1. In the case of this genre, however, the low score for Dimension 1 marks the absence of an affective or interactive focus rather than the presence of a highly informational focus *per se*. That is, broadcasts have neither a primary involved focus nor a primary informational focus, because they deal almost exclusively with reportage of events in progress.[2] Text 7.5 illustrates these characteristics:

Text 7.5: Broadcast of state funeral (LL:10,5)

B: *flanked* #
      by its escort of the Royal Air Force #
      the gun carriage #
      bearing the coffin # [*pause*]
      draped with the Union Jack # [*pause*]
      on it #
      the gold #
      and enamel #
      of the insignia of the Garter # [*pause*]
      and as it breasts #
      the slight rise # [*pause*]
      the naval crew that draws it #
      presents #
      an overwhelming impression #
      of strength #
      and solidarity # [*pause*]

Text 7.5 illustrates the specialized characteristics of Broadcasts with respect to Dimension 1. The grammatical structure of these texts is very reduced, but there are relatively many different words, and frequent

---

[2] More recent forms of radio and television broadcasts have developed in different ways. For example, sports broadcasts presently seem to include more affective commentary (opinions of plays and players), interpersonal interaction (between multiple commentators), and propositional information (concerning fine points of the game) than the broadcasts in the London–Lund corpus.

nouns and prepositions. The focus is event-oriented. Despite this event orientation, however, there are relatively few verbs, because many of the verbs are deleted due to time constraints, or to give the impression of action that moves so fast that there is no time for a full description (Ferguson 1983). The few verbs found in these texts are in the present tense, describing action that is on-going at the time of discourse production. The surprising fact that broadcasts have a more literate score than spontaneous and prepared speeches with respect to Dimension 1 might be explained by the reduced grammatical structure common in texts of this genre, leaving, essentially, only noun phrases and pre-positional phrases. Speeches, on the other hand, depend on elaborated grammatical structure, and thus they are more typical of informational discourse. In addition, speeches are addressed to specific, physically-present audiences, permitting some interaction and affective content, whereas broadcasts are directed to an unseen, relatively unknown, audience. Thus, broadcasts are a specialized genre, which is spoken and produced in real-time, but has the characteristics of informational production.

Overall, we have seen that the interpretation of Dimension 1 as 'Informational versus Involved Production' fits the relations among genres defined by this dimension. Highly interactive, affective discourse produced under real-time constraints, whether spoken or written, has a high score on this dimension; highly informational discourse produced without time constraints has a markedly low score on this dimension. Although the linguistic features co-occurring on this dimension can be associated with a basic oral/literate distinction, the relations among genres seen here in no way correspond to speech versus writing. Rather, the underlying communicative functions associated with this dimension cut directly across any distinction between the written and spoken modes.

7.2.2 Relations along Dimension 2

Figure 7.2 shows the relations among genres with respect to Dimension 2, 'Narrative versus Non-narrative Concerns'. The fiction genres have by far the highest mean scores on this dimension, while broadcasts, professional letters, academic prose, hobbies, and official documents all have very low scores. Table 6.1 shows that the genres with high scores on Dimension 2 are characterized by frequent occurrences of past tense and perfect aspect verbs, third person pronouns, public verbs, present

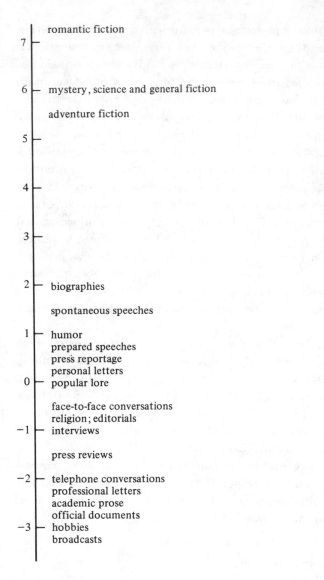

Figure 7.2 *Mean scores of Dimension 2 for each of the genres*
Dimension 2: 'Narrative versus Non-Narrative Concerns'

participial clauses, and synthetic negation, together with markedly
infrequent occurrences of present tense verbs and attributive adjectives.
Genres with low scores on Dimension 2 have the opposite characteristics.
The large separation of the fiction genres from all other genres seen on

Figure 7.2 indicates that the proposed interpretation of a narrative versus non-narrative dimension is an accurate description of the underlying function here. Text 7.6 illustrates the characteristics of texts with high scores on Dimension 2:

Text 7.6: General fiction (LOB:K,6)

> *It was difficult to tell whether he was unable to speak or whether he could see no point. Sometimes he started to say things in a hoarse whisper, looking ahead as if there might be people to either side who would stop him, but never got further than one or two words. Most of the time he lay on his back with his eyes open. After three days there seemed nothing Martin could do and he went to the office again.*
>
> *They had given the speech to Burridge. They would be able, later, when time had become a little confused, to explain his failure by his father's illness, if they wanted to.*

This text sample is straight narrative. It is written throughout in the past tense, to report past events, and it uses past perfects (e.g., *had given*, *had become*) to mark past events with continuing results (e.g., *They had given the speech to Burridge*, and he still had it at the present time). There are frequent third person personal pronouns, referring to the story participants. There are frequent public verbs of speaking (e.g., *tell*, *speak*, *say*, *explain*), even though there is no dialogue in this sample. In addition, this text illustrates the use of present participial clauses for depictive imagery (e.g., *looking ahead as if there might be people . . .*). Text 7.6 is representative of all five fiction genres, which have high narrative concerns and use the linguistic features on Dimension 2 to develop narrative structures.

In contrast, the genres with low scores on Dimension 2 are similar to one another only in that they do not have narrative concerns. That is, the frequent use of past tense, third person pronouns, etc., can be considered as the marked value of Dimension 2, being reserved for narrative discourse, while the frequent use of present tense and adjectives, coupled with infrequent use of past tense, etc., can be considered as the unmarked value of Dimension 2, which is associated with any of several different communicative purposes. These non-narrative purposes include (1) the presentation of expository information, which has few verbs and few animate referents; (2) the presentation of procedural information, which uses many imperative and infinitival verb forms to give a step-by-step description of what to do, rather than what somebody else has done; and (3) description of actions actually in progress, that is, action in the present tense. These three non-narrative purposes are illustrated by texts 7.7–7.9, taken from official documents, hobbies, and broadcasts, respectively:

Text 7.7: Official document (LOB:H,3 – government report)

> *In order to give a more detailed appraisal of the work done in modern language courses, it is convenient to consider separately the different facets of language study. Nevertheless it must be emphasized that, if language teaching is to be successful, there can be no question of dividing up the work into rigid compartments . . .*
>
> *The initial oral training is too rarely continued and developed in the later stages and many pupils do not progress beyond the standard of speech they had reached by the end of the second year. Many teachers feel that they cannot afford the time necessary for the development of oral work, but in most cases it is not additional time which is required so much as more systematic and purposeful training in the correct use of more difficult speech forms.*

Text 7.8: Hobbies (LOB:E,2)

> *A great deal of modern furniture has tapered legs, and in reproduction period pieces they are frequently used. The simpler varieties are extremely easy to work, the four sides being simply planed to give the required taper . . .*
>
> *When a leg has a simple taper the procedure of making it is straightforward. The wood is first planed parallel to the largest section, and pencil lines marking the beginning of the taper squared round on to all four sides. At the bottom end the extent of the taper is gauged in, again on all four sides . . .*
>
> *For convenience in handling it is convenient to work the hollow moulding before planing the taper of the toe. Mark in with pencil the depth of the hollow, using the pencil and finger as a gauge, and cut a chamfer with a keen chisel on all four sides as at (D). Cut*

inwards with the chisel from each side so that the far corner does
not splinter . . .

Text 7.9: Broadcasts (LL:10,7,c – scientific demonstration)

> *right* #
> *so what I'm going to demonstrate here* #
> *is the difference* #
> *between* #
> *transverse wave* #
> *and a longitudinal wave* #
> *and I'm going to use this gadget*#
> *which some of you may know* #
> *and may have played with* #
> *in your younger days* # [*pause*]
> *which is called a slinky* # [*pause*]
> *it's in effect* #
> *a special kind of spring* #
> *and it has rather nice properties* #
> *you can stand it up* # [*pause*]
> *on end* #
> *rather like that* # [*pause*]
> *and then if you bring the other end over* # [*pause*]
> *then the whole lot will just turn itself* #
> *from one side to the other* # [*pause*] . . .
> *so we've got a system here* #
> *which can transmit a wave* #
> *and if it's a transverse one* #
> *then it's like this* #
> *I can just send a pulse down* # [*long pause*]
> *that sort* # [*pause*]

Text 7.7, taken from an official document, is expository, presenting a straightforward and concise packaging of information. There are relatively few verbs, and those that do exist are often infinitival or passive constructions. Throughout, if tense is marked, it is in the present, emphasizing that this is a description of current findings or the current state of affairs (e.g., *training is too rarely continued; teachers feel; more systematic training is required*). There are many attributive adjectives in this type of discourse, which provide descriptive details that elaborate and specify the exact nature of the nominal referents (e.g., *detailed appraisal*; *modern language*; *rigid compartments*; *initial oral training*; *systematic and purposeful training*). Overall, discourse of this type is nominal, and descriptive or argumentative, rather than verbal and narrative.

Text 7.8 is taken from a hobbies magazine. It describes the procedure for making a certain type of table leg. This text has both descriptive and procedural portions, although most of the text is procedural. Descriptive portions are consistently in the present tense (e.g., *modern furniture has tapered legs*), while the procedural portions use either present passive forms (e.g., *wood is first planed*; *extent of the taper is gauged in*) or imperative forms (e.g., *mark in with pencil*; *cut a chamfer*; *cut inwards*). Attributive adjectives are used throughout to specify the particular referent intended (e.g., *the largest section*; *the bottom end*; *the hollow moulding*). Procedural discourse differs from expository discourse in that it is event-driven and concrete rather than conceptual and abstract, but with respect to Dimension 2 these two types of discourse are similar in that they frequently use non-past verbal forms and attributive adjectives rather than past tense forms, third person animate referents, etc.

Broadcasts illustrate yet another non-narrative concern. Text 7.9 is from a scientific demonstration, and thus it represents informational broadcast, while text 7.5 (discussed in Section 7.2.1) illustrates a broadcast with a non-informational focus, the more typical case. In either case, broadcasts report events actually in progress, and they thus have strictly non-narrative concerns. In Section 7.2.1, I noted that text 7.5 has few verbs, but those that do occur are exclusively in the present tense (e.g., *as it breasts the slight rise*; *the naval crew that draws it presents an overwhelming impression*). The attributive adjectives in this case are not so much for exact identification, as in the official document and procedural text, but for a more vivid description of the events (e.g., *slight rise*; *overwhelming impression*). Text 7.9 has a greater informational focus, but still reports events in progress in that it informs by demonstrating. Throughout, it uses present tense and present progressive forms, emphasizing the on-going nature of the events. There are no animate referents and thus no third person personal pronouns. Attributive adjectives are used for both identificatory and descriptive purposes (e.g., *transverse wave*; *longitudinal wave*; and *younger days*; *special kind*; *nice properties*). Thus, broadcasts have low scores on Dimension 2 because they report events actually in progress, whether for informational or entertainment purposes. They are grouped with official documents and procedural texts on this dimension because they have non-narrative concerns, although each of these genres is 'immediate' in a different sense.

In addition to these two poles on Dimension 2, several genres have intermediate values, indicating both narrative and non-narrative concerns. These genres include prepared and spontaneous speeches, biographies, personal letters, humor, face-to-face conversation, and press reportage. Text 7.10, from a spontaneous speech, illustrates the mixing of narrative and non-narrative concerns:

Text 7.10: Spontaneous speech (LL:11,3,d)

D: *well #*
I shall have to [pause] take you to a period of my life #
    [pause]
which I'm not very proud of actually # [pause]
when I was a professional Scrabble player #[pause]
mm [pause]
it happened #
at a small hotel in Sussex #
where I happened to be staying #
after dinner #
they used to all go in the lounge #
and all play Scrabble #
like crazy #
and as I got in through the doors #
a strange woman #
rushed up to me #
and said you're just the man I want # [pause]

Text 7.10 is taken from a spontaneous speech in which the speaker presents a personal narrative. The narrative is framed in terms of the present interaction between speaker and audience (*I shall have to take you*; *I'm not very proud of*). As the speaker begins his story, however, he switches to the past tense (*when I was a professional Scrabble player*; *it happened*), and the story itself uses the linguistic features characteristic of narrative discourse: past tense (e.g., *I got in*; *woman rushed up to me and said*), third person personal pronouns (e.g., *they*), and public verbs (e.g., *said*). The other genres with intermediate values on Dimension 2, such as biographies and personal letters, combine narrative and non-narrative concerns in similar ways.

Overall, Dimension 2 distinguishes between narrative and non-narrative discourse. The imaginative fiction genres are the only texts included in the present study with an extreme narrative concern. The dialogue portions in fiction are subordinate to the narrative purpose rather than marking a separate interactional purpose. Other genres, such as official documents, hobbies, and broadcasts, have strictly non-narrative concerns, but they differ from one another as to their specific purpose. Finally, genres such as public speeches, personal letters, and conversation have both narrative and non-narrative concerns. In these cases, narratives are typically framed within some larger interactive or expository discourse, and thus the narrative is in some sense subordinate to a larger purpose, although the text can be described as having both narrative and non-narrative emphases.

7.2.3   Relations along Dimension 3

Figure 7.3 shows the relations among genres with respect to Dimension 3, 'Explicit versus Situation-Dependent Reference'. Official documents and professional letters have the highest scores, while broadcasts have by far the lowest score. Press reviews, academic prose, and religion have moderately high scores on this dimension, and the conversational genres, fiction genres, and personal letters have moderately low scores. From the interpretation of Dimension 3 in Chapter 6, it will be recalled that texts with high scores on this dimension are characterized by frequent occurrences of WH relative clauses, pied-piping constructions, phrasal coordination, and nominalizations, together with infrequent occurrences of place and time adverbials and other adverbs; texts with low scores on this dimension have the opposite characteristics. I interpreted this distribution of features as representing a dimension that distinguishes highly explicit and elaborated, endophoric reference from situation-dependent, exophoric reference. The overall distribution of genres seen in Figure 3 supports this interpretation; genres such as official documents, professional letters, and academic prose require highly explicit, text-internal reference, while genres such as broadcasts and conversation

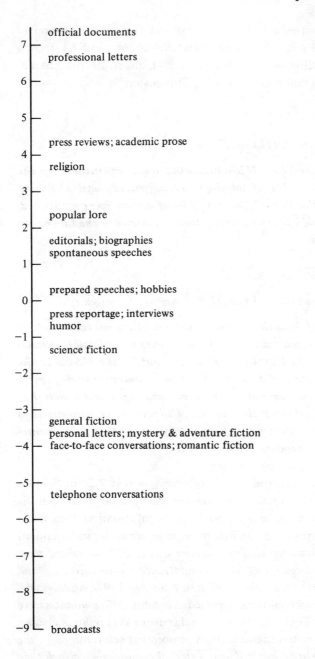

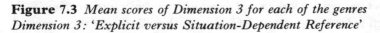

Figure 7.3 *Mean scores of Dimension 3 for each of the genres Dimension 3: 'Explicit versus Situation-Dependent Reference'*

permit extensive reference to the physical and temporal situation of discourse. Texts 7.11 and 7.12, from official documents, and 7.4, from a professional letter (discussed in Section 7.2.1), illustrate the characteristics of genres having high scores for Dimension 3:

Text 7.11: Official document (LOB:H, 26 – annual report)

> **During the past year 347 candidates were examined by the Surgical Section, 321 of whom were approved, and 352 were examined by the Dental Section, 230 of whom were approved, making a total of 230 candidates who were awarded the Licence in Dental Surgery.**

Text 7.12: Official document (LOB:H,29 – university bulletin)

> **Students must follow throughout the terms the courses for which they are registered and attend such classes and such examinations as required by the University and by the Heads of the Departments concerned . . . Students must enter on their registration form particulars of any external examinations which they propose to take during the session. University examinations of any kind will in all cases take priority over any other examinations which a student wishes to take.**

Text 7.11 is taken from the same document as text 7.2 (in Section 7.2.1). In text 7.11, WH relative clauses are used for nominal identification and elaboration. Relative clauses pack information into noun phrases instead of expressing the information as separate, independent clauses (e.g., *347 candidates were examined . . ., 321 of whom were approved* could be expressed as *347 candidates were examined . . ., and 320 of them were approved*; similarly, *making a total of 230 candidates who were awarded the Licence* could be expressed as *in total, 230 candidates were awarded the Licence*). Text 7.12 shows a similar use of WH relative clauses for explicit and elaborated identification of nominal referents (e.g., *the courses for which they are registered*; *any external examinations which they propose to take*; *any other examination which a student wishes to take*). Text 7.4, which is from a professional letter, further illustrates these uses of

WH relative clauses. This sample uses pied-piping constructions (e.g., *a financial base on which to work*), WH relatives on subject position (e.g., *directors who are competent . . .*), and WH relatives on object positions (e.g., *the goals which we indicated; other areas where we have L*). In all of these cases, WH relative clauses are used for elaborated, explicit identification of nominal referents.

In addition, text 7.12 shows the use of phrasal coordination to integrate information into a text (e.g., *such classes and such examinations; by the University and by the Heads*). This use of phrasal coordination is further illustrated by text 7.13, from a press review:

Text 7.13: Press reviews (LOB:C,10)

> **Somewhere in the middle of all this – the clowning and the prettiness, the slapstick and whimsy and phantasmagoria – Verdi's simplicity and honesty have fallen by the wayside . . . Mr. Evans continues to ripen and improve his distinguished Falstaff, but we cannot expect to see this impersonation at its best until it figures within a less confusing framework.**

This text sample shows extreme use of phrasal coordination, to pack high amounts of information into each phrase and clause (e.g., *the clowning and the prettiness, the slapstick and whimsy and phantasmagoria; simplicity and honesty; to ripen and improve*). In addition, both texts 7.12 and 7.13 illustrate relatively frequent use of nominalizations, emphasizing the prominence of informational, nominal content in these texts (text 7.12: *examinations, departments, registration*; text 7.13: *prettiness, simplicity, honesty, impersonation*). Taken together these texts illustrate informational discourse that is highly elaborated and explicit in its nominal reference.

In contrast, broadcasts report events actually in progress, thus encouraging direct reference to the physical and temporal situation of discourse. In the London–Lund corpus, these texts are recorded from radio broadcasts, and therefore the speaker and listener do not actually share the same physical situation. The speaker's physical surroundings, however, are well-known to the listener and therefore can be referred to directly. The extent of this exophoric reference is illustrated by text 7.14, from a sports broadcast:

Text 7.14: Sports broadcast (LL:10,2 – soccer match)

just over ten minutes gone # [*pause*]
into this second half # [*pause*]
and still #
nil nil #
the situation of the game # [*pause*]
as from the hands of Stepney the ball comes out onto this near
side #
and from the foot of Hemsley #
the ball into touch #
just below us here # [*pause*]
a throw to be taken by Alan Gowling # [*pause*]
used to be reckoned #
a strike forward #
but of course now turned #
by manager O'Farrell #
as indeed Willy Morgan has been #
into a midfield player # [*pause*]
a free kick given #
a little bit of argybargy #
quickly taken by Brian Kydd #
Kydd now #
to number seven #
that's Willy Morgan # [*pause*]
Morgan to # [*pause*]
aaa Bobby Charlton #
Charlton flicking it even more laterally #
away from us #
to his left fullback #
that's Tony Dunn #
Dunn #
down the line now #
aiming for Best #
or Aston #
missed them both #
and it's Derby that take up the count #
with Curry #
on the far side of the field #
chips the ball forward # [*pause*]

This sample illustrates extensive reference to the physical situation of discourse. In order to understand this text, the listener must construct a mental map of the playing field. Phrases such as *flicking it even more laterally* and *down the line* make direct reference to the physical layout of the playing field. Phrases such as *this near side*, *just below us here*, *away from us*, and *on the far side of the field* require placement of the broadcaster's booth on the listener's mental map, with events occurring relative to that position. Throughout, the reference is situation-dependent and cannot be understood unless the listener is physically present or able to construct a mental map of the situation. Even the personal referents are context dependent: proper names are used throughout, assuming familiarity with the players and their positions. Because the purpose of sports broadcast is to report on-going events within a constrained physical situation, contextualized reference is extremely high in these texts.

Such reference is found in informational broadcast as well. For example, text 7.9, the scientific demonstration discussed in Section 7.2.2, has an informational focus but is highly dependent on the physical and temporal situation of discourse production. It makes extensive reference to the physical situation of discourse (e.g., *I'm going to demonstrate here*; *you can stand it up on end*; *from one side to the other*; *we've got a system here*; *send a pulse down*), and the speaker commonly uses deictics to refer to physical objects or actions (e.g., *this gadget*; *it*; *like that*; *like this*; *the other end*). Again, a listener must construct a mental map of the situation in order to understand this text. The situated nature of broadcast, whether for informational or entertainment purposes, results in extensive reference to the situation of discourse.

Conversation, fiction, and personal letters also include considerable reference to the physical and temporal situation of discourse production, even though it is only in conversation that speaker and addressee actually share this situation. In fact, in the case of personal letters, reader and writer share neither physical nor temporal context; yet familiarity with both is often assumed. For example, consider again text 7.3 (in Section 7.2.1), which makes extensive reference to the writer's situational context: temporal (e.g., *Friday*; *tomorrow*; *this week*; *last Monday*; *last night*) and physical (e.g., *I'm here at work*; *in my room*). Thus, in personal letters as in broadcasts and conversations, the speaker/writer assumes familiarity with the production situation.

The case of fiction is somewhat different, since reference is made to a text-internal physical and temporal situation. In its form, this reference appears to be exophoric because it refers directly to the situation of events; but, in this case, the context of discourse production is not the same as the context of events – rather, there is a fictional situation that is referred to directly in the text. For example, consider again text 7.6 (discussed in Section 7.2.2). This sample marks direct reference to both physical context (e.g., *looking ahead*; *to either side*) and temporal context (e.g., *after three days*). The reader understands this reference in terms of the internal physical and temporal situation developed in the text rather than any actually existing external context.

Overall this dimension distinguishes between informational texts that mark referents in an elaborated and explicit manner, and situated texts that depend on direct reference to, or extensive knowledge of, the physical and temporal situation of discourse production for understanding.

7.2.4. Relations along Dimension 4

In Chapter 6, Dimension 4 was interpreted as marking persuasion. The features grouped on this dimension are prediction modals, necessity modals, possibility modals, conditional clauses, suasive verbs, infinitives, and split auxiliaries. These features often simply mark the speaker's persuasion, that is, the speaker's own assessment of likelihood or advisability. Prediction and possibility modals mark intention when used with a first person agent (e.g., *I will go*; *I might do it*), and they can mark assessment of likelihood in other cases (e.g., *he will come*; *it might rain*). Other features, such as necessity modals and suasive verbs, can mark the speaker's attempts to persuade the addressee that certain events are desirable or probable (e.g., *you should go*). These functions can all be considered as overt markers of persuasion in one way or another.

The distribution of genres shown in Figure 7.4 lends support to the above interpretation. Professional letters and editorials are the two genres with high scores on Dimension 4, while broadcasts and press reviews have markedly low scores. Both professional letters and editorials are opinionated genres intended to persuade the reader. They are argumentative in that they consider several different possibilities but seek to convince the reader of the advisability or likelihood of one of them. For example, consider text 7.15 from an editorial, and text 7.16 from a professional letter:

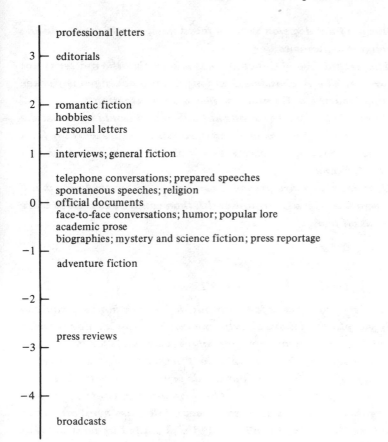

professional letters

3 — editorials

2 — romantic fiction
hobbies
personal letters

1 — interviews; general fiction

telephone conversations; prepared speeches
spontaneous speeches; religion
0 — official documents
face-to-face conversations; humor; popular lore
academic prose
biographies; mystery and science fiction; press reportage
−1 —

adventure fiction

−2 —

press reviews
−3 —

−4 —

broadcasts

Figure 7.4 *Mean scores of Dimension 4 for each of the genres*
Dimension 4: 'Overt Expression of Persuasion'

Text 7.15: Editorial (B,1 – Daily Herald, March 6, 1961)

**Prime Minister after Prime Minister speaks out in revulsion
against the South African Government's policy of apartheid as we
wait for the curtain to rise on the Commonwealth Conference in
London.**

**Will it end with South Africa's exclusion from the Com-
monwealth? The issue is touch and go.**

**There is a possibility that it will not be settled at this conference.
It may be agreed to wait until South Africa actually becomes a
republic later in the year.**

But if a final decision is to be faced now, on which side do the strongest arguments lie?

The Archbishop of Capetown has shown that the matter is not clear-cut. The Archbishop has long been a courageous fighter against apartheid. He must be heard with attention.

On purely practical grounds he holds that it would be a mistake to expel South Africa, weakening the whites who are working for a change of policy. In his view it would also be against the interests of the Africans.

He holds that more pressure can be put on South Africa while she remains in the Commonwealth than could be exercised were she cut off from it.

Text 7.16: Professional letter (private corpus, no. 1)

This resolution text is far from ideal. The parliamentarian can help you phrase it more clearly, and I'm sure you can do a lot with it yourself; my intent is only to suggest a vehicle for getting the notion in front of the membership. Furthermore, it would really be inappropriate for me to put words in your mouth. In short, you should really take the format of the resolution and put in your own thoughts . . . Please understand that while I am sympathetic to what you are trying to achieve, and that while I understand that certain N populations are more severely impacted than others, I am not at present entirely in sympathy with the notion.

Text 7.15 illustrates the features of a typical argumentative text written to persuade the reader. Several perspectives are considered, with arguments for and against them, but the overall discourse builds towards a final conclusion and attempts to convince the reader that this conclusion is superior to any other. Predictive modals are used to refer to the future, to consider events that will or will not occur (e.g., *will it end*; *it will not be settled*; *it would be a mistake to . . .*; *it would also be against the interests of the Africans*); possibility modals and conditional clauses are used to consider different perspectives on the issue (e.g., *it may be agreed*; *more pressure can be put . . . than could be exercised*; *if a final decision is to be faced now, on which side do the strongest arguments lie?*; see also *there is a possibility that*); necessity modals are directly persuasive (e.g., *he must be heard with attention*). Similar features are seen in text 7.16. This sample illustrates the expression of possibility (e.g., *the parliamentarian can help you*), direct expression of author's own intentions or persuasion (e.g., *my intent is only to suggest*; *it would really be inappropriate for me to put* . . .), and direct persuasion (e.g., *you should really take* . . .). Both of these samples have an overall persuasive tone, and particular aspects of this persuasion are marked by the features grouped on Dimension 4.

In contrast, broadcasts and press reviews are not persuasive. Broadcasts are a simple reportage of events and thus do not involve opinion or argumentation at all (see texts 7.5, 7.9, and 7.14). Press reviews are opinionated, but not intended to persuade. That is, the author's purpose in press reviews does not involve consideration of alternative points of view or argumentation that one point of view is superior to others. Rather, press reviews present directly the author's opinion as such, to be accepted or rejected as the reader wishes (see, e.g., text 7.13).

Overall, Dimension 4 distinguishes between persuasive and non-persuasive discourse. Figure 7.4 shows, however, that the genres are relatively undistinguished along this dimension. Four genres stand out: editorials and professional letters as persuasive, and broadcasts and press reviews as non-persuasive. With respect to most of the other genres, there is no general characterization as persuasive or not; rather, certain texts within these genres are persuasive, while others are not (see Chapter 8).

7.2.5 Relations along Dimension 5

Figure 7.5 plots the mean scores of the genres with respect to Dimension 5, 'Abstract versus Non-Abstract Information'. Academic prose and official documents have by far the highest scores on this dimension, while the fiction genres, personal letters, and the conversational genres have very low scores. Returning to Table 6.1, we can see that genres with high scores for Dimension 5 make frequent use of conjuncts, agentless and *by* passives, past participial clauses, WHIZ deletions, and certain types of adverbial subordination. Genres with low scores on Dimension 5 have the opposite characteristics. I interpret this dimension in Chapter 6 as distinguishing genres with an abstract and technical focus from the other genres; the separation of academic prose and official documents from the other genres seen on Figure 7.5 supports this interpretation. The characteristics of texts with high scores on this dimension are illustrated by texts 7.2 and 7.7 (discussed in Sections 7.2.1 and 7.2.2 respectively) and text 7.17 below. The former text portions are taken from official documents, while the latter is from an academic engineering text.

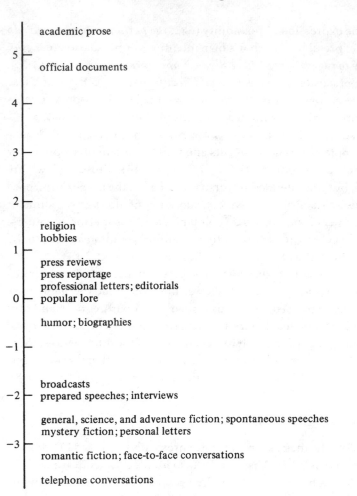

Figure 7.5 *Mean scores of Dimension 5 for each of the genres Dimension 5: 'Abstract versus Non-Abstract Information'*

Text 7.17: Academic prose (LOB:J,75 – engineering report)

> *It follows that the performance of down-draught systems can be improved by the influence of cross draughts only if the thermal currents are blown into exhaust air streams at higher velocities than the cross draughts, so that the resultant direction of all dust-bearing air streams is towards the grid . . .*
>
> *The exhaust air volume required by the 6-ft. × 4-ft. grid with the*

8-in. deep hot and cold moulds and the 16-in. deep cold moulds
tested in the absence of appreciable cross draughts exceeded the
volumes required by the 4-ft. 6-in. × 3-ft. 6-in. grid by between 25
and 40 per cent.

Text 7.17 is strictly informational; any human agents are quite incidental to the purpose of this text. Thus, several verbs are given without any agent specified (independent clauses such as *thermal currents are blown*, and WHIZ deletions such as *cold moulds tested in . . .*). When an agent is specified in a *by* phrase, it is typically inanimate and less closely tied to the discourse topic than the promoted patient (e.g., *performance . . . can be improved by the influence of cross-draughts*; *air volume required by the . . . grid*). Although this text sample is informational, there is considerable repetition of vocabulary because of the exact technical meanings associated with particular terms (e.g., *draught, stream, grid, mould*). In addition, although this text sample refers to some concrete entities (e.g., *grids* and *moulds*), the overall topic is conceptual and abstract rather than concrete, dealing with notions such as *performance* and the *exhaust air volume*. The Dimension 5 score for this text reflects its abstract conceptual focus.

Texts 7.2 and 7.7 show similar characteristics. Text 7.2 is an informational report of completed activities; the purpose is to document the annual activities undertaken by the Royal College of Surgeons. The human agents associated with these activities are largely unimportant to this purpose; in the first two clauses, the agent is irrelevant (e.g., *has been completed*) or can be inferred (e.g., *was lent*, probably by the College); in the third clause, the agent is important (e.g., *presented . . . by the President*), but it is still subordinate to the report of the activity itself. In text 7.7, a government document on language teaching, all passives are agentless; the agent is inferable as the author (e.g., *it must be emphasized*) or teachers (e.g., *the work done in modern language courses*; *initial oral training is too rarely continued and developed*), and in all cases, the agent is subordinate to the discourse topic, which is conceptual in nature (viz., *a more detailed appraisal of the work done in modern language courses*). In all of these texts, passives and other past participial clauses are used to emphasize abstract conceptual information over more concrete or active content.

Conversational and fiction genres have markedly low scores on Dimension 5, indicating an absence of the abstract and technical emphases found in academic prose and official documents. Text 7.1 (Section 7.2.1) from a conversation and text 7.6 (Section 7.2.2) from a fiction text illustrate the concrete, active emphases in these genres. Conversation is interactive and usually deals with immediate concerns, while fiction is carefully integrated and deals with narrative concerns; these two genres are similar with respect to Dimension 5 in that they both deal with active, human participants and concrete topics.

Overall, Dimension 5 distinguishes between highly abstract, technical discourse and non-abstract types of discourse. It can be seen from Figure 7.5 that many genres have intermediate scores on this dimension, indicating a mixture of the two content types. For example, hobby texts such as text 7.8 (Section 7.2.2) deal primarily with concrete referents (*table legs, pencils, chisels*, etc.) and concrete actions (*planing, gauging, marking, cutting*, etc.), yet no human agent is important to the discourse topic because the reader is the inferable agent throughout. Rather, the patient, the object being acted upon, is most central to the discourse topic, and therefore these texts use passive constructions relatively frequently (e.g., *wood is first planed*; *extent of the taper is first gauged in*). Similarly, press reportage, press reviews, and editorials show intermediate values on this dimension due to the twin purposes of these genres: reportage of events involving concrete, often human, referents; and abstract discussion of the implications of those events in conceptual terms. Overall, then, genres have high values on Dimension 5 to the extent that they focus on abstract, conceptual or technical subject matter.

7.2.6 Relations along Dimension 6

The co-occurrence pattern among linguistic features associated with Dimension 6, discussed in Section 6.2.6, is surprising: features with informational functions are included among both the positive and negative loadings, and subordination features co-occur with colloquial features such as final prepositions and demonstrative pronouns. The features with large positive weights on this dimension are *that* complements to verbs, *that* complements to adjectives, *that* relatives on object positions, and demonstratives (all with positive weights). Features with lesser positive weights are final prepositions, existential *there*, demonstrative pronouns, and WH relatives on object positions. The only feature with a negative weight is phrasal coordination, with a relatively small loading of $-.32$. The three subordination features with positive

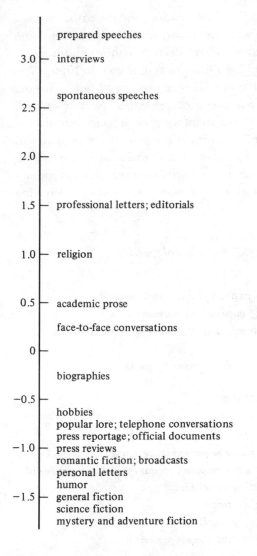

prepared speeches

3.0 — interviews

spontaneous speeches

2.5 —

2.0 —

1.5 — professional letters; editorials

1.0 — religion

0.5 — academic prose

face-to-face conversations

0 —

biographies

−0.5 —

hobbies
popular lore; telephone conversations
press reportage; official documents
−1.0 — press reviews
romantic fiction; broadcasts
personal letters
humor
−1.5 — general fiction
science fiction
mystery and adventure fiction

Figure 7.6 *Mean scores of Dimension 6 for each of the genres Dimension 6: 'On-Line Informational Elaboration'*

weights are all used for informational elaboration, and the co-occurrence pattern found on Dimension 6 was interpreted as indicating a dimension marking informational elaboration under strict real-time conditions.

The distribution of genres along Dimension 6, shown in Figure 7.6, largely supports this interpretation. Three genres stand out as having high scores on this dimension: prepared speeches, interviews, and spontaneous speeches. They all have an informational focus, but in all of them, the speaker must contend with real-time production constraints. The genre with the highest mean score for Dimension 6 is prepared speeches. Texts 7.18 and 7.19, taken from a political speech and a judge's final statement respectively, illustrate the characteristics of texts having high scores on this dimension:

Text 7.18: Prepared speech (LL:12, 5 – political speech)

> **A:** **does anyone believe ‡**
>   **that we would have accepted for the seventies ‡**
>   **a degree of freedom of capital movement ‡**
>   **that would have aggravated that power of speculative attack
>   on sterling ‡**
>   **which we had to fight in the sixties ‡ [pause] . . .**
>   **George Brown and I ‡**
>   **were reasonably satisfied ‡**
>   **that the permissive society ‡**
>   **they then described to us ‡**
>   **very intent on saying what a permissive society it was ‡**
>   **would allow a Labour government to carry out the regional
>   policies we regarded as essential ‡ . . .**
>   **and let me make clear ‡ [pause]**
>   **that we have to be utterly vigilant ‡**
>   **about new Common Market development ‡**

Text 7.19: Prepared speech (LL:12,4,a – judge's statement)

> **A:** **the plaintiff says ‡**
>   **that the defendant ‡**
>   **came up from behind ‡**
>   **notwithstanding the warning ‡**
>   **that he the plaintiff gave ‡**

that he was about to go across #
from his own side of the road #
towards the entrance of Hill Morris's factory # [*pause*]
and struck the plaintiff's cycle #
in such a way #
as to break the plaintiff's right leg # [*pause*]
the defendant says #
that there was and had been #
for some time before the accident #
a motor car #
ahead of him # [*pause*]
driving in the same direction #
as that in which the defendant was driving # [*pause*]
and that # [*pause*]
the [*short pause*] *that motor car* # [*pause*]
pulled out slightly #
to pass #
what proved to be the plaintiff on his cycle # [*pause*]
that the defendant #
followed the motor car #
in doing the same thing # [*pause*]
and that when # [*pause*]
the defendant was some thirty or forty yards #
before behind the plaintiff #
on his bicycle #
the plaintiff #
put out his hand # [*pause*]
and without more ado # [*pause*]
pulled # [*pause*]
across the main road # [*pause*]

Texts 7.18 and 7.19 are both highly informational, and both are produced under strict real-time constraints. The extreme use of pauses in text 7.19 reflects the planning required by the judge to express his final statement as carefully as possible. In both cases, *that* complements are used for informational elaboration in a way that does not integrate information tightly into the text. In text 7.18, *that* clauses are further used for indirect expressions of attitude (e.g., *does anyone believe that . . .; we were reasonably satisfied that . . .; let me make clear that . . .*). In text 7.19, *that* clauses are used primarily for reported speech, which is the primary linguistic device used by the judge to present the facts of the case. For example, the judge states: *the defendant says that there was . . . and that the* [pause] *that motor car pulled out slightly . . . that the defendant followed the motor car . . . and that when the defendant was . . .* – each of these *that* clauses reports further details of the defendant's statement, further elaborating the background facts of the case. Text 7.19 also illustrates the use of *that*-relatives for nominal elaboration (e.g., *the warning that he the plaintiff gave*). In both texts 7.18 and 7.19, *that* complements to verbs and adjectives, and *that* relatives, are used for informational elaboration in such a way that each additional piece of information is tacked on rather than integrated tightly into the text.

Similar use of these features is seen in interview texts. Thus, consider text 7.20:

Text 7.20: Interview (LL:5,2 – panel discussion)

F is the discussion moderator

Question: How did men think before speech was formed? ...

M: **and I believe ǂ**
that in Japanese and in Chinese ǂ
that the [short pause] when the Japanese took the Chinese script ǂ
they attached their own words ǂ
to the [short pause] the [short pause] id [short pause] id [pause] id [short pause] id id id id ideographs ǂ
...

Question:
when one thinks of the thousands of ancestors who've had a hand in our making we ought not be unduly surprised when our children do not resemble us in appearance or character couldn't the genealogist be of service here to the biologist and the psychologist ...

F: **Moncreiffe ǂ**

M: **could I br [gap] it's a long interest of mine ǂ**
and I've never been able to corner a biologist ǂ
over this ǂ pause]

> *but you know that what makes you a man #*
> *is that your father gives you a Y chromosome #*
> *mm and that only your father can*

F: *yes #*

M: *give that # [pause]*
> *now it's quite obvious that certain things can be sexlinked*
> *to the Y chromosome #*

In text 7.20, *that* complements are used for the elaboration of personal feelings or opinions (e.g., *I believe that . . .; you know that . . . and that . . .; it's quite obvious that . . .*). In fact, throughout texts 7.18–7.20, *that* complements to verbs and adjectives are used to express informational attitudes, opinions, or statements attributed to individuals or groups of people. In those cases where there is no explicit agent, the speaker can be inferred as the individual holding the stated opinion (e.g., *it's quite obvious that . . .*). Thus, the features grouped on this dimension enable a direct encoding of attitude or stance in addition to their use for informational elaboration.

It is seemingly for this reason that professional letters, editorials, and religion have moderately high scores on this dimension. Since these genres are not produced under real-time constraints, the interpretation given in Chapter 6 would not predict the relatively high scores shown for them on Figure 7.6. The information presented in these genres, however, is often given in relation to the attitudes, opinions, or statements of specific individuals, resulting in a moderately high use of the features on this dimension. For example, consider again text 7.15, from an editorial (in Section 7.2.4), and texts 7.4 and 7.16, from professional letters (in Sections 7.2.1 and 7.2.4 respectively). In the editorial, *that* complements are used to attribute certain arguments to the Archbishop of Capetown, adding weight to them because of his claimed expertise (e.g., *The Archbishop . . . has shown that*; *he holds that*). In the professional letters, the writers use *that* complements to express their feelings (7.4: *we felt that we needed . . .*) and to express an 'understanding' attitude (7.16: *please understand that while I am . . ., and that while I understand that . . .*).

We are now in a position to offer a fuller interpretation of the functions underlying this dimension. The primary use of *that* complements, to both verbs and adjectives, and *that* relative clauses on object position seems to be for informational elaboration under real-time production constraints. An important secondary use of these features, however, seems to be for the expression of opinions, attitudes, or personal statements of individuals. This finding indicates that those discourse tasks which involve the explicit marking of an individual's stance are frequently also tasks that demand informational production under real-time constraints. Thus, public speeches and interviews, which have especially high scores on this dimension, typically present high amounts of information in relation to an individual's beliefs or attitudes, framed in real-time; and the features grouped on this dimension are apparently well-suited to this combination of communicative demands. In the case of professional letters and editorials, there are no real-time production constraints, but since these genres often present information relative to the stance of the author or some other authority, they tend to have the characteristic features of this dimension.

7.3   Speech and writing; orality and literacy

Given these six dimensions of linguistic variation and the relations among genres with respect to each of them, it is possible now to return to the issues raised in Chapters 1 and 3 concerning the nature and extent of linguistic differences between speech and writing. The present study makes no simple two-way distinction between texts produced as speaking and those produced as writing, and it does not directly test overall or average differences between the two modes. That is, no a priori decision is made that all spoken texts should be grouped together as opposed to all written texts. Rather, the study includes a wide variety of genres from each mode and describes the relations among them. If the relations along any dimension distinguish between all written and spoken genres, then we have uncovered a true linguistic distinction between speech and writing. If no dimension makes an absolute distinction between all written and spoken genres, then it is reasonable to question the existence of an absolute linguistic difference between the two modes in English. In the present study, no absolute difference is observed; with respect to each dimension, written and spoken texts overlap. There do, however, seem to be some differences in the potential form of speech and writing, due to the different cognitive constraints on speakers and writers. I will return to this issue below.

Reviewing Figures 7.1–7.6, it can be seen that there is considerable overlap among written and spoken genres with respect to every dimension. Speech and writing are relatively well-distinguished along Dimensions 1, 3, and 5; but even in these cases, there is considerable overlap. Along Dimension 1, the spoken genres tend to have high scores (involved production), and the written genres tend to have low scores (informational production); but among the written genres, personal letters have a quite high score and the fiction genres have relatively high scores, while among the spoken genres, prepared speeches have a relatively low score and broadcasts have a quite low score. Along Dimension 3, written genres tend to have high scores (explicit reference) and spoken genres tend to have low scores (situation-dependent reference), but public speeches and interviews have relatively high scores while the fiction genres have relatively low scores. Along Dimension 5, written genres tend to have high scores (abstract information) and spoken genres tend to have low scores (non-abstract information), but the fiction genres and personal letters are among the lowest scores. Thus, no dimension defines an absolute spoken/written distinction.

This lack of an absolute difference between speech and writing shows that it is possible, within each mode, to override the salient situational characteristics of the mode. Speakers typically share space, time, and high amounts of knowledge with listeners, and they are typically constrained by real-time production considerations, but none of these characteristics prohibits production of dense, elaborated, or abstract discourse. Similarly, writing is well-suited to highly informational communicative tasks, because of the production and comprehension advantages of writers and readers over speakers and listeners, and it is not well-suited to interactional, attitudinal, or other involved purposes, because reader and writer do not typically share space, time, or intimate knowledge; but none of these characteristics require writing to be highly integrated and informational. In both cases, speakers and writers sometimes thwart the situational forces operating in each mode and produce discourse that is atypical for that mode.

Despite this fact, it is meaningful to discuss the typical or expected types of discourse in each mode, associated with the typical situational characteristics of speaking and writing. In Chapter 2, I use the term 'oral' discourse to refer to language produced in situations that are typical or expected for speaking, and the term 'literate' discourse to refer to language produced in situations that are typical for writing. From this point of view, face-to-face conversation is a stereotypically oral genre, having the characteristic situational features that are most typical of speech, while academic expository prose is considered one of the most literate genres, because it has the situational features most typically expected in writing.

Given this working definition of oral and literate discourse, it is possible to consider Dimensions 1, 3, and 5 of the present study as oral/literate dimensions. With respect to each of these dimensions, viz., 'Informational versus Involved Production', 'Explicit versus Situation-Dependent Reference', and 'Abstract versus Non-Abstract Information', the poles characterize academic exposition and conversation respectively (see Figures 7.1, 7.3, and 7.5). However, these three dimensions are by no means equivalent: each is defined by a different set of co-occurring linguistic features, and each defines a different set of relations among genres. For example, consider the relations among spontaneous speeches, fiction, professional letters, and broadcasts with respect to these three dimensions. Dimension I is composed of involved and generalized content features versus features indicating highly careful and precise lexical content; with respect to Dimension 1, spontaneous speeches are relatively involved and therefore oral, and the fiction genres, professional letters, and broadcasts all have similar, intermediate values not markedly oral or literate. Dimension 3 is composed of features marking explicit, elaborated reference, versus features marking situation-dependent reference. With respect to this dimension, the same four genres have quite different relations to one another and to the oral and literate poles: professional letters have one of the highest, most literate scores, marking highly explicit, elaborated reference; broadcasts have the lowest score by far, marking reference that is extremely situation-dependent and therefore oral; while spontaneous speeches have a moderately high, literate score, and the fiction genres have moderately low, oral scores. Finally, Dimension 5 is composed of abstract informational features such as passives and past participial clauses. This dimension shows yet another set of relations among these four genres: none of the four is abstract and therefore literate; professional letters has an intermediate score, while broadcasts, spontaneous speeches, and fiction all have non-abstract, oral values. Dimensions 1, 3, and 5 each distinguish between oral and literate discourse in some sense, but together they show that there is no single dimension of orality versus literacy. That is, even the notions of 'oral' and 'literate' texts, taken to represent typical speech and writing, are multi-dimensional constructs. The present analysis characterizes 'oral' discourse as involved production, situation-dependent reference, and non-abstract content, and 'literate' discourse as informational production, explicit, elaborated reference, and abstract, technical information. These characterizations are independent; it is only when we restrict our comparison to conversation and academic exposition that we observe a single set of genre relations. Consideration of other genres with respect to all three of these dimensions permits specification of the *extent* to which a genre is oral or literate.

Further consideration of Dimensions 1, 3, and 5, however, indicates that there is a difference between speech and writing in the *range* of forms that are produced in each mode. That is, there seems to be a cognitive ceiling on the frequency of certain syntactic constructions in speech, so that there is a difference in the *potential* forms of the two modes. Thus, with respect to all three of these dimensions, written exposition is considerably more literate than the most planned and informational forms of speech. On Dimension 1, the written expository genres have a greater informational density and more careful word choice than the most informational and carefully planned spoken genres. On Dimension 3, official documents and professional letters show a greater use of explicit reference than the informational speeches. On Dimension 5, none of the spoken genres are close to the written expository genres in their use of abstract information. With respect to all three of these dimensions, the characterizations of spoken and written genres overlap; there is no absolute difference between speech and writing. But with respect to all three dimensions, the most literate genres of speech and writing are systematically distinguished; there is a difference in the range of forms used in speech and writing, with the most informational and formal written genres using a greater frequency of literate features than any of the spoken genres. This difference might be due in part to the different social norms of spoken and written genres, but it seems to be related primarily to the processing constraints of speech – to the fact that even the most carefully planned and informational spoken genres are produced and comprehended in real-time, setting a cognitive ceiling for the syntactic and lexical complexity typically found in these genres.

The remaining three dimensions (2, 4, and 6) also define relations among spoken and written genres, but they in no way correspond to distinctions between oral and literate discourse. The poles on Dimension 2 ('Narrative versus Non-Narrative Concerns'; Figure 7.2) characterize the fiction genres on the one hand, and academic prose, official documents, hobbies, and broadcasts on the other, so that both poles might be considered literate. As discussed earlier, the fundamental distinction here is between narrative and non-narrative purposes, which has no relation to a distinction between oral and literate discourse. Similarly, on Dimension 4 ('Overt Expression of Persuasion'; Figure 7.4), the poles have no relation to oral and literate discourse, characterizing professional letters and editorials on the one hand, and press reviews and broadcasts on the other. In fact, typical speech (conversation) and typical writing (academic prose) have nearly the same score on this dimension, which is not marked for the presence or the absence of persuasive features. Finally, with respect to Dimension 6 ('On-Line Informational Elaboration'; Figure 7.6), academic prose and face-to-face conversation again have nearly the same intermediate score, while the positive pole characterizes public speeches and interviews, and the negative pole characterizes the fiction genres. All three of these dimensions define important, systematic relations among spoken and written genres, but none of them corresponds to a distinction between oral and literate discourse. An overall model of relations among texts in English must consider all six dimensions: Dimensions 1, 3, and 5, which correspond in some way to traditional notions of orality and literacy; and Dimensions 2, 4, and 6, which identify other parameters of variation among spoken and written texts.

7.4   A multi-dimensional description of textual relations in English

Figures 7.7 and 7.8 summarize the overall relations among seven of the genres included in the present study: face-to-face conversation, personal letters, spontaneous speeches, broadcasts, general fiction, professional letters, and official documents. These figures plot the mean dimension score of each of these genres for each dimension, presenting an overall characterization of each genre and enabling an assessment of the relations between any two genres. Both of these figures plot the same information, but Figure 7.7 highlights the scores for conversation, personal letters, spontaneous speeches, and broadcasts, while Figure 7.8 highlights the scores for official documents, professional letters, and general fiction.

Each of these genres has a different characterization with respect to the six dimensions. Conversation is involved (Dimension 1), depends on situation-dependent reference (Dimension 3), presents non-abstract information (Dimension 5), and has intermediate scores for the other

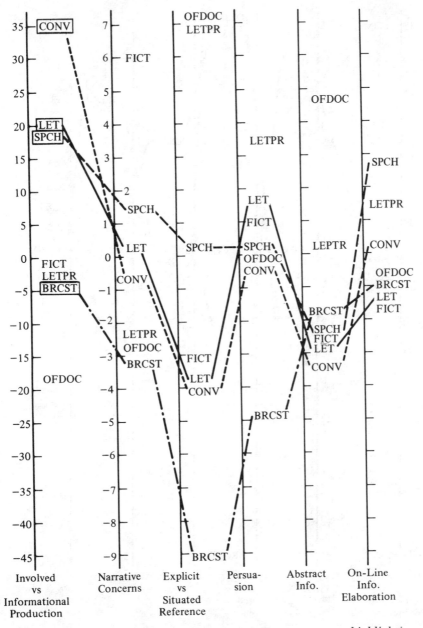

Figure 7.7 *Plot of the textual relations among seven genres, highlighting face-to-face conversation (– – – –), personal letters (———), spontaneous speeches (— — — —), and broadcasts (—— . ——).*
(Key: CONV = face-to-face conversation; LET = personal letters; LETPR = professional letters; SPCH = spontaneous speeches; FICT = general fiction; BRCST = broadcasts; OFDOC = official documents)

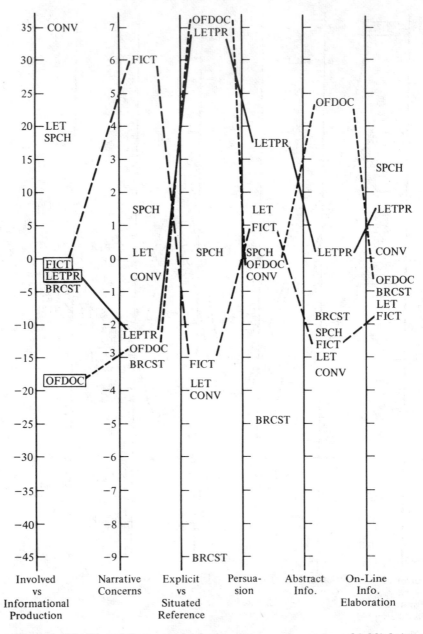

Figure 7.8 *Plot of the textual relations among seven genres, highlighting official documents (–––––), professional letters (————), and general fiction (— — — —).*
(Key: CONV = face-to-face conversation; LET = personal letters; LETPR = professional letters; SPCH = spontaneous speeches; FICT = general fiction; BRCST = broadcasts; OFDOC = official documents)

dimensions; that is, it is not marked with respect to narrative concerns (Dimension 2), expression of persuasion (Dimension 4), or on-line informational elaboration (Dimension 6). Personal letters are quite similar to conversation, being involved, situation-dependent, and non-abstract, and not having markedly high or low scores on the other dimensions. Spontaneous speeches are also similar to conversation in some respects, being relatively involved (Dimension 1), non-abstract (Dimension 5), and unmarked for persuasion (Dimension 4). Spontaneous speeches differ from conversation in that they have a moderately high score on Dimension 2, indicating a certain amount of narrative as well as non-narrative subject matter; they have an intermediate score on Dimension 3, indicating some use of both explicit, elaborated reference and situation-dependent reference; and they have the highest score on Dimension 6, marking a dependence on on-line elaboration strategies for the production of informational discourse.

At the other end of the spectrum are official documents. They are characterized by informational production (Dimension 1), a marked non-narrative concern (Dimension 2), highly explicit and elaborated reference (Dimension 3), highly abstract information (Dimension 5), and unmarked scores with respect to Dimensions 4 and 6. In some respects, professional letters are similar to official documents; on Dimension 2 they show a marked non-narrative concern, and on Dimension 3 they are characterized by markedly explicit and elaborated reference. They have intermediate scores on Dimension 1, indicating aspects of both involved and informational production, and on Dimension 5, indicating a certain amount of abstract information. Professional letters differ from official documents primarily on Dimensions 4 and 6. On Dimension 4, professional letters are characterized as the most persuasive genre, and on Dimension 6, they show a relatively high use of on-line informational elaboration for marking stance or associating particular statements with other individuals.

The remaining two genres, general fiction and broadcasts, are unlike any of the other genres. Fiction stands out as having a marked narrative concern (Dimension 2). It is non-abstract (Dimension 5) and depends on situation-dependent reference (Dimension 3), despite the fact that it has an intermediate score on Dimension 1, indicating characteristics of both informational and involved production. It has an unmarked score on Dimension 4 (persuasion), and it makes very little use of the informational elaboration devices associated with Dimension 6. Broadcasts have an intermediate score on Dimension 1, indicating an absence of either informational or involved production characteristics. They are highly marked with respect to Dimensions 2, 3, and 4, being the most non-narrative and non-persuasive genre, and depending the most on situated reference. They are not abstract (Dimension 5) and make little use of the informational elaboration features associated with Dimension 6.

The relation between any two genres is based on consideration of all six dimensions. If we considered only Dimension 1, which has been shown to be a very important and fundamental distinction between oral and literate types of discourse, we would conclude that personal letters and spontaneous speeches are relatively similar to conversation, and that fiction, professional letters, and broadcasts are quite similar to one another and relatively similar to official documents. If we considered only Dimension 3, on the other hand, we would conclude that broadcasts are unlike any other genre, that fiction, conversations, and personal letters are similar to one another, that official documents and professional letters are very similar to each other and very different from the other genres, and that spontaneous speeches are quite distinct from any of these genres. If we were to consider any of the other dimensions in isolation, we would develop yet another set 'of conclusions regarding the relations among these genres. But characterizations of similarity or difference with respect to any single dimension are inadequate, and often they are inaccurate. Comparisons along a single dimension are inaccurate when they lead to false conclusions of how two genres differ. For example, it is simply not correct to conclude that fiction and conversation are very different, as they are with respect to Dimensions 1 and 2, or that they are very similar, as they are with respect to Dimensions 3 and 5; rather, these two genres are similar in some respects and quite different in other respects. Further, even in cases where two genres have nearly the same relation with respect to all dimensions, as in the case of conversation and personal letters, it is still not adequate to simply describe the two genres as similar with respect to a single dimension. Rather, according to the model developed here, two genres are 'similar' to the extent that they are similarly characterized with respect to all dimensions; they are 'different' to the extent that they are distinguished along all dimensions. The relations among any two genres in this sense will be a relatively complex comparison of the genres with respect to all dimensions. This comparison will not be simple or easy to report, because the textual relations among genres are not simple. The dimensions given here enable comparison of spoken and written genres in terms of six basic parameters of variation. Each dimension is associated with a different set of underlying communicative functions, and each defines a different set of similarities and differences among genres. Consideration of all dimensions is required for an adequate description of the relations among spoken and written texts.

7.5 A note on simplicity of analysis

A fundamental tenet of recent American linguistics is that the linguistic structure of a language is best described by a small number of general, underlying rules or principles. This is the case in formal grammatical studies as well as in many sociolinguistic and discourse studies. The present study is also based on this approach, but it puts the goal of descriptive adequacy above the goal of simplicity. The resulting analysis is relatively complex. There is no simple dimension of variation posited here to account for the linguistic differences among texts; rather, six independent dimensions of variation are identified, each of which defines a different set of relations among texts. This degree of complexity is required to characterize adequately the relations among genres in English; as shown in the preceding sections, a simpler analysis would be misleading with respect to the overall relations among at least some genres.

The present analysis does, however, strive for the goal of simplicity of analysis. The six dimensions identified here are general, underlying parameters of variation. These dimensions do not represent all of the differences defined by the original 67 linguistic features. Rather the dimensions are abstractions, describing the underlying parameters of variation in relatively global terms. Consideration of the 67 features in isolation would not enable accurate generalizations concerning the relations among genres. Reducing these features to their underlying dimensions does enable such generalizations, resulting in an overall description of the textual relations among spoken and written genres in English.

8 Extending the description: variation within genres

8.1 Genres and text types

Genre categories are determined on the basis of external criteria relating to the speaker's purpose and topic; they are assigned on the basis of use rather than on the basis of form. It is also possible to consider groupings of texts that are derived on the basis of linguistic form. In other work (Biber forthcoming) I distinguish 'genres' from 'text types': genres characterize texts on the basis of external criteria, while text types represent groupings of texts that are similar in their linguistic form, irrespective of genre. For example, an academic article on Asian history represents formal, academic exposition in terms of the author's purpose, but its linguistic form might be narrative-like and more similar to some types of fiction than to scientific or engineering academic articles. The genre of such a text would be academic exposition, but its text type might be academic narrative.

Genres are not equally coherent in their linguistic characterizations. Some genres have several sub-classes which are quite different from one another; for example, academic prose includes engineering articles, political and historical analyses, and literary discussions. The linguistic form of texts in other genres is simply not highly constrained, and thus these genres permit a relatively wide range of variation; for example, the linguistic characteristics of face-to-face conversation in private academic settings, public social settings, and intimate settings are all different. In an analysis of text types, texts from different genres are grouped together when they are similar in their linguistic form; texts from a single genre might represent several different text types. It is beyond the scope of the present study to identify underlying text types in English; here I consider only the extent to which genre categories are internally coherent and the relations among several sub-genres.

170

8.2 Internal coherence of the genre categories

Figures 8.1–8.6 plot the range of dimension scores found within twelve of the genres used in the present study. These figures plot the maximum, minimum, and mean scores for each genre, taken from Table 7.1. For example, Figure 8.1 plots the range of scores on Dimension 1, 'Informational versus Involved Production'. The first column on this plot represents the range of scores in face-to-face conversation. It shows that the minimum score for a conversational text is around 18, the highest score for a conversational text is around 54, and the mean score for conversational texts is about 35; the actual scores (minimum: 17.7; maximum: 54.1; mean: 35.3) are given on Table 7.1.

A quick look at Figures 8.1–8.6 shows considerable variation in the score ranges. There are much greater ranges on some dimensions than others; for example, there are relatively large ranges on Dimensions 1 and 4, and a relatively small range on Dimension 5. In addition, some genres show much wider ranges than others; compare, for example, academic prose, which has a large range on every dimension, with personal letters, which has relatively small ránges. The range of scores indicates the internal coherence of a genre category – that is, the range of variation possible within a genre.[1] For example, Figures 8.1–8.6 show that academic prose texts can be quite different from one another and still be considered representative of their genre; personal letters are apparently much more similar to one another in their linguistic form.

Differences within genres can be considered from two perspectives. First, some of the genres used here include several well-defined sub-genres, and the variation within the genre is due in part to variation among the sub-genres. For example, in the LOB corpus, academic prose is divided into seven sub-categories: natural science, medical, mathematics, social science, politics/education, humanities, and technology/engineering. Due to the differences among these sub-genres, the dimension scores for academic prose have quite large ranges. Some other genres, however, are simply not well-constrained or defined. For example, conversation shows large ranges on most of the dimensions, even though there are no clear-cut sub-genre distinctions within conversation.

---

[1] Maximum and minimum scores plot the total range of variation within a genre; plots of the standard deviations would indicate how tightly the scores within a genre are grouped around the mean score; see Table 7.1 and the discussion in Section 7.1.

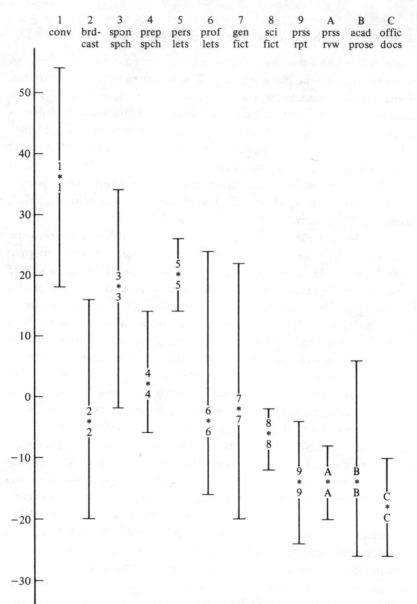

Figure 8.1 *Spread of scores along Dimension 1 ('Informational versus Involved Production') for selected genres (* marks the mean score of each genre)*

(Key: conv = face-to-face conversation; brdcast = broadcasts; spon spch = spontaneous speeches; prep spch = prepared speeches; pers lets = personal letters; prof lets = professional letters; gen fict = general fiction; sci fict = science fiction; prss rpt = press reportage; prss rvw = press reviews; acad prose = academic prose; offic docs = official documents.)

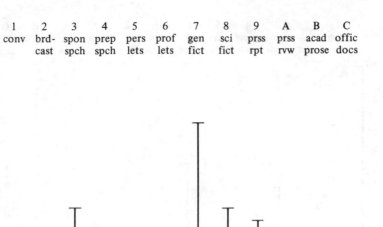
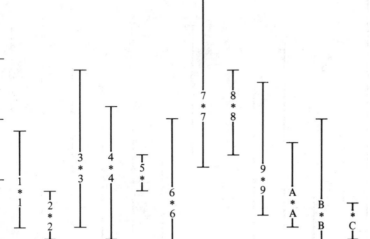

Figure 8.2 *Spread of scores along Dimension 2 ('Narrative versus Non-Narrative Concerns') for selected genres (* marks the mean score of each genre)*

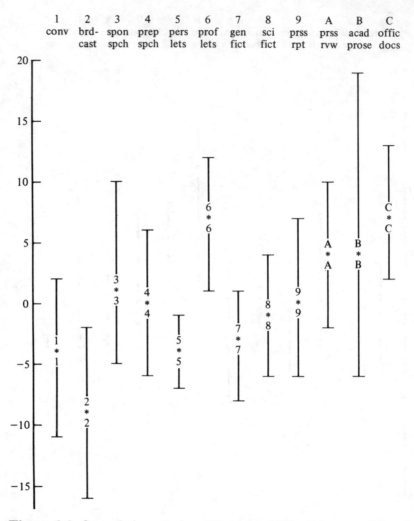

Figure 8.3 *Spread of scores along Dimension 3 ('Explicit versus Situation-Dependent Reference') for selected genres (* marks the mean score of each genre)*

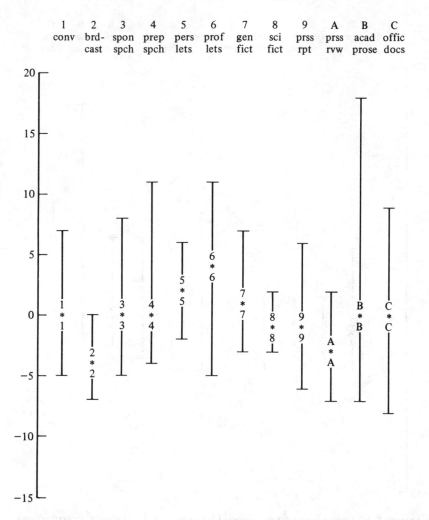

Figure 8.4 *Spread of scores along Dimension 4 ('Overt Expression of Persuasion') for selected genres (* marks the mean score of each genre)*

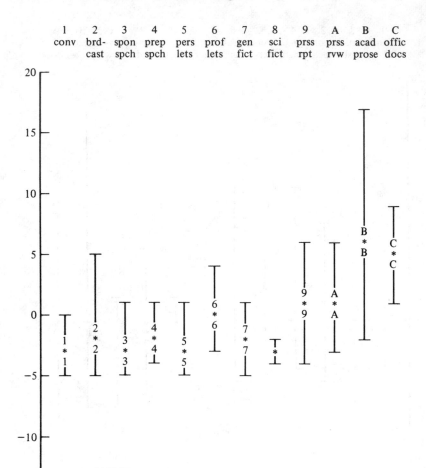

Figure 8.5 *Spread of scores along Dimension 5 ('Abstract versus Non-Abstract Information') for selected genres (* marks the mean score of each genre)*

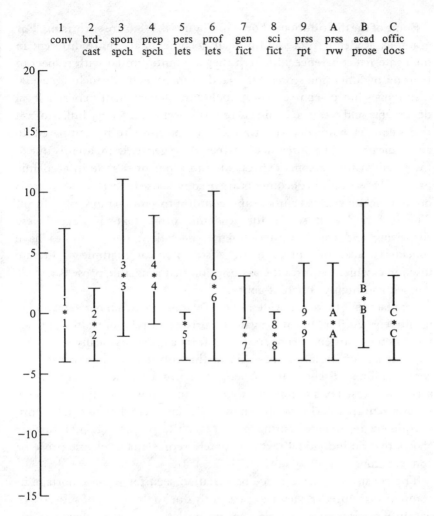

Figure 8.6 *Spread of scores along Dimension 6 ('On-Line Informational Elaboration') for selected genres (* marks the mean score of each genre)*

Some of the distributions shown in Figures 8.1–8.6 are surprising. For example, academic prose and official documents are quite different in their internal coherence, although they are quite similar with respect to their mean dimension scores. Official documents actually include several distinguishable discourse types, including government reports, legal documents and treaties, business reports, and a university bulletin; yet this genre is markedly constrained in linguistic form compared to academic prose. The difference between these genres is apparently due to the freedom for personal expression and a personal style in academic prose, whereas official documents are in some sense truly faceless (there is often no acknowledged author) and conform to a much more rigid form. The wide range of scores for academic prose texts is nevertheless surprising and contrary to popular expectation; many studies have considered academic prose to be a stereotypical example of literate discourse, which requires the assumption that academic prose is a well-defined and highly coherent genre.

The fact that there is a wide range of variation within conversation is intuitively sensible, but it is again surprising in relation to the characterization of particular conversational texts as stereotypically oral. The wide range of variation possible within both academic prose and conversation is disconcerting when we consider studies that use a few academic prose texts to represent writing and a few conversational texts to represent speech. I have shown in earlier chapters that no single genre adequately represents writing or speech; the present chapter further shows that no individual text adequately represents academic prose or conversation.

The consistently wide range of variation seen for press reportage in comparison to press reviews is apparently due to the range of sub-genres within press reportage (politics, sports, society, spot news, finance, and cultural events). Broadcasts show a wide range of variation on several dimensions because this genre includes coverage of sports events, non-sports events (such as a funeral and a wedding), and scientific demonstrations. On Dimension 2, 'Narrative versus Non-Narrative Concerns', there is very little variation among broadcast texts because they all report events actually in progress.

General fiction shows a considerably greater range of variation than science fiction. In this case, the small sample size for science fiction (only six texts) biases the comparison, since there is less opportunity for variation within that genre. However, the comparison also indicates that science fiction is more constrained than general fiction; that general fiction apparently deals with a broader range of topics and uses a broader range of styles than science fiction.

Both prepared speeches and spontaneous speeches include political and legal speeches. In addition, prepared speeches include sermons and a university lecture. Despite the greater range of purposes included in the category of prepared speeches, spontaneous speeches consistently show a greater range of scores. This difference might relate to the planning opportunities in the two genres, but it might also simply indicate a greater freedom for personal variation in spontaneous speeches.

Finally, the comparison of personal letters and professional letters is noteworthy: professional letters consistently have a much greater range of scores than personal letters. This is surprising, given the intuitive impression that personal letters are similar to conversation in being relatively unconstrained, and that professional letters are highly constrained. The actual distribution of texts in these two genres indicates that the opposite is the case: personal letters are apparently quite constrained in their linguistic form while professional letters show considerable variation. This generalization is based on only twenty letters, but the difference between these two genres is quite striking. The personal letters studied here have strictly interactional, affective purposes, and they therefore tolerate little variation in linguistic form. Professional letters, on the other hand, have both interactional and informational purposes, and apparently these two concerns can be weighted quite differently from one professional letter to the next, resulting in considerable variation within this genre.

The above characterizations consider the extent of variation possible within particular genres. We can also consider the extent of variation possible with respect to each dimension. Genres show the least internal variation with respect to Dimension 5, indicating that they are relatively uniform in their characterization as abstract or non-abstract. Academic prose is the only genre to show a wide range of variation on this dimension. The range of variation within most genres is also small with respect to Dimension 2, indicating that genres are relatively uniform in their characterization as narrative or non-narrative. Several genres, however, do show considerable ranges on Dimension 2; surprisingly, general fiction shows one of the largest score spreads on this dimension, perhaps due to variation in the amount of dialogue and description in these texts. The other dimensions show greater ranges within the genres.

On Dimension 1, only personal letters, science fiction, press reviews, and official documents show relatively small ranges. On Dimension 4, only broadcasts and science fiction show small ranges.

The standard deviations of the genre scores, which are also presented in Table 7.1, provide a different perspective on the coherence of the genre categories. The standard deviation shows how tightly a majority of texts are grouped around the genre mean score. A genre can have a small standard deviation, showing that a majority of texts in the genre are grouped tightly around the mean, yet have a large range, showing that at least some of the texts in the genre are quite different from the mean. This is in fact the case with respect to most of the genres studied here; Table 7.1 shows that most genres have relatively small standard deviations, but Figures 8.1–8.6 show that some texts in many of the genres differ greatly from the mean score, indicating that considerable variation is tolerated within most of these genres.

8.3   Relations among sub-genres

It was noted in the last section that the large range of variation within some genres is due to the inclusion of several sub-genres. In the present section, I consider the relations among some of these more specific genre categories.[2] Within the genre 'press reportage', the following sub-types of reportage are considered: political, sports, society, spot news, financial, and cultural; within the genre 'editorials', three sub-types are considered: institutional editorials, personal editorials, and letters to the editor; within the genre 'academic prose', seven sub-genres are considered: natural science, medical, mathematics, social science, politics/education/law, humanities, and technology/engineering; two types of 'broadcasts' are considered: sports and non-sports; and finally, three classes of 'telephone conversations' are considered: personal, between business associates, and between disparates.

Table 8.1 presents descriptive statistics for the dimension scores of each of these sub-genres. Similar to Table 7.1, this table presents the mean score, minimum and maximum scores, range, and standard deviation of each dimension score for each sub-genre. The data presented in this table thus enable comparison of the mean scores for different sub-genres as well as consideration of the internal coherence of the sub-genre

---

[2] The sub-genres considered here include all of the major sub-category distinctions made in the LOB or London–Lund corpus.

Table 8.1 *Descriptive statistics for specialized sub-genres*

Dimension 1:	'Involved versus Informational Production'
Dimension 2:	'Narrative versus Non-Narrative Concerns'
Dimension 3:	'Explicit versus Situation-Dependent Reference'
Dimension 4:	'Overt Expression of Persuasion'
Dimension 5:	'Abstract versus Non-Abstract Information'
Dimension 6:	'On-Line Informational Elaboration'

Dimension	Mean	Minimum value	Maximum value	Range	Standard deviation
-----------------------	Political	Press	Reportage	---------------------	
Dimension 1	-17.1	-22.6	-11.9	10.7	3.2
Dimension 2	0.8	-2.6	2.6	5.2	1.5
Dimension 3	-0.9	-6.2	5.6	11.7	3.5
Dimension 4	0.6	-3.4	3.4	6.7	2.0
Dimension 5	0.6	-1.6	2.8	4.5	1.7
Dimension 6	0.4	-2.8	3.9	6.7	1.9
-----------------------	Sports	Press	Reportage	---------------------	
Dimension 1	-14.7	-22.7	-10.2	12.4	4.1
Dimension 2	-0.4	-2.0	1.1	3.0	1.2
Dimension 3	-1.2	-4.1	1.6	5.7	2.1
Dimension 4	-0.5	-4.9	2.5	7.4	2.7
Dimension 5	0.1	-3.3	3.6	6.9	2.2
Dimension 6	-1.5	-3.1	0.8	3.9	1.4
-----------------------	Society	Press	Reportage	---------------------	
Dimension 1	-16.1	-22.4	-8.3	14.1	7.2
Dimension 2	-0.4	-2.5	1.0	3.5	1.9
Dimension 3	1.0	-2.1	6.5	8.6	4.8
Dimension 4	-2.1	-4.6	1.3	5.9	3.1
Dimension 5	-0.9	-1.6	0.3	2.0	1.1
Dimension 6	-2.1	-4.0	0.8	4.9	2.6
-----------------------	Spot	News	Reportage	---------------------	
Dimension 1	-13.9	-18.7	-7.6	11.1	3.7
Dimension 2	2.1	-0.4	7.7	8.1	2.5
Dimension 3	0.4	-3.7	4.4	8.0	3.0
Dimension 4	-1.2	-3.7	5.7	9.4	2.9
Dimension 5	1.6	-1.4	5.0	6.5	2.4
Dimension 6	-1.6	-3.6	0.6	4.2	1.4
-----------------------	Financial	Press	Reportage	---------------------	
Dimension 1	-17.6	-24.1	-12.4	11.7	4.9
Dimension 2	-2.0	-2.7	-1.3	1.3	0.5
Dimension 3	-0.2	-1.7	1.7	3.3	1.7
Dimension 4	-1.1	-6.0	3.4	9.5	4.0
Dimension 5	2.7	-1.5	5.5	7.0	3.1
Dimension 6	-0.8	-3.2	1.1	4.4	2.2

Table 8.1 (*cont.*)

Dimension	Mean	Minimum value	Maximum value	Range	Standard deviation
---------------------- Cultural Press Reportage --------------------					
Dimension 1	-11.7	-18.8	-3.1	15.7	5.5
Dimension 2	-0.4	-3.2	3.3	6.6	2.1
Dimension 3	0.3	-1.6	3.9	5.5	2.2
Dimension 4	-2.0	-5.5	0.7	6.2	2.1
Dimension 5	-0.6	-4.4	4.8	9.1	2.9
Dimension 6	-1.2	-3.1	0.2	3.3	1.4
---------------------- Institutional Editorials --------------------					
Dimension 1	-9.1	-14.7	1.6	16.2	4.6
Dimension 2	-0.6	-2.7	1.6	4.4	1.3
Dimension 3	1.8	-2.9	5.4	8.3	2.3
Dimension 4	4.0	-1.2	9.3	10.6	3.1
Dimension 5	0.1	-2.2	3.9	6.1	1.8
Dimension 6	1.9	0.3	5.7	5.4	1.7
---------------------- Personal Editorials ------------------------					
Dimension 1	-11.0	-18.0	-7.4	10.6	3.5
Dimension 2	-0.4	-3.2	1.8	4.9	1.6
Dimension 3	1.5	-0.4	4.5	4.9	1.7
Dimension 4	1.6	-1.8	7.4	9.3	3.2
Dimension 5	0.6	-2.2	4.5	6.8	2.2
Dimension 6	1.1	-1.8	3.6	5.4	1.6
---------------------- Letters to the Editor ----------------------					
Dimension 1	-9.9	-13.0	-6.0	7.0	2.8
Dimension 2	-1.6	-3.5	0.2	3.7	1.3
Dimension 3	2.5	-0.1	5.1	5.3	2.1
Dimension 4	3.8	-0.8	9.2	10.0	3.2
Dimension 5	0.4	-2.4	3.2	5.6	2.1
Dimension 6	1.5	-1.0	3.2	4.2	1.5
---------------------- Natural Science Academic Prose --------------					
Dimension 1	-18.2	-22.9	-11.2	11.7	3.9
Dimension 2	-2.6	-5.1	0.9	6.0	1.8
Dimension 3	2.7	-5.8	7.7	13.5	3.7
Dimension 4	-2.1	-7.1	4.4	11.4	3.0
Dimension 5	8.8	3.0	16.8	13.8	4.5
Dimension 6	-0.8	-3.1	4.1	7.2	2.4
---------------------- Medical Academic Prose ---------------------					
Dimension 1	-17.0	-22.5	-12.9	9.7	4.4
Dimension 2	-1.3	-5.9	0.5	6.3	2.6
Dimension 3	4.1	1.4	6.5	5.2	2.0
Dimension 4	-1.9	-6.8	3.9	10.7	4.6
Dimension 5	7.3	2.3	11.5	9.2	3.9
Dimension 6	1.1	-2.5	3.8	6.3	2.4

Table 8.1 (*cont.*)

Dimension	Mean	Minimum value	Maximum value	Range	Standard deviation
---------------------- Mathematics Academic Prose -------------------					
Dimension 1	-4.4	-12.9	1.6	14.5	6.4
Dimension 2	-3.1	-4.9	-1.0	3.9	1.7
Dimension 3	3.7	0.8	5.5	4.7	2.0
Dimension 4	-0.2	-4.4	1.6	6.0	2.8
Dimension 5	7.6	5.0	11.3	6.3	2.6
Dimension 6	3.6	0.1	9.2	9.0	4.1
---------------------- Social Science Academic Prose ----------------					
Dimension 1	-14.0	-21.3	-3.5	17.8	4.6
Dimension 2	-2.8	-6.1	1.5	7.7	2.2
Dimension 3	5.1	-1.0	18.6	19.6	4.9
Dimension 4	-1.8	-5.8	3.9	9.6	2.9
Dimension 5	3.4	-1.4	12.6	14.1	4.7
Dimension 6	0.7	-3.1	6.1	9.2	3.0
---------------------- Politics/Education Academic Prose -----------					
Dimension 1	-15.3	-26.5	-2.5	23.9	5.4
Dimension 2	-2.8	-5.3	0.4	5.7	1.7
Dimension 3	4.9	-0.4	10.3	10.6	3.6
Dimension 4	2.6	-6.0	14.8	20.8	5.1
Dimension 5	3.7	-2.4	10.6	13.0	3.1
Dimension 6	0.9	-3.1	5.4	8.5	2.7
---------------------- Humanities Academic Prose --------------------					
Dimension 1	-14.9	-22.8	7.1	29.9	7.9
Dimension 2	-1.5	-5.5	5.3	10.8	2.8
Dimension 3	3.8	-2.3	11.9	14.1	3.7
Dimension 4	-0.7	-6.2	17.5	23.6	6.3
Dimension 5	2.8	-1.6	15.2	16.9	4.1
Dimension 6	0.1	-3.3	6.9	10.2	2.5
------------------ Technology/Engineering Academic Prose ------------					
Dimension 1	-14.3	-21.3	-9.2	12.1	3.4
Dimension 2	-4.1	-6.2	0.3	6.6	1.8
Dimension 3	4.7	0.3	8.5	8.2	2.6
Dimension 4	-0.3	-4.8	6.6	11.5	3.6
Dimension 5	9.7	2.7	15.5	12.8	4.0
Dimension 6	0.2	-2.1	4.4	6.5	2.1
---------------------- Sports Broadcasts -------------------------------					
Dimension 1	-3.0	-16.0	7.0	23.0	7.0
Dimension 2	-3.0	-4.7	-0.6	4.1	1.3
Dimension 3	-11.4	-15.8	-3.7	12.1	4.1
Dimension 4	-4.8	-6.4	-2.1	4.3	1.5
Dimension 5	-1.5	-4.7	5.4	10.0	3.6
Dimension 6	-1.2	-3.6	1.7	5.3	1.7

Table 8.1 (*cont.*)

Dimension	Mean	Minimum value	Maximum value	Range	Standard deviation
----------------------		Non-Sports	Broadcasts	----------------------	
Dimension 1	-6.0	-19.6	16.9	36.6	14.4
Dimension 2	-3.7	-5.2	-2.3	2.9	1.2
Dimension 3	-6.2	-11.3	-2.2	9.1	2.8
Dimension 4	-3.8	-6.9	-0.3	6.5	2.4
Dimension 5	-2.0	-3.4	0.1	3.5	1.2
Dimension 6	-1.5	-2.8	1.2	4.0	1.5
------------	Telephone	Conversations /	Personal	Friends	-------------
Dimension 1	40.8	25.7	52.9	27.2	8.6
Dimension 2	-1.7	-4.1	4.7	8.8	2.5
Dimension 3	-6.2	-10.1	-3.8	6.4	2.2
Dimension 4	0.3	-4.9	8.4	13.3	3.7
Dimension 5	-3.8	-4.8	0.1	4.9	1.4
Dimension 6	-1.5	-4.8	3.3	8.1	2.4
------------	Telephone	Conversations /	Business	Associates	----------
Dimension 1	37.2	32.9	48.3	15.4	5.1
Dimension 2	-1.7	-3.2	1.7	4.9	1.8
Dimension 3	-4.3	-9.1	2.3	11.5	4.1
Dimension 4	1.0	-4.1	5.3	9.4	3.5
Dimension 5	-3.1	-4.2	-1.4	2.8	1.1
Dimension 6	-0.8	-3.7	1.2	5.0	1.7
------------	Telephone	Conversations /	Disparates	--------------------	
Dimension 1	29.3	7.2	45.3	38.2	13.8
Dimension 2	-3.4	-4.2	-1.6	2.6	1.1
Dimension 3	-4.1	-7.5	-1.9	5.6	1.9
Dimension 4	0.8	-4.9	6.8	11.8	4.0
Dimension 5	-4.2	-4.7	-3.5	1.2	0.5
Dimension 6	0.4	-1.8	2.6	4.4	1.7

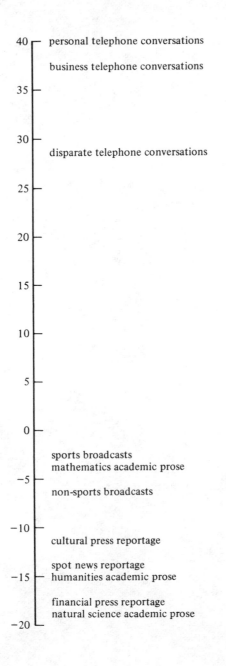

40 ┌ personal telephone conversations

business telephone conversations

35 ├

30 ├ disparate telephone conversations

25 ├

20 ├

15 ├

10 ├

5 ├

0 ├

sports broadcasts
mathematics academic prose
−5 ├ non-sports broadcasts

−10 ├ cultural press reportage

spot news reportage
−15 ├ humanities academic prose

financial press reportage
natural science academic prose
−20 └

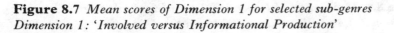

Figure 8.7 *Mean scores of Dimension 1 for selected sub-genres*
Dimension 1: 'Involved versus Informational Production'

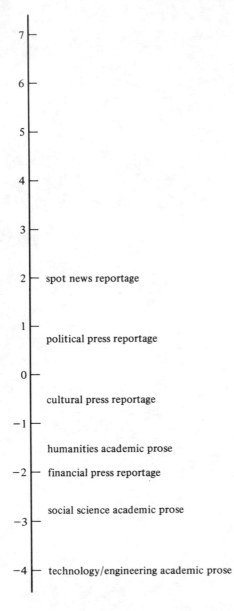

Figure 8.8 *Mean scores of Dimension 2 for selected sub-genres Dimension 2: 'Narrative versus Non-Narrative Concerns'*

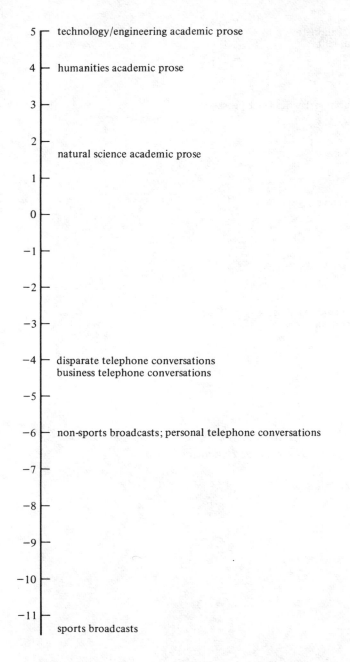

Figure 8.9 *Mean scores of Dimension 3 for selected sub-genres Dimension 3: 'Explicit versus Situation-Dependent Reference'*

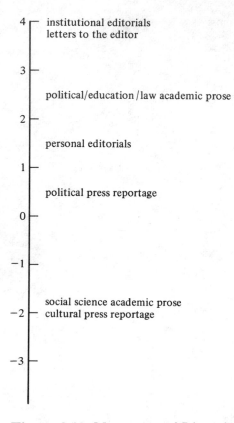

Figure 8.10 *Mean scores of Dimension 4 for selected sub-genres*
Dimension 4: 'Overt Expression of Persuasion'

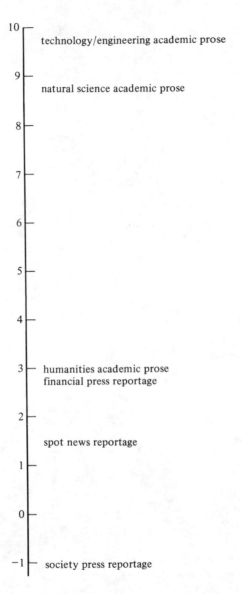

Figure 8.11 *Mean scores of Dimension 5 for selected sub-genres Dimension 5: 'Abstract versus Non-Abstract Information'*

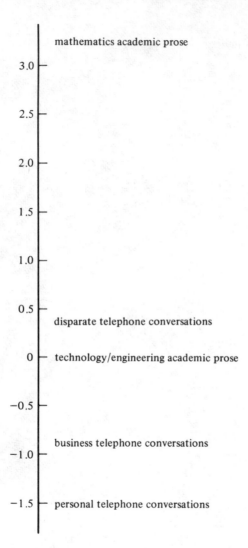

Figure 8.12 *Mean scores of Dimension 6 for selected sub-genres*
Dimension 6: 'On-Line Informational Elaboration'

categories. Figures 8.7–8.12 plot the mean dimension scores for some of these sub-genres. Although Table 8.1 gives descriptive statistics for all sub-genre categories, Figures 8.7–8.12 plot the mean scores of only a few sub-genres, to illustrate the major differences within genres on each dimension. These plots show that there are systematic patterns of variation within the major genre categories of press reportage, academic prose, editorials, broadcasts, and telephone conversations. In the following sections, I discuss each of these genres in turn.

8.3.1 Press reportage sub-genres

There are interesting differences among press reportage sub-genres with respect to Dimensions 1, 2, 4, and 5. Figure 8.7 plots the differences among cultural press reportage, spot news, and financial press reportage with respect to Dimension 1 ('Involved versus Informational Production'); the mean scores for the other press sub-genres on Dimension 1 are given in Table 8.1. Figure 8.7 shows that some types of press reportage are more colloquial, affective, and involved than other types. Cultural press reportage (e.g., reportage of theatre or music events) is the most involved type of reportage; financial reportage is the least involved; spot news, along with the other types of reportage not plotted here, have intermediate scores. In relation to the total range of genres on Dimension 1, none of the press sub-genres are involved, but among themselves there are small yet systematic differences with respect to this dimension.

Figure 8.8 plots the mean scores of spot news, political press, cultural press, and financial press along Dimension 2 ('Narrative versus Non-narrative Concerns'); again, the scores for the other press sub-genres are given in Table 8.1. Along Dimension 2, we see relatively large differences among the press reportage sub-genres with respect to their narrative concerns. Spot news has a markedly high narrative focus, presumably because this type of reportage deals primarily with the description of past events. Political, sports, society, and cultural reportage have intermediate scores on Dimension 2, indicating the presence of both narrative and non-narrative text portions; that is, these sub-genres typically include news analysis as well as description of past events. Finally, financial reportage has a markedly non-narrative focus, dealing almost exclusively with the analysis and current implications of past events and processes.

Press reportage is reputed to be a direct, factual reportage of information, suggesting that there should be little difference among press texts along the dimension 'Overt Expression of Persuasion' (Dimension 4). Figure 8.10, however, shows that there is considerable variation among press texts along this dimension. Political reportage has a relatively high score, indicating a substantial amount of persuasion and argumentation, while cultural reportage has a markedly low mean score. Table 8.1 shows that there is also considerable variation within each of the sub-genres along this dimension. Thus, for example, spot news has a maximum score of 5.7 on Dimension 4, and a minimum score of -3.7, making a range of 9.4. This distribution is quite surprising; it shows that spot news can vary considerably in its purpose, ranging from a strictly informational and factual presentation of past events to a more argumentative or persuasive consideration of possibilities. A quick look at almost any newspaper confirms this range of discourse purposes, but it disagrees with the stereotype of press reportage as factual, decontextualized, informational discourse.

Finally, Figure 8.11 shows that press texts differ considerably in their degree of abstractness (Dimension 5). Financial reportage has a high score along this dimension, indicating a considerable amount of abstract information. Spot news also has a relatively high score on this dimension. These two sub-genres are quite different from each other – financial reportage deals with primarily conceptual, abstract topics, while spot news deals with concrete events and human agents – but they are relatively similar in their characterization along this dimension. In financial reportage, an abstract form is used because there are few active agents, due to the nature of the subject matter. In spot news, on the other hand, the use of passives and other past participial constructions apparently reflects the greater topical relevance of 'patients' and events over agents, who are held constant throughout much of a typical news story. Most of the other press sub-genres have intermediate or low scores on this dimension, reflecting a more active, concrete presentation of information. (There are no striking differences among press sub-genres with respect to Dimensions 3 or 6.)

8.3.2 Academic prose sub-genres

Table 8.1 and Figures 8.7–8.12 show that the seven sub-genres of academic prose have systematic, and often large, differences among themselves. With respect to Dimension 1 ('Involved versus Informational Production'; Figure 8.7), these differences are relatively small;

except for mathematics, all academic sub-genres are characterized by the features of highly informational production (frequent nouns, prepositions, attributive adjectives, long words, and high lexical variety). Mathematics texts have a somewhat higher score, apparently because their subject matter is technical and sometimes non-linguistic, using mathematical expressions instead.

Like press reportage, academic prose texts show considerable variation in the extent to which they use narrative as a means of expression (Dimension 2; Figure 8.8). Humanities prose has a relatively high score on this dimension, showing a topical concern for concrete events and participants, while technology/engineering prose shows a markedly low score on this dimension, reflecting its concern with abstract concepts and findings rather than events in the past. Table 8.1 shows that the other academic sub-genres have intermediate scores between humanities and technology/engineering prose. This table also shows the range of scores possible within some of the sub-genres. In particular, humanities academic prose can be markedly narrative in focus (with a maximum score of 5.3) or markedly non-narrative (with a minimum score of − 5.5). This range seems to reflect the differences between historical and biographical studies, which describe and analyze events in the past, and philosophical and analytical studies, which deal exclusively with abstract, conceptual information.

Although all academic prose sub-genres have high scores on Dimension 3 ('Explicit versus Situation-Dependent Reference'), Figure 8.9 shows that there are some differences among them; further, Table 8.1 shows that there is considerable variation within some of the sub-genres with respect to this dimension. Technology/engineering prose has a very high mean score on Dimension 3, indicating a highly explicit and elaborated identification of referents, while natural science prose has a relatively low mean score. The range of texts within natural science is even more striking: the maximum score is 7.7, similar to the typical scores for technology/engineering, medical, and mathematics texts, but the minimum score is − 5.8, which is comparable to the mean scores for non-sports broadcasts and personal telephone conversations. These low scores for certain natural science texts seem to reflect situation-dependent reference rather than inexplicit reference. These texts are taken from disciplines such as geology, meteorology, and biology, which deal with specific aspects of the physical environment and thus make extensive reference to that environment. 'Situation-dependent reference' in these texts is not in relation to the situation of text production, but to the physical environment being analyzed as the discourse topic.

Along Dimension 4 ('Overt Expression of Persuasion'; Figure 8.10), we see considerable variation among academic texts in the extent to which they argue for a particular point of view, rather than simply presenting informational findings. Political/education/law academic prose is quite persuasive relative to the other academic sub-genres, while social science prose is more typical of academic exposition in being non-persuasive. In fact, Table 8.1 shows that some political/education/law texts and some humanities texts are extremely persuasive or argumentative in purpose: the political/education/law sub-genre shows a maximum of 14.8 and a minimum of −6.0; humanities shows a maximum of 17.5 and a minimum of −6.2. The differences within these sub-genres reflect both personal style and purpose; these scores indicate the extent to which an author considers alternative points of view and argues persuasively for a particular perspective. Studies that depend on logical development and argumentation, such as political, legal, or philosophical analyses, make considerable use of this style of argumentation; studies that are more experimental or empirical in nature (natural sciences, social sciences, etc.) depend less on the logical comparison of alternatives and the use of persuasive form.

Figure 8.11 shows that there are large differences among academic prose sub-genres with respect to Dimension 5, marking abstract, technical information. Sub-genres such as technology/engineering, natural science, and mathematics prose have extremely high scores on this dimension, while sub-genres such as humanities, social science, and political prose have considerably lower scores. A primary distinction here seems to be between those sub-genres that are strictly technical and abstract, and therefore do not deal with specific participants or events, and those that are less technical in nature. The extremely abstract form for scientific and engineering prose might also reflect the linguistic norms that are explicitly taught to scientists and engineers: that empirical studies are factual, and therefore faceless and agentless. Conversely, humanists are taught (and teach) that passives are dispreferred constructions and that good writing is active. In fact, all academic prose sub-genres are quite abstract in form when compared to the full range of English genres, but technical and scientific prose represents extreme use of these forms.

Finally, on Dimension 6 ('On-Line Informational Elaboration';

Figure 8.12), mathematics prose is distinguished from the other sub-genres of academic prose, similar to the distribution along Dimension 1. In the interpretation of this dimension, I suggested that features like *that* complements to verbs, *that* complements to adjectives, and *that* relative clauses are used for informational elaboration in discourse that cannot be carefully planned and integrated; and that these features are also used to mark stance in those same types of discourse. The relatively high score for mathematics prose reflects primarily the use of *that* complements to mark logical development or emphasis. Logical development is marked by constructions such as: *it follows that* . . .; *this shows that* . . .; *if we* . . ., *we find that* . . .; emphasis is marked by constructions such as *note that* . . . The extremely dense use of mathematical formulas and argumentation in this type of prose apparently makes it difficult to integrate the marking of logical relations, resulting in a relatively frequent use of these features. In fact, all academic prose sub-genres use these features to some extent. The interpretation of Dimension 6 as on-line informational elaboration was not meant to exclude the use of these features in other types of discourse, but rather indicates a primary use of these features in genres such as public speeches and interviews, which are informational but must be produced in an on-line manner.

8.3.3   Editorial sub-genres

Overall, editorials are relatively homogeneous, but the sub-genres within this category show interesting differences along Dimension 4 ('Overt Expression of Persuasion'; Figure 8.10). All three editorial sub-genres are persuasive when compared to the other major genres in this study, but institutional editorials and letters to the editor are even more persuasive in focus than personal editorials. Institutional editorials, which are the official opinions of a newspaper, generally make no attempt at objectivity; they are overt expressions of opinion intended to persuade readers. Letters to the editor are also highly opinionated and persuasive. They are reactions to a previous news article or editorial and thus, like institutional editorials, assume no obligation to discuss all sides of an issue; rather they present a personal opinion written to persuade potential readers. Personal editorials are also persuasive, but approach the task more covertly, considering a broad range of perspectives on a given issue, and arguing for the superiority of one perspective on logical grounds. In form, personal editorials are therefore less opinionated and persuasive than the other two editorial sub-genres. However, as with most other genres, Table 8.1 shows that the scores within all three editorial types vary considerably on Dimension 4. For institutional editorials, the maximum score is 9.3, the minimum score is − 1.2; for personal editorials, the maximum is 7.4, the minimum is − 1.8; for letters to the editor, the maximum is 9.2, the minimum is − 0.8. Thus, in all three sub-genres, texts can range from extremely persuasive and argumentative to markedly non-persuasive.

8.3.4   Broadcast sub-genres

Broadcasts are divided into two groups, sports broadcasts and non-sports broadcasts. The latter includes coverage of non-sports public events, such as weddings or parades, as well as informational broadcasts, such as scientific demonstrations. On most dimensions, the two types of broadcasts are quite similar, but there is a noteworthy difference along Dimension 1 and a quite large difference along Dimension 3. With respect to Dimension 1 ('Involved versus Informational Production'; Figure 8.7), both sports and non-sports broadcasts have a relatively low score because they lack a specific addressee and are focused on external events; they are therefore not highly interactive, affective, or involved, although they are not highly informational either. The slightly higher score for sports broadcasts on this dimension indicates greater involvement in this sub-genre than in non-sports broadcasts. Table 8.1 shows, however, that there is a very large range of variation within non-sports broadcasts. The maximum score for a non-sports broadcast on Dimension 1 is 16.9, compared to a maximum of 7.0 for sports broadcasts; the minimum score for non-sports broadcasts is − 19.6, compared to a minimum of − 16.0 for sports broadcasts. This extremely high amount of variation within non-sports broadcasts with respect to Dimension 1 probably reflects the difference between involved reportage of events that have very high emotional import, such as a wedding or funeral, and the more detached reportage of informational broadcasts.

With respect to Dimension 3 ('Explicit versus Situation-Dependent Reference'; Figure 8.9), both sub-genres of broadcasts are highly situated in their reference, but sports broadcasts show extreme dependence on the external situation. These texts are produced under severe real-time constraints, because of the rapid succession of events in a typical sports situation (Ferguson 1983). In the reportage of sports such as boxing, where events actually occur at a relatively slow pace, broadcasters often package the reportage in a way that gives the impression of strict time constraints and a high level of excitement. There is thus not time, or desire, for elaborated, explicit reference in these broadcasts; and due to the fact that the situation of reference is constrained to the playing-field, sports broadcasters can make extreme use of situation-dependent reference. Some non-sports broadcasts also make a very high use of situation-dependent reference. For example, the referential frame for a wedding in a well-known church is constrained in a similar way to a playing-field for a sports event. In general, though, non-sports broadcasts depend less on the production situation than do sports broadcasts.

8.3.5 Telephone conversation sub-genres

Three types of telephone conversations are included in the London–Lund corpus, which are ranked along scales of intimacy and formality: conversations between personal friends (the most intimate and least formal), between business acquaintances, and between disparates (the least intimate and most formal). These three types of conversation have similar speech situations in most respects; they differ primarily in the social role relations between participants, the amount of background knowledge shared by participants, and the purpose of communication (affective versus informational). Although these situational differences are relatively minor in relation to the possible differences among genres, they are associated with systematic linguistic differences on Dimensions 1, 3, and 6.

On Dimension 1 ('Involved versus Informational Production'; Figure 8.7), personal telephone conversations are the most involved, followed by conversations with business acquaintances and those with disparates. Conversations with disparates are considerably less involved than the other two types, reflecting a lesser expression of affect and a greater informational emphasis in those texts. All three types of conversation are equally constrained by real-time production, but the social relations between participants differ in each case and seem to be the major influence on the differences among these sub-genres with respect to Dimension 1.

On Dimension 3 ('Explicit versus Situation-Dependent Reference'; Figure 8.9), personal conversations are markedly more situated in reference than disparate or business conversations. On Dimension 6

('On-Line Informational Elaboration'; Figure 8.12), conversations between disparates show considerably higher scores than business or personal conversations. In both cases, this distribution seems to be related to two factors: (1) the greater amounts of specific background knowledge shared by personal friends in comparison to business associates or disparates, and (2) the more formal and informational purposes of disparate conversations compared to conversations between business associates and personal friends. High amounts of shared background knowledge and an informal, non-informational purpose, as in personal telephone conversations, permit highly situated reference (on Dimension 3), even when participants do not share physical space; the opposite characteristics of less shared background knowledge and a more formal, informational purpose, as in conversations between disparates, result in more on-line informational elaboration (Dimension 6). Thus, with respect to Dimensions 1, 3, and 6, we see that social role relations are also associated with systematic differences in linguistic form.

8.3.6   Summary of sub-genre variation

Sub-genre differences account for a considerable amount of the variation existing within the major genre categories. This is especially the case with respect to academic prose: Figures 8.1–8.6 show that academic prose taken as a single genre has a large range of variation on all six dimensions, and Figures 8.7–8.12 show that the seven academic sub-genres are quite different from one another with respect to each of the six dimensions. With respect to some of the dimensions, however, consideration of sub-genre categories is not very helpful in explaining the range of variation within genres. Dimension 4 in particular does not distinguish neatly among genres or sub-genres; the range of scores within sub-genres on Dimension 4 is usually larger than the differences among the sub-genre mean scores. In these cases, textual distinctions other than those captured by traditional genre categories seem to be at work. For example, the difference between persuasive prose and factual prose seems to cut directly across traditional genre categories. Future research is required to investigate the salient groupings of texts with respect to dimensions like Dimension 4.

9 Afterword: applying the model

9.1 Overview of the study

The analysis presented here was undertaken to describe the relationship between speech and writing in English. Previous studies have offered a wide range of conclusions concerning this relationship; some studies conclude that speech and writing are not very different from a linguistic perspective, while others conclude that they are fundamentally different; some studies conclude that the differences between speech and writing are due to one set of features, while others focus on a different set of features. The present study sorts out these contradictory findings and arrives at an overall account of the textual relations in spoken and written English. To accomplish this task, the study analyzes the distribution of many functionally diverse linguistic features in many different types of spoken and written texts. This analysis shows that there is no single, absolute difference between speech and writing in English; rather there are several dimensions of variation, and particular types of speech and writing are more or less similar with respect to each dimension. In all, six dimensions of variation are identified here, which are interpreted in functional terms and labelled: Dimension 1: 'Involved versus Informational Production', Dimension 2: 'Narrative versus Non-Narrative Concerns', Dimension 3: 'Explicit versus Situation-Dependent Reference', Dimension 4: 'Overt Expression of Persuasion', Dimension 5: 'Abstract versus Non-Abstract Information', and Dimension 6: 'On-Line Informational Elaboration'.

Each dimension defines a different set of relations among texts. For example, on Dimension 1 conversation and personal letters are involved, and official documents and press reportage are informational; on Dimension 2, fiction is highly narrative, while telephone conversations and official documents are both non-narrative; on Dimension 3, official documents and professional letters both use highly explicit and elaborated forms of reference, while broadcasts are by far the most situation-dependent in reference; on Dimension 4, professional letters and editorials are both persuasive, while broadcasts and press reviews are not (even though the reviews are opinionated); on Dimension 5, academic prose and official documents are extremely abstract, while fiction and conversations are markedly non-abstract; finally, on Dimension 6, prepared speeches and interviews have frequent features of on-line informational elaboration, fiction and personal letters have markedly few of these features, and academic prose is similar to face-to-face conversation in having an intermediate score.

Although this study began as an investigation of speech and writing, the final analysis presents an overall description of the relations among texts in English, and it can therefore be used as a basis for the investigation of several related issues. That is, since the texts used in this study cover many of the possible discourse types in English, and the linguistic features used here cover many of the communicative functions marked by surface features in English, the resulting dimensions are not strictly parameters of variation between speech and writing; rather they are fundamental parameters of linguistic variation among English texts. As such, the dimensions can be used to specify the relations among many different types of texts, for example, texts from different historical periods, texts from different social dialects, or texts from student writers of differing abilities. Similarly, the general MF/MD approach to textual variation, which I apply here to the relations among spoken and written texts in English, can be used to investigate a number of other discourse issues. In particular, this approach can be used to specify the relations among texts in other languages and provide a basis for cross-linguistic comparisons of text types. In the concluding sections of this book, I discuss several specific applications of the model of textual relations developed here and the MF/MD approach in general: dialect comparisons (Section 9.2), discourse, stylistic, and historical comparisons (Section 9.3), composition research (Section 9.4), comparison of stance types (Section 9.5), cross-linguistic textual comparisons (Section 9.6), and a typology of English texts (Section 9.7).

9.2   Dialect comparisons

Most studies of dialect variation, whether social or regional, have been restricted to analysis of phonological differences. In contrast, the textual dimensions identified here enable comparison of English dialects at a textual level, in terms of systematic variation among lexical and syntactic features. I illustrate the value of this approach in a comparison of nine written genres from British and American English (Biber 1987). The findings of that study show that there are highly systematic differences between British and American written texts with respect to two underlying textual dimensions: American written genres are consistently more colloquial and involved than British written genres, while at the same time American written genres are consistently more nominal and jargony than British genres. I suggest that these two patterns reflect a single underlying functional priority, relating to a greater influence of grammatical and stylistic prescriptions in British writing and editing. With respect to the first dimension, the prescriptions restrict the use of interactional and colloquial features in British writing; with respect to the second dimension, prescriptions discourage the use of a heavily nominal style in British writing. These proposed explanations need further confirmation, but the relations among British and American genres along these two dimensions are highly systematic, indicating that this analysis captures significant differences between the British and American dialects at a textual level.

Similar analyses can be undertaken with respect to social dialect comparisons or gender comparisons. Although mainstream work on social dialect variation (e.g. Labov 1972) has focused on phonological features, some previous research on 'code elaboration' examines social dialects from a textual perspective (see Labov 1969; Bernstein 1970; Poole 1973; Poole and Field 1976). The six dimensions identified here can be used to gain new insights into the textual relations among social dialects. This would require analysis of spoken and written texts from several genres produced by speakers and writers of different social dialects. Dimension scores for each genre in each dialect could be computed, enabling specification of the relations among the genres and dialects. The results of the present study predict that the relations among social dialects will not be simple or unidimensional; rather, each dimension potentially defines a different set of relations.

Many studies of gender differences in English have been restricted in similar ways to previous research on speech and writing; they typically consider only a few linguistic features in a few texts that represent only one or two speaking situations. The MF/MD approach can enable new insights into this area of research by providing overall characterizations of male and female speech as well as comparison of female–female, male–male, female–male, and male–female interactions. Similar to other text-related issues, an MF/MD analysis of gender differences would be based on consideration of texts from several speaking and writing situations, with special emphasis on the different role relations between men and women.

9.3   Discourse, stylistic, and historical comparisons

Several studies have investigated discourse issues during an MF/MD approach. For example, Finegan and Biber (1986b) show that the notion of 'discourse complexity' is not a unified construct; rather, it comprises at least two relatively independent dimensions. The first dimension shows that certain types of structural elaboration, represented by subordination features such as *that*-complements to verbs, WH-clauses, and *if*-clauses, occur in a largely complementary pattern to complexity and elaboration in lexical content, represented by high type/token ratio and frequent long words. Public speeches and conversations make frequent use of the structural elaboration associated with this dimension, while more planned, written genres such as official documents, academic prose, and fiction depend on lexical elaboration. Both positive and negative features on this dimension have been taken as markers of discourse complexity in other research; the fact that they occur in a largely complementary pattern shows that there are different types of complexity, and that it is not adequate to simply characterize particular genres as complex or not – rather, different genres are complex in different ways to different extents. The discourse complexity of spoken informational genres takes the form of structural elaboration, while the complexity of planned, written genres takes the form of lexical elaboration and precision. (The second dimension in this study identifies yet another aspect of discourse complexity relating to abstractness of content.)

Other discourse issues can be addressed using this approach as well. Finegan and Biber (1986a) identify two dimensions of sociolinguistic prestige using an MF/MD approach. The one dimension is associated with differences between speech and writing; the other dimension seems to be associated with differences in formality. Grabe (1984a) uses an MF/MD approach to analyze the salient text type distinctions within English expository prose. This study analyzes exposition from social sciences, humanities, and engineering texts, including both introductory textbooks as well as advanced academic articles.

In other studies, the model of textual relations developed here has been used for stylistic comparisons (Biber and Finegan 1988b, 1988c). These studies have two major emphases. In the one case, they focus on the stylistic distinctiveness of particular authors by considering the position of an author's works relative to the range of texts in the same genre – this can be done simply by plotting the factor score of particular texts on Figures 8.1–8.6. For example, on Dimension 1 Mark Twain's fiction is relatively colloquial and involved relative to the range of twentieth-century general fiction; D.H. Lawrence's fiction is informational and non-involved relative to the same range. By considering particular authors, and particular works, relative to all six dimensions, we achieve a macroscopic analysis of an author's stylistic distinctiveness. The second major emphasis of these stylistic studies is to trace the historical evolution of written texts in English. By comparing fiction and exposition from the eighteenth, nineteenth, and twentieth centuries with respect to the six dimensions, we achieve a macroscopic description of the historical shifts in discourse style over the last three centuries. This analysis indicates that the discourse norms for fictional narrative and expository essays are relatively independent; for example, on Dimension 3 fiction has shifted to less explicit, more situation-dependent forms of reference, while essays have remained essentially constant; on Dimension 5, both fiction and essays have shifted to less abstract, passive forms of presentation.

9.4 Application to composition research

A discourse issue that has received much attention concerns the comparison of student compositions and an assessment of the linguistic characteristics of 'good' and 'poor' writing (Hillocks 1986). Some previous analyses note that compositions from different genres must be studied separately; that is, since the linguistic characteristics of narrative, exposition, argumentation, and description are all different, the composition tasks used in any particular study must be considered when evaluating the results and conclusions. An MF/MD approach is ideally suited to research issues of this type, because it enables a comparison of good and poor writing from several different composition tasks in a single, coherent analysis. Grabe and Biber (1987) use the model of textual relations developed here in a pilot study of the linguistic characteristics of good and poor essays written by native and non-native writers of English. That study finds almost no difference between native and non-native essays and only small differences between good and poor essays. The most striking result, however, is that student essays are unlike any of the published genres of English; they use the surface forms of academic writing (e.g., passives), but they are relatively non-informational and involved, and they are extremely persuasive in form. This finding indicates that compositions do not have a well-defined discourse norm in English.

The research issues surrounding written compositions are quite complex, including differences due to composition task, planning opportunities, classroom practices, amount of in-class and out-of-class writing, amount of in-class and out-of-class reading, extent and type of comments given on compositions, and the social background and home culture of the student. In addition, the relation of good compositions to different types of published exposition is crucially important. MF/MD analyses can help provide a macroscopic characterization of student compositions with respect to these different parameters.

9.5   Comparison of stance types

In other studies I have used an MF/MD approach for the analysis of stance types, that is, the ways in which an author or speaker overtly expresses attitudes, feelings, judgments, or commitment concerning the message. Biber and Finegan (1988a) focus exclusively on the adverbial marking of stance, analyzing the distribution of six classes of adverbials (such as *surely* adverbials, *actually* adverbials, and *maybe* adverbials) in order to group texts into text types that are similar in the ways that they mark stance. Biber and Finegan (forthcoming) extend this research to include verbs and adjectives as markers of stance. Both of these studies use a multivariate statistical technique called cluster analysis to group together texts that are similar in their linguistic form, irrespective of their genre classification. The resulting clusters of texts are interpreted as stance styles by considering the characteristic linguistic features in each cluster, the particular kinds of texts grouped in each cluster, and micro-analyses of the stance features in particular texts. In the interpretation, functional labels are proposed for the different styles; for example, in Biber and Finegan (1988a), eight stance styles are identified and given labels such as 'Cautious', 'Secluded from Dispute', and 'Faceless'.

9.6 Cross-linguistic textual comparisons

The approach to macroscopic textual variation developed here is not restricted to English language studies. For example, Besnier (1986a) uses an MF/MD approach to analyse textual variation in Nukulaelae Tuvaluan, a Polynesian language. From a mechanical point of view, the application of an MF/MD approach is identical from one language to the next. However, analyses of other languages often require considerable research into the range of speech situations and the functions of linguistic features before attempting a macroscopic analysis. Thus, Besnier undertook a careful ethnographic analysis to determine the situational characteristics of each genre according to the patterns of usage in Tuvaluan, rather than assuming a set of situational characteristics from English. Similarly, he determined the communicative functions served by particular linguistic features in Tuvaluan, independently of the functions of seemingly similar features in English. For example, Tuvaluan participants in conversation rarely express affect towards one another or concerning themselves. In contrast, writers of personal letters in Tuvaluan often express intimate feelings and display affect towards the recipient. Thus, in this sense personal letters are more intimate and interactive than face-to-face conversation in Tuvaluan, so that the situational characterization of these genres is different from the characterization commonly assumed for the closest equivalent in English.

Not surprisingly, Besnier found that the situational contrasts between conversations and personal letters are associated with different linguistic characterizations in Tuvaluan and English. Similar to the present study of English, Besnier finds that no dimension of variation in Tuvaluan correlates with a simple spoken/written contrast. For instance, with respect to the first dimension identified by Besnier, which is associated with the extent of involvement (e.g., first and second person pronouns, emphatic particles), both the most involved and the least involved texts are from written genres, while the spoken genres all have intermediate scores. That is, personal letters are by far the most involved genre in Tuvaluan, while written sermon notes are by far the least involved. Conversation is the most involved of the spoken genres on this dimension, but is far less involved than personal letters. Similar relations are shown with respect to the two other dimensions identified in Besnier's study. In general, the dimensions of variation identified in Tuvaluan are quite similar to the dimensions identified in English, but the relations among genres are quite different due to the differing situational characterizations of genres in English and Tuvaluan. Besnier's study on Tuvaluan is the first to analyze the overall textual relations among spoken and written genres in a non-Western language. It makes a very important contribution to the study of speech and writing, showing that Western sociolinguistic norms cannot be assumed to prevail in other cultures; the study thus paves the way for cross-linguistic comparisons of textual variation.

9.7   Towards a typology of English texts

In all of the above applications, different types of discourse are compared from different theoretical perspectives. One of the final goals of this line of research is the development of an overall typology of texts that can be used to specify the interrelations existing among texts in terms of their exploitation of linguistic features for functional purposes. Such a typology is required as a foundation for discourse research, which typically undertakes analyses of particular sets of texts without specifying their relations to other kinds of texts, often making the unwarranted assumption that findings can be generalized to discourse as a whole. We have seen earlier that discourse researchers have often undertaken comparisons of spoken and written texts without adequate consideration of the genres chosen for analysis in relation to other genres. Researchers in discourse comprehension have overgeneralized in a similar way, often analyzing only the comprehension of stories but generalizing their findings to all discourse processing. In fact, any research issue that involves particular types of text in relation to other texts (for example, any of the research areas discussed in Sections 9.2–9.6) requires a typology of texts to place findings in their proper perspective with respect to the possible types of discourse.

Discourse types can be considered from at least two perspectives. In the present study, I use the term 'genre' for classes of texts that are determined on the basis of external criteria relating to author's or speaker's purpose. In other studies (e.g., Biber forthcoming), I use the term 'text type' to refer to classes of texts that are grouped on the basis of similarities in linguistic form, irrespective of their genre classifications. For example, particular texts from press reportage, biographies, and academic prose might be very similar in having a narrative linguistic form, and they would thus be grouped together as a single text type, even though they represent three different genres. In a fully developed typology of texts, genres and text types will be distinguished, and the relations among and between them will be identified and explained.

The present study has identified six dimensions of variation among texts in English, and it has specified the relations among genres with respect to those dimensions.

The present study has identified six dimensions of variation among texts in English, and it has specified the relations among genres with respect to those dimensions. Biber (forthcoming) uses a cluster analysis to develop a typology of English texts in terms of these same dimensions. The 'types' are identified empirically such that the texts grouped in each type are maximally similar in their linguistic characterizations (with respect to the dimensions). In all, eight text types are identified. The types are interpreted by considering the salient linguistic characteristics of each type together with the shared situational, communicative, and processing characteristics of the texts grouped in each type. The typology identifies several interesting differences among English texts. For example, there is no single interactive text type. Rather, two major types are identified: 'Intimate Interpersonal Interaction' and 'Informational Interaction'. Similarly, there is no single expository text type; rather, the analysis distinguishes among 'Scientific Exposition', 'Learned Exposition', and 'General Narrative Exposition'. The other three types in the analysis are labelled 'Imaginative Narrative', 'Situated Reportage', and 'Involved Persuasion'. Overall, this typology provides a theoretical basis for a variety of discourse comparisons in English.

Additional research is required concerning the relations among texts with respect to other linguistic systems, such as the marking of cohesion, coherence, and information structure. However, the present model of variation, as well as the approach to variation developed here, should continue to prove useful to the investigation of many related discourse issues in English, and it is hoped that it will provide a foundation for cross-linguistic research to identify universal dimensions of variation among texts.

Texts used in the study

As noted in Chapter 4, not all texts from the London–Lund and LOB corpora were included in the study, because of the time involved in editing the tagged texts. All genres included in the corpora, however, are represented in the study.

In addition, many of the text samples in the London–Lund corpus were divided. Texts were divided for one of two reasons. The first is that many of these texts, which are 5,000 words long, actually comprise two or more shorter texts. For example, a typical telephone 'text' consists of several conversations which are juxtaposed so that the total number of words in the text sample exceeds 5,000. In these cases, each conversation (or speech, broadcast, etc.) was separated and treated as a distinct text. If a text thus separated was shorter than 400 words, it was excluded from the analysis. (For this same reason, several of the letters that had been collected were excluded.)

Text samples that did not consist of several different texts were divided to obtain two samples of approximately 2,500 (continuous) words each. For this reason, these are not 'texts' in the sense that they are not bounded and do not contain all of the structural (textual) properties of a text. Many of the 2,000-word samples in the LOB corpus are of this type also; the text samples do not represent entire books, articles, or even chapters, and so do not represent entire 'texts'. Rather they are representative 2,000-word (continuous) samples from those texts. In the same way, it was felt that dividing the 5,000 word spoken text samples into two portions would not alter the validity of these samples. In the case of some of these samples, the original text was not bounded in the first place. (For example, it is difficult to determine when a conversation begins and ends; rather participants come and go, topics gradually shift, but the conversation continues for long periods.) In all cases where a sample was divided, it was done at a turn boundary, and, when possible, it was done at a place where there seemed to be some kind of topic shift also.

The LOB and London–Lund corpora have specific identifiers for each of the genres, and, within each genre, the texts are numbered consecutively. The following list identifies the individual texts used in the present study.

Press reportage: all texts in LOB category A

Editorials: all texts in LOB category B

Press reviews: all texts in LOB category C

Religion: all texts in LOB category D

Skills and hobbies: the first 30,000 words (texts 1–14) from LOB category E

Popular lore: the first 30,000 words (texts 1–14) from LOB category F

Biographies: the first 30,000 words (texts 1–14) from LOB category G

Official documents: texts 1–6 (government reports), 13–14 (acts and treaties), 25–30 (other official reports and documents) from LOB category H

Academic prose: all texts in LOB category J

General fiction: all texts in LOB category K

Mystery fiction: the first 30,000 words (texts 1–14) from LOB category L

Science fiction: all texts in LOB category M

Adventure and western fiction: the first 30,000 words (texts 1–14) from LOB category N

Romance fiction: the first 30,000 words (texts 1–14) from LOB category P

Humor: all texts in LOB category R

Face-to-face conversation: from the London–Lund corpus, texts 1.1 (divided), 1.2 (4 sub-texts), 1.3 (divided), 1.4 (divided), 1.5 (divided), 1.6 (divided), 1.7 (divided), 1.8 (divided), 1.9 (divided), 1.10 (divided), 1.11 (2 sub-texts), 1.12 (divided), 1.13 (divided), 1.14 (2 sub-texts), 3.1 (3 sub-texts), 3.2 (3 sub-texts), 3.3 (divided), 3.4 (divided), 3.5 (2 sub-texts), 3.6 (divided)

Telephone conversation: from the London–Lund corpus (texts shorter than 400 words are excluded), texts 7.1 (5 sub-texts), 7.2 (5 sub-texts), 7.3 (3 sub-texts), 8.1 (3 sub-texts), 8.2 (1 sub-text), 8.3 (3 sub-texts), 8.4 (1 sub-text), 9.1 (3 sub-texts), 9.2 (2 sub-texts), 9.3 (1 sub-text)

Public conversations, debates, interviews: from the London–Lund corpus, 5.1 (divided), 5.2 (divided), 5.3 (divided), 5.5 (divided), 5.6 (divided), 5.7 (divided), 6.1 (3 sub-texts), 6.3 (divided), 6.4a (1 sub-text), 6.5 (divided), 6.6 (divided) – texts 5.8–5.11, 6.2, and 6.4b are excluded because they are not public conversations – 5.4 was excluded accidentally – 6.6 is actually a narrative monologue

Broadcasts: from the London–Lund corpus, 10.1 (divided), 10.2 (divided), 10.3 (divided), 10.4 (4 sub-texts), 10.5 (divided), 10.6 (2 sub-texts), 10.7 (3 sub-texts), 10.8 (1 sub-text – 1 sub-text excluded because it was too short)

Spontaneous speeches: from the London–Lund corpus, 11.1 (divided), 11.2 (divided), 11.3 (7 sub-texts), 11.4 (divided), 11.5 (divided)

Prepared speeches: from the London–Lund corpus, 12.1 (4 sub-texts), 12.2 (2 sub-texts), 12.3 (divided), 12.4 (2 sub-texts), 12.5 (divided), 12.6 (divided)

Linguistic features: algorithms and functions

II.1 Development of computer programs for grammatical analysis

One of the distinctive characteristics of the present study is inclusion of a large number of linguistic features representing the range of functional possibilities in English. Further, these features are counted in a large number of texts and genres, to exclude idiosyncratic variation and to insure inclusion of the range of situational and linguistic variation existing within speaking and writing in English.

The use of computerized text corpora and computer programs for the automatic identification of linguistic features made it possible to carry out a study of this scope. The programs, which are written in PL/1, use the untagged versions of the LOB and London–Lund corpora as input. In a tagged corpus, such as the Brown corpus, the words in a text are all marked, or 'tagged', for their grammatical category, greatly facilitating automatic syntactic analysis. A tagged version of the LOB corpus became available during the course of the present study, but it was not used because there is no comparable version of the London–Lund corpus (the spoken texts). That is, programs that took advantage of the grammatical tagging in the LOB corpus would identify features with a greater accuracy than could be identified in the London–Lund corpus, thus skewing the comparison of spoken and written genres. Therefore, the untagged versions of both corpora were used, and a single set of programs was developed for the analysis of both.

There are two major steps involved in the automatic identification of linguistic features. The first is to identify, or tag, the grammatical category of each word, as a noun, verb, adjective, preposition, WH pronoun, etc. This step requires a computerized dictionary, so that the program can 'look up' words in the dictionary and find their grammatical category. The tags resulting from this procedure provide the basis for the second step, which identifies particular sequences of words as instances of a linguistic feature. For example, if a noun is followed by a WH pronoun and not preceded by the verb *tell* or *say*, it can be identified as a relative clause; the sequence *tell/say* + noun phrase + WH pronoun might be either a relative clause or a WH clause (e.g., *Tell the man who came that I'm not home* versus *Tell the man who came last night*).

Work on the programs used for the frequency counts, which was spread over the years 1983–6, progressed in two major stages. Programs resulting from the first stage provided the basis for the analyses in Biber (1984, 1986a). These earlier programs were hampered by the lack of a dictionary; to identify linguistic constructions, they relied on small lists of words built into the program structure itself. These lists included prepositions, conjuncts, pronominal forms, auxiliary forms, the 120 most common adjectives occurring in the Brown corpus, and the 150 most common verbs in the Brown corpus. Since these word lists were relatively restricted, the grammatical category of many words in texts could not be accurately identified, and therefore these programs did not identify all of the occurrences of some linguistic features. The programs were designed to avoid skewing the frequency counts of features in one genre or another, so that the relative frequencies were accurate. The main disadvantage of this earlier approach was that certain linguistic features could not be counted at all. For example, there was no way to compute a simple frequency count for the total nouns in a text, because nouns could not be identified. For these reasons, a second set of programs was developed.

The second stage of program development took place during the year 1985–6. The approach used in this stage differed from that of the first stage. First, a general tagging program to identify the grammatical category of each word in a text was developed. The goal at this point was to develop a program that was general enough to be used for tagging both written and spoken texts; thus, for example, the program could not depend on upper case letters or sentence punctuation.

This goal is achieved by using a large-scale dictionary together with a number of context-dependent disambiguating algorithms. Because the Brown corpus exists in a tagged version (i.e., each word in this corpus has an identifier marking the grammatical category of the word in its context), it was sorted into alphabetical order and used as a dictionary. Duplicate entries (the same lexical entry with the same grammatical tag) were deleted, and the resulting dictionary contains 50,624 lexical entries from the four major categories of noun, verb, adjective, and adverb. The closed grammatical categories (e.g., prepositions, pronouns, conjuncts, auxiliaries) are identified directly by the tagging program. Using the dictionary and the word-lists of closed category items built into the program, the initial identification of most words in the LOB and London–Lund corpora was relatively straightforward.

The major problem that had to be solved was that many of the most common words in English are ambiguous as to their grammatical category. Words like *account* can be either nouns or verbs; words like *absent* can be either adjectives or verbs; words like *acid* can be either nouns or adjectives; words like *abstract* can function as a noun, adjective, or verb. There are 3,440 such words in the dictionary compiled from the Brown corpus. In addition, all past and present participial forms can function as noun (gerund), adjective, or verb. A simple word like *that* can function as a demonstrative, demonstrative pronoun, relative pronoun, complementizer, or adverbial subordinator. Using Quirk *et al.* (1985) as a grammatical reference, I developed algorithms to disambiguate occurrences of these (and other) words, depending on their surrounding contexts. For example, a participial form preceded by an article, demonstrative, quantifier, numeral, adjective, or possessive pronoun is functioning as a noun or adjective (i.e., it is not functioning as a verb in this context); given this preceding context, if the form is followed by a noun or adjective then it will be tagged as an adjective; if it is followed by a verb or preposition, then it will be tagged as a noun.

Tagged texts enable automatic identification of a broad range of linguistic features that are important for distinguishing among genres in English. The tagged texts are subsequently used as input to other programs that count the frequencies of certain tagged items (e.g., nouns, adjectives, adverbs) and compute the frequencies of particular syntactic constructions (e.g., relativization on subject versus non-subject position). This approach enables a higher degree of accuracy than the approach used in my earlier analyses, plus it enables inclusion of many features that could not be accurately identified by the previous set of programs. The resulting analysis is thus considerably more complete than earlier analyses.

In section II.2, I describe the major outlines of the tagging program used for the present analysis. In section II.3, then, I describe the particular algorithm used for each linguistic feature. In addition, the primary functions that have been associated with each feature are presented in this section, providing the background for the factor interpretations in Chapter 6.

II.2   General description of the tagging program

The tagging program operates in two steps: (1) initial identification of the grammatical category of each word, and (2) in cases where the dictionary lists more than one possible grammatical category for a word, resolution of ambiguities. There is not space here for a complete description of this program, but I will briefly summarize the major components.

The program first identifies words belonging to any of the following closed grammatical categories:

DO: *do, does, did, don't, doesn't, didn't, doing, done*

HAVE: *have, has, had, having, -'ve♯, -'d♯, haven't, hasn't, hadn't*

BE: *am, is, are, was, were, being, been -'m ♯, -'ve ♯, isn't, aren't, wasn't, weren't*

MODAL: *can, may, shall, will, -'ll♯, could, might, should, would, must, can't, won't, couldn't, mightn't, shouldn't, wouldn't, mustn't*

AUX: MODAL/DO/HAVE/BE/-*'s*

Subject pronouns: *I, we, he, she, they* (plus contracted forms)

Object pronouns: *me, us, him, them* (plus contracted forms)

Possessive pronouns: *my, our, your, his, their, its* (plus contracted forms)

Reflexive pronouns: *himself, themselves, herself, itself*

Other personal pronouns: *you, her, it* (plus contracted forms)

Subordinators (e.g., *since, while, because*)

Prepositions (e.g., *at, among*)

Conjuncts (e.g., *furthermore, therefore*)

Amplifiers (e.g., *absolutely, greatly*)

Downtoners (e.g., *almost, nearly*)

Place adverbials (e.g., *beneath, downstairs*)

Time adverbials (e.g., *early, tonight*)

WH pronouns: *who, whom, whose, which*

Other WH words: *what, where, when, how, whether, why, whoever, whomever, whichever, wherever, whenever, whatever, however*

Nominalizations: all words ending in *-tion♯, -ment♯, -ness♯,* or *-ity♯* (plus plurals)

Articles: *a, an, the, (dhi)*

Demonstratives: *this, that, these, those*

Quantifiers: *each, all, every, many, much, few, several, some, any*

Numerals: *one . . . twenty, hundred, thousand*

Ordinal numerals: *first . . . tenth*

Quantifier pronouns: *everybody, somebody, anybody, everyone, someone, anyone, everything, something, anything*

Titles: *mr, ms, miss, mrs, dr*

Clause punctuation (Cl-P): '.', '!', '?', ':', ';', '–'

Failing to match a word with one of these closed categories, the program then attempts to locate the word in the dictionary, which contains nouns, verbs, adjectives, and adverbs. If there is a single entry for the lexical item in the dictionary, then it is simply tagged. If there are multiple entries, then the item must be disambiguated. If the lexical item is not found in the dictionary, and if it is longer than six letters, there is one final check: if the word ends in *ing*, it is tagged as a present participle; if it ends in *ly*, it is tagged as an adverb; if it ends in *ed*, it is tagged as a past tense form of a verb. Words that match none of the above criteria are left untagged.

There is a separate disambiguating algorithm for each possible ambiguity: adjective–noun (e.g., *assistant, kind*), adjective–verb (e.g., *appropriate, approximate*), noun–verb (e.g., *abuse, acts*), adjective–noun–verb (e.g., *abstract, average, base*), adverb–adjective (e.g., *late, long*), adverb–noun (e.g., *more*), adverb–adjective–verb (e.g., *close, clean, slow*), adverb–adjective–noun (e.g., *flat, high*), and adverb–adjective–verb–noun (e.g., *fine, light*). In addition, present and past participial forms are disambiguated according to their function as noun, verb, or adjective.

For example, noun–verb–adjective forms are disambiguated as follows:

(1) if the preceding word is a form of the verb *be, seem*, or *appear*, then tag the item as an adjective;
(2) else (having not met condition 1), if the preceding word is an article, demonstrative, quantifier, numeral, adjective, possessive noun or pronoun, preposition, or verb, then do the following:
    (2a) if (having met condition 2), the following word is an adjective, noun, or an ambiguity of the types ADJ–N, N–V, or ADJ–N–V, then tag the item as an adjective;
    (2b) else (having met condition 2 but not 2a), tag the item as a noun;
(3) else (having not met conditions 1 or 2), if the preceding word is a subject pronominal form, the pronoun *you* or *it*, a modal, or a form of the verb *do*, then tag the item as a verb;
(4) else (having not met conditions 1, 2, or 3), if the following word is unambiguously a noun or adjective, tag the item as an adjective;
(5) else (having not met conditions 1, 2, 3, or 4), if the following word is a verb, auxiliary, or participial form, then tag the item as a noun;
(6) else (having failed to meet any of the above conditions), if the preceding word is a WH pronoun or a subject pronoun, or the following word is an object pronoun, possessive pronoun, reflexive pronoun, quantifier pronoun, *it, you*, article, demonstrative, quantifier, numeral, or adverb, then tag the item as a verb;
(7) else (having failed the above conditions), if the following word is *of* then tag the item as a noun;
(8) else, failing to meet each of these conditions, the item remains untagged.

Similar algorithms have been developed for the other ambiguities (some of them even more complex than this one). In addition to the basic categories listed above, several other lexical and syntactic features are marked by the tagging program. These include: demonstrative pronouns, passives, perfect aspect, past tense, present tense, infinitives, participial and non-participial adjectives in attributive versus predicative positions, nominalizations, gerunds, causative subordinators, conditional subordinators, concessive subordinators, *that* complements to verbs and adjectives, contractions, analytic and synthetic negation, *be* as main verb, necessity modals, possibility modals, prediction modals, public verbs, private verbs, suasive verbs, discourse particles, hedges, emphatics, sentence relatives, WH questions, phrasal coordination, non-phrasal coordination, WHIZ deletions, participial clauses, and existential *there*. More details of the algorithms for specific features are given in the next section. An example of the output of the tagging program is given as Table II.1. This example is from the tagged version of text K–13, where K is the genre identifier for general fiction and 13 marks this as text no. 13 in that genre.

The tagging of some lexical items was so problematic that they were systematically excluded. For example, the item *as* can function as an adverb, preposition, conjunction, particle, subordinator, or even relative, and it is very difficult to decide among these functions (even for a human analyst!). This lexical item was thus not tagged, to avoid producing incorrectly tagged items in texts. In addition, I carried out some hand-editing of the tagged texts to correct certain inaccuracies. For example, in the spoken texts a *that* immediately following an intonation unit boundary was ambiguous because there was no way to determine if it was clause-initial or clause-internal; it was not possible to automatically decide whether *that* in this position was functioning as a demonstrative, complementizer, or relative pronoun. All occurrences of *that* in this position were therefore checked by hand. Similarly, it was not possible to determine automatically whether *which* following an intonation unit boundary or a comma was functioning as a relative pronoun modifying a specific noun or as a sentence relative pronoun; these items were also checked by hand. Finally, past and present participial forms were checked by hand. Although the tagging program includes elaborate algorithms to distinguish among gerunds, participial adjectives, WHIZ deletions, participial clauses, passives and perfects (in the case of past participles), and main active verbs (present or past), a high percentage of these forms was incorrectly tagged. For example, it is extremely difficult, without the aid of semantic content, to distinguish between active past tense forms and passive WHIZ deletions in constructions such as: (1) . . .

the Americans ranked close in importance . . .; (2) . . . *the woman asked for her fare* . . .; versus (3) . . . *the equation solved in the last section* . . . As human readers, we expect human referents to be agents of verbs and abstract referents to be patients of verbs. Thus, the verb form in example no. 3 is unambiguously a past participle WHIZ deletion construction, and in example nos. 1 and 2 the verb forms are most straightforwardly past tense active verbs, although they can also be past participle heads of WHIZ deletion constructions. To a computer program without access to semantic information, however, there is no difference between these constructions, and thus at least one of the two cases will be tagged incorrectly. Similar problems were found in attempting to disambiguate the other functions of present and past participial forms; as a result, all participial forms were checked by hand.

Spot checks of the tagged texts indicate that the accuracy of the tagging program is quite good. To provide a quantitative assessment of the accuracy, after the hand-editing described above, I examined the tags in twelve randomly selected 100-word passages: three from each of conversation, prepared speeches, general fiction, and academic prose. (The sample output in Table II.1 is taken from one of these general fiction passages.) Out of the 1,200 words examined, five items were incorrectly tagged and 56 items were left untagged (twelve of these were in a single sample). Translating these figures into percentages, the program incorrectly tagged less than one per cent of the items in these text samples, and left untagged approximately five per cent. It is not possible to claim that these twelve samples are representative of the entire corpus used in the study, but even a conservative interpretation of these results indicates that the tagging program (plus editing of participial forms, etc.) achieves coverage of 90 per cent or better.

A general survey of the corpus and analysis of the specific mistags and untagged items in the twelve sample texts indicates that the errors are relatively idiosyncratic or specialized; that there is no serious skewing of results in one genre or another; and that the major features used in the present study are identified with a very high accuracy. The incorrectly tagged items in the sample texts are distributed one in each of five text samples: one of the conversation samples, two of the fiction samples, and two of the academic prose samples. In the conversational mistag, the program failed to recognize *one* in the form *one's* as a pronoun, and instead tagged the form as a possessive noun on the basis of the *'s* ending. In one of the academic prose mistags, the item *a* was tagged as an article when in fact it was simply a label (*classes a and b*). The remaining three mistags are more problematic. In two of them (from two of the fictional samples), a *that* following a noun is incorrectly classified as a relative pronoun. In one

Table II.1 *Sample output from the tagging program, taken from general fiction (genre 'K'), text no. 13 (*** marks incorrectly tagged items)*

k 13	his	p3p			
k 13	short		adj		
k 13	speech		nn		
k 13	which		whp		
k 13	followed	vbn	vbd		
k 13	,				
k 13	showed	vbn	vbd	prv	v
k 13	clearly		adv	rb	
k 13	where		who		
k 13	his	p3p			
k 13	sympathies		nns		
k 13	lay	vbn	vbd		
k 13	.		clp		
k 13	the		art		
k 13	burgomaster's		n		
k 13	question		n	nom	
k 13	had		vbd	hv	aux
k 13	come	prf	vbn		v
k 13	as				
k 13	no		qan	neg	
k 13	surprise		nn		
k 13	to		pp		
k 13	him	p3o			
k 13	;		clp		
k 13	he	p3s			
k 13	had		vbd	hv	aux
k 13	been	prf	vbn	be	aux
k 13	warned	psv	vbn	pub	v
k 13	before		adv	rb	
k 13	the		art		
k 13	reception		n	nom	
k 13	that		tht	rel	***
k 13	he	p3s			
k 13	would		prd	mod	aux
k 13	be		vb	be	aux
k 13	challenged	psv	vbn		v
k 13	,				
k 13	and		hand		
k 13	vicky		np		
k 13	,				
k 13	who		whp		
k 13	was		vbd	be	v

Table II.1 (*cont.*)

k 13	with		pp	
k 13	him	p3o		
k 13	,			
k 13	had		vbd	hv	aux
k 13	implored	prf	vbn	v
k 13	him	3po		
k 13	to		inf	
k 13	make		vb	
k 13	his	p3p		
k 13	position		n	nom
k 13	plain		adj	
k 13	.		clp	
k 13	they	p3s		
k 13	had		vbd	hv	v
k 13	their	p3p		
k 13	own		adj	
k 13	following	vbg	n	
k 13	,			
k 13	she	p3s		
k 13	argued	vbn	vbd	pub
k 13	,			
k 13	though		sub	con
k 13	it	it		
k 13	might		pos	mod	aux
k 13	be		vb	be	v
k 13	a		art	
k 13	minority		n	nom
k 13	following	vbg	n	
k 13	,			
k 13	and		hand	
k 13	fritz		np	
k 13	owed	vbn	vbd	
k 13	it	it		
k 13	to		pp	
k 13	them	p3o		
k 13	to		inf	
k 13	show		vb	prv
k 13	that		tht	thcl
k 13	he	p3s		
k 13	was		vbd	be	aux
k 13	not	not		adv
k 13	involved	psv	vbn	v

case, the *that* is rather the head of a clefted clause, and in the other case, the *that* is the complementizer of a displaced *that*-clause (*he had been warned before the reception that* . . .; where *that* is complementizer to the verb *warned*). In both of these cases, the tagging program analyzed a NOUN + *that* sequence as a relative clause when in fact the *that* was associated with some other more distant entity. The final mistag is from another of the academic prose samples, in which a noun–verb ambiguity was incorrectly analyzed as a verb (*change* in the phrase *free energy change per mole*). None of these mistags represents a fundamental problem in the tagging program; rather, they all represent specialized ambiguities that cannot be readily disambiguated by an automated analysis.

The untagged items are similarly very specialized. A large number of these items are proper nouns that do not occur in the dictionary, because they do not occur in the Brown corpus. These include *Gibraltar*, *Pompidou*, *Duffield*, *Stoke Poges*, and *Gilliatt*; some of these items occur multiple times in a single sample. Other untagged items were archaic forms, unusual spellings, or British spellings, such as *thou*, *shouldest*, *wilful*, and *colour*. Some of the untagged items were simply uncommon nouns, such as *centurion, hominem, frigates, churchwarden, cricketers, gas-constant*, and *diabetics*. The program made no attempt to tag numerals and dates (e.g., 1959, 25, 54, etc.), because they are not needed to identify any of the relevant linguistic features. For the reasons noted above, occurrences of *as* were not tagged. Finally, a few of the untagged items are due to ambiguities that could not be resolved. Three occurrences of *it's* could not be resolved between *it has* and *it is* and so were tagged only as *it* plus auxiliary. Three occurrences of *this* or *that* were tagged as demonstratives but not identified as pronominal in their function. The sequence *appropriate values*, in which both items are ambiguous as to their class, was not resolved and both items were left untagged.

Overall, these results indicate that the tagging program is quite accurate. First, there are very few mistags; the majority of 'errors' are untagged items, which do not introduce misleading analyses, and even untagged items are relatively uncommon. Secondly, there is no serious skewing of mistags in any particular genre so that the results are accurate in relative terms; that is, the results enable accurate comparisons across texts because the same word types are left untagged in all texts. Finally, the few mistags and untagged items that do exist are of a very specialized or idiosyncratic nature, and often these items have no bearing on the linguistic features counted for the analysis of textual dimensions. The tagged texts produced by this program thus provide a good basis for the automatic identification of linguistic features. As discussed in Chapter 4, only the potentially important linguistic features are actually counted, those features that have been associated with particular communicative functions in previous research. The grammatical tags on each word enable identification of these linguistic features, and we turn now to a discussion of the particular algorithm used for each feature and the communicative functions that have been associated with each feature in previous research.

II.3 Discussion of the individual linguistic features

To this point, the linguistic features used in the present study have been discussed in only general terms. The earlier part of this appendix indicates the algorithms for their automatic identification but does not present specific details. Similarly, Chapters 2 and 4 indicate some of the functions that have been associated with linguistic features but present no details about particular features. This section provides these additional details; for each linguistic feature, this section gives the algorithm for its automatic identification, a description of the functions associated with the feature, and a list of previous studies that discuss the feature in functional terms or as a marker of situational differences among genres. The algorithms are given so that interested readers can determine exactly which forms were counted as instances of each feature. The functional discussion is given as the background to the dimension interpretations in Chapters 6–8.

Many linguistic features are included in the present study that are not used in my earlier investigations of speech and writing (Biber 1984, 1986a). Most of these features could not be identified without the use of a tagging program and large-scale dictionary. The additional features include: gerunds, total other nouns, existential *there*, *be* as main verb, *that* adjective complements, present and past participial clauses, relativization on different positions and *that* versus WH relatives, WHIZ deletion constructions, subclasses of adverbial subordination (causative, concessive), participial adjectives, attributive versus predicative adjectives, phrasal and independent clause coordination, synthetic and analytic negation, sub-classes of modals (possibility, necessity, and predictive), verb sub-classes (public, private, and suasive), demonstrative pronouns, *any* and *none* as pronouns, and demonstratives. In addition, some linguistic features that were included in earlier studies have been excluded here, because I determined that they cannot be accurately identified by automatic analysis in spoken texts where there is no sentence or clause punctuation. Excluded features include: *it*-clefts, WH-clefts, fronted *that*-clauses, fronted prepositional phrases, relative pronoun deletions, and direct questions. In all, the 67 linguistic features listed in

Table 4.4 were counted. These features include all features that: (1) have been assigned distinctive functions by previous research, and (2) can be automatically identified in spoken and written texts. Each of these features is discussed in turn here.

The following notation is used in the descriptions of the algorithms:

+ : used to separate constituents
(): marks optional constituents
/: marks disjunctive options
xxx: stands for any word
#: marks a word boundary
T#: marks a 'tone unit' boundary, as defined in Quirk *et al.* (1972: 937–8) for use in the London–Lund corpus.[1]
DO: *do, does, did, don't, doesn't, didn't, doing, done*
HAVE: *have, has, had, having, -'ve#, -'d#, haven't, hasn't, hadn't*
BE: *am, is, are, was, were, being, been -'m#, -'re#, isn't, aren't, wasn't, weren't*
MODAL: *can, may, shall, will, -'ll#, could, might, should, would, must, can't, won't, couldn't, mightn't, shouldn't, wouldn't, mustn't*
AUX: MODAL/DO/HAVE/BE/-'s
SUBJPRO: *I, we, he, she, they* (plus contracted forms)
OBJPRO: *me, us, him, them* (plus contracted forms)
POSSPRO: *my, our, your, his, their, its* (plus contracted forms)
REFLEXPRO: *myself, ourselves, himself, themselves, herself, yourself, yourselves, itself*
PRO: SUBJPRO/OBJPRO/POSSPRO/REFLEXPRO/*you/her/it*
PREP: prepositions (e.g. *at, among* – see no. 39)
CONJ: conjuncts (e.g. *furthermore, therefore* – see no. 45)
ADV: adverbs (see no. 42)
ADJ: adjectives (see nos. 40, 41)
N: nouns (see nos. 14, 15, 16)
VBN: any past tense or irregular past participial verb
VBG: *-ing* form of verb
VB: base form of verb
VBZ: third person, present tense form of verb
PUB: 'public' verbs (see no. 55)
PRV: 'private' verbs (see no. 56)
SUA: 'suasive' verbs (see no. 57)
V: any verb

In general, a tone unit corresponds to a simple sentence, unless: (1) it begins with a phrasal or clausal adverbial element, (2) it contains a medial phrase or clause (such as a non-restrictive relative clause), (3) it contains a vocative, disjunct, or polysyllabic conjunct, (4) it has a clause or long noun phrase as subject, (5) it contains clausal coordination. In these cases, the structure in question often constitutes an additional tone unit.

WHP: WH pronouns – *who, whom, whose, which*

WHO: other WH words – *what, where, when, how, whether, why, whoever, whomever, whichever, wherever, whenever, whatever, however*

ART: articles – *a, an, the, (dhi)*

DEM: demonstratives – *this, that, these, those*

QUAN: quantifiers – *each, all, every, many, much, few, several, some, any*

NUM: numerals – *one . . . twenty, hundred, thousand*

DET: ART/DEM/QUAN/NUM

ORD: ordinal numerals – *first . . . tenth*

QUANPRO: quantifier pronouns – *everybody, somebody, anybody, everyone, someone, anyone, everything, something, anything*

TITLE: address titles

CL-P: clause punctuation ('.', '!', '?', ':', ';', '–')

ALL-P: all punctuation (CL-P plus ',')

In the following discussion, the 67 linguistic features have been grouped into sixteen major categories: (A) tense and aspect markers, (B) place and time adverbials, (C) pronouns and pro-verbs, (D) questions, (E) nominal forms, (F) passives, (G) stative forms, (H) subordination features, (I) adjectives and adverbs, (J) lexical specificity, (K) specialized lexical classes, (L) modals, (M) specialized verb classes, (N) reduced or dispreferred forms, (O) coordination, and (P) negation. The order of discussion here follows that of Tables 4.4 and 4.5.

(A) TENSE AND ASPECT MARKERS (nos. 1–3)

1. **past tense**

Any past tense form that occurs in the dictionary, or any word not otherwise identified that is longer than six letters and ends in *ed#*. Past tense forms have been edited by hand to distinguish between those forms with past participial functions and those with past tense functions.

Past tense forms are usually taken as the primary surface marker of narrative. Schiffrin (1981) describes alternations between past tense forms and the historical present within narratives. Studies that use frequency counts of past tense verbs in register comparisons include Blankenship (1962), Marckworth and Baker (1974), Biber (1986a).

2. **perfect aspect**

(a) HAVE + (ADV) + (ADV) + VBN

(b) HAVE + N/PRO + VBN   (questions)

(includes contracted forms of HAVE)

Perfect aspect forms mark actions in past time with 'current relevance' (Quirk *et al.* 1985:189ff). They have been associated with narrative/descriptive texts and with certain types of academic writing

(Feigenbaum 1978). Biber (1986a) and Marckworth and Baker (1974) find that perfect aspect forms co-occur frequently with past tense forms as markers of narrative.

3. present tense

All VB (base form) or VBZ (third person singular present) verb forms in the dictionary, excluding infinitives.

Present tense verbs deal with topics and actions of immediate relevance. They can also be used in academic styles to focus on the information being presented and remove focus from any temporal sequencing. In contrast, use of the past tense places focus on the temporal sequence, even when used for informational purposes. Ochs (1979) associates the more ready use of present tense forms in unplanned speech styles with the fact that they are acquired before past or future tense forms in English. Weber (1985) notes that cognitive verbs (verbs describing the speaker's mental processes) typically occur in the present tense. Biber (1986a) and Grabe (1986) describe present tense forms as a marker of immediate, as opposed to removed, situations.

(B) PLACE AND TIME ADVERBIALS (nos. 4–5)

mark direct reference to the physical and temporal context of the text, or in the case of fiction, to the text-internal physical and temporal world. Chafe and Danielewicz (1986) include place and time adverbials as markers of involvement. Biber (1986a) interprets their distribution as marking situated, as opposed to abstract, textual content.

4. place adverbials

aboard, above, abroad, across, ahead, alongside, around, ashore, astern, away, behind, below, beneath, beside, downhill, downstairs, downstream, east, far, hereabouts, indoors, inland, inshore, inside, locally, near, nearby, north, nowhere, outdoors, outside, overboard, overland, overseas, south, underfoot, underground, underneath, uphill, upstairs, upstream, west

This list is taken from Quirk *et al.* (1985:514ff). Items with other major functions, for example, *in, on*, which often mark logical relations in a text, have been excluded from the list.

5. time adverbials

afterwards, again, earlier, early, eventually, formerly, immediately, initially, instantly, late, lately, later, momentarily, now, nowadays, once, originally, presently, previously, recently, shortly, simultaneously, soon, subsequently, today, tomorrow, tonight, yesterday

This list is taken from Quirk *et al.* (1985:526ff). Items with other major functions, for example, *last, next*, which often mark logical relations within a text, have been excluded from the list.

(C) PRONOUNS AND PRO-VERBS (nos. 6–12)

Some studies have grouped all pronominal forms together as a single category which is interpreted as marking a relatively low informational load, a lesser precision in referential identification, or a less formal style (e.g., Kroch and Hindle 1982; Brainerd 1972). Other studies have grouped all personal pronouns into a single category, and interpret that category as marking interpersonal focus (Carroll 1960; Poole 1973; Poole and Field 1976). In the present analysis, I separate personal and impersonal pronominal forms, as well as each of the persons within the personal pronouns.

(C1) PERSONAL PRONOUNS

6. **first person pronouns**

I, me, we, us, my, our, myself, ourselves
(plus contracted forms)

First person pronouns have been treated as markers of ego-involvement in a text. They indicate an interpersonal focus and a generally involved style (Chafe 1982, 1985). Weber (1985) points out that the subjects of cognitive verbs are usually first person pronouns, indicating that discussion of mental processes is a personal matter often associated with high ego-involvement. Numerous studies have used first person pronouns for comparison of spoken and written registers (Poole 1973; Poole and Field 1976; Blankenship 1974; Hu 1984; Chafe and Danielewicz 1986; Biber 1986a).

7. **second person pronouns**

you, your, yourself, yourselves (plus contracted forms)

Second person pronouns require a specific addressee and indicate a high degree of involvement with that addressee (Chafe 1985). They have been used as a marker of register differences by Hu (1984), Finegan (1982), and Biber (1986a).

8. **third person personal pronouns**

she, he, they, her, him, them, his, their, himself, herself, themselves (plus contracted forms)

Third person personal pronouns mark relatively inexact reference to persons outside of the immediate interaction. They have been used in register comparisons by Poole and Field (1976) and Hu (1984). Biber (1986a) finds that third person pronouns co-occur frequently with past tense and perfect aspect forms, as a marker of narrative, reported (versus immediate) styles.

(C2) IMPERSONAL PRONOUNS

9. **pronoun *it***

It is the most generalized pronoun, since it can stand for referents ranging from animate beings to abstract concepts. This pronoun can be substituted for nouns, phrases, or whole clauses. Chafe and Danielewicz (1986) and Biber (1986a) treat a frequent use of this pronoun as marking a relatively inexplicit lexical content due to strict time constraints and a non-informational focus. Kroch and Hindle (1982) associate greater generalized pronoun use with the limited amounts of information that can be produced and comprehended in typical spoken situations.

10. **demonstrative pronouns** (e.g., *this is ridiculous*)

(a)   *that/this/these/those* + V/AUX/CL-P/T♯/WHP/*and*
        (where *that* is not a relative pronoun)

(b)   *that's*

(c)   *T♯ + that*
        (*that* in this last context was edited by hand to distinguish among demonstrative pronouns, relative pronouns, complementizers, etc.)

Demonstrative pronouns can refer to an entity outside the text, an exophoric referent, or to a previous referent in the text itself. In the latter case, it can refer to a specific nominal entity or to an inexplicit, often abstract, concept (e.g., *this shows* . . .). Chafe (1985; Chafe and Danielewicz 1986) characterizes those demonstrative pronouns that are used without nominal referents as errors typically found in speech due to faster production and the lack of editing. Demonstrative pronouns have also been used for register comparisons by Carroll (1960) and Hu (1984).

11. **indefinite pronouns**
anybody, anyone, anything, everybody, everyone, everything, nobody, none, nothing, nowhere, somebody, someone, something (Quirk *et al.* 1985:376ff)

These forms have not been used frequently for register comparison. They are included here as markers of generalized pronominal reference, in a similar way to *it* and the demonstrative pronouns.

(C3) PRO-VERBS

12. **pro-verb *do*** (e.g., *the cat did it*)
DO when NOT in the following constructions:
DO + (ADV) + V   (DO as auxiliary)
ALL-P/T♯/WHP + DO   (DO as question)

This feature was included in Biber (1986a) as a marker of register differences. *Do* as pro-verb substitutes for an entire clause, reducing the informational density of a text and indicating a lesser informational focus, due to processing constraints or a higher concern with interpersonal matters.

(D) QUESTIONS (no. 13)

Questions, like second person pronouns, indicate a concern with interpersonal functions and involvement with the addressee (Marckworth and Baker 1974; Biber 1986a). *Yes/no* questions were excluded from the present analysis because they could not be accurately identified by automatic analysis in formal spoken genres, where every phrase tends to be a separate intonation unit; that is, many intonation units begin with an auxiliary and therefore are identical in form to direct questions.

13. **direct WH-questions**
CL-P/T♯ + WHO + AUX
(where AUX is not part of a contracted form)

(E) NOMINAL FORMS (nos. 14–16)

The overall nominal characterization of a text and the distinction between nominal and verbal styles is identified as one of the most fundamental distinctions among registers by Wells (1960) and Brown and Fraser (1979). A high nominal content in a text indicates a high (abstract) informational focus, as opposed to primarily interpersonal or narrative foci. Nominalizations, including gerunds, have particularly been taken as markers of conceptual abstractness.

14. **nominalizations**
All words ending in -*tion*♯, -*ment*♯, -*ness*♯, or -*ity*♯ (plus plural forms).

Nominalizations have been used in many register studies. Chafe (1982, 1985, and Danielewicz 1986) focuses on their use to expand idea units and integrate information into fewer words. Biber (1986a) finds that they tend to co-occur with passive constructions and prepositions and thus interprets their function as conveying highly abstract (as opposed to situated) information. Janda (1985) shows that nominalizations are used during note-taking to reduce full sentences to more compact and efficient series of noun phrases. Other references: Carroll (1960), DeVito (1967), Marckworth and Baker (1974), Grabe (1986).

15. **gerunds**
All participle forms serving nominal functions – these are edited by hand.

Gerunds (or verbal nouns) are verbal forms serving nominal functions. As such, they are closely related to nominalizations in their functions. Some researchers (e.g., Chafe 1982) do not distinguish among the different participial functions, treating gerunds, participial adjectives (nos. 40–1), and participial clauses (nos. 25–8) as a single feature. In the present study, these functions are treated separately. Studies that have used gerunds as a distinguishing marker of register are Carroll (1960) and O'Donnell (1974).

16. **total other nouns**

All nouns included in the dictionary, excluding those forms counted as nominalizations or gerunds.

This count provides an overall nominal assessment of a text. Nominalizations and gerunds are excluded from the total noun count so that the three features will be statistically independent. In addition to Wells (1960), overall noun counts have been used by Carroll (1960) and Blankenship (1974).

(F) PASSIVES (nos. 17–18)

Passives have been taken as one of the most important surface markers of the decontextualized or detached style that stereotypically characterizes writing. In passive constructions, the agent is demoted or dropped altogether, resulting in a static, more abstract presentation of information. Passives are also used for thematic purposes (Thompson 1982; Finegan 1982; Weiner and Labov 1983; Janda 1985). From this perspective, agentless passives are used when the agent does not have a salient role in the discourse; *by*-passives are used when the patient is more closely related to the discourse theme than the patient. Studies that have used passives for register comparisons include Carroll (1960), Blankenship (1962), Poole (1973), Poole and Field (1976), O'Donnell (1974), Marckworth and Baker (1974), Ochs (1979), Brown and Yule (1983), Young (1985), Chafe (1982, 1985), Chafe and Danielewicz (1986), Biber (1986a), and Grabe (1986).

17. **agentless passives**   18. ***by*-passives****

(a) BE + (ADV) + (ADV) + VBN + (*by*)**

(b) BE + N/PRO + VBN + (*by*)**   (question form)

(** no. 18 with the *by*-phrase)

(G) STATIVE FORMS (nos. 19–20)

Only a few studies have used stative forms for register comparisons. These forms might be considered as markers of the static, informational style common in writing, since they preclude the presence of an active verb. Conversely, they can be considered as non-complex constructions with a reduced informational load, and therefore might be expected to be more characteristic of spoken styles. Kroch and Hindle (1982) analyze existential *there* as being used to introduce a new entity while adding a minimum of other information. Janda (1985) notes that stative or predicative constructions (X *be* Y) are used frequently in note-taking, although the *be* itself is often dropped. Predicative constructions with *be*-ellipsis are also common in sports announcer talk (Ferguson 1983). These predicative constructions might be characterized as fragmented, because they are typically alternatives to more integrated attributive constructions (e.g., *the house is big* versus *the big house*). *Be* as main verb is used for register comparisons by Carroll (1960) and Marckworth and Baker (1974).

19. ***be* as main verb**
BE + DET/POSSPRO/TITLE/PREP/ADJ
20. **existential *there*** (e.g., *there are several explanations* . . .)
(a) *there* + (xxx) + BE
(b) *there's*

(H) SUBORDINATION (nos. 21–38)
Subordination has perhaps been the most discussed linguistic feature used for register comparisons. It has generally been taken as an index of structural complexity and therefore supposed to be more commonly used in typical writing than typical speech. Some researchers, though, have found higher use of subordination in speech than writing (e.g., Poole and Field 1976). Halliday (1979) claims that even conversational speech has more subordination than written styles, because the two modes have different types of complexities: spoken language, because it is created and perceived as an on-going process, is characterized by 'an intricacy of movement [and by] complex sentence structures with low lexical density (more clauses, but fewer high-content words per clause)'; written language, in which the text is created and perceived as an object, is characterized by 'a denseness of matter [and by] simple sentence structures with high lexical density (more high-content words per clause, but fewer clauses)'.

Thompson (1983, 1984, 1985; Thompson and Longacre 1985; Ford and Thompson to appear) has carried out some of the most careful research into the discourse functions of subordination. She distinguishes between dependent clauses (complementation and relative clauses) and other types of subordination (e.g., adverbial clauses) that function to frame discourse information in different ways. Her studies have focused on the discourse functions of detached participial clauses, adverbial clauses in general, purpose clauses, and conditional clauses (see below). In all of these studies, Thompson emphasizes that subordination is not a unified construct, that different types of structural dependency have different discourse functions, and that particular subordination features are therefore used to different degrees in different types of discourse.

Beaman (1984) and Biber (1986a) also find that different subordination forms are distributed differently. Based on an analysis of spoken and written narratives, Beaman observes that there are more finite nominal clauses (*that*-clauses and WH-clauses) in speech and more non-finite nominal clauses (infinitives and participial clauses) in writing. She also discusses the distribution of relative and adverbial clauses in these texts (see below). In my own earlier studies, I find that *that*-clauses, WH-clauses, and adverbial subordinators co-occur frequently with interpersonal and reduced-content features such as first and second person pronouns, questions, contractions, hedges, and emphatics. These types of subordination occur frequently in spoken genres, both interactional (conversation) and informational (speeches), but they occur relatively infrequently in informational written genres. Relative clauses and infinitive were found to have a separate distribution from the other types of subordination, but they did not form a strong enough co-occurrence pattern for interpretation. These same features are discussed from the perspective of discourse complexity in Finegan and Biber (1986b).

These studies by Thompson and Beaman, and my own earlier studies, all show that different types of subordination function in different ways. Based on these analyses, I have divided the subordination features used in the present study into four sub-classes: complementation (H1), participial forms (H2), relative clauses (H3), and adverbial clauses (H4). Each of these is now discussed in turn.

(H1) COMPLEMENTATION (nos. 21–4)

21. **that verb complements** (e.g., *I said that he went*)

(a) *and/nor/but/or/also*/ALL-P + *that* +
DET/PRO/*there*/plural noun/proper noun/TITLE
(these are *that*-clauses in clause-initial positions)

(b) PUB/PRV/SUA/SEEM/APPEAR + *that* + xxx
(where xxx is NOT: V/AUX/CL-P/T#/*and*)

(*that*-clauses as complements to verbs which are not included in the above verb classes are not counted – see Quirk *et al.* 1985:1179ff.)

(c) PUB/PRV/SUA + PREP + xxx + N + *that*
(where xxx is any number of words, but NOT = N)

(This algorithm allows an intervening prepositional phrase between a verb and its complement.)

(d) T# + *that*
(This algorithm applies only to spoken texts. Forms in this context are checked by hand, to distinguish among *that* complements, relatives, demonstrative pronouns and subordinators.)

Chafe (1982, 1985) identifies *that*-complements as one of the indices of integration, used for idea-unit expansion in typical writing. Ochs (1979) describes complementation as a relatively complex construction used to a greater extent in planned than unplanned discourse. In contrast, Beaman (1984) finds more *that* complementation in her spoken than written narratives. Biber (1986a) finds that *that*-complements co-occur frequently with interactive features such as first and second person pronouns and questions, and that all of these features are more common in spoken than written genres. In that paper and in Finegan and Biber (1986b), this distribution is interpreted in a similar way to Halliday's characterization: that this type of structural complexity is used in typical speech, where there is little opportunity for careful production or revision, while other types of linguistic complexity, notably lexical variety and density, are used in typical academic writing, which provides considerable opportunity for production and revision.

Other studies that have used *that*-complements for register comparisons include Carroll (1960), O'Donnell (1974), Frawley (1982), and Weber (1985). Winter (1982) notes that both verb and adjective *that*-complements provide a way to talk about the information in the dependent clause, with the speaker's evaluation (commitment, etc.) being given in the main clause and the propositional information in the *that*-clause.

Some verb complements do not have an overt complementizer (e.g., *I think he went*); these are counted as a separate feature (no. 60).

22. **that adjective complements** (e.g., *I'm glad that you like it*)
ADJ + (T#) + *that*
(complements across intonation boundaries were edited by hand)

Most studies of *that*-clauses consider only verb complements. Winter (1982) points out, however, that verb and adjective complements seem to have similar discourse functions, and so both should be important for register comparisons. Because there is no a priori way to know if *that* verb and adjective complements are distributed in the same way among genres, they are included as separate features here. Householder (1964) has compiled a list of adjectives that occur before *that*-clauses; Quirk *et al.* (1985:1222–5) give a grammatical and discourse description of these constructions.

23. **WH-clauses** (e.g., *I believed what he told me*)
PUB/PRV/SUA + WHP/WHO + xxx
(where xxx is NOT = AUX – this excludes WH questions)

This algorithm captures only those WH clauses that occur as object complements to the restricted verb classes described below in nos. 55–7; see Quirk *et al.* 1985:1184–5. Other WH clauses could not be identified reliably by automatic analysis and so were not counted.

Similar to *that*-clauses, WH-clauses are complements to verbs. Chafe (1985) analyzes them as being used for idea unit expansion, and thus they should be more frequent in typical writing. Beaman (1984) did not find WH-clauses in her written narratives; she writes that they resemble questions and serve interpersonal functions in discourse, accounting for their use in spoken but not written narratives. Winter (1982) notes that WH complements provide a way to talk about questions in the same way that *that*-complements provide a way to talk about statements, that is, with the speaker's evaluation, commitment, etc. provided in the main clause. Biber (1986a) finds WH-clauses to be distributed in a similar pattern to *that*-clauses, both of which co-occur frequently with interpersonal features such as first and second person pronouns and questions.

24. **infinitives**

to + (ADV) + VB

Infinitives are the final form of complementation to be included in the present study. The algorithm above groups together all infinitival forms: complements to nouns, adjectives, and verbs, as well as 'purpose' adverbial clauses (see below). The distribution and discourse functions of infinitives seem to be less marked than that of other types of subordination. Chafe (1982, 1985) includes infinitives as one of the devices used to achieve integration and idea-unit expansion in typical writing. Beaman (1984) finds that infinitives co-occur with other non-finite nominal clauses (especially participial clauses), and that they are more common in written than spoken narratives. Biber (1986a) finds a weak co-occurrence relationship between infinitives and relative clauses. Finally, Thompson (1985) carefully distinguishes between those infinitives functioning as complements and those functioning as adverbial purpose clauses, and she analyzes the thematic discourse functions of the latter in some detail. Although this is an important functional distinction, it is not made here because of the limitations of the automatic analysis. Other references include: Carroll (1960), O'Donnell (1974), and Dubuisson *et al.* (1983).

(H2) PARTICIPIAL FORMS (nos. 25-8)

Participles are among the most difficult forms to analyze. They can function as nouns, adjectives, or verbs, and within their use as verbs, they can function as main verbs (present progressive, perfect, or passive), complement clauses, adjectival clauses, or adverbial clauses. Some studies do not distinguish among these functions, counting all participial forms (excluding main verbs) as a single feature (e.g., Chafe 1982; Beaman 1984). Many studies also do not distinguish between present and past participial clauses, or they count only present participle forms. In the present analysis, each of the different grammatical functions of participles is treated as a separate linguistic feature, since these grammatical functions are likely to be associated with different discourse functions.

Studies that consider participles typically find that they occur more frequently in writing than in speech; the usual interpretation associated with this distribution is that participles are used for integration or structural elaboration. References include Carroll (1960), O'Donnell (1974), Winter (1982), Chafe (1985), Young (1985), Chafe and Danielewicz (1986), Bäcklund (1986), Quirk *et al.* (1985).

Thompson (1983) distinguishes syntactically detached participial clauses (e.g., *Stuffing his mouth with cookies, Joe ran out the door*) from other participial functions. She shows how these clauses are used for depictive functions, that is, for discourse that describes by creating an image. No. 25 and no. 26 below are algorithms for detached participial clauses (present and past). These forms were edited by hand to exclude participial forms not having an adverbial function. Participial clauses functioning as reduced relatives, also known as WHIZ deletions, are treated separately (nos. 27 and 28). Janda (1985) notes the use of these forms in note-taking to replace full relative clauses, apparently because they are more compact and integrated and therefore well-suited to the production of highly informational discourse under severe time constraints. In the present analysis, these forms were also edited by hand to distinguish between subordinate clause functions and other functions; in particular, past participles following a noun can represent either a simple past tense form or the head of a reduced relative clause, and these forms thus needed to be checked by hand. Finally, participles functioning as nouns and adjectives were distinguished (nos. 15 and 40–1 respectively); these forms were also edited by hand to verify their grammatical function.

25. **present participial clauses**
(e.g., *Stuffing his mouth with cookies, Joe ran out the door*)
T#/ALL-P + VBG + PREP/DET/WHP/WHO/PRO/ADV
(these forms were edited by hand)

26. **past participial clauses**
(e.g., *Built in a single week, the house would stand for fifty years.*)
T#/ALL-P + VBN + PREP/ADV
(these forms were edited by hand)

27. **past participial WHIZ deletion relatives**
(e.g., *the solution produced by this process*)
N/QUANPRO + VBN + PREP/BE/ADV
(these forms were edited by hand)

28. **present participial WHIZ deletion relatives**
(e.g., *the event causing this decline is . . .*)
N + VBG
(these forms were edited by hand)

(H3) RELATIVES (nos. 29–34)

Relative clauses have been used frequently as a marker of register differences. Relatives provide a way to talk about nouns, either for identification or simply to provide additional information (Winter 1982; Beaman 1984). Ochs (1979) notes that referents are marked differently in planned and unplanned discourse: simple determiners are preferred in unplanned discourse while relative clauses are used for more exact and explicit reference in planned discourse. Chafe (1982, 1985) states that relative clauses are also used as a device for integration and idea unit expansion. Other references include Carroll (1960), Poole (1973), Poole and Field (1976), O'Donnell (1974), Kroll (1977), Frawley (1982), Dubuisson *et al.* (1983), Biber (1986a), and Grabe (1986).

In general, these studies find that relative clauses occur more frequently in writing than in speech. Some studies, however, do not treat all relative clauses as a single feature and consequently do not find a uniform distribution. Kroch and Hindle (1982) and Beaman (1984) provide two of the fullest discussions. Beaman analyzes *that* relatives separately from WH relatives and finds more *that* relatives in her spoken narratives but more WH relatives in her written narratives; further, she finds more relativization on subject position in her spoken narratives versus more relativization on object positions in her written narratives. In contrast, Kroch and Hindle find more relativization on subject position in their written texts and more relativization on object position in their spoken texts. They attribute this to a greater use of pronouns in subject position in speech, making this position unavailable for relativization. Both of these studies also analyze pied-piping constructions separately, finding more in written than in spoken texts. In the present analysis, I separate *that* from WH relatives, and relativization on subject position from relativization on object position. Pied-piping constructions are also treated separately.

29. ***that* relative clauses on subject position**

(e.g., *the dog that bit me*)

N + (T#) + *that* + (ADV) + AUX/V

(*that* relatives across intonation boundaries are identified by hand.)

30. ***that* relative clauses on object position**

(e.g., *the dog that I saw*)

N + (T#) + *that* + DET/SUBJPRO/POSSPRO/*it*/ADJ/plural noun/ proper noun / possessive noun / TITLE

(This algorithm does not distinguish between *that* complements to nouns and true relative clauses.)

(In spoken texts, *that* relatives sometimes span two intonation units; these are identified by hand.)

31. WH relative clauses on subject position

(e.g., *the man who likes popcorn*)

xxx + yyy + N + WHP + (ADV) + AUX/V

(where xxx is NOT any form of the verbs ASK or TELL; to exclude indirect WH questions like *Tom asked the man who went to the store*)

32. WH relative clauses on object positions

(e.g., *the man who Sally likes*)

xxx + yyy + N + WHP + zzz

(where xxx is NOT any form of the verbs ASK or TELL, to exclude indirect WH questions, and zzz is not ADV, AUX or V, to exclude relativization on subject position)

33. pied-piping relative clauses

(e.g., *the manner in which he was told*)

PREP + WHP

34. sentence relatives

(e.g., *Bob likes fried mangoes, which is the most disgusting thing I've ever heard of*)

T#/, + *which*

(These forms are edited by hand to exclude non-restrictive relative clauses.)

Sentence relatives do not have a nominal antecedent, referring instead to the entire predication of a clause (Quirk *et al.* 1985:1118–20). They function as a type of comment clause, and they are not used for identificatory functions in the way that other relative clauses are. A preliminary analysis of texts suggested that these constructions were considerably more frequent in certain spoken genres than in typical writing, and they are therefore included here as a separate feature.

(H4) ADVERBIAL CLAUSES (nos. 35–8)

Adverbial clauses appear to be an important device for indicating informational relations in a text. Overall, Thompson (1984) and Biber (1986a) find more adverbial clauses in speech than in writing. Several studies, though, separate preposed from postposed adverbial clauses, and find that these two types have different scopes, functioning to mark global versus local topics, and that they have different distributions (Winter 1982; Chafe 1984a; Thompson 1985; Thompson and Longacre 1985; Ford and Thompson 1986). Other references include Carroll (1960), O'Donnell (1974), Marckworth and Baker (1974), Beaman (1984), Chafe (1985), Altenberg (1984, 1986), and Grabe (1986).

There are several subclasses of adverbial clauses, including condition, reason/cause, purpose, comparison, and concession (Quirk *et al.* 1985:1077–18; Tottie 1986; Smith and Frawley 1983). The most common types, causative, concessive, and conditional adverbials, can be identified unambiguously by machine (nos. 35–7); the other subordinators are grouped together as a general category (no. 38).

35.　**causative adverbial subordinators:** *because*

Because is the only subordinator to function unambiguously as a causative adverbial. Other forms, such as *as*, *for*, and *since*, can have a range of functions, including causative. Most researchers find more causative adverbials in speech (Beaman 1984; Tottie 1986), although the functional reasons for this distribution are not clear. Tottie (1986) and Altenberg (1984) both provide detailed analyses of these subordination constructions. For example, Tottie notes that while there is more causative subordination overall in speech, the form *as* is used as a causative subordinator more in writing. Other references: Smith and Frawley (1983), Schiffrin (1985b).

36.　**concessive adverbial subordinators:** *although, though*

Following a general pattern for adverbial clauses, concessive adverbials can also be used for framing purposes or to introduce background information, and they have different functions in pre- and post-posed positions (McClure and Geva 1983; Altenberg 1986). Both Altenberg and Tottie (1986) find more concessive subordination overall in writing.

37.　**conditional adverbial subordinators:** *if, unless*

Conditional clauses are also used for discourse framing and have differing functions when they are in pre- or post-posed position (Ford and Thompson 1986). Finegan (1982) finds a very frequent use of conditional clauses in legal wills, due to the focus on the possible conditions existing when the will is executed. Several researchers have found more conditional clauses in speech than in writing (Beaman 1984; Tottie 1986; Biber 1986a; Ford and Thompson 1986), but the functional reasons for this distribution are not clear.

38.　**other adverbial subordinators: (having multiple functions)**

since, while, whilst, whereupon, whereas, whereby, such that, so that xxx, such that xxx, inasmuch as, forasmuch as, insofar as, insomuch as, as long as, as soon as
(where xxx is NOT: N/ADJ)

(I1) PREPOSITIONAL PHRASES (no. 39)

39.　**total prepositional phrases**

against, amid, amidst, among, amongst, at, besides, between, by, despite, during, except, for, from, in, into, minus, notwithstanding, of, off, on, onto, opposite, out, per, plus, pro, re, than, through, throughout, thru, to, toward, towards, upon, versus, via, with, within, without

This list of prepositions is taken from Quirk *et al.* (1985:665–7), excluding those lexical items that have some other primary function, such as place or time adverbial, conjunct, or subordinator (e.g., *down, after, as*).

Prepositions are an important device for packing high amounts of information into academic nominal discourse. Chafe (1982, 1985; and Danielewicz 1986) describes prepositions as a device for integrating information into idea units and expanding the amount of information contained within an idea unit. Biber (1986a) finds that prepositions tend to co-occur frequently with nominalizations and passives in academic prose, official documents, professional letters, and other informational types of written discourse. Other references include: Carroll (1960), Blankenship (1974), Marckworth and Baker (1974), and Dubuisson *et al.* (1983).

(12) ADJECTIVES AND ADVERBS (nos. 40–2)

Adjectives and adverbs also seem to expand and elaborate the information presented in a text. Chafe (1982, 1985; and Danielewicz 1986) groups adjectives together with prepositional phrases and subordination constructions as devices used for idea unit integration and expansion. However, the descriptive kinds of information presented by adjectives and adverbs do not seem equivalent to the logical, nominal kinds of information often presented in prepositional phrases. In my earlier work (e.g., Biber 1986a), I find that prepositions, subordination features, adjectives, and adverbs are all distributed differently; for example, prepositional phrases occur frequently in formal, abstract styles, while many types of subordination occur frequently in highly interactive, unplanned discourse; adjectives and adverbs are distributed in yet other ways. All of these features elaborate information in one way or another, but the type of information being elaborated is apparently different in each case. Other relevant studies include: Carroll (1960), Drieman (1962), Poole (1973), Poole and Field (1976), Blankenship (1974), O'Donnell (1974), Marckworth and Baker (1974), Dubuisson *et al.* (1983), Tottie (1986), and Grabe (1986).

Some studies distinguish between attributive and predicative adjectives (e.g., Drieman, O'Donnell, and Chafe). Attributive adjectives are highly integrative in their function, while predicative adjectives might be considered more fragmented. In addition, predicative adjectives are frequently used for marking stance (as heads of *that* or *to* complements; see Winter 1982). The present analysis distinguishes between attributive and predicative adjectives, including both participial and non-participial forms.

40. **attributive adjectives** (e.g., *the big horse*)

ADJ + ADJ/N

(+ any ADJ not identified as predicative – no. 41)

41. **predicative adjectives** (e.g., *the horse is big*)

(a) BE + ADJ + xxx

(where xxx is NOT ADJ, ADV, or N)

(b) BE + ADJ + ADV + xxx

(where xxx is NOT ADJ or N)

42. **total adverbs**

Any adverb form occurring in the dictionary, or any form that is longer than five letters and ends in *-ly*. The count for total adverbs excludes those adverbs counted as instances of hedges, amplifiers, downtoners, amplifiers, place adverbials, and time adverbials.

(J) LEXICAL SPECIFICITY (nos. 43–4)

Two measures of lexical specificity or diversity are commonly used: type/token ratio and word length. Unlike structural elaboration, differences in lexical specificity seem to truly correlate with the production differences between speaking and writing; the high levels of lexical diversity and specificity that are found in formal academic writing are apparently not possible in spoken texts due to the restrictions of on-line production (Chafe and Danielewicz 1986; Biber 1986a). Type/token ratio (the number of different words per text) was a favorite measure of psychologists and researchers in communication studying linguistic differences between speech and writing (Osgood 1960; Drieman 1962; Horowitz and Newman 1964; Gibson *et al.* 1966; Preston and Gardner 1967; Blankenship 1974). Longer words also convey more specific, specialized meanings than shorter ones; Zipf (1949) has shown that words become shorter as they are more frequently used and more general in meaning. Osgood, Drieman and Blankenship include measures of word length in their studies. These two features are found to co-occur frequently in planned written genres by Biber (1986a), and this distributional pattern is interpreted as marking a highly exact presentation of information, conveying maximum content in the fewest words.

43. **type/token ratio**

the number of different lexical items in a text, as a percentage

This feature is computed by counting the number of different lexical items that occur in the first 400 words of each text, and then dividing by four; texts shorter than 400 words are not included in the present analysis. In a preliminary version of the computer programs used here, I computed this feature by counting the number of different lexical items in a text, dividing by the total number of words in the text, and then multiplying by 100. If the texts in the analysis were all nearly the same length, these two methods of computing type/token ratio would give nearly equivalent results. If text length varies widely, however, these two methods will give quite different results, because the relation between the number of 'types' (different lexical items) and the total number of words in a text is not linear. That is, a large number of the different words used in the first 100 words of a text will be repeated in each successive 100-word chunk of text. The result is that each additional 100 words of text adds fewer and fewer additional types. In a comparison of very short texts and very long texts, the type/token ratio computed over the entire text will thus appear to be much higher in the short texts than in the long texts. To avoid this skewing, the present study computes the number of types in the first 400 words of each text, regardless of the total text length.

44. **word length**
mean length of the words in a text, in orthographic letters

(K) LEXICAL CLASSES (nos. 45–51)
45. **conjuncts**
alternatively, altogether, consequently, conversely, eg, e.g., else, further-more, hence, however, i.e., instead, likewise, moreover, namely, neverthe-less, nonetheless, notwithstanding, otherwise, rather, similarly, therefore, thus, viz.

  in + comparison/contrast/particular/addition/conclusion/consequence
/sum/summary/any event/any case/other words
  for + example/instance
  by + contrast/comparison
  as a + result/consequence
  on the + contrary/other hand
  ALL-P/T♯ + *that is/else/altogether* + T♯/,
  ALL-P/T♯ + *rather* + T♯/,/xxx
(where xxx is NOT: ADJ/ADV)

Conjuncts explicitly mark logical relations between clauses, and as such they are important in discourse with a highly informational focus. Quirk *et al.* (1985:634–6) list the following functional classes of conjuncts: listing, summative, appositive, resultive, inferential, con-'trastive, and transitional. Despite their importance in marking logical relations, few register comparisons have analysed the distribution of conjuncts. Ochs (1979) notes that they are more formal and therefore more common in planned discourse than unplanned. Biber (1986a) finds that they co-occur frequently with prepositions, passives, and nominalizations in highly informational genres such as academic prose, official documents, and professional letters. Altenberg (1986) looks at concessive and antithetic conjuncts and finds that they are generally more common in writing than speech.

46. downtoners

almost, barely, hardly, merely, mildly, nearly, only, partially, partly, practically, scarcely, slightly, somewhat

Downtoners 'have a general lowering effect on the force of the verb' (Quirk *et al.*, 1985:597–602). Chafe and Danielewicz (1986) characterize these forms as 'academic hedges', since they are commonly used in academic writing to indicate probability. Chafe (1985) notes that downtoners are among those evidentials used to indicate reliability. Holmes (1984) notes that these forms can mark politeness or deference towards the addressee in addition to marking uncertainty towards a proposition.

47. hedges

at about/something like/more or less/almost/maybe/xxx *sort of*/xxx *kind of* (where xxx is NOT: DET/ADJ/POSSPRO/WHO – excludes *sort* and *kind* as true nouns)

Hedges are informal, less specific markers of probability or uncertainty. Downtoners give some indication of the degree of uncertainty; hedges simply mark a proposition as uncertain. Chafe (1982) discusses the use of these forms to mark fuzziness in involved discourse, and Chafe and Danielewicz (1986) state that the use of hedges in conversational discourse indicates an awareness of the limited word choice that is possible under the production restrictions of speech. Biber (1986a) finds hedges co-occurring with interactive features (e.g., first and second person pronouns and questions) and with other features marking reduced or generalized lexical content (e.g., general emphatics, pronoun *it*, contractions). Other references include Aijmer (1984), Schourup (1985), and Grabe (1986).

48. amplifiers

absolutely, altogether, completely, enormously, entirely, extremely, fully, greatly, highly, intensely, perfectly, strongly, thoroughly, totally, utterly, very

Amplifiers have the opposite effect of downtoners, boosting the force of the verb (Quirk *et al.* 1985:590–7). They are used to indicate, in positive terms, the reliability of propositions (Chafe 1985). Holmes (1984) notes that, similar to downtoners, amplifiers can be used for non-propositional functions; in particular, they can signal solidarity with the listener in addition to marking certainty or conviction towards the proposition.

49. emphatics
for sure/a lot/such a/real + ADJ/*so* + ADJ/DO + V/*just/really/most /more*

The relation between emphatics and amplifiers is similar to that between hedges and downtoners: emphatics simply mark the presence (versus absence) of certainty while amplifiers indicate the degree of certainty towards a proposition. Emphatics are characteristic of informal, colloquial discourse, marking involvement with the topic (Chafe 1982, 1985). As noted above, Biber (1986a) finds emphatics and hedges co-occurring frequently in the conversational genres. Labov (1984) discusses forms of this type under the label of 'intensity': the 'emotional expression of social orientation toward the linguistic proposition'. Other studies of emphatics include Stenström's (1986) analysis of *really* and Aijmer's (1985) analysis of *just*.

50. discourse particles
CL-P/T# + *well/now/anyway/anyhow/anyways*

Discourse particles are used to maintain conversational coherence (Schiffrin 1982, 1985a). Chafe (1982, 1985) describes their role as 'monitoring the information flow' in involved discourse. They are very generalized in their functions and rare outside of the conversational genres. Other studies include: Hu (1984), Schourup (1985), and Perera (1986).

51. demonstratives
that/this/these/those

(This count excludes demonstrative pronouns (no. 10) and *that* as relative, complementizer, or subordinator.)

Demonstratives are used for both text-internal deixis (Kurzon 1985) and for exophoric, text-external, reference. They are an important device for marking referential cohesion in a text (Halliday and Hasan 1976). Ochs (1979) notes that demonstratives are preferred to articles in unplanned discourse.

(L) MODALS (nos. 52–4)
It is possible to distinguish three functional classes of modals: (1) those marking permission, possibility, or ability; (2) those marking obligation or necessity; and (3) those marking volition or prediction (Quirk *et al.* 1985:219–36; Coates 1983; Hermeren 1986). Tottie (1985; Tottie and Overgaard 1984) discusses particular aspects of modal usage, including the negation of necessity modals and the use of *would*. Chafe (1985) includes possibility modals among the evidentials that mark reliability, and necessity modals among those evidentials that mark some aspect of the reasoning process.

52. possibility modals
can/may/might/could (+ contractions)

53. **necessity modals**
ought/should/must (+ contractions)
54. **predictive modals**
will/would/shall (+ contractions)

(M) SPECIALIZED VERB CLASSES (nos. 55–8)

Certain restricted classes of verbs can be identified as having specific functions. Several researchers refer to 'verbs of cognition', those verbs that refer to mental activities (Carroll 1960; Weber 1985). Chafe (1985) discusses the use of 'sensory' verbs (e.g., *see, hear, feel*) to mark knowledge from a particular kind of evidence. In the present analysis, I distinguish four specialized classes of verbs: public, private, suasive, and *seem/appear*. Public verbs involve actions that can be observed publicly; they are primarily speech act verbs, such as *say* and *explain*, and they are commonly used to introduce indirect statements. Private verbs express intellectual states (e.g., *believe*) or nonobservable intellectual acts (e.g., *discover*); this class corresponds to the 'verbs of cognition' used in other studies. Suasive verbs imply intentions to bring about some change in the future (e.g., *command, stipulate*). All present and past tense forms of these verbs are included in the counts.

55. **public verbs**
(e.g., *acknowledge, admit, agree, assert, claim, complain, declare, deny, explain, hint, insist, mention, proclaim, promise, protest, remark, reply, report, say, suggest, swear, write*)

  This class of verbs is taken from Quirk *et al.* (1985:1180–1).

56. **private verbs**
(e.g., *anticipate, assume, believe, conclude, decide, demonstrate, determine, discover, doubt, estimate, fear, feel, find, forget, guess, hear, hope, imagine, imply, indicate, infer, know, learn, mean, notice, prove, realize, recognize, remember, reveal, see, show, suppose, think, understand*)

  This class of verbs is taken from Quirk *et al.* (1985:1181–2).

57. **suasive verbs**
(e.g., *agree, arrange, ask, beg, command, decide, demand, grant, insist, instruct, ordain, pledge, pronounce, propose, recommend, request, stipulate, suggest, urge*)

  This class of verbs is taken from Quirk *et al.* (1985:1182–3).

58. *seem/appear*
These are 'perception' verbs (Quirk *et al.* 1985:1033, 1183). They can be used to mark evidentiality with respect to the reasoning process (Chafe 1985), and they represent another strategy used for academic hedging (see the discussion of downtoners – no. 46).

(N) REDUCED FORMS AND DISPREFERRED STRUCTURES (nos. 59–63)

Several linguistic constructions, such as contractions, stranded prepositions, and split infinitives, are dispreferred in edited writing. Linguists typically disregard the prescriptions against these constructions as arbitrary. Finegan (1980, 1987; Finegan and Biber 1986a), however, shows that grammatical prescriptions tend to be systematic if considered from a strictly linguistic point of view: they tend to disprefer those constructions that involve a mismatch between surface form and underlying representation, resulting in either a reduced surface form (due to contraction or deletion) or a weakened isomorphism between form and meaning (e.g., split infinitives). Biber (1986a) finds that these features tend to co-occur frequently with interactive features (e.g., first and second person pronouns) and with certain types of subordination. Chafe (1984b) discusses the linguistic form of grammatical prescriptions and analyzes the historical evolution of certain prescriptions in speech and writing. Features 59–63 are all dispreferred in edited writing; nos. 59–60 involve surface reduction of form and nos. 61–3 involve a weakened isomorphism between form and meaning.

59. **contractions**
(1) all contractions on pronouns
(2) all contractions on auxiliary forms (negation)
(3) *'s* suffixed on nouns is analyzed separately (to exclude possessive forms):

N's + V/AUX/ADV+V/ADV+AUX/DET/POSSPRO/
PREP/ADJ+CL-P/ADJ+T#

Contractions are the most frequently cited example of reduced surface form. Except for certain types of fiction, they are dispreferred in formal, edited writing; linguists have traditionally explained their frequent use in conversation as being a consequence of fast and easy production. Finegan and Biber (1986a), however, find that contractions are distributed as a cline: used most frequently in conversation; least frequently in academic prose; and with intermediate frequencies in broadcast, public speeches, and press reportage. Biber (1987) finds that contractions are more frequent in American writing than in British writing, apparently because of greater attention to grammatical prescriptions by British writers. Chafe and Danielewicz (1986) also find that there is no absolute difference between speech and writing in the use of contractions. Thus, the use of contractions seems to be tied to appropriateness considerations as much as to the differing production circumstances of speech and writing. Other references include: Marckworth and Baker (1974), Chafe (1985), and Biber (1986a).

60. **subordinator-*that* deletion**
(e.g., *I think* [*that*] *he went to* . . .)
(1) PUB/PRV/SUA+(T#)+demonstrative pro/SUBJPRO
(2) PUB/PRV/SUA+PRO/N+AUX/V
(3) PUB/PRV/SUA+ADJ/ADV/DET/POSSPRO+(ADJ)+N+
AUX/V

While contractions are a form of phonological (or orthographic) reduction, subordinator-*that* deletion is a form of syntactic reduction. There are very few of these deletions in edited writing, even though few explicit prescriptions prohibit this form. Apparently the concern for elaborated and explicit expression in typical edited writing is the driving force preventing this reduction. Studies that discuss the distribution of *that*-deletions include Frawley (1982), Finegan and Biber (1986a), Elsness (1984), Beaman (1984), Weber (1985), and Biber (1986a).

61. **stranded prepositions**
(e.g., *the candidate that I was thinking of*)
PREP+ALL-P/T#

Stranded prepositions represent a mismatch between surface and underlying representations, since the relative pronoun and the preposition belong to the same phrase in underlying structure. Chafe (1985) cites these forms as an example of spoken 'errors' due to the production constraints of speech.

62. **split infinitives**
(e.g., *he wants to convincingly prove that* . . .)
to + ADV + (ADV) + VB

Split infinitives are the most widely cited prescription against surface–underlying mismatches. This notoriety suggests that writers *would* use split infinitives if it were not for the prescriptions against them, but these forms in fact seem to be equally uncommon in spoken and written genres (Biber 1986a; Chafe 1984b). This feature did not co-occur meaningfully with the other features included in the present study, and it was therefore dropped from the factor analysis (Chapter 5).

63. **split auxiliaries**
(e.g., *they are objectively shown to* . . .)
AUX + ADV + (ADV) + VB

Split auxiliaries are analogous to split infinitives, but they have not received much attention from prescriptive grammarians. They are actually more common in certain written genres than in typical conversation; Biber (1986a) finds that they frequently co-occur with passives, prepositions, and nominalizations.

(O) COORDINATION (nos. 64–5)

Phrase and clause coordination have complementary functions, so that any overall count of coordinators would be hopelessly confounded. *And* as a clause coordinator is a general purpose connective that can mark many different logical relations between two clauses. Chafe (1982, 1985) relates the fragmented style resulting from this simple chaining of ideas to the production constraints of speech. *And* as a phrase coordinator, on the other hand, has an integrative function and is used for idea unit expansion (Chafe 1982, 1985; Chafe and Danielewicz 1986). Other studies that analyze the distribution and uses of *and* include Marckworth and Baker (1974), Schiffrin (1982), and Young (1985). The algorithms used in the present study identify only those uses of *and* that are clearly phrasal or clausal connectives.

64. **phrasal coordination**

xxxx1 + *and* + xxxx2

(where xxx1 and xxx2 are both: ADV/ADJ/V/N)

65. **independent clause coordination**

(a) T#/, + *and* + *it/so/then/you/there*+BE/demonstrative pronoun /SUBJPRO

(b) CL-P + *and*

(c) *and* + WHP/WHO/adverbial subordinator (nos. 35–8)/discourse particle (no. 50)/conjunct (no. 45)

(P) NEGATION (nos. 66–7)

There is twice as much negation overall in speech as in writing, a distribution that Tottie (1981, 1982, 1983b) attributes to the greater frequency of repetitions, denials, rejections, questions, and mental verbs in speech. Tottie (1983a) distinguishes between synthetic and analytic negation. Synthetic negation is more literary, and seemingly more integrated; analytic negation is more colloquial and seems to be more fragmented.

66. **synthetic negation**

(a) *no* + QUANT/ADJ/N

(b) *neither, nor*

(excludes *no* as a response)

67. **analytic negation:** *not*

(also contracted forms)

Mean frequency counts of all features in each genre

This appendix presents descriptive statistics for the frequency count of each linguistic feature in each genre. The frequency counts are all normalized to a text length of 1,000 words (except for type/token ratio and word length – see Appendix II). Further discussion of the normalization procedure is given in Section 4.5.

Mean frequencies for Press Reportage

Linguistic feature	Mean	Minimum value	Maximum value	Range	Standard deviation
past tense	45.1	7.0	110.0	103.0	21.6
perfect aspect verbs	8.0	3.0	14.0	11.0	2.8
present tense	55.8	22.0	82.0	60.0	15.9
place adverbials	4.7	0.0	24.0	24.0	4.5
time adverbials	6.5	1.0	13.0	12.0	3.1
first person pronouns	9.5	0.0	32.0	32.0	8.7
second person pronouns	1.1	0.0	5.0	5.0	1.4
third person pronouns	28.7	5.0	57.0	52.0	13.2
pronoun IT	5.8	1.0	13.0	12.0	2.9
demonstrative pronouns	1.6	0.0	5.0	5.0	1.2
indefinite pronouns	0.6	0.0	6.0	6.0	1.0
DO as pro-verb	1.3	0.0	5.0	5.0	1.3
WH questions	0.0	0.0	1.0	1.0	0.2
nominalizations	19.2	5.0	43.0	38.0	9.3
gerunds	7.8	3.0	16.0	13.0	3.2
nouns	220.5	186.0	273.0	87.0	18.5
agentless passives	11.0	2.0	22.0	20.0	4.6
BY passives	1.6	0.0	5.0	5.0	1.2
BE as main verb	20.7	10.0	38.0	28.0	5.6
existential THERE	1.8	0.0	5.0	5.0	1.3
THAT verb complements	3.3	0.0	10.0	10.0	2.4
THAT adj. complements	0.1	0.0	1.0	1.0	0.3
WH clauses	0.4	0.0	2.0	2.0	0.5
infinitives	13.8	5.0	22.0	17.0	4.3
present participial clauses	0.6	0.0	3.0	3.0	0.7
past participial clauses	0.2	0.0	1.0	1.0	0.4
past prt. WHIZ deletions	3.1	0.0	14.0	14.0	2.3
present prt. WHIZ deletions	2.5	0.0	6.0	6.0	1.4
THAT relatives: subj. position	0.2	0.0	1.0	1.0	0.4
THAT relatives: obj. position	0.8	0.0	3.0	3.0	0.9
WH relatives: subj. position	2.0	0.0	4.0	4.0	1.0
WH relatives: obj. position	1.0	0.0	3.0	3.0	1.0
WH relatives: pied pipes	0.6	0.0	3.0	3.0	0.8
sentence relatives	0.0	0.0	0.0	0.0	0.0
adv. subordinator - cause	0.5	0.0	3.0	3.0	0.8
adv. sub. - concession	0.4	0.0	2.0	2.0	0.5
adv. sub. - condition	1.4	0.0	5.0	5.0	1.3
adv. sub. - other	1.0	0.0	3.0	3.0	0.8
prepositions	116.6	90.0	148.0	58.0	13.1
attributive adjectives	64.5	30.0	90.0	60.0	14.0
predicative adjectives	3.0	0.0	8.0	8.0	1.8
adverbs	52.8	27.0	83.0	56.0	12.2
type/token ratio	55.3	46.0	63.0	17.0	4.4
word length	4.7	4.2	4.9	0.7	0.2
conjuncts	0.6	0.0	4.0	4.0	1.0
downtoners	1.6	0.0	5.0	5.0	1.4
hedges	0.2	0.0	1.0	1.0	0.4
amplifiers	0.9	0.0	4.0	4.0	1.1
emphatics	4.2	1.0	10.0	9.0	2.1
discourse particles	0.0	0.0	1.0	1.0	0.2
demonstratives	7.4	2.0	16.0	14.0	2.8
possibility modals	3.2	0.0	8.0	8.0	1.8
necessity modals	1.7	0.0	8.0	8.0	1.6
predictive modals	6.1	1.0	13.0	12.0	2.8
public verbs	12.0	2.0	28.0	26.0	6.5
private verbs	10.4	3.0	23.0	20.0	4.1
suasive verbs	3.0	0.0	7.0	7.0	1.8
SEEM/APPEAR	0.5	0.0	2.0	2.0	0.7
contractions	1.8	0.0	10.0	10.0	3.1
THAT deletion	2.0	0.0	9.0	9.0	2.0
stranded prepositions	0.5	0.0	3.0	3.0	0.8
split infinitives	0.0	0.0	0.0	0.0	0.0
split auxiliaries	5.4	1.0	10.0	9.0	2.2
phrasal coordination	4.1	0.0	8.0	8.0	2.0
non-phrasal coordination	2.3	0.0	6.0	6.0	1.7
synthetic negation	1.5	0.0	6.0	6.0	1.3
analytic negation	4.7	0.0	9.0	9.0	2.2

Mean frequencies for Press Editorials

Linguistic feature	Mean	Minimum value	Maximum value	Range	Standard deviation
past tense	18.1	3.0	61.0	58.0	12.2
perfect aspect verbs	9.7	5.0	16.0	11.0	3.0
present tense	81.8	49.0	104.0	55.0	12.6
place adverbials	4.0	1.0	13.0	12.0	2.7
time adverbials	4.2	1.0	7.0	6.0	1.9
first person pronouns	11.2	2.0	34.0	32.0	7.6
second person pronouns	1.6	0.0	10.0	10.0	2.6
third person pronouns	21.9	8.0	58.0	50.0	10.8
pronoun IT	9.3	4.0	17.0	13.0	3.2
demonstrative pronouns	2.9	0.0	7.0	7.0	1.6
indefinite pronouns	0.6	0.0	2.0	2.0	0.8
DO as pro-verb	1.9	0.0	4.0	4.0	1.2
WH questions	0.3	0.0	2.0	2.0	0.6
nominalizations	27.6	14.0	45.0	31.0	7.9
gerunds	7.4	3.0	14.0	11.0	2.7
nouns	201.0	178.0	233.0	55.0	16.6
agentless passives	11.7	7.0	19.0	12.0	2.9
BY passives	0.8	0.0	4.0	4.0	0.9
BE as main verb	28.9	17.0	43.0	26.0	5.8
existential THERE	3.2	1.0	7.0	6.0	1.8
THAT verb complements	3.9	0.0	8.0	8.0	2.1
THAT adj. complements	0.4	0.0	1.0	1.0	0.5
WH clauses	0.4	0.0	2.0	2.0	0.6
infinitives	17.6	9.0	25.0	16.0	3.6
present participial clauses	0.3	0.0	2.0	2.0	0.6
past participial clauses	0.1	0.0	1.0	1.0	0.3
past prt. WHIZ deletions	2.9	1.0	5.0	4.0	1.3
present prt. WHIZ deletions	2.0	0.0	6.0	6.0	1.5
THAT relatives: subj. position	0.4	0.0	2.0	2.0	0.6
THAT relatives: obj. position	1.4	0.0	4.0	4.0	0.9
WH relatives: subj. position	3.1	1.0	7.0	6.0	1.5
WH relatives: obj. position	1.6	0.0	4.0	4.0	1.4
WH relatives: pied pipes	0.7	0.0	4.0	4.0	0.9
sentence relatives	0.1	0.0	1.0	1.0	0.3
adv. subordinator - cause	0.7	0.0	4.0	4.0	1.0
adv. sub. - concession	0.3	0.0	2.0	2.0	0.6
adv. sub. - condition	2.7	0.0	6.0	6.0	1.8
adv. sub. - other	0.8	0.0	3.0	3.0	0.8
prepositions	116.3	101.0	138.0	37.0	8.4
attributive adjectives	74.4	47.0	89.0	42.0	8.9
predicative adjectives	5.6	3.0	10.0	7.0	1.9
adverbs	60.4	46.0	77.0	31.0	8.5
type/token ratio	54.4	48.0	62.0	14.0	3.3
word length	4.7	4.4	4.9	0.6	0.1
conjuncts	1.6	0.0	6.0	6.0	1.6
downtoners	2.6	0.0	6.0	6.0	1.6
hedges	0.3	0.0	2.0	2.0	0.7
amplifiers	1.1	0.0	3.0	3.0	0.8
emphatics	5.9	2.0	12.0	10.0	2.3
discourse particles	0.2	0.0	2.0	2.0	0.5
demonstratives	11.7	7.0	17.0	10.0	2.4
possibility modals	6.4	2.0	10.0	8.0	2.1
necessity modals	4.0	0.0	8.0	8.0	2.4
predictive modals	7.7	3.0	21.0	18.0	3.7
public verbs	6.8	2.0	12.0	10.0	2.8
private verbs	11.4	6.0	17.0	11.0	2.8
suasive verbs	4.0	1.0	11.0	10.0	2.3
SEEM/APPEAR	0.7	0.0	4.0	4.0	1.0
contractions	0.8	0.0	7.0	7.0	1.9
THAT deletion	0.8	0.0	4.0	4.0	1.1
stranded prepositions	0.3	0.0	3.0	3.0	0.7
split infinitives	0.0	0.0	0.0	0.0	0.0
split auxiliaries	7.2	2.0	11.0	9.0	2.0
phrasal coordination	4.4	2.0	9.0	7.0	1.7
non-phrasal coordination	2.1	0.0	6.0	6.0	1.6
synthetic negation	2.8	1.0	6.0	5.0	1.2
analytic negation	6.6	2.0	10.0	8.0	2.2

Mean frequencies for Press Reviews

Linguistic feature	Mean	Minimum value	Maximum value	Range	Standard deviation
past tense	18.2	2.0	39.0	37.0	11.4
perfect aspect verbs	6.8	3.0	11.0	8.0	2.4
present tense	70.9	45.0	91.0	46.0	12.9
place adverbials	1.9	0.0	4.0	4.0	1.1
time adverbials	4.3	2.0	8.0	6.0	1.8
first person pronouns	7.5	1.0	20.0	19.0	5.7
second person pronouns	1.2	0.0	6.0	6.0	1.7
third person pronouns	33.6	15.0	62.0	47.0	12.1
pronoun IT	7.9	4.0	17.0	13.0	3.3
demonstrative pronouns	1.9	0.0	6.0	6.0	1.6
indefinite pronouns	1.0	0.0	3.0	3.0	1.0
DO as pro-verb	1.1	0.0	3.0	3.0	1.1
WH questions	0.0	0.0	0.0	0.0	0.0
nominalizations	21.6	11.0	36.0	25.0	7.6
gerunds	8.2	4.0	13.0	9.0	2.9
nouns	208.3	180.0	250.0	70.0	21.5
agentless passives	8.6	5.0	12.0	7.0	2.1
BY passives	1.4	0.0	4.0	4.0	1.2
BE as main verb	25.5	13.0	36.0	23.0	6.4
existential THERE	1.2	0.0	3.0	3.0	0.9
THAT verb complements	1.8	0.0	6.0	6.0	1.4
THAT adj. complements	0.1	0.0	1.0	1.0	0.3
WH clauses	0.4	0.0	1.0	1.0	0.5
infinitives	11.6	8.0	17.0	9.0	2.7
present participial clauses	0.5	0.0	2.0	2.0	0.7
past participial clauses	0.2	0.0	1.0	1.0	0.4
past prt. WHIZ deletions	3.8	1.0	6.0	5.0	1.4
present prt. WHIZ deletions	2.5	0.0	5.0	5.0	1.5
THAT relatives: subj. position	0.6	0.0	2.0	2.0	0.8
THAT relatives: obj. position	0.9	0.0	3.0	3.0	0.8
WH relatives: subj. position	3.5	1.0	6.0	5.0	1.5
WH relatives: obj. position	2.6	0.0	5.0	5.0	1.6
WH relatives: pied pipes	1.5	0.0	4.0	4.0	1.2
sentence relatives	0.0	0.0	0.0	0.0	0.0
adv. subordinator - cause	0.2	0.0	1.0	1.0	0.4
adv. sub. - concession	0.7	0.0	2.0	2.0	0.8
adv. sub. - condition	1.1	0.0	3.0	3.0	0.9
adv. sub. - other	0.8	0.0	3.0	3.0	1.0
prepositions	119.3	102.0	141.0	39.0	12.3
attributive adjectives	82.3	62.0	100.0	38.0	12.5
predicative adjectives	3.2	0.0	7.0	7.0	1.9
adverbs	60.8	34.0	77.0	43.0	12.1
type/token ratio	56.5	49.0	64.0	15.0	4.4
word length	4.7	4.5	4.9	0.5	0.1
conjuncts	1.2	0.0	4.0	4.0	1.2
downtoners	2.3	0.0	4.0	4.0	1.2
hedges	0.4	0.0	1.0	1.0	0.5
amplifiers	2.0	0.0	4.0	4.0	1.2
emphatics	6.5	2.0	9.0	7.0	1.9
discourse particles	0.2	0.0	1.0	1.0	0.4
demonstratives	8.7	3.0	13.0	10.0	3.1
possibility modals	3.5	1.0	7.0	6.0	1.7
necessity modals	1.1	0.0	4.0	4.0	1.2
predictive modals	3.0	1.0	13.0	12.0	2.9
public verbs	4.9	1.0	10.0	9.0	2.8
private verbs	11.3	7.0	14.0	7.0	2.5
suasive verbs	1.9	0.0	4.0	4.0	1.3
SEEM/APPEAR	1.4	0.0	4.0	4.0	1.1
contractions	1.9	0.0	13.0	13.0	3.6
THAT deletion	0.5	0.0	2.0	2.0	0.6
stranded prepositions	0.5	0.0	2.0	2.0	0.7
split infinitives	0.0	0.0	0.0	0.0	0.0
split auxiliaries	4.8	1.0	9.0	8.0	2.2
phrasal coordination	6.5	2.0	12.0	10.0	2.4
non-phrasal coordination	1.8	0.0	4.0	4.0	1.0
synthetic negation	2.0	0.0	5.0	5.0	1.5
analytic negation	6.0	1.0	13.0	12.0	3.0

Mean frequencies for Religion

Linguistic feature	Mean	Minimum value	Maximum value	Range	Standard deviation
past tense	26.1	4.0	85.0	81.0	19.1
perfect aspect verbs	6.1	1.0	12.0	11.0	3.4
present tense	79.4	30.0	106.0	76.0	20.3
place adverbials	2.2	0.0	11.0	11.0	2.7
time adverbials	3.1	0.0	6.0	6.0	2.0
first person pronouns	16.6	0.0	35.0	35.0	12.5
second person pronouns	2.9	0.0	20.0	20.0	5.4
third person pronouns	22.5	5.0	60.0	55.0	13.1
pronoun IT	9.6	5.0	15.0	10.0	3.6
demonstrative pronouns	3.6	0.0	10.0	10.0	2.4
indefinite pronouns	0.9	0.0	5.0	5.0	1.4
DO as pro-verb	2.2	0.0	10.0	10.0	3.1
WH questions	0.1	0.0	1.0	1.0	0.3
nominalizations	26.8	11.0	50.0	39.0	10.8
gerunds	9.3	3.0	19.0	16.0	4.6
nouns	187.7	149.0	225.0	76.0	22.4
agentless passives	14.6	8.0	25.0	17.0	5.1
BY passives	1.1	0.0	3.0	3.0	1.1
BE as main verb	30.4	19.0	44.0	25.0	6.2
existential THERE	2.5	0.0	7.0	7.0	1.9
THAT verb complements	4.3	1.0	10.0	9.0	2.3
THAT adj. complements	0.2	0.0	1.0	1.0	0.4
WH clauses	0.8	0.0	5.0	5.0	1.2
infinitives	14.9	6.0	33.0	27.0	7.4
present participial clauses	0.4	0.0	2.0	2.0	0.6
past participial clauses	0.1	0.0	1.0	1.0	0.2
past prt. WHIZ deletions	3.4	0.0	7.0	7.0	2.3
present prt. WHIZ deletions	1.4	0.0	4.0	4.0	1.3
THAT relatives: subj. position	0.6	0.0	4.0	4.0	1.1
THAT relatives: obj. position	0.6	0.0	3.0	3.0	0.9
WH relatives: subj. position	2.8	0.0	7.0	7.0	1.9
WH relatives: obj. position	2.3	0.0	7.0	7.0	1.9
WH relatives: pied pipes	0.9	0.0	3.0	3.0	1.1
sentence relatives	0.0	0.0	0.0	0.0	0.0
adv. subordinator - cause	0.6	0.0	3.0	3.0	0.9
adv. sub. - concession	0.4	0.0	2.0	2.0	0.7
adv. sub. - condition	2.1	0.0	9.0	9.0	2.7
adv. sub. - other	0.8	0.0	3.0	3.0	1.2
prepositions	117.7	83.0	135.0	52.0	15.3
attributive adjectives	59.5	31.0	97.0	66.0	16.6
predicative adjectives	5.2	2.0	12.0	10.0	2.7
adverbs	54.1	32.0	84.0	52.0	14.5
type/token ratio	50.1	44.0	55.0	11.0	3.3
word length	4.5	4.2	5.0	0.8	0.2
conjuncts	1.9	0.0	5.0	5.0	1.5
downtoners	2.6	0.0	6.0	6.0	1.6
hedges	0.0	0.0	0.0	0.0	0.0
amplifiers	1.5	0.0	4.0	4.0	1.2
emphatics	4.0	1.0	10.0	9.0	2.1
discourse particles	0.1	0.0	1.0	1.0	0.2
demonstratives	13.5	6.0	21.0	15.0	4.4
possibility modals	5.4	2.0	12.0	10.0	2.8
necessity modals	2.2	0.0	7.0	7.0	1.8
predictive modals	6.0	2.0	15.0	13.0	4.0
public verbs	9.4	4.0	25.0	21.0	5.5
private verbs	14.5	7.0	24.0	17.0	5.7
suasive verbs	2.9	0.0	7.0	7.0	2.2
SEEM/APPEAR	0.5	0.0	4.0	4.0	1.1
contractions	1.8	0.0	30.0	30.0	7.3
THAT deletion	0.9	0.0	4.0	4.0	1.2
stranded prepositions	0.5	0.0	2.0	2.0	0.6
split infinitives	0.0	0.0	0.0	0.0	0.0
split auxiliaries	5.9	2.0	9.0	7.0	2.2
phrasal coordination	5.0	0.0	12.0	12.0	3.0
non-phrasal coordination	2.9	0.0	12.0	12.0	2.9
synthetic negation	2.8	0.0	7.0	7.0	2.2
analytic negation	7.0	3.0	21.0	18.0	4.6

Mean frequencies for Hobbies

Linguistic feature	Mean	Minimum value	Maximum value	Range	Standard deviation
past tense	17.6	0.0	54.0	54.0	16.8
perfect aspect verbs	5.6	1.0	11.0	10.0	3.1
present tense	79.7	46.0	102.0	56.0	18.1
place adverbials	3.4	0.0	9.0	9.0	2.5
time adverbials	4.4	1.0	9.0	8.0	2.5
first person pronouns	14.9	0.0	59.0	59.0	15.2
second person pronouns	4.2	0.0	16.0	16.0	5.3
third person pronouns	14.1	4.0	44.0	40.0	10.9
pronoun IT	7.6	2.0	14.0	12.0	3.8
demonstrative pronouns	3.2	0.0	8.0	8.0	2.2
indefinite pronouns	0.8	0.0	2.0	2.0	0.6
DO as pro-verb	1.2	0.0	6.0	6.0	1.7
WH questions	0.0	0.0	0.0	0.0	0.0
nominalizations	13.1	8.0	20.0	12.0	4.1
gerunds	10.4	5.0	17.0	12.0	3.4
nouns	199.1	174.0	237.0	63.0	20.5
agentless passives	15.4	8.0	30.0	22.0	6.9
BY passives	0.8	0.0	2.0	2.0	0.9
BE as main verb	24.0	13.0	32.0	19.0	6.1
existential THERE	1.5	0.0	4.0	4.0	1.2
THAT verb complements	2.7	1.0	6.0	5.0	1.3
THAT adj. complements	0.2	0.0	1.0	1.0	0.4
WH clauses	0.1	0.0	1.0	1.0	0.3
infinitives	18.3	9.0	27.0	18.0	5.3
present participial clauses	1.6	0.0	3.0	3.0	0.9
past participial clauses	0.2	0.0	3.0	3.0	0.8
past prt. WHIZ deletions	2.7	0.0	6.0	6.0	2.0
present prt. WHIZ deletions	1.6	0.0	5.0	5.0	1.7
THAT relatives: subj. position	0.4	0.0	1.0	1.0	0.5
THAT relatives: obj. position	0.4	0.0	3.0	3.0	0.8
WH relatives: subj. position	1.6	0.0	4.0	4.0	1.1
WH relatives: obj. position	1.6	0.0	9.0	9.0	2.4
WH relatives: pied pipes	0.9	0.0	5.0	5.0	1.3
sentence relatives	0.0	0.0	0.0	0.0	0.0
adv. subordinator - cause	0.5	0.0	3.0	3.0	0.9
adv. sub. - concession	0.6	0.0	2.0	2.0	0.8
adv. sub. - condition	2.5	0.0	9.0	9.0	2.6
adv. sub. - other	1.0	0.0	3.0	3.0	1.1
prepositions	114.6	106.0	132.0	26.0	7.8
attributive adjectives	72.0	55.0	87.0	32.0	10.6
predicative adjectives	5.4	2.0	12.0	10.0	2.4
adverbs	62.1	38.0	89.0	51.0	14.5
type/token ratio	53.2	44.0	59.0	15.0	4.4
word length	4.5	4.2	4.8	0.6	0.2
conjuncts	1.3	0.0	5.0	5.0	1.4
downtoners	2.2	0.0	6.0	6.0	1.8
hedges	0.4	0.0	2.0	2.0	0.8
amplifiers	2.3	0.0	6.0	6.0	1.8
emphatics	6.1	2.0	13.0	11.0	3.4
discourse particles	0.2	0.0	1.0	1.0	0.4
demonstratives	10.2	3.0	17.0	14.0	3.7
possibility modals	6.8	1.0	14.0	13.0	3.9
necessity modals	3.1	0.0	9.0	9.0	3.0
predictive modals	5.7	0.0	12.0	12.0	3.0
public verbs	3.3	0.0	9.0	9.0	2.4
private verbs	10.3	6.0	15.0	9.0	3.3
suasive verbs	2.9	0.0	8.0	8.0	2.2
SEEM/APPEAR	0.6	0.0	3.0	3.0	1.1
contractions	1.4	0.0	11.0	11.0	2.9
THAT deletion	0.5	0.0	3.0	3.0	0.9
stranded prepositions	0.9	0.0	5.0	5.0	1.3
split infinitives	0.0	0.0	0.0	0.0	0.0
split auxiliaries	6.6	2.0	12.0	10.0	3.2
phrasal coordination	4.4	2.0	9.0	7.0	2.2
non-phrasal coordination	2.6	0.0	7.0	7.0	2.2
synthetic negation	1.1	0.0	4.0	4.0	1.4
analytic negation	4.3	0.0	9.0	9.0	2.6

Mean frequencies for Popular Lore

Linguistic feature	Mean	Minimum value	Maximum value	Range	Standard deviation
past tense	40.0	1.0	87.0	86.0	28.1
perfect aspect verbs	8.0	2.0	28.0	26.0	6.7
present tense	65.9	22.0	127.0	105.0	32.6
place adverbials	2.8	0.0	5.0	5.0	1.7
time adverbials	3.4	1.0	9.0	8.0	2.3
first person pronouns	11.7	0.0	55.0	55.0	16.9
second person pronouns	12.0	0.0	67.0	67.0	23.5
third person pronouns	33.9	15.0	70.0	55.0	15.6
pronoun IT	8.4	3.0	15.0	12.0	3.7
demonstrative pronouns	2.1	0.0	5.0	5.0	1.7
indefinite pronouns	1.0	0.0	4.0	4.0	1.1
DO as pro-verb	1.5	0.0	4.0	4.0	1.1
WH questions	0.1	0.0	1.0	1.0	0.3
nominalizations	21.8	4.0	49.0	45.0	12.3
gerunds	9.6	5.0	13.0	8.0	3.1
nouns	195.4	161.0	229.0	68.0	23.2
agentless passives	10.6	2.0	18.0	16.0	5.1
BY passives	0.9	0.0	4.0	4.0	1.3
BE as main verb	24.3	12.0	35.0	23.0	6.0
existential THERE	1.6	0.0	4.0	4.0	1.4
THAT verb complements	2.7	0.0	8.0	8.0	2.6
THAT adj. complements	0.2	0.0	1.0	1.0	0.4
WH clauses	0.6	0.0	3.0	3.0	0.9
infinitives	17.3	11.0	30.0	19.0	5.7
present participial clauses	1.0	0.0	3.0	3.0	1.0
past participial clauses	0.0	0.0	0.0	0.0	0.0
past prt. WHIZ deletions	3.7	0.0	12.0	12.0	3.3
present prt. WHIZ deletions	2.6	0.0	7.0	7.0	2.1
THAT relatives: subj. position	0.4	0.0	1.0	1.0	0.5
THAT relatives: obj. position	1.1	0.0	3.0	3.0	1.0
WH relatives: subj. position	3.0	0.0	6.0	6.0	1.8
WH relatives: obj. position	1.5	0.0	5.0	5.0	1.3
WH relatives: pied pipes	1.0	0.0	4.0	4.0	1.2
sentence relatives	0.0	0.0	0.0	0.0	0.0
adv. subordinator - cause	0.5	0.0	3.0	3.0	0.9
adv. sub. - concession	0.7	0.0	3.0	3.0	1.1
adv. sub. - condition	2.1	0.0	10.0	10.0	2.9
adv. sub. - other	0.6	0.0	2.0	2.0	0.8
prepositions	114.8	92.0	148.0	56.0	16.0
attributive adjectives	68.5	40.0	96.0	56.0	17.1
predicative adjectives	4.1	1.0	7.0	6.0	2.0
adverbs	57.6	37.0	76.0	39.0	10.4
type/token ratio	53.7	47.0	58.0	11.0	3.8
word length	4.6	4.1	5.3	1.2	0.3
conjuncts	1.6	0.0	4.0	4.0	1.3
downtoners	1.7	0.0	4.0	4.0	1.1
hedges	0.6	0.0	3.0	3.0	0.9
amplifiers	1.6	0.0	3.0	3.0	1.0
emphatics	5.4	1.0	11.0	10.0	2.7
discourse particles	0.1	0.0	1.0	1.0	0.3
demonstratives	6.6	3.0	10.0	7.0	2.2
possibility modals	4.4	1.0	10.0	9.0	3.3
necessity modals	1.6	0.0	11.0	11.0	2.9
predictive modals	5.4	0.0	13.0	13.0	4.2
public verbs	6.1	2.0	13.0	11.0	2.8
private verbs	17.3	7.0	33.0	26.0	8.0
suasive verbs	2.4	0.0	8.0	8.0	2.2
SEEM/APPEAR	0.6	0.0	1.0	1.0	0.5
contractions	2.6	0.0	12.0	12.0	4.5
THAT deletion	1.9	0.0	7.0	7.0	2.2
stranded prepositions	0.6	0.0	2.0	2.0	0.7
split infinitives	0.0	0.0	0.0	0.0	0.0
split auxiliaries	5.1	2.0	10.0	8.0	2.3
phrasal coordination	4.4	1.0	9.0	8.0	2.3
non-phrasal coordination	2.9	0.0	10.0	10.0	3.0
synthetic negation	2.0	0.0	6.0	6.0	2.0
analytic negation	5.1	1.0	13.0	12.0	3.4

Mean frequencies for Biographies

Linguistic feature	Mean	Minimum value	Maximum value	Range	Standard deviation
past tense	68.4	35.0	94.0	59.0	16.4
perfect aspect verbs	10.6	1.0	29.0	28.0	6.7
present tense	35.9	17.0	90.0	73.0	18.2
place adverbials	2.0	0.0	5.0	5.0	1.5
time adverbials	5.0	1.0	10.0	9.0	2.3
first person pronouns	22.1	0.0	80.0	80.0	24.1
second person pronouns	0.6	0.0	3.0	3.0	0.9
third person pronouns	34.3	9.0	85.0	76.0	20.2
pronoun IT	7.6	4.0	12.0	8.0	2.7
demonstrative pronouns	0.9	0.0	3.0	3.0	0.9
indefinite pronouns	1.0	0.0	4.0	4.0	1.1
DO as pro-verb	1.2	0.0	5.0	5.0	1.4
WH questions	0.0	0.0	0.0	0.0	0.0
nominalizations	20.6	5.0	33.0	28.0	9.6
gerunds	6.9	3.0	11.0	8.0	2.2
nouns	192.4	144.0	226.0	82.0	20.7
agentless passives	9.9	5.0	15.0	10.0	3.1
BY passives	0.9	0.0	2.0	2.0	0.8
BE as main verb	24.2	15.0	37.0	22.0	6.0
existential THERE	1.9	0.0	4.0	4.0	1.2
THAT verb complements	2.5	0.0	5.0	5.0	1.6
THAT adj. complements	0.3	0.0	2.0	2.0	0.6
WH clauses	0.6	0.0	7.0	7.0	1.9
infinitives	16.9	7.0	23.0	16.0	4.1
present participial clauses	1.3	0.0	3.0	3.0	1.3
past participial clauses	0.0	0.0	0.0	0.0	0.0
past prt. WHIZ deletions	1.8	0.0	6.0	6.0	1.7
present prt. WHIZ deletions	1.6	0.0	4.0	4.0	1.2
THAT relatives: subj. position	0.4	0.0	4.0	4.0	1.2
THAT relatives: obj. position	0.6	0.0	2.0	2.0	0.6
WH relatives: subj. position	2.5	0.0	7.0	7.0	2.0
WH relatives: obj. position	1.9	0.0	5.0	5.0	1.6
WH relatives: pied pipes	1.0	0.0	3.0	3.0	1.0
sentence relatives	0.0	0.0	0.0	0.0	0.0
adv. subordinator - cause	0.3	0.0	2.0	2.0	0.6
adv. sub. - concession	0.3	0.0	2.0	2.0	0.6
adv. sub. - condition	0.9	0.0	3.0	3.0	0.9
adv. sub. - other	1.1	0.0	3.0	3.0	1.1
prepositions	122.6	105.0	149.0	44.0	13.8
attributive adjectives	66.4	49.0	90.0	41.0	12.1
predicative adjectives	3.1	0.0	6.0	6.0	1.8
adverbs	65.9	43.0	100.0	57.0	14.2
type/token ratio	55.2	51.0	60.0	9.0	2.6
word length	4.5	4.2	4.8	0.6	0.2
conjuncts	1.0	0.0	5.0	5.0	1.5
downtoners	1.7	0.0	4.0	4.0	1.1
hedges	0.1	0.0	1.0	1.0	0.4
amplifiers	2.7	0.0	7.0	7.0	2.1
emphatics	4.2	1.0	8.0	7.0	2.2
discourse particles	0.0	0.0	0.0	0.0	0.0
demonstratives	10.7	6.0	22.0	16.0	4.3
possibility modals	4.0	1.0	7.0	6.0	1.7
necessity modals	1.3	0.0	3.0	3.0	1.1
predictive modals	3.3	0.0	7.0	7.0	1.8
public verbs	7.1	2.0	14.0	12.0	3.3
private verbs	13.6	8.0	22.0	14.0	3.5
suasive verbs	3.2	0.0	8.0	8.0	2.3
SEEM/APPEAR	0.8	0.0	2.0	2.0	0.8
contractions	0.9	0.0	3.0	3.0	1.3
THAT deletion	1.2	0.0	6.0	6.0	2.0
stranded prepositions	0.6	0.0	3.0	3.0	0.9
split infinitives	0.0	0.0	0.0	0.0	0.0
split auxiliaries	6.6	4.0	12.0	8.0	2.0
phrasal coordination	4.9	2.0	9.0	7.0	1.8
non-phrasal coordination	2.4	0.0	8.0	8.0	2.2
synthetic negation	2.6	0.0	6.0	6.0	1.8
analytic negation	6.2	2.0	13.0	11.0	2.9

Mean frequencies for Official Documents

Linguistic feature	Mean	Minimum value	Maximum value	Range	Standard deviation
past tense	16.2	0.0	44.0	44.0	15.1
perfect aspect verbs	7.9	2.0	18.0	16.0	5.1
present tense	59.1	21.0	84.0	63.0	19.1
place adverbials	2.1	0.0	6.0	6.0	1.9
time adverbials	3.4	0.0	9.0	9.0	2.5
first person pronouns	10.0	0.0	38.0	38.0	15.0
second person pronouns	1.4	0.0	10.0	10.0	3.0
third person pronouns	10.1	3.0	16.0	13.0	4.4
pronoun IT	3.2	0.0	6.0	6.0	1.9
demonstrative pronouns	1.1	0.0	5.0	5.0	1.4
indefinite pronouns	0.2	0.0	1.0	1.0	0.4
DO as pro-verb	0.6	0.0	2.0	2.0	0.8
WH questions	0.0	0.0	0.0	0.0	0.0
nominalizations	39.8	14.0	69.0	55.0	17.7
gerunds	10.6	2.0	16.0	14.0	4.1
nouns	206.5	183.0	257.0	74.0	23.2
agentless passives	18.6	8.0	31.0	23.0	6.5
BY passives	2.1	0.0	5.0	5.0	1.4
BE as main verb	16.5	7.0	27.0	20.0	6.8
existential THERE	2.0	0.0	5.0	5.0	1.5
THAT verb complements	1.4	0.0	4.0	4.0	1.3
THAT adj. complements	0.2	0.0	1.0	1.0	0.4
WH clauses	0.2	0.0	1.0	1.0	0.4
infinitives	13.4	2.0	24.0	22.0	6.0
present participial clauses	0.3	0.0	1.0	1.0	0.5
past participial clauses	0.5	0.0	3.0	3.0	0.9
past prt. WHIZ deletions	7.5	4.0	11.0	7.0	2.3
present prt. WHIZ deletions	4.0	0.0	9.0	9.0	2.7
THAT relatives: subj. position	0.2	0.0	1.0	1.0	0.4
THAT relatives: obj. position	0.7	0.0	2.0	2.0	0.6
WH relatives: subj. position	2.7	0.0	5.0	5.0	1.6
WH relatives: obj. position	3.0	1.0	6.0	5.0	1.5
WH relatives: pied pipes	2.0	0.0	4.0	4.0	1.4
sentence relatives	0.1	0.0	1.0	1.0	0.3
adv. subordinator - cause	0.1	0.0	1.0	1.0	0.4
adv. sub. - concession	0.4	0.0	3.0	3.0	0.9
adv. sub. - condition	1.0	0.0	3.0	3.0	1.0
adv. sub. - other	0.9	0.0	3.0	3.0	0.9
prepositions	150.9	109.0	209.0	100.0	25.3
attributive adjectives	77.9	52.0	110.0	58.0	16.7
predicative adjectives	4.3	2.0	11.0	9.0	2.3
adverbs	43.7	22.0	66.0	44.0	10.5
type/token ratio	47.8	38.0	55.0	17.0	5.7
word length	4.9	4.5	5.1	0.6	0.2
conjuncts	1.2	0.0	3.0	3.0	1.0
downtoners	1.9	0.0	7.0	7.0	2.0
hedges	0.0	0.0	0.0	0.0	0.0
amplifiers	0.9	0.0	3.0	3.0	1.1
emphatics	4.0	0.0	15.0	15.0	4.7
discourse particles	0.0	0.0	0.0	0.0	0.0
demonstratives	9.6	2.0	18.0	16.0	4.1
possibility modals	5.0	0.0	14.0	14.0	4.2
necessity modals	2.2	0.0	13.0	13.0	3.4
predictive modals	4.9	0.0	16.0	16.0	5.0
public verbs	4.9	1.0	12.0	11.0	3.3
private verbs	7.8	2.0	13.0	11.0	3.7
suasive verbs	5.2	0.0	13.0	13.0	3.3
SEEM/APPEAR	0.4	0.0	2.0	2.0	0.6
contractions	0.0	0.0	0.0	0.0	0.0
THAT deletion	0.8	0.0	4.0	4.0	1.2
stranded prepositions	0.3	0.0	1.0	1.0	0.5
split infinitives	0.0	0.0	0.0	0.0	0.0
split auxiliaries	5.7	1.0	11.0	10.0	2.6
phrasal coordination	7.3	1.0	12.0	11.0	3.0
non-phrasal coordination	1.2	0.0	6.0	6.0	1.8
synthetic negation	1.5	0.0	3.0	3.0	1.3
analytic negation	3.4	0.0	8.0	8.0	2.2

Mean frequencies for Academic Prose

Linguistic feature	Mean	Minimum value	Maximum value	Range	Standard deviation
past tense	21.9	0.0	84.0	84.0	21.1
perfect aspect verbs	4.9	0.0	16.0	16.0	3.5
present tense	63.7	12.0	114.0	102.0	23.1
place adverbials	2.4	0.0	21.0	21.0	3.3
time adverbials	2.8	0.0	10.0	10.0	2.1
first person pronouns	5.7	0.0	29.0	29.0	7.4
second person pronouns	0.2	0.0	13.0	13.0	1.5
third person pronouns	11.5	0.0	46.0	46.0	10.6
pronoun IT	5.9	1.0	16.0	15.0	3.4
demonstrative pronouns	2.5	0.0	9.0	9.0	1.9
indefinite pronouns	0.2	0.0	10.0	10.0	1.2
DO as pro-verb	0.7	0.0	9.0	9.0	1.3
WH questions	0.0	0.0	0.0	0.0	0.0
nominalizations	35.8	11.0	71.0	60.0	13.3
gerunds	8.5	2.0	23.0	21.0	4.2
nouns	188.1	84.0	242.0	158.0	24.0
agentless passives	17.0	7.0	38.0	31.0	7.4
BY passives	2.0	0.0	8.0	8.0	1.7
BE as main verb	23.8	11.0	49.0	38.0	6.7
existential THERE	1.8	0.0	11.0	11.0	1.7
THAT verb complements	3.2	0.0	10.0	10.0	2.4
THAT adj. complements	0.4	0.0	3.0	3.0	0.7
WH clauses	0.3	0.0	4.0	4.0	0.8
infinitives	12.8	4.0	34.0	30.0	6.0
present participial clauses	1.3	0.0	7.0	7.0	1.5
past participial clauses	0.4	0.0	3.0	3.0	0.7
past prt. WHIZ deletions	5.6	0.0	21.0	21.0	3.8
present prt. WHIZ deletions	2.5	0.0	9.0	9.0	2.2
THAT relatives: subj. position	0.2	0.0	3.0	3.0	0.5
THAT relatives: obj. position	0.8	0.0	5.0	5.0	1.0
WH relatives: subj. position	2.6	0.0	10.0	10.0	2.1
WH relatives: obj. position	2.0	0.0	9.0	9.0	1.7
WH relatives: pied pipes	1.3	0.0	7.0	7.0	1.2
sentence relatives	0.0	0.0	0.0	0.0	0.0
adv. subordinator - cause	0.3	0.0	4.0	4.0	0.7
adv. sub. - concession	0.5	0.0	2.0	2.0	0.7
adv. sub. - condition	2.1	0.0	9.0	9.0	2.1
adv. sub. - other	1.8	0.0	6.0	6.0	1.5
prepositions	139.5	95.0	185.0	90.0	16.7
attributive adjectives	76.9	32.0	115.0	83.0	16.1
predicative adjectives	5.0	1.0	11.0	10.0	2.1
adverbs	51.8	30.0	77.0	47.0	10.3
type/token ratio	50.6	39.0	62.0	23.0	5.2
word length	4.8	4.0	5.3	1.3	0.2
conjuncts	3.0	0.0	12.0	12.0	2.1
downtoners	2.5	0.0	10.0	10.0	1.8
hedges	0.2	0.0	2.0	2.0	0.5
amplifiers	1.4	0.0	6.0	6.0	1.5
emphatics	3.6	0.0	10.0	10.0	2.3
discourse particles	0.0	0.0	2.0	2.0	0.2
demonstratives	11.4	4.0	22.0	18.0	4.6
possibility modals	5.6	0.0	14.0	14.0	3.1
necessity modals	2.2	0.0	11.0	11.0	2.3
predictive modals	3.7	0.0	14.0	14.0	3.4
public verbs	5.7	0.0	28.0	28.0	4.7
private verbs	12.5	2.0	30.0	28.0	5.8
suasive verbs	4.0	0.0	36.0	36.0	5.8
SEEM/APPEAR	1.0	0.0	4.0	4.0	1.2
contractions	0.1	0.0	4.0	4.0	0.6
THAT deletion	0.4	0.0	3.0	3.0	0.7
stranded prepositions	1.1	0.0	23.0	23.0	2.9
split infinitives	0.0	0.0	0.0	0.0	0.0
split auxiliaries	5.8	1.0	11.0	10.0	2.5
phrasal coordination	4.2	0.0	10.0	10.0	2.4
non-phrasal coordination	1.9	0.0	6.0	6.0	1.4
synthetic negation	1.3	0.0	6.0	6.0	1.3
analytic negation	4.3	0.0	15.0	15.0	3.0

Mean frequencies for General Fiction

Linguistic feature	Mean	Minimum value	Maximum value	Range	Standard deviation
past tense	85.6	41.0	113.0	72.0	15.7
perfect aspect verbs	12.3	4.0	30.0	26.0	5.5
present tense	53.4	25.0	100.0	75.0	18.8
place adverbials	4.4	1.0	14.0	13.0	3.2
time adverbials	5.8	2.0	10.0	8.0	2.0
first person pronouns	32.0	1.0	83.0	82.0	23.5
second person pronouns	11.1	0.0	35.0	35.0	9.1
third person pronouns	67.2	21.0	124.0	103.0	26.3
pronoun IT	11.5	5.0	24.0	19.0	4.6
demonstrative pronouns	2.1	0.0	7.0	7.0	1.8
indefinite pronouns	1.5	0.0	5.0	5.0	1.6
DO as pro-verb	3.3	0.0	12.0	12.0	2.5
WH questions	0.1	0.0	1.0	1.0	0.4
nominalizations	10.0	3.0	25.0	22.0	5.5
gerunds	6.5	2.0	11.0	9.0	2.0
nouns	160.7	112.0	216.0	104.0	25.7
agentless passives	5.7	0.0	12.0	12.0	3.2
BY passives	0.2	0.0	1.0	1.0	0.4
BE as main verb	25.6	15.0	35.0	20.0	5.7
existential THERE	1.7	0.0	4.0	4.0	1.2
THAT verb complements	2.1	0.0	7.0	7.0	1.9
THAT adj. complements	0.1	0.0	1.0	1.0	0.3
WH clauses	0.9	0.0	4.0	4.0	1.0
infinitives	16.6	6.0	26.0	20.0	4.7
present participial clauses	2.7	0.0	7.0	7.0	2.1
past participial clauses	0.0	0.0	0.0	0.0	0.0
past prt. WHIZ deletions	0.7	0.0	3.0	3.0	0.8
present prt. WHIZ deletions	1.1	0.0	4.0	4.0	1.3
THAT relatives: subj. position	0.3	0.0	2.0	2.0	0.6
THAT relatives: obj. position	0.4	0.0	2.0	2.0	0.6
WH relatives: subj. position	1.0	0.0	3.0	3.0	1.0
WH relatives: obj. position	0.9	0.0	4.0	4.0	1.2
WH relatives: pied pipes	0.2	0.0	2.0	2.0	0.5
sentence relatives	0.0	0.0	0.0	0.0	0.0
adv. subordinator - cause	0.4	0.0	3.0	3.0	0.8
adv. sub. - concession	1.1	0.0	5.0	5.0	1.3
adv. sub. - condition	2.6	0.0	6.0	6.0	1.9
adv. sub. - other	0.9	0.0	4.0	4.0	1.0
prepositions	92.8	67.0	134.0	67.0	15.8
attributive adjectives	50.7	31.0	80.0	49.0	9.9
predicative adjectives	5.3	2.0	12.0	10.0	2.3
adverbs	74.1	49.0	108.0	59.0	13.2
type/token ratio	52.7	46.0	61.0	15.0	3.8
word length	4.2	3.8	4.7	0.9	0.2
conjuncts	0.5	0.0	3.0	3.0	0.8
downtoners	2.1	0.0	8.0	8.0	1.7
hedges	0.4	0.0	4.0	4.0	0.9
amplifiers	1.7	0.0	5.0	5.0	1.4
emphatics	4.9	0.0	12.0	12.0	2.9
discourse particles	0.2	0.0	2.0	2.0	0.6
demonstratives	7.8	2.0	13.0	11.0	3.2
possibility modals	5.2	1.0	13.0	12.0	2.7
necessity modals	1.9	0.0	4.0	4.0	1.3
predictive modals	6.2	0.0	14.0	14.0	2.9
public verbs	10.3	2.0	23.0	21.0	5.1
private verbs	20.6	10.0	36.0	26.0	6.9
suasive verbs	2.5	0.0	7.0	7.0	1.6
SEEM/APPEAR	1.1	0.0	4.0	4.0	1.2
contractions	11.2	0.0	42.0	42.0	11.4
THAT deletion	3.0	0.0	9.0	9.0	2.5
stranded prepositions	1.3	0.0	5.0	5.0	1.3
split infinitives	0.0	0.0	0.0	0.0	0.0
split auxiliaries	7.0	2.0	15.0	13.0	3.0
phrasal coordination	3.4	0.0	6.0	6.0	1.6
non-phrasal coordination	3.6	0.0	8.0	8.0	2.2
synthetic negation	2.7	0.0	8.0	8.0	2.0
analytic negation	10.4	3.0	17.0	14.0	3.9

Mean frequencies for Mystery Fiction

Linguistic feature	Mean	Minimum value	Maximum value	Range	Standard deviation
past tense	93.6	72.0	116.0	44.0	12.4
perfect aspect verbs	14.9	2.0	29.0	27.0	7.7
present tense	46.4	22.0	66.0	44.0	16.3
place adverbials	4.8	1.0	13.0	12.0	3.7
time adverbials	5.6	1.0	9.0	8.0	2.2
first person pronouns	29.2	4.0	89.0	85.0	24.3
second person pronouns	10.5	0.0	26.0	26.0	8.1
third person pronouns	57.8	5.0	81.0	76.0	20.5
pronoun IT	13.9	6.0	29.0	23.0	5.7
demonstrative pronouns	3.2	0.0	7.0	7.0	1.7
indefinite pronouns	2.7	0.0	6.0	6.0	2.3
DO as pro-verb	3.5	0.0	5.0	5.0	1.7
WH questions	0.0	0.0	0.0	0.0	0.0
nominalizations	8.3	3.0	13.0	10.0	3.7
gerunds	4.9	2.0	7.0	5.0	1.6
nouns	165.7	127.0	212.0	85.0	25.7
agentless passives	4.9	1.0	12.0	11.0	3.4
BY passives	0.1	0.0	1.0	1.0	0.3
BE as main verb	28.0	19.0	43.0	24.0	7.5
existential THERE	2.5	0.0	7.0	7.0	1.9
THAT verb complements	1.8	0.0	5.0	5.0	1.6
THAT adj. complements	0.0	0.0	0.0	0.0	0.0
WH clauses	0.6	0.0	3.0	3.0	0.9
infinitives	14.5	7.0	24.0	17.0	4.7
present participial clauses	2.8	0.0	11.0	11.0	3.0
past participial clauses	0.0	0.0	0.0	0.0	0.0
past prt. WHIZ deletions	1.0	0.0	6.0	6.0	1.7
present prt. WHIZ deletions	1.3	0.0	4.0	4.0	1.4
THAT relatives: subj. position	0.8	0.0	3.0	3.0	0.9
THAT relatives: obj. position	0.7	0.0	3.0	3.0	0.9
WH relatives: subj. position	1.1	0.0	4.0	4.0	1.3
WH relatives: obj. position	0.6	0.0	5.0	5.0	1.4
WH relatives: pied pipes	0.4	0.0	4.0	4.0	1.1
sentence relatives	0.0	0.0	0.0	0.0	0.0
adv. subordinator - cause	0.2	0.0	1.0	1.0	0.4
adv. sub. - concession	0.5	0.0	2.0	2.0	0.8
adv. sub. - condition	3.2	0.0	6.0	6.0	2.0
adv. sub. - other	0.8	0.0	3.0	3.0	1.1
prepositions	93.0	68.0	132.0	64.0	15.8
attributive adjectives	50.4	32.0	73.0	41.0	13.3
predicative adjectives	5.4	2.0	10.0	8.0	2.4
adverbs	73.6	55.0	94.0	39.0	11.1
type/token ratio	53.2	47.0	59.0	12.0	3.7
word length	4.2	3.8	4.5	0.7	0.2
conjuncts	0.3	0.0	2.0	2.0	0.6
downtoners	2.2	0.0	4.0	4.0	1.2
hedges	0.7	0.0	4.0	4.0	1.1
amplifiers	1.1	0.0	3.0	3.0	1.2
emphatics	5.1	0.0	11.0	11.0	2.8
discourse particles	0.2	0.0	1.0	1.0	0.4
demonstratives	6.6	2.0	11.0	9.0	2.6
possibility modals	6.1	1.0	14.0	13.0	4.1
necessity modals	1.6	0.0	4.0	4.0	1.3
predictive modals	4.5	0.0	10.0	10.0	3.3
public verbs	8.3	1.0	16.0	15.0	5.3
private verbs	19.2	10.0	33.0	23.0	6.0
suasive verbs	2.5	0.0	8.0	8.0	2.3
SEEM/APPEAR	0.7	0.0	4.0	4.0	1.3
contractions	18.1	1.0	31.0	30.0	10.2
THAT deletion	3.2	0.0	8.0	8.0	2.2
stranded prepositions	1.9	0.0	4.0	4.0	1.3
split infinitives	0.0	0.0	0.0	0.0	0.0
split auxiliaries	4.5	1.0	10.0	9.0	2.8
phrasal coordination	2.4	0.0	6.0	6.0	1.7
non-phrasal coordination	2.0	0.0	6.0	6.0	1.6
synthetic negation	2.8	1.0	7.0	6.0	2.0
analytic negation	9.4	2.0	16.0	14.0	3.7

Mean frequencies for Science Fiction

Linguistic feature	Mean	Minimum value	Maximum value	Range	Standard deviation
past tense	74.2	63.0	89.0	26.0	11.2
perfect aspect verbs	8.8	7.0	12.0	5.0	2.1
present tense	51.2	31.0	64.0	33.0	10.9
place adverbials	4.5	3.0	7.0	4.0	1.4
time adverbials	5.3	2.0	8.0	6.0	2.2
first person pronouns	22.2	8.0	57.0	49.0	17.6
second person pronouns	7.3	0.0	18.0	18.0	6.3
third person pronouns	44.5	25.0	66.0	41.0	14.6
pronoun IT	11.3	7.0	14.0	7.0	3.0
demonstrative pronouns	1.8	0.0	5.0	5.0	1.8
indefinite pronouns	0.7	0.0	1.0	1.0	0.5
DO as pro-verb	3.3	0.0	8.0	8.0	2.7
WH questions	0.0	0.0	0.0	0.0	0.0
nominalizations	14.0	7.0	24.0	17.0	6.0
gerunds	7.0	1.0	12.0	11.0	3.7
nouns	171.7	153.0	188.0	35.0	14.5
agentless passives	5.8	4.0	9.0	5.0	2.1
BY passives	0.0	0.0	0.0	0.0	0.0
BE as main verb	25.2	21.0	32.0	11.0	3.9
existential THERE	1.5	0.0	3.0	3.0	1.2
THAT verb complements	1.5	1.0	4.0	3.0	1.2
THAT adj. complements	0.2	0.0	1.0	1.0	0.4
WH clauses	0.3	0.0	1.0	1.0	0.5
infinitives	12.5	9.0	15.0	6.0	2.1
present participial clauses	6.7	4.0	10.0	6.0	2.3
past participial clauses	0.0	0.0	0.0	0.0	0.0
past prt. WHIZ deletions	1.8	0.0	5.0	5.0	1.8
present prt. WHIZ deletions	1.5	0.0	3.0	3.0	1.4
THAT relatives: subj. position	0.8	0.0	2.0	2.0	1.0
THAT relatives: obj. position	0.2	0.0	1.0	1.0	0.4
WH relatives: subj. position	1.3	0.0	4.0	4.0	1.4
WH relatives: obj. position	1.3	0.0	4.0	4.0	1.8
WH relatives: pied pipes	0.7	0.0	3.0	3.0	1.2
sentence relatives	0.0	0.0	0.0	0.0	0.0
adv. subordinator - cause	0.3	0.0	2.0	2.0	0.8
adv. sub. - concession	1.2	0.0	2.0	2.0	0.8
adv. sub. - condition	2.5	0.0	5.0	5.0	2.1
adv. sub. - other	0.8	0.0	2.0	2.0	0.8
prepositions	94.3	74.0	110.0	36.0	14.5
attributive adjectives	62.8	46.0	86.0	40.0	14.0
predicative adjectives	4.0	1.0	9.0	8.0	2.7
adverbs	70.5	57.0	80.0	23.0	7.8
type/token ratio	55.2	47.0	61.0	14.0	4.7
word length	4.4	4.2	4.6	0.4	0.1
conjuncts	0.2	0.0	1.0	1.0	0.4
downtoners	1.7	0.0	4.0	4.0	1.6
hedges	0.3	0.0	1.0	1.0	0.5
amplifiers	1.7	0.0	6.0	6.0	2.4
emphatics	4.7	1.0	8.0	7.0	2.3
discourse particles	0.3	0.0	1.0	1.0	0.5
demonstratives	9.2	4.0	14.0	10.0	3.8
possibility modals	5.2	1.0	10.0	9.0	3.4
necessity modals	1.8	0.0	3.0	3.0	1.3
predictive modals	4.0	1.0	9.0	8.0	2.8
public verbs	8.7	5.0	13.0	8.0	3.0
private verbs	17.5	13.0	23.0	10.0	3.9
suasive verbs	3.8	1.0	6.0	5.0	1.7
SEEM/APPEAR	1.2	0.0	3.0	3.0	1.5
contractions	6.5	0.0	14.0	14.0	5.8
THAT deletion	1.7	0.0	4.0	4.0	1.5
stranded prepositions	2.0	0.0	6.0	6.0	2.2
split infinitives	0.0	0.0	0.0	0.0	0.0
split auxiliaries	5.2	1.0	9.0	8.0	2.7
phrasal coordination	4.2	0.0	10.0	10.0	3.3
non-phrasal coordination	3.3	1.0	7.0	6.0	2.3
synthetic negation	2.8	0.0	6.0	6.0	2.4
analytic negation	7.5	4.0	12.0	8.0	2.7

Mean frequencies for Adventure Fiction

Linguistic feature	Mean	Minimum value	Maximum value	Range	Standard deviation
past tense	84.8	67.0	119.0	52.0	14.2
perfect aspect verbs	12.2	3.0	21.0	18.0	4.8
present tense	55.2	29.0	81.0	52.0	16.0
place adverbials	5.0	1.0	11.0	10.0	2.9
time adverbials	5.2	2.0	9.0	7.0	2.2
first person pronouns	35.2	11.0	67.0	56.0	19.4
second person pronouns	13.1	2.0	27.0	25.0	8.3
third person pronouns	55.2	32.0	79.0	47.0	15.4
pronoun IT	10.8	5.0	19.0	14.0	3.4
demonstrative pronouns	2.0	0.0	6.0	6.0	1.7
indefinite pronouns	1.7	0.0	5.0	5.0	1.5
DO as pro-verb	3.5	0.0	8.0	8.0	2.4
WH questions	0.1	0.0	1.0	1.0	0.3
nominalizations	7.8	3.0	13.0	10.0	3.8
gerunds	6.0	2.0	11.0	9.0	2.5
nouns	165.6	133.0	194.0	61.0	17.3
agentless passives	4.6	1.0	9.0	8.0	2.3
BY passives	0.1	0.0	1.0	1.0	0.3
BE as main verb	25.7	18.0	36.0	18.0	5.0
existential THERE	2.1	0.0	4.0	4.0	1.3
THAT verb complements	1.8	0.0	5.0	5.0	1.5
THAT adj. complements	0.2	0.0	1.0	1.0	0.4
WH clauses	1.2	0.0	4.0	4.0	1.1
infinitives	15.3	10.0	26.0	16.0	5.4
present participial clauses	3.2	0.0	8.0	8.0	2.7
past participial clauses	0.0	0.0	0.0	0.0	0.0
past prt. WHIZ deletions	0.3	0.0	1.0	1.0	0.5
present prt. WHIZ deletions	1.1	0.0	4.0	4.0	1.3
THAT relatives: subj. position	0.5	0.0	4.0	4.0	1.1
THAT relatives: obj. position	0.1	0.0	1.0	1.0	0.3
WH relatives: subj. position	1.2	0.0	3.0	3.0	1.2
WH relatives: obj. position	0.4	0.0	4.0	4.0	1.1
WH relatives: pied pipes	0.1	0.0	1.0	1.0	0.3
sentence relatives	0.0	0.0	0.0	0.0	0.0
adv. subordinator - cause	0.4	0.0	2.0	2.0	0.8
adv. sub. - concession	0.5	0.0	3.0	3.0	1.0
adv. sub. - condition	2.3	0.0	6.0	6.0	1.7
adv. sub. - other	1.3	0.0	3.0	3.0	1.1
prepositions	94.3	73.0	112.0	39.0	13.9
attributive adjectives	46.5	38.0	58.0	20.0	7.1
predicative adjectives	5.2	1.0	9.0	8.0	2.4
adverbs	69.8	59.0	88.0	29.0	8.5
type/token ratio	52.8	48.0	59.0	11.0	3.5
word length	4.1	3.9	4.5	0.6	0.2
conjuncts	0.5	0.0	2.0	2.0	0.8
downtoners	1.5	0.0	5.0	5.0	1.5
hedges	0.5	0.0	3.0	3.0	1.0
amplifiers	0.9	0.0	2.0	2.0	1.0
emphatics	5.8	3.0	10.0	7.0	2.1
discourse particles	0.2	0.0	1.0	1.0	0.4
demonstratives	7.5	2.0	13.0	11.0	3.6
possibility modals	6.1	4.0	10.0	6.0	2.0
necessity modals	1.8	0.0	5.0	5.0	1.8
predictive modals	4.2	1.0	9.0	8.0	2.4
public verbs	10.0	4.0	20.0	16.0	5.6
private verbs	18.8	11.0	31.0	20.0	5.9
suasive verbs	2.3	0.0	6.0	6.0	1.8
SEEM/APPEAR	0.8	0.0	3.0	3.0	1.1
contractions	17.5	4.0	30.0	26.0	8.5
THAT deletion	1.8	0.0	4.0	4.0	1.4
stranded prepositions	2.2	0.0	6.0	6.0	1.7
split infinitives	0.0	0.0	0.0	0.0	0.0
split auxiliaries	4.1	1.0	9.0	8.0	2.4
phrasal coordination	2.0	0.0	5.0	5.0	1.7
non-phrasal coordination	2.4	0.0	5.0	5.0	1.9
synthetic negation	2.7	0.0	7.0	7.0	2.1
analytic negation	9.2	3.0	17.0	14.0	4.3

Mean frequencies for Romantic Fiction

Linguistic feature	Mean	Minimum value	Maximum value	Range	Standard deviation
past tense	83.7	64.0	105.0	41.0	11.1
perfect aspect verbs	13.6	8.0	30.0	22.0	5.5
present tense	65.8	46.0	90.0	44.0	11.8
place adverbials	3.6	0.0	8.0	8.0	2.3
time adverbials	6.8	3.0	10.0	7.0	2.3
first person pronouns	32.4	18.0	56.0	38.0	11.4
second person pronouns	18.6	9.0	31.0	22.0	7.2
third person pronouns	78.5	49.0	102.0	53.0	13.9
pronoun IT	9.8	6.0	16.0	10.0	2.9
demonstrative pronouns	2.6	1.0	5.0	4.0	1.4
indefinite pronouns	2.3	0.0	5.0	5.0	1.6
DO as pro-verb	3.7	2.0	8.0	6.0	1.5
WH questions	0.2	0.0	2.0	2.0	0.6
nominalizations	8.5	5.0	15.0	10.0	2.9
gerunds	5.8	3.0	9.0	6.0	1.8
nouns	146.8	119.0	173.0	54.0	17.6
agentless passives	5.0	4.0	7.0	3.0	1.1
BY passives	0.0	0.0	0.0	0.0	0.0
BE as main verb	28.1	23.0	33.0	10.0	3.2
existential THERE	1.5	0.0	4.0	4.0	1.5
THAT verb complements	2.5	0.0	7.0	7.0	2.5
THAT adj. complements	0.4	0.0	2.0	2.0	0.7
WH clauses	0.5	0.0	2.0	2.0	0.7
infinitives	19.0	14.0	27.0	13.0	3.3
present participial clauses	4.5	0.0	9.0	9.0	2.8
past participial clauses	0.1	0.0	1.0	1.0	0.3
past prt. WHIZ deletions	0.1	0.0	1.0	1.0	0.3
present prt. WHIZ deletions	0.5	0.0	3.0	3.0	1.0
THAT relatives: subj. position	0.3	0.0	1.0	1.0	0.5
THAT relatives: obj. position	0.2	0.0	1.0	1.0	0.4
WH relatives: subj. position	0.8	0.0	3.0	3.0	1.0
WH relatives: obj. position	0.4	0.0	1.0	1.0	0.5
WH relatives: pied pipes	0.1	0.0	1.0	1.0	0.3
sentence relatives	0.0	0.0	0.0	0.0	0.0
adv. subordinator - cause	0.2	0.0	2.0	2.0	0.6
adv. sub. - concession	0.4	0.0	2.0	2.0	0.7
adv. sub. - condition	3.2	0.0	8.0	8.0	2.0
adv. sub. - other	0.8	0.0	2.0	2.0	0.8
prepositions	82.0	69.0	97.0	28.0	8.5
attributive adjectives	41.9	36.0	56.0	20.0	5.9
predicative adjectives	7.0	4.0	11.0	7.0	1.7
adverbs	78.4	65.0	93.0	28.0	10.0
type/token ratio	52.9	47.0	59.0	12.0	3.5
word length	4.1	3.9	4.3	0.3	0.1
conjuncts	0.1	0.0	1.0	1.0	0.3
downtoners	1.8	0.0	4.0	4.0	1.1
hedges	0.1	0.0	1.0	1.0	0.3
amplifiers	2.2	0.0	5.0	5.0	1.4
emphatics	6.8	2.0	11.0	9.0	2.6
discourse particles	0.0	0.0	0.0	0.0	0.0
demonstratives	7.3	4.0	12.0	8.0	2.4
possibility modals	6.5	3.0	11.0	8.0	2.4
necessity modals	1.9	0.0	6.0	6.0	2.1
predictive modals	8.5	4.0	17.0	13.0	3.5
public verbs	8.6	3.0	15.0	12.0	4.0
private verbs	24.2	12.0	31.0	19.0	5.4
suasive verbs	2.6	0.0	8.0	8.0	2.3
SEEM/APPEAR	0.8	0.0	3.0	3.0	0.9
contractions	19.0	4.0	41.0	37.0	11.3
THAT deletion	5.2	2.0	14.0	12.0	3.1
stranded prepositions	1.5	0.0	5.0	5.0	1.3
split infinitives	0.0	0.0	0.0	0.0	0.0
split auxiliaries	6.0	2.0	9.0	7.0	1.8
phrasal coordination	3.2	1.0	7.0	6.0	1.8
non-phrasal coordination	2.8	0.0	7.0	7.0	1.8
synthetic negation	2.5	0.0	7.0	7.0	2.4
analytic negation	12.7	7.0	20.0	13.0	4.2

Mean frequencies for Humor

Linguistic feature	Mean	Minimum value	Maximum value	Range	Standard deviation
past tense	56.1	6.0	89.0	83.0	30.4
perfect aspect verbs	8.0	4.0	12.0	8.0	2.4
present tense	59.8	32.0	112.0	80.0	27.9
place adverbials	3.2	1.0	7.0	6.0	2.2
time adverbials	5.3	0.0	10.0	10.0	3.2
first person pronouns	29.7	5.0	58.0	53.0	18.3
second person pronouns	8.7	0.0	24.0	24.0	8.0
third person pronouns	33.0	9.0	53.0	44.0	13.2
pronoun IT	8.2	2.0	14.0	12.0	4.2
demonstrative pronouns	1.9	1.0	3.0	2.0	0.9
indefinite pronouns	1.3	0.0	3.0	3.0	1.1
DO as pro-verb	1.8	0.0	4.0	4.0	1.2
WH questions	0.3	0.0	2.0	2.0	0.7
nominalizations	12.1	6.0	17.0	11.0	3.4
gerunds	7.3	3.0	12.0	9.0	3.0
nouns	190.2	142.0	243.0	101.0	29.1
agentless passives	7.8	6.0	10.0	4.0	1.4
BY passives	0.3	0.0	2.0	2.0	0.7
BE as main verb	26.3	17.0	43.0	26.0	7.7
existential THERE	1.9	0.0	5.0	5.0	2.0
THAT verb complements	2.1	0.0	5.0	5.0	1.7
THAT adj. complements	0.0	0.0	0.0	0.0	0.0
WH clauses	0.4	0.0	2.0	2.0	0.7
infinitives	16.3	10.0	24.0	14.0	4.5
present participial clauses	1.7	0.0	3.0	3.0	0.9
past participial clauses	0.2	0.0	1.0	1.0	0.4
past prt. WHIZ deletions	2.8	1.0	5.0	4.0	1.4
present prt. WHIZ deletions	1.4	0.0	3.0	3.0	1.1
THAT relatives: subj. position	0.1	0.0	1.0	1.0	0.3
THAT relatives: obj. position	0.4	0.0	3.0	3.0	1.0
WH relatives: subj. position	2.1	0.0	3.0	3.0	1.1
WH relatives: obj. position	1.3	0.0	4.0	4.0	1.2
WH relatives: pied pipes	0.7	0.0	3.0	3.0	1.0
sentence relatives	0.0	0.0	0.0	0.0	0.0
adv. subordinator - cause	0.4	0.0	2.0	2.0	0.7
adv. sub. - concession	0.2	0.0	1.0	1.0	0.4
adv. sub. - condition	2.0	1.0	4.0	3.0	1.3
adv. sub. - other	0.7	0.0	3.0	3.0	1.0
prepositions	111.7	96.0	127.0	31.0	10.0
attributive adjectives	65.0	55.0	81.0	26.0	7.6
predicative adjectives	4.1	2.0	6.0	4.0	1.5
adverbs	68.2	55.0	84.0	29.0	11.8
type/token ratio	55.3	49.0	59.0	10.0	3.2
word length	4.5	4.3	4.6	0.4	0.1
conjuncts	1.6	0.0	5.0	5.0	1.4
downtoners	2.2	0.0	5.0	5.0	1.6
hedges	0.1	0.0	1.0	1.0	0.3
amplifiers	1.6	0.0	3.0	3.0	1.1
emphatics	4.8	1.0	12.0	11.0	3.3
discourse particles	0.3	0.0	2.0	2.0	0.7
demonstratives	8.9	4.0	14.0	10.0	3.3
possibility modals	4.4	2.0	9.0	7.0	2.2
necessity modals	1.1	0.0	3.0	3.0	0.9
predictive modals	5.7	0.0	15.0	15.0	4.2
public verbs	6.6	3.0	12.0	9.0	3.4
private verbs	13.8	10.0	20.0	10.0	3.5
suasive verbs	2.7	0.0	7.0	7.0	2.2
SEEM/APPEAR	0.9	0.0	2.0	2.0	0.8
contractions	6.1	0.0	16.0	16.0	6.5
THAT deletion	1.1	0.0	2.0	2.0	0.6
stranded prepositions	2.0	0.0	5.0	5.0	1.7
split infinitives	0.0	0.0	0.0	0.0	0.0
split auxiliaries	5.9	3.0	11.0	8.0	2.3
phrasal coordination	3.6	1.0	6.0	5.0	1.7
non-phrasal coordination	2.4	1.0	4.0	3.0	1.0
synthetic negation	2.1	1.0	4.0	3.0	1.3
analytic negation	7.8	4.0	14.0	10.0	3.4

Mean frequencies for Personal Letters

Linguistic feature	Mean	Minimum value	Maximum value	Range	Standard deviation
past tense	43.8	14.0	65.0	51.0	19.9
perfect aspect verbs	11.2	6.0	20.0	14.0	5.5
present tense	127.7	103.0	143.0	40.0	16.0
place adverbials	2.0	0.0	5.0	5.0	1.8
time adverbials	8.3	3.0	14.0	11.0	4.0
first person pronouns	62.0	37.0	91.0	54.0	22.5
second person pronouns	20.2	5.0	43.0	38.0	13.4
third person pronouns	52.8	28.0	75.0	47.0	19.7
pronoun IT	11.0	6.0	16.0	10.0	3.6
demonstrative pronouns	3.7	0.0	6.0	6.0	2.1
indefinite pronouns	2.3	0.0	6.0	6.0	2.2
DO as pro-verb	4.3	0.0	8.0	8.0	2.9
WH questions	0.2	0.0	1.0	1.0	0.4
nominalizations	5.2	2.0	8.0	6.0	2.8
gerunds	3.5	1.0	6.0	5.0	1.6
nouns	156.7	124.0	195.0	71.0	26.1
agentless passives	2.8	0.0	6.0	6.0	2.3
BY passives	0.0	0.0	0.0	0.0	0.0
BE as main verb	39.3	35.0	49.0	14.0	5.2
existential THERE	1.2	0.0	3.0	3.0	1.3
THAT verb complements	1.3	0.0	4.0	4.0	1.5
THAT adj. complements	0.2	0.0	1.0	1.0	0.4
WH clauses	1.0	1.0	1.0	0.0	0.0
infinitives	19.8	16.0	23.0	7.0	2.6
present participial clauses	0.2	0.0	1.0	1.0	0.4
past participial clauses	0.0	0.0	0.0	0.0	0.0
past prt. WHIZ deletions	0.2	0.0	1.0	1.0	0.4
present prt. WHIZ deletions	0.0	0.0	0.0	0.0	0.0
THAT relatives: subj. position	0.0	0.0	0.0	0.0	0.0
THAT relatives: obj. position	0.5	0.0	1.0	1.0	0.5
WH relatives: subj. position	0.7	0.0	2.0	2.0	0.8
WH relatives: obj. position	0.2	0.0	1.0	1.0	0.4
WH relatives: pied pipes	0.2	0.0	1.0	1.0	0.4
sentence relatives	0.2	0.0	1.0	1.0	0.4
adv. subordinator - cause	2.7	0.0	4.0	4.0	1.4
adv. sub. - concession	1.7	0.0	4.0	4.0	1.6
adv. sub. - condition	3.5	0.0	9.0	9.0	3.4
adv. sub. - other	1.7	0.0	6.0	6.0	2.3
prepositions	72.0	54.0	82.0	28.0	10.3
attributive adjectives	44.2	36.0	54.0	18.0	6.4
predicative adjectives	8.3	6.0	13.0	7.0	2.5
adverbs	80.7	70.0	89.0	19.0	6.7
type/token ratio	52.5	50.0	56.0	6.0	2.6
word length	3.9	3.8	4.0	0.2	0.1
conjuncts	0.2	0.0	1.0	1.0	0.4
downtoners	1.2	0.0	2.0	2.0	0.8
hedges	3.3	0.0	7.0	7.0	2.7
amplifiers	2.2	0.0	5.0	5.0	1.9
emphatics	11.2	4.0	17.0	13.0	5.1
discourse particles	1.2	0.0	4.0	4.0	1.6
demonstratives	9.0	3.0	16.0	13.0	5.0
possibility modals	9.0	4.0	16.0	12.0	4.8
necessity modals	1.5	0.0	5.0	5.0	2.1
predictive modals	9.8	3.0	16.0	13.0	4.4
public verbs	6.7	3.0	11.0	8.0	3.2
private verbs	27.2	20.0	33.0	13.0	5.0
suasive verbs	1.0	0.0	3.0	3.0	1.3
SEEM/APPEAR	2.2	0.0	6.0	6.0	2.3
contractions	22.2	12.0	48.0	36.0	13.9
THAT deletion	12.8	8.0	21.0	13.0	4.4
stranded prepositions	1.3	0.0	3.0	3.0	1.0
split infinitives	0.2	0.0	1.0	1.0	0.4
split auxiliaries	5.5	3.0	7.0	4.0	1.6
phrasal coordination	5.7	1.0	11.0	10.0	4.3
non-phrasal coordination	6.3	2.0	11.0	9.0	4.2
synthetic negation	0.7	0.0	2.0	2.0	0.8
analytic negation	12.0	3.0	19.0	16.0	5.6

Mean frequencies for Professional Letters

Linguistic feature	Mean	Minimum value	Maximum value	Range	Standard deviation
past tense	10.1	0.0	20.0	20.0	6.7
perfect aspect verbs	10.3	0.0	24.0	24.0	8.7
present tense	94.7	71.0	123.0	52.0	16.8
place adverbials	1.6	0.0	6.0	6.0	2.0
time adverbials	2.0	0.0	4.0	4.0	1.7
first person pronouns	40.9	16.0	68.0	52.0	14.8
second person pronouns	15.2	0.0	42.0	42.0	13.8
third person pronouns	8.7	0.0	24.0	24.0	9.1
pronoun IT	7.1	1.0	28.0	27.0	8.1
demonstrative pronouns	2.4	0.0	10.0	10.0	3.1
indefinite pronouns	1.1	0.0	8.0	8.0	2.5
DO as pro-verb	2.6	0.0	12.0	12.0	3.6
WH questions	0.0	0.0	0.0	0.0	0.0
nominalizations	44.2	24.0	60.0	36.0	12.0
gerunds	11.7	4.0	23.0	19.0	6.3
nouns	172.6	143.0	221.0	78.0	22.8
agentless passives	7.3	1.0	15.0	14.0	4.3
BY passives	0.6	0.0	2.0	2.0	0.8
BE as main verb	27.0	13.0	45.0	32.0	10.2
existential THERE	0.7	0.0	4.0	4.0	1.3
THAT verb complements	4.3	0.0	14.0	14.0	4.3
THAT adj. complements	0.5	0.0	3.0	3.0	1.1
WH clauses	1.0	0.0	5.0	5.0	1.8
infinitives	24.1	12.0	32.0	20.0	6.0
present participial clauses	0.3	0.0	2.0	2.0	0.7
past participial clauses	0.2	0.0	1.0	1.0	0.4
past prt. WHIZ deletions	1.3	0.0	3.0	3.0	1.2
present prt. WHIZ deletions	2.5	0.0	11.0	11.0	3.4
THAT relatives: subj. position	0.7	0.0	3.0	3.0	1.1
THAT relatives: obj. position	1.1	0.0	7.0	7.0	2.2
WH relatives: subj. position	3.4	0.0	15.0	15.0	4.6
WH relatives: obj. position	2.9	0.0	9.0	9.0	3.4
WH relatives: pied pipes	0.9	0.0	3.0	3.0	1.1
sentence relatives	0.0	0.0	0.0	0.0	0.0
adv. subordinator - cause	2.9	0.0	11.0	11.0	3.8
adv. sub. - concession	0.5	0.0	4.0	4.0	1.3
adv. sub. - condition	2.0	0.0	6.0	6.0	2.3
adv. sub. - other	1.4	0.0	4.0	4.0	1.7
prepositions	118.9	96.0	157.0	61.0	21.8
attributive adjectives	76.5	56.0	101.0	45.0	17.1
predicative adjectives	7.4	1.0	19.0	18.0	5.3
adverbs	49.8	36.0	74.0	38.0	12.6
type/token ratio	53.0	45.0	60.0	15.0	4.2
word length	4.8	4.5	5.1	0.6	0.2
conjuncts	2.5	0.0	10.0	10.0	3.1
downtoners	1.6	0.0	7.0	7.0	2.1
hedges	0.3	0.0	2.0	2.0	0.7
amplifiers	1.9	0.0	8.0	8.0	2.6
emphatics	7.8	1.0	20.0	19.0	6.3
discourse particles	0.2	0.0	2.0	2.0	0.6
demonstratives	12.0	2.0	22.0	20.0	5.2
possibility modals	7.7	1.0	20.0	19.0	5.6
necessity modals	2.2	0.0	6.0	6.0	2.3
predictive modals	11.9	0.0	30.0	30.0	10.1
public verbs	9.2	0.0	26.0	26.0	8.1
private verbs	17.1	11.0	30.0	19.0	6.3
suasive verbs	3.7	0.0	10.0	10.0	3.9
SEEM/APPEAR	1.0	0.0	4.0	4.0	1.3
contractions	4.7	0.0	26.0	26.0	8.1
THAT deletion	1.9	0.0	7.0	7.0	2.7
stranded prepositions	0.1	0.0	1.0	1.0	0.3
split infinitives	0.0	0.0	0.0	0.0	0.0
split auxiliaries	6.0	2.0	10.0	8.0	2.9
phrasal coordination	5.8	0.0	12.0	12.0	4.3
non-phrasal coordination	1.5	0.0	4.0	4.0	1.6
synthetic negation	1.0	0.0	3.0	3.0	1.3
analytic negation	7.2	0.0	14.0	14.0	4.4

Mean frequencies for Face-to-face Conversations

Linguistic feature	Mean	Minimum value	Maximum value	Range	Standard deviation
past tense	37.4	10.0	72.0	62.0	17.3
perfect aspect verbs	10.4	3.0	22.0	19.0	3.6
present tense	128.4	66.0	182.0	116.0	22.2
place adverbials	2.0	0.0	14.0	14.0	2.2
time adverbials	5.1	1.0	8.0	7.0	1.9
first person pronouns	57.9	28.0	86.0	58.0	13.5
second person pronouns	30.8	10.0	55.0	45.0	11.2
third person pronouns	29.2	4.0	70.0	66.0	16.0
pronoun IT	20.0	6.0	42.0	36.0	7.7
demonstrative pronouns	13.1	5.0	28.0	23.0	4.5
indefinite pronouns	3.9	1.0	9.0	8.0	2.1
DO as pro-verb	9.0	1.0	18.0	17.0	3.6
WH questions	0.7	0.0	4.0	4.0	1.0
nominalizations	9.2	2.0	25.0	23.0	5.3
gerunds	4.7	1.0	13.0	12.0	2.2
nouns	137.4	110.0	164.0	54.0	15.6
agentless passives	4.2	1.0	11.0	10.0	2.1
BY passives	0.1	0.0	1.0	1.0	0.3
BE as main verb	39.5	24.0	65.0	41.0	7.2
existential THERE	2.8	0.0	10.0	10.0	1.9
THAT verb complements	4.0	0.0	8.0	8.0	2.0
THAT adj. complements	0.1	0.0	2.0	2.0	0.4
WH clauses	1.3	0.0	3.0	3.0	1.0
infinitives	13.8	7.0	22.0	15.0	3.7
present participial clauses	0.0	0.0	1.0	1.0	0.2
past participial clauses	0.0	0.0	0.0	0.0	0.0
past prt. WHIZ deletions	0.1	0.0	2.0	2.0	0.4
present prt. WHIZ deletions	0.4	0.0	2.0	2.0	0.6
THAT relatives: subj. position	0.4	0.0	2.0	2.0	0.5
THAT relatives: obj. position	0.9	0.0	3.0	3.0	0.9
WH relatives: subj. position	0.9	0.0	4.0	4.0	1.0
WH relatives: obj. position	0.5	0.0	3.0	3.0	0.7
WH relatives: pied pipes	0.2	0.0	2.0	2.0	0.5
sentence relatives	0.7	0.0	3.0	3.0	0.9
adv. subordinator - cause	3.5	1.0	8.0	7.0	1.7
adv. sub. - concession	0.3	0.0	3.0	3.0	0.7
adv. sub. - condition	3.9	0.0	8.0	8.0	2.1
adv. sub. - other	0.8	0.0	4.0	4.0	1.0
prepositions	85.0	64.0	112.0	48.0	12.4
attributive adjectives	40.8	30.0	68.0	38.0	7.9
predicative adjectives	4.2	0.0	9.0	9.0	1.9
adverbs	86.0	62.0	115.0	53.0	11.6
type/token ratio	46.1	39.0	60.0	21.0	3.6
word length	4.1	3.8	4.3	0.5	0.1
conjuncts	0.3	0.0	3.0	3.0	0.7
downtoners	1.5	0.0	5.0	5.0	1.3
hedges	2.1	0.0	10.0	10.0	2.1
amplifiers	6.0	2.0	12.0	10.0	2.3
emphatics	12.2	4.0	20.0	16.0	3.7
discourse particles	3.9	0.0	8.0	8.0	2.0
demonstratives	11.1	5.0	20.0	15.0	3.9
possibility modals	7.9	2.0	21.0	19.0	3.4
necessity modals	1.9	0.0	7.0	7.0	1.5
predictive modals	5.8	1.0	16.0	15.0	3.5
public verbs	8.8	3.0	19.0	16.0	4.0
private verbs	35.4	22.0	53.0	31.0	8.0
suasive verbs	1.5	0.0	8.0	8.0	1.6
SEEM/APPEAR	0.4	0.0	2.0	2.0	0.6
contractions	46.2	27.0	71.0	44.0	10.8
THAT deletion	9.6	3.0	23.0	20.0	4.6
stranded prepositions	4.8	1.0	13.0	12.0	2.4
split infinitives	0.0	0.0	0.0	0.0	0.0
split auxiliaries	4.8	1.0	9.0	8.0	1.7
phrasal coordination	1.3	0.0	5.0	5.0	1.3
non-phrasal coordination	9.5	4.0	20.0	16.0	4.4
synthetic negation	0.9	0.0	4.0	4.0	0.9
analytic negation	18.5	8.0	32.0	24.0	5.1

Mean frequencies for Telephone Conversations

Linguistic feature	Mean	Minimum value	Maximum value	Range	Standard deviation
past tense	28.3	3.0	70.0	67.0	15.9
perfect aspect verbs	8.8	0.0	20.0	20.0	5.2
present tense	142.6	110.0	182.0	72.0	19.5
place adverbials	1.7	0.0	7.0	7.0	2.1
time adverbials	7.4	1.0	15.0	14.0	3.9
first person pronouns	70.7	28.0	104.0	76.0	18.7
second person pronouns	34.3	19.0	72.0	53.0	11.2
third person pronouns	21.7	0.0	62.0	62.0	14.4
pronoun IT	22.2	6.0	47.0	41.0	10.8
demonstrative pronouns	11.5	3.0	30.0	27.0	6.3
indefinite pronouns	3.6	0.0	13.0	13.0	3.3
DO as pro-verb	7.4	0.0	22.0	22.0	5.0
WH questions	1.1	0.0	4.0	4.0	1.2
nominalizations	6.6	0.0	17.0	17.0	5.0
gerunds	3.3	0.0	8.0	8.0	2.1
nouns	134.8	106.0	250.0	144.0	31.1
agentless passives	3.4	0.0	13.0	13.0	3.0
BY passives	0.0	0.0	1.0	1.0	0.2
BE as main verb	43.5	30.0	72.0	42.0	9.7
existential THERE	3.2	0.0	10.0	10.0	2.8
THAT verb complements	3.0	0.0	9.0	9.0	2.8
THAT adj. complements	0.3	0.0	2.0	2.0	0.5
WH clauses	1.1	0.0	6.0	6.0	1.4
infinitives	13.3	1.0	23.0	22.0	4.8
present participial clauses	0.0	0.0	1.0	1.0	0.2
past participial clauses	0.0	0.0	0.0	0.0	0.0
past prt. WHIZ deletions	0.1	0.0	1.0	1.0	0.3
present prt. WHIZ deletions	0.1	0.0	1.0	1.0	0.4
THAT relatives: subj. position	0.4	0.0	3.0	3.0	0.7
THAT relatives: obj. position	0.4	0.0	3.0	3.0	0.7
WH relatives: subj. position	0.9	0.0	8.0	8.0	1.8
WH relatives: obj. position	0.3	0.0	5.0	5.0	1.0
WH relatives: pied pipes	0.1	0.0	3.0	3.0	0.6
sentence relatives	0.3	0.0	3.0	3.0	0.7
adv. subordinator - cause	2.6	0.0	7.0	7.0	1.6
adv. sub. - concession	0.3	0.0	2.0	2.0	0.5
adv. sub. - condition	4.6	0.0	13.0	13.0	3.7
adv. sub. - other	0.3	0.0	2.0	2.0	0.5
prepositions	71.8	50.0	102.0	52.0	12.9
attributive adjectives	38.9	21.0	70.0	49.0	11.3
predicative adjectives	6.0	0.0	16.0	16.0	3.6
adverbs	88.5	63.0	125.0	62.0	14.8
type/token ratio	45.8	40.0	55.0	15.0	3.3
word length	4.0	3.7	4.4	0.6	0.2
conjuncts	0.5	0.0	4.0	4.0	1.0
downtoners	1.6	0.0	5.0	5.0	1.5
hedges	2.7	0.0	8.0	8.0	2.2
amplifiers	5.4	0.0	11.0	11.0	3.1
emphatics	11.3	4.0	22.0	18.0	4.8
discourse particles	6.6	0.0	15.0	15.0	3.7
demonstratives	8.4	0.0	19.0	19.0	4.5
possibility modals	9.1	3.0	17.0	14.0	4.1
necessity modals	2.6	0.0	8.0	8.0	2.1
predictive modals	6.6	0.0	16.0	16.0	3.7
public verbs	6.2	1.0	13.0	12.0	3.0
private verbs	35.6	12.0	54.0	42.0	10.4
suasive verbs	2.0	0.0	7.0	7.0	2.2
SEEM/APPEAR	0.7	0.0	4.0	4.0	1.2
contractions	54.4	21.0	89.0	68.0	12.3
THAT deletion	10.0	3.0	24.0	21.0	4.7
stranded prepositions	3.7	0.0	9.0	9.0	2.1
split infinitives	0.0	0.0	0.0	0.0	0.0
split auxiliaries	4.6	0.0	9.0	9.0	2.3
phrasal coordination	1.0	0.0	3.0	3.0	0.9
non-phrasal coordination	7.5	3.0	15.0	12.0	3.2
synthetic negation	0.9	0.0	8.0	8.0	1.7
analytic negation	16.9	7.0	29.0	22.0	6.4

Mean frequencies for Interviews

Linguistic feature	Mean	Minimum value	Maximum value	Range	Standard deviation
past tense	30.1	4.0	102.0	98.0	24.9
perfect aspect verbs	9.4	3.0	18.0	15.0	4.2
present tense	104.9	39.0	140.0	101.0	28.2
place adverbials	1.6	0.0	8.0	8.0	1.9
time adverbials	5.5	0.0	14.0	14.0	3.2
first person pronouns	50.5	25.0	90.0	65.0	15.8
second person pronouns	19.5	1.0	58.0	57.0	14.6
third person pronouns	22.2	11.0	44.0	33.0	9.8
pronoun IT	11.9	1.0	20.0	19.0	4.8
demonstrative pronouns	8.7	1.0	14.0	13.0	3.4
indefinite pronouns	2.8	0.0	8.0	8.0	2.4
DO as pro-verb	4.6	1.0	8.0	7.0	2.2
WH questions	0.5	0.0	2.0	2.0	0.7
nominalizations	17.7	4.0	34.0	30.0	8.2
gerunds	6.9	2.0	23.0	21.0	4.9
nouns	160.9	109.0	204.0	95.0	23.8
agentless passives	8.0	4.0	14.0	10.0	3.0
BY passives	0.3	0.0	2.0	2.0	0.6
BE as main verb	36.3	22.0	52.0	30.0	7.1
existential THERE	3.4	0.0	8.0	8.0	1.8
THAT verb complements	7.1	2.0	15.0	13.0	3.6
THAT adj. complements	0.4	0.0	2.0	2.0	0.6
WH clauses	0.6	0.0	3.0	3.0	0.7
infinitives	16.4	8.0	28.0	20.0	5.8
present participial clauses	0.0	0.0	0.0	0.0	0.0
past participial clauses	0.0	0.0	0.0	0.0	0.0
past prt. WHIZ deletions	0.3	0.0	2.0	2.0	0.6
present prt. WHIZ deletions	1.0	0.0	3.0	3.0	1.1
THAT relatives: subj. position	1.7	0.0	7.0	7.0	2.0
THAT relatives: obj. position	2.2	0.0	7.0	7.0	1.7
WH relatives: subj. position	2.3	0.0	7.0	7.0	2.0
WH relatives: obj. position	2.0	0.0	5.0	5.0	1.6
WH relatives: pied pipes	1.0	0.0	5.0	5.0	1.3
sentence relatives	0.5	0.0	2.0	2.0	0.7
adv. subordinator - cause	2.7	0.0	8.0	8.0	2.1
adv. sub. - concession	0.4	0.0	3.0	3.0	0.8
adv. sub. - condition	3.6	0.0	7.0	7.0	1.8
adv. sub. - other	0.8	0.0	2.0	2.0	0.7
prepositions	108.0	88.0	150.0	62.0	17.7
attributive adjectives	55.3	38.0	72.0	34.0	10.1
predicative adjectives	5.3	1.0	10.0	9.0	2.5
adverbs	71.8	53.0	88.0	35.0	11.6
type/token ratio	48.4	44.0	55.0	11.0	3.0
word length	4.4	4.1	4.8	0.8	0.2
conjuncts	1.0	0.0	4.0	4.0	1.0
downtoners	1.8	0.0	5.0	5.0	1.7
hedges	0.4	0.0	3.0	3.0	0.9
amplifiers	6.8	2.0	14.0	12.0	3.0
emphatics	9.7	3.0	18.0	15.0	3.9
discourse particles	3.0	0.0	8.0	8.0	2.0
demonstratives	11.0	6.0	17.0	11.0	3.3
possibility modals	7.3	1.0	15.0	14.0	3.0
necessity modals	2.7	0.0	6.0	6.0	1.4
predictive modals	7.0	2.0	17.0	15.0	3.9
public verbs	8.5	1.0	17.0	16.0	4.1
private verbs	23.7	13.0	42.0	29.0	8.0
suasive verbs	2.2	0.0	6.0	6.0	1.8
SEEM/APPEAR	0.7	0.0	3.0	3.0	0.9
contractions	25.4	4.0	49.0	45.0	12.3
THAT deletion	4.3	0.0	8.0	8.0	2.4
stranded prepositions	5.4	0.0	15.0	15.0	4.0
split infinitives	0.0	0.0	0.0	0.0	0.0
split auxiliaries	5.0	1.0	10.0	9.0	2.2
phrasal coordination	0.9	0.0	3.0	3.0	0.9
non-phrasal coordination	9.1	1.0	19.0	18.0	3.9
synthetic negation	1.4	0.0	4.0	4.0	1.4
analytic negation	12.6	5.0	22.0	17.0	5.3

Mean frequencies for Broadcasts

Linguistic feature	Mean	Minimum value	Maximum value	Range	Standard deviation
past tense	18.5	3.0	34.0	31.0	11.0
perfect aspect verbs	6.4	2.0	12.0	10.0	2.9
present tense	74.8	40.0	125.0	85.0	21.1
place adverbials	9.9	0.0	20.0	20.0	5.7
time adverbials	13.9	3.0	24.0	21.0	5.9
first person pronouns	11.8	0.0	40.0	40.0	9.9
second person pronouns	2.7	0.0	12.0	12.0	3.5
third person pronouns	31.7	0.0	57.0	57.0	14.1
pronoun IT	9.9	2.0	23.0	21.0	7.1
demonstrative pronouns	5.7	1.0	17.0	16.0	4.4
indefinite pronouns	0.5	0.0	1.0	1.0	0.5
DO as pro-verb	1.1	0.0	4.0	4.0	1.4
WH questions	0.1	0.0	1.0	1.0	0.3
nominalizations	8.2	1.0	42.0	41.0	9.8
gerunds	3.8	0.0	9.0	9.0	1.9
nouns	229.8	138.0	298.0	160.0	44.8
agentless passives	3.6	0.0	9.0	9.0	2.5
BY passives	0.7	0.0	4.0	4.0	1.3
BE as main verb	21.9	13.0	41.0	28.0	7.3
existential THERE	2.2	0.0	6.0	6.0	1.4
THAT verb complements	1.0	0.0	5.0	5.0	1.5
THAT adj. complements	0.2	0.0	2.0	2.0	0.5
WH clauses	0.1	0.0	1.0	1.0	0.2
infinitives	9.8	2.0	20.0	18.0	4.5
present participial clauses	0.0	0.0	0.0	0.0	0.0
past participial clauses	0.0	0.0	0.0	0.0	0.0
past prt. WHIZ deletions	4.3	0.0	15.0	15.0	4.8
present prt. WHIZ deletions	1.2	0.0	6.0	6.0	1.5
THAT relatives: subj. position	0.6	0.0	5.0	5.0	1.2
THAT relatives: obj. position	0.2	0.0	1.0	1.0	0.4
WH relatives: subj. position	1.1	0.0	5.0	5.0	1.5
WH relatives: obj. position	0.4	0.0	2.0	2.0	0.6
WH relatives: pied pipes	0.0	0.0	0.0	0.0	0.0
sentence relatives	0.0	0.0	0.0	0.0	0.0
adv. subordinator - cause	0.4	0.0	2.0	2.0	0.6
adv. sub. - concession	0.3	0.0	2.0	2.0	0.6
adv. sub. - condition	1.3	0.0	5.0	5.0	1.5
adv. sub. - other	0.6	0.0	4.0	4.0	1.0
prepositions	118.0	96.0	135.0	39.0	10.6
attributive adjectives	61.1	39.0	87.0	48.0	11.7
predicative adjectives	3.0	0.0	16.0	16.0	3.8
adverbs	86.3	56.0	114.0	58.0	18.0
type/token ratio	49.7	42.0	55.0	13.0	3.5
word length	4.4	4.2	4.8	0.6	0.2
conjuncts	0.2	0.0	2.0	2.0	0.5
downtoners	1.9	0.0	9.0	9.0	2.4
hedges	0.7	0.0	3.0	3.0	0.9
amplifiers	4.7	3.0	9.0	6.0	2.0
emphatics	7.5	2.0	14.0	12.0	3.7
discourse particles	2.1	0.0	7.0	7.0	1.9
demonstratives	10.8	5.0	19.0	14.0	3.3
possibility modals	3.2	0.0	14.0	14.0	3.5
necessity modals	0.6	0.0	2.0	2.0	0.8
predictive modals	2.1	0.0	7.0	7.0	2.1
public verbs	1.9	0.0	8.0	8.0	2.2
private verbs	10.1	1.0	28.0	27.0	6.4
suasive verbs	1.9	0.0	5.0	5.0	1.6
SEEM/APPEAR	0.4	0.0	2.0	2.0	0.7
contractions	21.5	2.0	50.0	48.0	11.7
THAT deletion	1.3	0.0	8.0	8.0	2.2
stranded prepositions	4.6	0.0	12.0	12.0	3.1
split infinitives	0.0	0.0	0.0	0.0	0.0
split auxiliaries	2.7	0.0	6.0	6.0	1.9
phrasal coordination	1.3	0.0	6.0	6.0	1.6
non-phrasal coordination	8.9	2.0	17.0	15.0	4.1
synthetic negation	0.8	0.0	4.0	4.0	1.3
analytic negation	4.3	0.0	14.0	14.0	4.2

Mean frequencies for Spontaneous Speeches

Linguistic feature	Mean	Minimum value	Maximum value	Range	Standard deviation
past tense	63.9	9.0	109.0	100.0	40.3
perfect aspect verbs	7.6	2.0	12.0	10.0	3.3
present tense	80.4	48.0	109.0	61.0	16.3
place adverbials	1.8	0.0	5.0	5.0	1.6
time adverbials	5.1	0.0	11.0	11.0	2.7
first person pronouns	60.4	22.0	122.0	100.0	29.9
second person pronouns	14.6	0.0	42.0	42.0	12.5
third person pronouns	31.9	8.0	73.0	65.0	19.1
pronoun IT	13.6	6.0	22.0	16.0	6.3
demonstrative pronouns	9.1	4.0	15.0	11.0	3.4
indefinite pronouns	1.6	0.0	4.0	4.0	1.7
DO as pro-verb	4.4	0.0	14.0	14.0	3.9
WH questions	1.0	0.0	4.0	4.0	1.2
nominalizations	18.2	0.0	41.0	41.0	14.1
gerunds	4.3	0.0	8.0	8.0	3.0
nouns	157.7	135.0	188.0	53.0	16.8
agentless passives	6.2	0.0	18.0	18.0	4.2
BY passives	0.1	0.0	1.0	1.0	0.3
BE as main verb	35.2	16.0	48.0	32.0	7.9
existential THERE	3.6	0.0	9.0	9.0	3.1
THAT verb complements	7.1	0.0	20.0	20.0	5.2
THAT adj. complements	0.4	0.0	3.0	3.0	1.0
WH clauses	1.2	0.0	4.0	4.0	1.5
infinitives	15.1	4.0	28.0	24.0	7.2
present participial clauses	0.2	0.0	1.0	1.0	0.4
past participial clauses	0.0	0.0	0.0	0.0	0.0
past prt. WHIZ deletions	0.8	0.0	3.0	3.0	0.9
present prt. WHIZ deletions	0.8	0.0	6.0	6.0	1.6
THAT relatives: subj. position	0.2	0.0	1.0	1.0	0.4
THAT relatives: obj. position	1.4	0.0	4.0	4.0	1.4
WH relatives: subj. position	4.5	0.0	8.0	8.0	2.9
WH relatives: obj. position	2.1	0.0	7.0	7.0	2.1
WH relatives: pied pipes	0.6	0.0	4.0	4.0	1.1
sentence relatives	0.3	0.0	2.0	2.0	0.6
adv. subordinator - cause	3.1	0.0	7.0	7.0	2.3
adv. sub. - concession	0.1	0.0	1.0	1.0	0.2
adv. sub. - condition	3.1	0.0	8.0	8.0	2.3
adv. sub. - other	0.8	0.0	3.0	3.0	1.0
prepositions	94.6	66.0	128.0	62.0	20.6
attributive adjectives	44.2	16.0	67.0	51.0	15.4
predicative adjectives	4.4	1.0	10.0	9.0	2.1
adverbs	65.4	47.0	86.0	39.0	11.3
type/token ratio	44.9	35.0	50.0	15.0	3.9
word length	4.2	3.8	4.7	0.9	0.3
conjuncts	0.4	0.0	3.0	3.0	0.8
downtoners	1.7	0.0	7.0	7.0	1.9
hedges	0.5	0.0	4.0	4.0	1.0
amplifiers	5.1	0.0	12.0	12.0	3.2
emphatics	5.8	1.0	10.0	9.0	2.3
discourse particles	3.6	1.0	9.0	8.0	2.4
demonstratives	11.6	4.0	18.0	14.0	4.0
possibility modals	6.6	2.0	13.0	11.0	3.1
necessity modals	1.4	0.0	5.0	5.0	1.6
predictive modals	9.1	2.0	25.0	23.0	6.1
public verbs	14.0	0.0	40.0	40.0	9.8
private verbs	21.6	14.0	39.0	25.0	6.0
suasive verbs	2.7	0.0	5.0	5.0	1.9
SEEM/APPEAR	0.4	0.0	2.0	2.0	0.7
contractions	17.8	8.0	40.0	32.0	9.5
THAT deletion	5.6	1.0	16.0	15.0	3.8
stranded prepositions	4.5	1.0	13.0	12.0	3.3
split infinitives	0.0	0.0	0.0	0.0	0.0
split auxiliaries	4.1	1.0	10.0	9.0	2.7
phrasal coordination	1.7	0.0	8.0	8.0	1.9
non-phrasal coordination	14.9	3.0	44.0	41.0	11.5
synthetic negation	1.6	0.0	4.0	4.0	1.3
analytic negation	9.1	1.0	27.0	26.0	6.9

Mean frequencies for Prepared Speeches

Linguistic feature	Mean	Minimum value	Maximum value	Range	Standard deviation
past tense	48.3	14.0	87.0	73.0	22.5
perfect aspect verbs	11.3	2.0	40.0	38.0	9.1
present tense	70.5	28.0	104.0	76.0	21.1
place adverbials	1.9	0.0	8.0	8.0	2.1
time adverbials	7.1	3.0	20.0	17.0	4.4
first person pronouns	41.8	10.0	95.0	85.0	21.4
second person pronouns	5.1	0.0	14.0	14.0	4.9
third person pronouns	37.1	16.0	58.0	42.0	15.3
pronoun IT	8.9	4.0	18.0	14.0	4.4
demonstrative pronouns	6.9	2.0	9.0	7.0	2.1
indefinite pronouns	1.5	0.0	3.0	3.0	1.2
DO as pro-verb	2.4	0.0	7.0	7.0	2.3
WH questions	0.3	0.0	2.0	2.0	0.6
nominalizations	20.6	6.0	46.0	40.0	11.5
gerunds	5.1	2.0	9.0	7.0	1.9
nouns	189.1	153.0	221.0	68.0	21.6
agentless passives	9.6	4.0	20.0	16.0	3.9
BY passives	0.2	0.0	1.0	1.0	0.4
BE as main verb	30.5	19.0	38.0	19.0	5.8
existential THERE	3.1	1.0	6.0	5.0	1.4
THAT verb complements	7.0	1.0	13.0	12.0	4.5
THAT adj. complements	0.6	0.0	2.0	2.0	0.7
WH clauses	0.2	0.0	1.0	1.0	0.4
infinitives	16.2	6.0	36.0	30.0	6.6
present participial clauses	0.2	0.0	2.0	2.0	0.6
past participial clauses	0.0	0.0	0.0	0.0	0.0
past prt. WHIZ deletions	0.9	0.0	5.0	5.0	1.4
present prt. WHIZ deletions	1.4	0.0	5.0	5.0	1.2
THAT relatives: subj. position	0.3	0.0	2.0	2.0	0.7
THAT relatives: obj. position	1.6	0.0	4.0	4.0	1.4
WH relatives: subj. position	2.4	0.0	9.0	9.0	2.3
WH relatives: obj. position	2.5	1.0	8.0	7.0	1.8
WH relatives: pied pipes	1.1	0.0	6.0	6.0	1.6
sentence relatives	0.1	0.0	1.0	1.0	0.3
adv. subordinator - cause	1.6	0.0	5.0	5.0	1.7
adv. sub. - concession	0.1	0.0	1.0	1.0	0.4
adv. sub. - condition	2.4	0.0	4.0	4.0	1.1
adv. sub. - other	0.8	0.0	5.0	5.0	1.4
prepositions	112.6	92.0	137.0	45.0	12.5
attributive adjectives	48.9	28.0	72.0	44.0	13.6
predicative adjectives	3.6	1.0	6.0	5.0	1.6
adverbs	62.2	45.0	78.0	33.0	9.8
type/token ratio	49.0	43.0	56.0	13.0	3.4
word length	4.4	4.1	4.8	0.7	0.2
conjuncts	0.5	0.0	2.0	2.0	0.7
downtoners	1.5	0.0	4.0	4.0	0.9
hedges	0.2	0.0	2.0	2.0	0.6
amplifiers	3.1	1.0	8.0	7.0	2.1
emphatics	4.8	0.0	10.0	10.0	3.2
discourse particles	2.4	0.0	6.0	6.0	2.4
demonstratives	12.9	7.0	20.0	13.0	4.2
possibility modals	5.6	1.0	12.0	11.0	3.1
necessity modals	2.6	0.0	10.0	10.0	2.9
predictive modals	5.0	0.0	11.0	11.0	3.0
public verbs	7.9	1.0	15.0	14.0	4.8
private verbs	17.6	9.0	26.0	17.0	4.9
suasive verbs	3.3	0.0	14.0	14.0	3.5
SEEM/APPEAR	0.5	0.0	2.0	2.0	0.7
contractions	13.3	3.0	45.0	42.0	10.4
THAT deletion	1.9	0.0	6.0	6.0	1.6
stranded prepositions	3.7	1.0	7.0	6.0	1.9
split infinitives	0.0	0.0	0.0	0.0	0.0
split auxiliaries	5.3	2.0	11.0	9.0	2.9
phrasal coordination	1.1	0.0	4.0	4.0	1.2
non-phrasal coordination	8.6	4.0	16.0	12.0	3.4
synthetic negation	1.8	0.0	4.0	4.0	1.4
analytic negation	8.4	1.0	16.0	15.0	4.3

Pearson correlation coefficients for all linguistic features

Key to abbreviations

PASTTNSE	*past tense*	SUB CND	*adv. sub. – condition*
PERFECTS	*perfect aspect verbs*	SUB OTHR	*adv. sub. – other*
PRES	*present tense*	PREP	*prepositions*
PL ADV	*place adverbials*	ADJ ATTR	*attributive adjectives*
TM ADV	*time adverbials*	ADJ PRED	*predicative adjective*
PRO1	*first person pronouns*	ADVS	*adverbs*
PRO2	*second person pronouns*	TYPETOKN	*type/token ratio*
PRO3	*third person pronouns*	WRDLNGTH	*word length*
IT	*pronoun IT*	CONJNCTS	*conjuncts*
PDEM	*demonstrative pronouns*	DOWNTONE	*downtoners*
PANY	*indefinite pronouns*	GEN HDG	*hedges*
PRO DO	*DO as pro-verb*	AMPLIFR	*amplifiers*
WH QUES	*WH questions*	GEN EMPH	*emphatics*
N NOM	*nominalizations*	PRTCLE	*discourse particles*
N VBG	*gerunds*	DEM	*demonstratives*
N	*nouns*	POS MOD	*possibility modals*
AGLS PSV	*agentless passives*	NEC MOD	*necessity modals*
BY PASV	*BY passives*	PRD MOD	*predictive modals*
BE STATE	*BE as main verb*	PUB VB	*public verbs*
EX THERE	*existential THERE*	PRV VB	*private verbs*
TH CL	*THAT verb complements*	SUA VB	*suasive verbs*
ADJ CL	*THAT adj complements*	SEEM	*SEEM/APPEAR*
WH CL	*WH clauses*	CONTRAC	*contractions*
INF	*infinitives*	THAT DEL	*THAT deletion*
CL VBG	*pres participial clauses*	FINLPREP	*stranded prepositions*
CL VBN	*past participial clauses*	SPL INF	*split infinitives*
WHIZ VBN	*past prt. WHIZ del.*	SPL AUX	*split auxiliaries*
WHIZ VBG	*pres prt. WHIZ del.*	P AND	*phrasal coordination*
THTREL S	*THAT relatives: subj position*	O AND	*nonphrasal coord.*
THTREL O	*THAT relatives: obj positions*	SYNTHNEG	*synthetic negation*
REL SUBJ	*WH relatives: subj position*	NOT NEG	*analytic negation*
REL OBJ	*WH relatives: obj positions*		
REL PIPE	*WH relatives: pied pipes*		
SENT REL	*sentence relatives*		
SUB COS	*adv. subordinator – cause*		
SUB CON	*adv. sub. – concession*		

	PASTTNSE	PERFECTS	PRES	PL_ADV	TM_ADV	PRO1	PRO2	PRO3
PASTTNSE	1.00000	0.38826	-0.46964	0.09066	0.15146	0.20767	0.08508	0.68004
PERFECTS	0.38826	1.00000	-0.01617	-0.03059	0.16140	0.21244	0.17447	0.43958
PRES	-0.46964	-0.01617	1.00000	-0.21840	0.06683	0.54563	0.67463	-0.15668
PL_ADV	0.09066	-0.03059	-0.21840	1.00000	0.28275	-0.17839	-0.18327	0.05336
TM_ADV	0.15146	0.16140	0.06683	0.28275	1.00000	0.12390	0.12174	0.24769
PRO1	0.20767	0.21244	0.54563	-0.17839	0.12390	1.00000	0.66061	0.08237
PRO2	0.08508	0.17447	0.67463	-0.18327	0.12174	0.66061	1.00000	0.13895
PRO3	0.68004	0.43958	-0.15668	0.05336	0.24769	0.08237	0.13895	1.00000
IT	0.08175	0.11223	0.58245	-0.05338	0.13827	0.50378	0.58159	0.08256
PDEM	-0.13191	0.05327	0.67766	-0.14327	0.10339	0.53254	0.55424	-0.08677
PANY	0.15696	0.13283	0.43828	-0.13895	0.10865	0.50442	0.50826	0.20325
PRO_DO	0.10575	0.15091	0.61756	-0.15280	0.11347	0.58898	0.67461	0.17509
WH_QUES	0.01222	0.03829	0.39071	-0.11654	0.06070	0.35024	0.42875	0.03803
N_NOM	-0.46718	-0.24976	-0.20716	-0.17102	-0.39779	-0.45439	-0.44851	-0.50054
N_VBG	-0.25545	-0.16471	-0.17400	-0.06217	-0.25199	-0.33963	-0.32936	-0.23809
N	-0.18952	-0.22218	-0.54609	0.23642	0.00726	-0.64921	-0.64032	-0.22198
AGLS_PSV	-0.30246	-0.21462	-0.30988	-0.05442	-0.31527	-0.53324	-0.49729	-0.43401
BY_PASV	-0.25643	-0.19183	-0.27027	0.06501	-0.23745	-0.44721	-0.39437	-0.32813
BE_STATE	-0.01317	0.13137	0.67526	-0.24266	0.06773	0.52650	0.54589	0.07502
EX_THERE	0.00779	0.07520	0.24527	-0.03222	0.02522	0.14773	0.13732	-0.04950
TH_CL	-0.06171	0.09107	0.17289	-0.18172	-0.06717	0.14792	0.09175	-0.04531
ADJ_CL	-0.10634	0.11158	0.06687	-0.05342	-0.00010	-0.04023	-0.07704	-0.08351
WH_CL	0.10693	0.06669	0.30136	-0.10515	-0.04286	0.29494	0.32610	0.17048
INF	-0.00349	0.07889	0.13390	-0.15376	-0.07708	0.13200	0.08617	0.12034
CL_VBG	0.35917	0.05858	-0.31088	0.16726	-0.03561	-0.09968	-0.06359	0.34559
CL_VBN	-0.21787	-0.18393	-0.08737	-0.01068	-0.20037	-0.19572	-0.16818	-0.22565
WHIZ_VBN	-0.36383	-0.29656	-0.33674	0.11109	-0.19716	-0.52418	-0.46549	-0.42543
WHIZ_VBG	-0.15894	-0.17916	-0.35192	0.09160	-0.17633	-0.37919	-0.40021	-0.27958
THTREL_S	-0.09222	0.08081	0.11680	0.04083	0.00244	0.07057	0.06329	-0.05561
THTREL_O	-0.17682	0.06182	0.10433	-0.08907	-0.12932	0.02058	-0.05491	-0.11063
REL_SUBJ	-0.20742	-0.12933	-0.09653	-0.09257	-0.19170	-0.22820	-0.26886	-0.22284
REL_OBJ	-0.25629	-0.06956	-0.13278	-0.15400	-0.22583	-0.20847	-0.30368	-0.19753
REL_PIPE	-0.25790	-0.08099	-0.11872	-0.09351	-0.26097	-0.27557	-0.31400	-0.25780
SENT_REL	-0.05454	0.06389	0.40776	-0.08671	-0.01592	0.36091	0.31829	-0.05719
SUB_COS	-0.02387	0.07929	0.50706	-0.20644	0.05969	0.53056	0.51424	-0.00053
SUB_CON	0.07856	0.00944	-0.05924	-0.01716	-0.01155	-0.08964	-0.10116	0.14291
SUB_CND	-0.10718	0.04562	0.49314	-0.13874	-0.01222	0.30867	0.37454	0.06064
SUB_OTHR	-0.09788	-0.05035	-0.09061	-0.05159	-0.13090	-0.13466	-0.14774	-0.11600
PREP	-0.40885	-0.32014	-0.48861	0.03419	-0.27893	-0.64065	-0.65536	-0.50758
ADJ_ATTR	-0.41144	-0.29199	-0.37374	0.05141	-0.23382	-0.59229	-0.58074	-0.44570
ADJ_PRED	-0.03803	0.06175	0.26537	-0.13684	-0.09467	0.15768	0.21056	0.09366
ADVS	0.23039	0.20289	0.44484	0.20120	0.47032	0.52539	0.53574	0.32039
TYPETOKN	0.13215	0.04725	-0.45028	0.10789	0.01433	-0.35157	-0.39225	0.13939
WRDLNGTH	-0.40526	-0.26674	-0.47190	0.01614	-0.28139	-0.72163	-0.66034	-0.45480
CONJNCTS	-0.36426	-0.21571	-0.03696	-0.11496	-0.28790	-0.30885	-0.26962	-0.36039
DOWNTONE	-0.04323	-0.01081	-0.09045	-0.01456	-0.08060	-0.10304	-0.11607	-0.06267
GEN_HDG	0.00798	0.06736	0.43885	-0.04599	0.10351	0.41146	0.42659	0.04862
AMPLIFR	-0.05670	0.01666	0.47346	-0.10865	0.17105	0.48020	0.48378	-0.02743
GEN_EMPH	-0.06028	0.10107	0.63177	-0.13763	0.19199	0.49564	0.60566	0.07795
PRTCLE	-0.09094	0.09962	0.63208	-0.14472	0.31489	0.56157	0.59313	-0.03474
DEM	-0.30321	-0.03756	0.15560	-0.09785	-0.06162	-0.00996	-0.06862	-0.28221
POS_MOD	-0.16127	0.04442	0.51447	-0.21145	-0.09755	0.39220	0.39297	-0.03998
NEC_MOD	-0.21667	-0.05843	0.20159	-0.13289	-0.12389	0.02760	-0.01716	-0.11132
PRD_MOD	-0.12123	0.00715	0.27767	-0.08913	-0.03027	0.18452	0.14547	0.00764
PUB_VB	0.31804	0.17866	0.00875	-0.08672	-0.02844	0.16168	0.13743	0.25848
PRV_VB	0.16308	0.22484	0.66623	-0.21205	0.05489	0.68798	0.75392	0.24709
SUA_VB	-0.09767	-0.09035	-0.06883	-0.07080	-0.12561	-0.12319	-0.14871	-0.10397
SEEM	0.03733	0.05795	-0.00408	-0.01308	-0.04100	-0.04479	-0.04053	0.08981
CONTRAC	0.07162	0.22584	0.73228	-0.09693	0.26306	0.71809	0.78950	0.15458
THAT_DEL	0.15968	0.20932	0.64584	-0.15507	0.14620	0.66963	0.70122	0.21105
FINLPREP	0.01620	0.01360	0.38137	0.00068	0.21747	0.39486	0.35019	0.02595
SPL_INF	-0.03914	0.10029	0.08171	-0.00186	0.08781	0.07311	0.04007	0.00225
SPL_AUX	-0.07418	0.15357	-0.01256	-0.08823	-0.11512	-0.09936	-0.13630	-0.00993
P_AND	-0.12138	-0.12812	-0.35569	0.01021	-0.25447	-0.38114	-0.39155	-0.12814
O_AND	0.14402	0.09914	0.34629	-0.06129	0.21315	0.57964	0.40155	0.09991
SYNTHNEG	0.23031	0.20833	-0.16484	0.01178	-0.04100	-0.08553	-0.11496	0.23635
NOT_NEG	0.16515	0.24730	0.62933	-0.22265	0.11472	0.59457	0.67825	0.30780

	IT	PDEM	PANY	PRO_DO	WH_QUES	N_NOM	N_VBG	N
PASTTNSE	0.08175	-0.13191	0.15696	0.10575	0.01222	-0.46718	-0.25545	-0.18952
PERFECTS	0.11223	0.05327	0.13283	0.15091	0.03829	-0.24976	-0.16471	-0.22218
PRES	0.58245	0.67766	0.43828	0.61756	0.39071	-0.20716	-0.17400	-0.54609
PL_ADV	-0.05338	-0.14327	-0.13895	-0.15280	-0.11654	-0.17102	-0.06217	0.23642
TM_ADV	0.13827	0.10339	0.10865	0.11347	0.06070	-0.39779	-0.25199	0.00726
PRO1	0.50378	0.53254	0.50442	0.58898	0.35024	-0.45439	-0.33963	-0.64921
PRO2	0.58159	0.55424	0.50826	0.67461	0.42875	-0.44851	-0.32936	-0.64032
PRO3	0.08256	-0.08677	0.20325	0.17509	0.03803	-0.50054	-0.23809	-0.22198
IT	1.00000	0.56752	0.48445	0.62067	0.25244	-0.39380	-0.28411	-0.59379
PDEM	0.56752	1.00000	0.40492	0.58543	0.39301	-0.28655	-0.28251	-0.50991
PANY	0.48445	0.40492	1.00000	0.60047	0.25584	-0.39614	-0.22400	-0.52269
PRO_DO	0.62067	0.58543	0.60047	1.00000	0.40148	-0.42756	-0.26482	-0.60887
WH_QUES	0.25244	0.39301	0.25584	0.40148	1.00000	-0.19412	-0.15085	-0.28806
N_NOM	-0.39380	-0.28655	-0.39614	-0.42756	-0.19412	1.00000	0.36435	0.24086
N_VBG	-0.28411	-0.28251	-0.22400	-0.26482	-0.15085	0.36435	1.00000	0.19944
N	-0.59379	-0.50991	-0.52269	-0.60887	-0.28806	0.24086	0.19944	1.00000
AGLS_PSV	-0.46271	-0.32492	-0.41763	-0.45148	-0.23469	0.57572	0.37407	0.34418
BY_PASV	-0.37880	-0.29945	-0.35410	-0.36913	-0.19259	0.44639	0.26233	0.37035
BE_STATE	0.60417	0.63818	0.42389	0.51604	0.35928	-0.32736	-0.28196	-0.58848
EX_THERE	0.25036	0.31228	0.14422	0.18325	0.17340	-0.13277	-0.11568	-0.17155
TH_CL	0.09111	0.25278	0.05890	0.12820	0.06625	0.13699	-0.03724	-0.24515
ADJ_CL	-0.05692	0.04808	-0.08718	-0.09465	-0.03609	0.16307	0.04774	-0.06269
WH_CL	0.31056	0.25221	0.28850	0.38307	0.15112	-0.20930	-0.13329	-0.33131
INF	0.03428	-0.03732	0.13716	0.15438	-0.08213	0.06707	0.14262	-0.19750
CL_VBG	-0.13136	-0.26240	-0.01676	-0.11052	-0.14631	-0.09307	0.06272	-0.07320
CL_VBN	-0.19046	-0.15487	-0.16763	-0.18140	-0.08350	0.30114	0.16118	0.08322
WHIZ_VBN	-0.43935	-0.35327	-0.39339	-0.45580	-0.21221	0.47368	0.29987	0.45947
WHIZ_VBG	-0.38955	-0.31308	-0.31929	-0.39096	-0.20403	0.37331	0.20716	0.37838
THTREL_S	0.05872	0.11837	0.10466	0.05512	0.12853	0.01179	0.08791	-0.07083
THTREL_O	-0.04126	0.12412	0.04126	0.04731	0.05002	0.19717	0.11587	-0.02739
REL_SUBJ	-0.20842	-0.07123	-0.16871	-0.17671	-0.04964	0.29988	0.19892	0.22856
REL_OBJ	-0.23270	-0.14485	-0.26604	-0.26781	-0.11524	0.43330	0.19917	0.19372
REL_PIPE	-0.21094	-0.13470	-0.21872	-0.24581	-0.08636	0.42272	0.26822	0.21323
SENT_REL	0.35021	0.47358	0.25305	0.34428	0.26043	-0.17224	-0.13674	-0.28235
SUB_COS	0.43280	0.50330	0.39583	0.51728	0.26320	-0.24201	-0.22930	-0.43103
SUB_CON	-0.03098	-0.10413	-0.02237	-0.03630	-0.05903	-0.02294	0.07030	-0.00402
SUB_CND	0.36470	0.32808	0.37571	0.33287	0.06805	-0.12692	-0.12101	-0.44737
SUB_OTHR	-0.17064	-0.08499	-0.15069	-0.11548	-0.06327	0.21583	0.11803	0.01464
PREP	-0.56201	-0.41997	-0.54637	-0.60890	-0.33918	0.67927	0.39344	0.56834
ADJ_ATTR	-0.47257	-0.44817	-0.45845	-0.54825	-0.29692	0.57585	0.35724	0.51276
ADJ_PRED	0.08649	0.05845	0.06418	0.12369	0.08284	0.01589	0.00743	-0.32839
ADVS	0.55075	0.44553	0.45422	0.52866	0.25348	-0.60056	-0.35021	-0.56324
TYPETOKN	-0.38328	-0.48124	-0.26031	-0.39834	-0.24304	0.02640	0.14942	0.42958
WRDLNGTH	-0.59789	-0.48634	-0.54139	-0.60367	-0.28995	0.76343	0.44058	0.63217
CONJNCTS	-0.22815	-0.14260	-0.24361	-0.25352	-0.16742	0.50419	0.27541	0.04078
DOWNTONE	-0.07943	-0.06469	-0.13416	-0.11316	-0.07865	0.02928	0.07951	0.06349
GEN_HDG	0.38358	0.36472	0.47786	0.44408	0.21954	-0.30244	-0.22823	-0.39770
AMPLIFR	0.38447	0.58933	0.37816	0.44172	0.28824	-0.27921	-0.27022	-0.36763
GEN_EMPH	0.48632	0.51019	0.49368	0.56036	0.33493	-0.38657	-0.22527	-0.48304
PRTCLE	0.53498	0.69441	0.44932	0.60065	0.38904	-0.32713	-0.33620	-0.47180
DEM	0.04829	0.22779	-0.02442	-0.01469	-0.00394	0.25260	0.09815	-0.11790
POS_MOD	0.29547	0.33204	0.36169	0.37890	0.16201	-0.03543	-0.07722	-0.48899
NEC_MOD	0.04796	0.06118	-0.00241	0.02177	0.07097	0.21669	0.09114	-0.10784
PRD_MOD	0.10417	0.13758	0.13007	0.13887	0.09828	0.05516	0.00234	-0.15288
PUB_VB	0.08498	0.04029	0.15253	0.14968	0.13752	-0.07981	-0.07189	-0.19017
PRV_VB	0.62632	0.60033	0.55724	0.69143	0.40173	-0.43092	-0.29698	-0.74585
SUA_VB	-0.14103	-0.15583	-0.01137	-0.04416	-0.11445	0.26985	0.26818	0.07973
SEEM	0.04008	-0.06919	0.03240	0.03249	-0.06158	0.03998	0.00788	-0.14403
CONTRAC	0.69432	0.70670	0.55695	0.71694	0.40299	-0.51898	-0.41476	-0.62905
THAT_DEL	0.56910	0.58955	0.52159	0.65689	0.42177	-0.45604	-0.32020	-0.59845
FINLPREP	0.34546	0.57438	0.31640	0.39112	0.31576	-0.29929	-0.24537	-0.37139
SPL_INF	-0.02783	-0.00557	-0.00999	0.00057	-0.01753	-0.05368	-0.04767	0.01861
SPL_AUX	-0.10258	-0.14036	-0.07481	-0.08455	-0.16498	0.18878	0.15763	-0.04923
P_AND	-0.37876	-0.46896	-0.32003	-0.37624	-0.22611	0.30522	0.30452	0.41172
O_AND	0.34821	0.46526	0.33914	0.35708	0.30159	-0.38073	-0.34427	-0.34560
SYNTHNEG	-0.04182	-0.17931	-0.00139	-0.07831	-0.04402	-0.04479	0.04640	-0.03729
NOT_NEG	0.59400	0.56545	0.55855	0.73304	0.34282	-0.42409	-0.34022	-0.68202

	AGLS_PSV	BY_PASV	BE_STATE	EX_THERE	TH_CL	ADJ_CL	WH_CL	INF
PASTTNSE	-0.30246	-0.25643	-0.01317	0.00779	-0.06171	-0.10634	0.10693	-0.00349
PERFECTS	-0.21462	-0.19183	0.13137	0.07520	0.09107	0.11158	0.06669	0.07889
PRES	-0.30988	-0.27027	0.67526	0.24527	0.17289	0.06687	0.30136	0.13390
PL_ADV	-0.05442	0.06501	-0.24266	-0.03222	-0.18172	-0.05342	-0.10515	-0.15376
TM_ADV	-0.31527	-0.23745	0.06773	0.02522	-0.06717	-0.00010	-0.04286	-0.07708
PRO1	-0.53324	-0.44721	0.52650	0.14773	0.14792	-0.04023	0.29494	0.13200
PRO2	-0.49729	-0.39437	0.54589	0.13732	0.09175	-0.07704	0.32610	0.08617
PRO3	-0.43401	-0.32813	0.07502	-0.04950	-0.04531	-0.08351	0.17048	0.12034
IT	-0.46271	-0.37880	0.60417	0.25036	0.09111	-0.05692	0.31056	0.03428
PDEM	-0.32492	-0.29945	0.63818	0.31228	0.25278	0.04808	0.25221	-0.03732
PANY	-0.41763	-0.35410	0.42389	0.14422	0.05890	-0.08718	0.28850	0.13716
PRO_DO	-0.45148	-0.36913	0.51604	0.18325	0.12820	-0.09465	0.38307	0.15438
WH_QUES	-0.23469	-0.19259	0.35928	0.17340	0.06625	-0.03609	0.15112	-0.08213
N_NOM	0.57572	0.44639	-0.32736	-0.13277	0.13699	0.16307	-0.20930	0.06707
N_VBG	0.37407	0.26233	-0.28196	-0.11568	-0.03724	0.04774	-0.13329	0.14262
N	0.34418	0.37035	-0.58848	-0.17155	-0.24515	-0.06269	-0.33131	-0.19750
AGLS_PSV	1.00000	0.54097	-0.37758	-0.04527	0.07078	0.09538	-0.23534	-0.07089
BY_PASV	0.54097	1.00000	-0.38180	-0.16374	-0.04221	0.05751	-0.19296	-0.23197
BE_STATE	-0.37758	-0.38180	1.00000	0.43751	0.23875	0.12706	0.27170	0.09000
EX_THERE	-0.04527	-0.16374	0.43751	1.00000	0.12178	0.08144	0.14457	-0.05660
TH_CL	0.07078	-0.04221	0.23875	0.12178	1.00000	0.21122	0.02286	0.20472
ADJ_CL	0.09538	0.05751	0.12706	0.08144	0.21122	1.00000	-0.08245	0.03112
WH_CL	-0.23534	-0.19296	0.27170	0.14457	0.02286	-0.08245	1.00000	0.12417
INF	-0.07089	-0.23197	0.09000	-0.05660	0.20472	0.03112	0.12417	1.00000
CL_VBG	-0.00159	-0.01450	-0.21063	-0.12786	-0.18357	-0.05800	-0.01810	-0.01381
CL_VBN	0.33531	0.35214	-0.20412	-0.08127	-0.07683	0.00701	-0.09464	-0.08744
WHIZ_VBN	0.56125	0.56301	-0.45470	-0.16850	-0.14983	0.01544	-0.23186	-0.28238
WHIZ_VBG	0.42297	0.37657	-0.42524	-0.07526	-0.11630	-0.05604	-0.24441	-0.19599
THTREL_S	-0.01745	-0.05369	0.05708	0.08068	0.02705	0.05035	0.05633	-0.00386
THTREL_O	0.04511	-0.01663	0.10734	0.07206	0.44801	0.13178	0.00079	0.17883
REL_SUBJ	0.19836	0.17183	-0.05081	0.09760	0.07765	0.05293	0.01374	0.06235
REL_OBJ	0.24907	0.16815	-0.14566	-0.04515	0.12455	0.08730	-0.08466	0.08697
REL_PIPE	0.35460	0.25588	-0.12087	0.04589	0.09194	0.10279	-0.16019	-0.02472
SENT_REL	-0.18281	-0.15332	0.32134	0.20127	0.05037	-0.04623	0.23472	-0.07389
SUB_COS	-0.30468	-0.24305	0.47163	0.16811	0.19924	-0.03172	0.32470	0.11999
SUB_CON	0.01244	0.02862	-0.01825	-0.06953	-0.04640	-0.03269	-0.01446	0.00888
SUB_CND	-0.16992	-0.20069	0.42306	0.12062	0.21367	0.14899	0.16139	0.30321
SUB_OTHR	0.23628	0.18059	-0.07762	-0.06689	0.10402	0.17524	-0.08156	-0.01889
PREP	0.58273	0.51390	-0.55925	-0.14770	-0.04000	0.06371	-0.34626	-0.21716
ADJ_ATTR	0.44720	0.38529	-0.41951	-0.19157	-0.18188	0.06172	-0.29424	-0.08339
ADJ_PRED	-0.02421	-0.02699	0.39152	0.01593	0.08931	0.18460	0.00070	0.19998
ADVS	-0.55569	-0.48427	0.47581	0.11124	0.00569	-0.03935	0.23748	0.04522
TYPETOKN	0.02327	0.08520	-0.38867	-0.24008	-0.23486	-0.03398	-0.21584	-0.00505
WRDLNGTH	0.59398	0.50884	-0.55161	-0.20036	-0.05438	0.08220	-0.31525	-0.09416
CONJNCTS	0.42966	0.35286	-0.08362	-0.05974	0.10050	0.24313	-0.09691	-0.00341
DOWNTONE	0.08182	0.08249	-0.02695	0.03753	-0.03411	0.08582	-0.03696	-0.08725
GEN_HDG	-0.28711	-0.19900	0.29143	0.03803	-0.02957	-0.07814	0.17742	-0.04914
AMPLIFR	-0.31351	-0.24142	0.51194	0.21195	0.18894	-0.00985	0.20810	-0.04996
GEN_EMPH	-0.47067	-0.37119	0.49263	0.16055	0.00794	-0.01060	0.26296	0.09755
PRTCLE	-0.36544	-0.31556	0.54448	0.26530	0.19606	0.02649	0.18692	-0.05127
DEM	0.11165	-0.00652	0.15683	0.11435	0.26711	0.21637	0.06385	-0.01173
POS_MOD	-0.09702	-0.15700	0.35205	0.09062	0.17304	0.01727	0.23714	0.29473
NEC_MOD	0.15988	0.06424	0.10691	0.07232	0.18261	0.18087	0.01510	0.30720
PRD_MOD	-0.08748	-0.15590	0.14367	0.00553	0.16176	0.09292	0.14123	0.33962
PUB_VB	-0.12146	-0.09715	0.06830	0.10640	0.25632	-0.02620	0.23231	0.12793
PRV_VB	-0.47198	-0.37646	0.62005	0.19279	0.22514	0.00161	0.42957	0.12233
SUA_VB	0.20656	0.07315	-0.13007	-0.05069	0.09720	0.02029	-0.01055	0.31460
SEEM	-0.04468	-0.04795	0.00940	0.04293	0.07650	0.06302	-0.00524	0.12019
CONTRAC	-0.55108	-0.39708	0.63155	0.25305	0.03943	-0.03612	0.32786	-0.05114
THAT_DEL	-0.47393	-0.34769	0.55711	0.17683	0.05366	-0.06320	0.33187	0.05872
FINLPREP	-0.31985	-0.26903	0.40777	0.25784	0.13017	-0.00911	0.15948	-0.08231
SPL_INF	-0.05926	-0.03049	0.09936	-0.05530	0.01063	0.06161	0.01835	0.03383
SPL_AUX	0.24998	0.09257	-0.03576	-0.10178	0.14095	0.14227	-0.01948	0.30278
P_AND	0.27357	0.23256	-0.38136	-0.15916	-0.25930	-0.06546	-0.11810	-0.00505
O_AND	-0.37278	-0.29791	0.39080	0.20908	0.17397	-0.03598	0.23637	-0.07334
SYNTHNEG	-0.01418	-0.10676	0.04504	0.17278	0.07682	0.07913	0.13862	0.09331
NOT_NEG	-0.46781	-0.39302	0.62309	0.19554	0.21415	0.01284	0.37251	0.14087

	CL_VBG	CL_VBN	WHIZ_VBN	WHIZ_VBG	THTREL_S	THTREL_O	REL_SUBJ	REL_OBJ
PASTTNSE	0.35917	-0.21787	-0.36383	-0.15894	-0.09222	-0.17682	-0.20742	-0.25629
PERFECTS	0.05858	-0.18393	-0.29656	-0.17916	0.08081	0.06182	-0.12933	-0.06956
PRES	-0.31088	-0.08737	-0.33674	-0.35192	0.11680	0.10433	-0.09653	-0.13278
PL_ADV	0.16726	-0.01068	0.11109	0.09160	0.04083	-0.08907	-0.09257	-0.15400
TM_ADV	-0.03561	-0.20037	-0.19716	-0.17633	0.00244	-0.12932	-0.19170	-0.22583
PRO1	-0.09968	-0.19572	-0.52418	-0.37919	0.07057	0.02058	-0.22820	-0.20847
PRO2	-0.06359	-0.16818	-0.46549	-0.40021	0.06329	-0.05491	-0.26886	-0.30368
PRO3	0.34559	-0.22565	-0.42543	-0.27958	-0.05561	-0.11063	-0.22284	-0.19753
IT	-0.13136	-0.19046	-0.43935	-0.38955	0.05872	-0.04126	-0.20842	-0.23270
PDEM	-0.26240	-0.15487	-0.35327	-0.31308	0.11837	0.12412	-0.07123	-0.14485
PANY	-0.01676	-0.16763	-0.39339	-0.31929	0.10466	0.04126	-0.16871	-0.26604
PRO_DO	-0.11052	-0.18140	-0.45580	-0.39096	0.05512	0.04731	-0.17671	-0.26781
WH_QUES	-0.14631	-0.08350	-0.21221	-0.20403	0.12853	0.05002	-0.04964	-0.11524
N_NOM	-0.09307	0.30114	0.47368	0.37331	0.01179	0.19717	0.29988	0.43330
N_VBG	0.06272	0.16118	0.29987	0.20716	0.08791	0.11587	0.19892	0.19917
N	-0.07320	0.08322	0.45947	0.37838	-0.07083	-0.02739	0.22856	0.19372
AGLS_PSV	-0.00159	0.33531	0.56125	0.42297	-0.01745	0.04511	0.19836	0.24907
BY_PASV	-0.01450	0.35214	0.56301	0.37657	-0.05369	-0.01663	0.17183	0.16815
BE_STATE	-0.21063	-0.20412	-0.45470	-0.42524	0.05708	0.10734	-0.05081	-0.14566
EX_THERE	-0.12786	-0.08127	-0.16850	-0.07526	0.08068	0.07206	0.09760	-0.04515
TH_CL	-0.18357	-0.07683	-0.14983	-0.11630	0.02705	0.44801	0.07765	0.12455
ADJ_CL	-0.05800	0.00701	0.01544	-0.05604	0.05035	0.13178	0.05293	0.08730
WH_CL	-0.01810	-0.09464	-0.23186	-0.24441	0.05633	0.00079	0.01374	-0.08466
INF	-0.01381	-0.08744	-0.28238	-0.19599	-0.00386	0.17883	0.06235	0.08697
CL_VBG	1.00000	0.05891	0.02159	0.07503	-0.00508	-0.18810	-0.16192	-0.12532
CL_VBN	0.05891	1.00000	0.35105	0.20279	-0.07040	-0.04851	0.05160	0.09771
WHIZ_VBN	0.02159	0.35105	1.00000	0.41357	-0.06458	-0.02644	0.11645	0.13765
WHIZ_VBG	0.07503	0.20279	0.41357	1.00000	-0.01459	-0.07698	0.15319	0.18943
THTREL_S	-0.00508	-0.07040	-0.06458	-0.01459	1.00000	0.25104	0.00541	-0.00061
THTREL_O	-0.18810	-0.04851	-0.02644	-0.07698	0.25104	1.00000	0.15561	0.15668
REL_SUBJ	-0.16192	0.05160	0.11645	0.15319	0.00541	0.15561	1.00000	0.36910
REL_OBJ	-0.12532	0.09771	0.13765	0.18943	-0.00061	0.15668	0.36910	1.00000
REL_PIPE	-0.08815	0.14642	0.21925	0.26028	0.06279	0.18015	0.37096	0.74998
SENT_REL	-0.14632	-0.07366	-0.18745	-0.18382	0.08677	0.05296	-0.07798	-0.07251
SUB_COS	-0.23860	-0.09286	-0.34611	-0.27444	-0.03028	0.08980	-0.08761	-0.10654
SUB_CON	0.11206	-0.02482	-0.02034	-0.00597	0.06128	-0.02645	0.01522	0.00014
SUB_CND	-0.08483	-0.02777	-0.29293	-0.23329	0.08264	0.05865	-0.13929	-0.11127
SUB_OTHR	0.10640	0.19116	0.15926	0.18712	-0.05199	0.00973	0.00849	0.11228
PREP	-0.03356	0.30297	0.64904	0.48921	0.01474	0.11655	0.28696	0.39587
ADJ_ATTR	-0.04023	0.19860	0.49772	0.33613	-0.00832	0.04851	0.31553	0.26275
ADJ_PRED	0.11576	0.03240	-0.08538	-0.16130	-0.04037	0.03177	-0.13821	-0.10600
ADVS	-0.00933	-0.26795	-0.49461	-0.41098	0.04384	-0.10324	-0.31091	-0.35032
TYPETOKN	0.14928	-0.09190	0.07562	0.13777	-0.06120	-0.08946	0.00729	0.03078
WRDLNGTH	-0.07818	0.22212	0.55912	0.46403	-0.03365	0.11603	0.34836	0.37529
CONJNCTS	0.02044	0.22316	0.33687	0.20699	0.02229	0.09381	0.13466	0.24635
DOWNTONE	-0.03909	0.00268	0.08469	-0.00102	-0.02874	0.08018	0.04830	0.07255
GEN_HDG	-0.14638	-0.11696	-0.23814	-0.22048	0.00972	-0.03078	-0.16404	-0.21682
AMPLIFR	-0.25295	-0.14187	-0.29483	-0.28613	0.07977	0.13409	-0.03768	-0.12235
GEN_EMPH	-0.19033	-0.21391	-0.43386	-0.34451	0.13268	-0.02340	-0.15707	-0.24656
PRTCLE	-0.26249	-0.15178	-0.34909	-0.30183	0.05245	0.07819	-0.11638	-0.19278
DEM	-0.17412	0.03640	0.07078	-0.03889	0.15671	0.22008	0.13652	0.19602
POS_MOD	-0.08142	-0.00686	-0.24403	-0.24909	0.10787	0.04959	-0.03991	-0.06560
NEC_MOD	-0.06599	0.00874	-0.01603	-0.03930	-0.00267	0.12564	0.02186	0.11652
PRD_MOD	-0.07090	-0.01875	-0.17558	-0.08917	0.12097	0.15332	0.00979	0.03637
PUB_VB	0.01657	-0.11536	-0.21305	-0.12917	-0.06681	0.08852	-0.12329	-0.12651
PRV_VB	-0.06823	-0.15880	-0.50619	-0.43588	0.05565	0.02105	-0.20493	-0.24928
SUA_VB	0.02830	0.05978	0.16040	0.04152	0.00383	0.14251	0.07739	0.09584
SEEM	0.04054	-0.02011	-0.07407	-0.04505	-0.01812	0.02650	0.00945	0.09197
CONTRAC	-0.15134	-0.20153	-0.45852	-0.42530	0.08596	-0.04886	-0.33063	-0.34271
THAT_DEL	-0.13853	-0.16403	-0.45484	-0.37422	0.00139	-0.04618	-0.25942	-0.31410
FINLPREP	-0.06955	-0.11597	-0.28888	-0.13691	0.23360	0.14386	-0.09512	-0.08667
SPL_INF	-0.02688	-0.01358	-0.03734	-0.04148	-0.02255	0.00777	-0.04877	-0.01161
SPL_AUX	-0.04974	0.03529	0.00257	-0.04706	-0.03616	0.08935	0.07698	0.13822
P_AND	0.09670	0.15562	0.32971	0.30000	-0.05240	-0.09140	0.13646	0.25514
O_AND	-0.23061	-0.17587	-0.32174	-0.26704	0.04528	-0.01211	-0.07730	-0.13562
SYNTHNEG	0.17171	-0.09841	-0.07945	-0.02437	0.04249	0.10740	0.02142	0.00312
NOT_NEG	-0.11266	-0.18271	-0.50385	-0.41836	0.03339	0.07045	-0.27593	-0.26092

	REL_PIPE	SENT_REL	SUB_COS	SUB_CON	SUB_CND	SUB_OTHR	PREP	ADJ_ATTR
PASTTNSE	-0.25790	-0.05454	-0.02387	0.07856	-0.10718	-0.09788	-0.40885	-0.41144
PERFECTS	-0.08099	0.06389	0.07929	0.00944	0.04562	-0.05035	-0.32014	-0.29199
PRES	-0.11872	0.40776	0.50706	-0.05924	0.49314	-0.09061	-0.48861	-0.37374
PL_ADV	-0.09351	-0.08671	-0.20644	-0.01716	-0.13874	-0.05159	0.03419	0.05141
TM_ADV	-0.26097	-0.01592	0.05969	-0.01555	-0.01222	-0.13090	-0.27893	-0.23382
PRO1	-0.27557	0.36091	0.53056	-0.08964	0.30867	-0.13466	-0.64065	-0.59229
PRO2	-0.31400	0.31829	0.51424	-0.10116	0.37454	-0.14774	-0.65536	-0.58074
PRO3	-0.25780	-0.05719	-0.00053	0.14291	0.06064	-0.11600	-0.50758	-0.44570
IT	-0.21094	0.35021	0.43280	-0.03098	0.36470	-0.17064	-0.56201	-0.47257
PDEM	-0.13470	0.47358	0.50330	-0.10413	0.32808	-0.08499	-0.41997	-0.44817
PANY	-0.21872	0.25305	0.39583	-0.02237	0.37551	-0.15069	-0.54637	-0.45845
PRO_DO	-0.24581	0.34428	0.51728	-0.03630	0.33287	-0.11548	-0.60890	-0.54825
WH_QUES	-0.08636	0.26043	0.26320	-0.05903	0.06805	-0.06327	-0.33918	-0.29692
N_NOM	0.42272	-0.17224	-0.24201	-0.02294	-0.12692	0.21583	0.67927	0.57585
N_VBG	0.26822	-0.13674	-0.22930	0.07030	-0.12101	0.11803	0.39344	0.35724
N	0.21323	-0.28235	-0.43103	-0.00402	-0.44737	0.01464	0.56834	0.51276
AGLS_PSV	0.35460	-0.18281	-0.30468	0.01244	-0.16992	0.23628	0.58273	0.44720
BY_PASV	0.25588	-0.15332	-0.24305	0.02862	-0.20069	0.18059	0.51390	0.38529
BE_STATE	-0.12087	0.32134	0.47163	-0.01825	0.42306	-0.07762	-0.55925	-0.41951
EX_THERE	0.04589	0.20127	0.16811	-0.06953	0.12062	-0.06689	-0.14770	-0.19157
TH_CL	0.09194	0.05037	0.19924	-0.04640	0.21367	0.10402	-0.04000	-0.18188
ADJ_CL	0.10279	-0.04623	-0.03172	-0.03269	0.14899	0.17524	0.06371	0.06172
WH_CL	-0.16019	0.23472	0.32470	-0.01446	0.16139	-0.08156	-0.34626	-0.29424
INF	-0.02472	-0.07389	0.11999	0.00888	0.30321	-0.01889	-0.21716	-0.08339
CL_VBG	-0.08815	-0.14632	-0.23860	0.11206	-0.08483	0.10640	-0.03356	-0.04023
CL_VBN	0.14642	-0.07366	-0.09286	-0.02482	-0.02777	0.19116	0.30297	0.19860
WHIZ_VBN	0.21925	-0.18745	-0.34611	-0.02034	-0.29293	0.15926	0.64904	0.49772
WHIZ_VBG	0.26028	-0.18382	-0.27444	-0.00597	-0.23329	0.18712	0.48921	0.33613
THTREL_S	0.06279	0.08677	-0.03028	0.06128	0.08264	-0.05199	0.01474	-0.00832
THTREL_O	0.18015	0.05296	0.08980	-0.02645	0.05865	0.00973	0.11655	0.04851
REL_SUBJ	0.37096	-0.07798	-0.08761	0.01522	-0.13929	0.00849	0.28696	0.31553
REL_OBJ	0.74998	-0.07251	-0.10654	0.00014	-0.11127	0.11228	0.39587	0.26275
REL_PIPE	1.00000	-0.06292	-0.18088	0.04669	-0.07390	0.11405	0.43439	0.27582
SENT_REL	-0.06292	1.00000	0.31502	0.01530	0.21015	-0.11290	-0.24219	-0.23688
SUB_COS	-0.18088	0.31502	1.00000	-0.05823	0.23082	-0.07514	-0.39850	-0.37237
SUB_CON	0.04669	0.01530	-0.05823	1.00000	-0.04423	0.03442	-0.03274	0.07670
SUB_CND	-0.07390	0.21015	0.23082	-0.04423	1.00000	0.01123	-0.37445	-0.33738
SUB_OTHR	0.11405	-0.11290	-0.07514	0.03442	0.01123	1.00000	0.21830	0.09267
PREP	0.43439	-0.24219	-0.39850	-0.03274	-0.37445	0.21830	1.00000	0.64506
ADJ_ATTR	0.27582	-0.23688	-0.37237	0.07670	-0.33738	0.09267	0.64506	1.00000
ADJ_PRED	-0.06590	-0.02834	0.15839	0.04535	0.26768	0.15581	-0.19344	-0.12045
ADVS	-0.35121	0.24875	0.35221	0.05075	0.32582	-0.16684	-0.65997	-0.44539
TYPETOKN	0.00514	-0.18910	-0.36995	0.14254	-0.28386	-0.03124	0.14695	0.37674
WRDLNGTH	0.38770	-0.25259	-0.41817	0.05171	-0.36046	0.18729	0.77988	0.80901
CONJNCTS	0.28636	-0.11054	-0.16715	0.04465	0.06673	0.31515	0.43247	0.34708
DOWNTONE	0.04504	-0.05243	0.00891	0.12650	-0.05750	0.10887	0.11651	0.18394
GEN_HDG	-0.16591	0.19631	0.31743	0.03589	0.21168	-0.11105	-0.40781	-0.31591
AMPLIFR	-0.16531	0.28938	0.50015	-0.06013	0.20101	-0.09128	-0.34612	-0.30264
GEN_EMPH	-0.22382	0.30418	0.42918	0.05952	0.30470	-0.13370	-0.50803	-0.31658
PRTCLE	-0.18180	0.34523	0.47500	-0.11554	0.31765	-0.19531	-0.46622	-0.47044
DEM	0.17651	0.04672	0.06576	0.01176	0.05102	0.11675	0.20729	0.11614
POS_MOD	-0.07496	0.14946	0.32543	0.01015	0.45647	-0.00861	-0.34250	-0.22580
NEC_MOD	0.11899	0.08290	0.03843	-0.00644	0.32156	0.11080	-0.01624	0.05086
PRD_MOD	-0.04765	0.08758	0.10677	0.01277	0.32875	0.03109	-0.21265	-0.20704
PUB_VB	-0.12395	0.11953	0.07959	-0.01128	0.05456	-0.07128	-0.25720	-0.31672
PRV_VB	-0.24902	0.38937	0.49441	0.01378	0.38781	-0.11377	-0.67237	-0.60171
SUA_VB	0.10852	-0.11157	-0.08148	-0.04411	0.12185	0.08461	0.12092	0.04153
SEEM	0.08597	-0.00870	-0.07372	0.16331	0.02771	0.01149	-0.01100	0.07107
CONTRAC	-0.31589	0.44966	0.53200	-0.08817	0.38010	-0.21384	-0.67803	-0.62477
THAT_DEL	-0.26732	0.43533	0.50057	-0.00240	0.32138	-0.15608	-0.66118	-0.60001
FINLPREP	-0.06591	0.30842	0.33734	-0.06075	0.25376	0.00404	-0.23232	-0.40593
SPL_INF	0.01126	-0.01301	0.05135	-0.02796	0.01099	0.19895	-0.05126	-0.03090
SPL_AUX	0.10045	-0.05347	0.00219	0.09270	0.15055	0.10846	0.01359	0.13521
P_AND	0.25508	-0.21662	-0.30005	0.03133	-0.30978	0.11242	0.40050	0.47516
O_AND	-0.20455	0.32551	0.49205	-0.08851	0.19057	-0.13886	-0.44177	-0.42407
SYNTHNEG	-0.01463	-0.12890	-0.12807	-0.04264	0.01148	-0.04703	-0.07248	-0.01622
NOT_NEG	-0.25755	0.33185	0.49227	-0.02521	0.46208	-0.15676	-0.67072	-0.59850

	ADJ_PRED	ADVS	TYPETOKN	WRDLNGTH	CONJNCTS	DOWNTONE	GEN_HDG	AMPLIFR
PASTTNSE	-0.03803	0.23039	0.13215	-0.40526	-0.36426	-0.04323	0.00798	-0.05670
PERFECTS	0.06175	0.20289	0.04725	-0.26674	-0.21571	-0.01081	0.06736	0.01666
PRES	0.26537	0.44484	-0.45028	-0.47190	-0.03696	-0.09045	0.43885	0.47346
PL_ADV	-0.13684	0.20120	0.10789	0.01614	-0.11496	-0.01456	-0.04599	-0.10865
TM_ADV	-0.09467	0.47032	0.01433	-0.28139	-0.28790	-0.08060	0.10351	0.17105
PRO1	0.15768	0.52539	-0.35157	-0.72163	-0.30885	-0.10304	0.41146	0.48020
PRO2	0.21056	0.53574	-0.39225	-0.66034	-0.26962	-0.11607	0.42659	0.48378
PRO3	0.09366	0.32039	0.13939	-0.45480	-0.36039	-0.06267	0.04862	-0.02743
IT	0.08649	0.55075	-0.38328	-0.59789	-0.22815	-0.07943	0.38358	0.38447
PDEM	0.05845	0.44553	-0.48124	-0.48634	-0.14260	-0.06469	0.36472	0.58933
PANY	0.06418	0.45422	-0.26031	-0.54139	-0.24361	-0.13416	0.47786	0.37816
PRO_DO	0.12369	0.52866	-0.39834	-0.60367	-0.25352	-0.11316	0.44408	0.44172
WH_QUES	0.08284	0.25348	-0.24304	-0.28995	-0.16742	-0.07865	0.21954	0.28824
N_NOM	0.01589	-0.60056	0.02640	0.76343	0.50419	0.02928	-0.30244	-0.27921
N_VBG	0.00743	-0.35021	0.14942	0.44058	0.27541	0.07951	-0.22823	-0.27022
N	-0.32839	-0.56324	0.42958	0.63217	0.04078	0.06349	-0.39770	-0.36763
AGLS_PSV	-0.02421	-0.55569	0.02327	0.59398	0.42966	0.08182	-0.28711	-0.31351
BY_PASV	-0.02699	-0.48427	0.08520	0.50884	0.35286	0.08249	-0.19900	-0.24142
BE_STATE	0.39152	0.47581	-0.38867	-0.55161	-0.08362	-0.02695	0.29143	0.51194
EX_THERE	0.01593	0.11124	-0.24008	-0.20036	-0.05974	0.03753	0.03803	0.21195
TH_CL	0.08931	0.00569	-0.23486	-0.05438	0.10050	-0.03411	-0.02957	0.18894
ADJ_CL	0.18460	-0.03935	-0.03398	0.08220	0.24313	0.08582	-0.07814	-0.00985
WH_CL	0.00070	0.23748	-0.21584	-0.31525	-0.09691	-0.03696	0.17742	0.20810
INF	0.19998	0.04522	-0.00505	-0.09416	-0.00341	-0.08725	-0.04914	-0.04996
CL_VBG	0.11576	-0.00933	0.14928	-0.07818	0.02044	-0.03909	-0.14638	-0.25295
CL_VBN	0.03240	-0.26795	-0.09190	0.22212	0.22316	0.00268	-0.11696	-0.14187
WHIZ_VBN	-0.08538	-0.49461	0.07562	0.55912	0.33687	0.08469	-0.23814	-0.29483
WHIZ_VBG	-0.16130	-0.41098	0.13777	0.46403	0.20699	-0.00102	-0.22048	-0.28613
THTREL_S	-0.04037	0.04384	-0.06120	-0.03365	0.02229	-0.02874	0.00972	0.07977
THTREL_O	0.03177	-0.10324	-0.08946	0.11603	0.09381	0.08018	-0.03078	0.13409
REL_SUBJ	-0.13821	-0.31091	0.00729	0.34836	0.13466	0.04830	-0.16404	-0.03768
REL_OBJ	-0.10600	-0.35032	0.03078	0.37529	0.24635	0.07255	-0.21682	-0.12235
REL_PIPE	-0.06590	-0.35121	0.00514	0.38770	0.28636	0.04504	-0.16591	-0.16531
SENT_REL	-0.02834	0.24875	-0.18910	-0.25259	-0.11054	-0.05243	0.19631	0.28938
SUB_COS	0.15839	0.35221	-0.36995	-0.41817	-0.16715	0.00891	0.31743	0.50015
SUB_CON	0.04535	0.05075	0.14254	0.05171	0.04465	0.12650	0.03589	-0.06013
SUB_CND	0.26768	0.32582	-0.28386	-0.36046	0.06673	-0.05750	0.21168	0.20101
SUB_OTHR	0.15581	-0.16684	-0.03124	0.18729	0.31515	0.10887	-0.11105	-0.09128
PREP	-0.19344	-0.65997	0.14695	0.77988	0.43247	0.11651	-0.40781	-0.34612
ADJ_ATTR	-0.12045	-0.44539	0.37674	0.80901	0.34708	0.18394	-0.31591	-0.30264
ADJ_PRED	1.00000	0.11962	-0.14365	-0.19471	0.11563	0.10812	0.03542	0.04321
ADVS	0.11962	1.00000	-0.20600	-0.63647	-0.29380	0.03695	0.46047	0.46909
TYPETOKN	-0.14365	-0.20600	1.00000	0.36472	-0.02295	0.07614	-0.20726	-0.35979
WRDLNGTH	-0.19471	-0.63647	0.36472	1.00000	0.39906	0.13647	-0.39351	-0.37654
CONJNCTS	0.11563	-0.29380	-0.02295	0.39906	1.00000	0.10011	-0.15205	-0.20167
GEN_HDG	0.03542	0.46047	-0.20726	-0.39351	-0.15205	-0.00538	1.00000	0.25814
AMPLIFR	0.04321	0.46909	-0.35979	-0.37654	-0.20167	-0.00792	0.25814	1.00000
GEN_EMPH	0.12317	0.59629	-0.26820	-0.47515	-0.19812	-0.03897	0.45953	0.46886
PRTCLE	0.03263	0.48692	-0.42774	-0.48025	-0.21308	-0.09642	0.43194	0.52874
DEM	0.02584	-0.05915	-0.22333	0.12367	0.31151	0.13254	-0.06813	0.06716
POS_MOD	0.30765	0.27194	-0.27931	-0.31773	0.06220	0.04145	0.25767	0.20622
NEC_MOD	0.17465	0.02210	-0.07657	0.04219	0.22828	0.00803	-0.02768	-0.02134
PRD_MOD	0.19578	0.00549	-0.14511	-0.13655	0.04520	-0.07373	0.06081	0.02719
PUB_VB	0.01024	-0.01160	-0.09496	-0.19088	-0.16925	-0.14442	-0.01023	-0.03838
PRV_VB	0.20714	0.57979	-0.41191	-0.68072	-0.20807	-0.11483	0.46880	0.46075
SUA_VB	0.02407	-0.20627	-0.09282	0.15476	0.22174	-0.01014	-0.14535	-0.15336
SEEM	0.03776	0.09233	0.03883	0.02360	0.11387	0.05067	0.05308	-0.07247
CONTRAC	0.14549	0.65949	-0.43388	-0.70681	-0.31360	-0.12730	0.53865	0.54840
THAT_DEL	0.14098	0.51491	-0.39615	-0.65680	-0.30526	-0.15256	0.44288	0.42739
FINLPREP	-0.03818	0.37069	-0.37300	-0.42115	-0.09238	-0.12516	0.28939	0.37977
SPL_INF	0.07528	0.04261	-0.01000	-0.06409	-0.03327	-0.05573	-0.02199	0.02332
SPL_AUX	0.13455	0.05225	0.05792	0.13586	0.21466	0.16732	-0.04495	-0.10280
P_AND	-0.04946	-0.43608	0.34294	0.46940	0.10549	0.04331	-0.23766	-0.36789
O_AND	-0.02639	0.43039	-0.36203	-0.49800	-0.24764	-0.07314	0.32827	0.49339
SYNTHNEG	0.08028	0.02020	0.10228	-0.03846	-0.07156	0.06105	-0.08401	-0.12154
NOT_NEG	0.22773	0.60358	-0.37274	-0.64892	-0.22872	-0.08420	0.40539	0.41316

	GEN_EMPH	PRTCLE	DEM	POS_MOD	NEC_MOD	PRD_MOD	PUB_VB	PRV_VB
PASTTNSE	-0.06028	-0.09094	-0.30321	-0.16127	-0.21667	-0.12123	0.31804	0.16308
PERFECTS	0.10107	0.09962	-0.03756	0.04442	-0.05843	0.00715	0.17866	0.22484
PRES	0.63177	0.63208	0.15560	0.51447	0.20159	0.27767	0.00875	0.66623
PL_ADV	-0.13763	-0.14472	-0.09785	-0.21145	-0.13289	-0.08913	-0.08672	-0.21205
TM_ADV	0.19199	0.31489	-0.06162	-0.09755	-0.12389	-0.03027	-0.02844	0.05489
PRO1	0.49564	0.56157	-0.00996	0.39220	0.02760	0.18452	0.16168	0.68798
PRO2	0.60566	0.59313	-0.06862	0.39297	-0.01716	0.14547	0.13743	0.75392
PRO3	0.07795	-0.03474	-0.28221	-0.03998	-0.11132	0.00764	0.25848	0.24709
IT	0.48632	0.53498	0.04829	0.29547	0.04796	0.10417	0.08498	0.62632
PDEM	0.51019	0.69441	0.22779	0.33204	0.06118	0.13758	0.04029	0.60033
PANY	0.49368	0.44932	-0.02442	0.36169	-0.00241	0.13007	0.15253	0.55724
PRO_DO	0.56036	0.60065	-0.01469	0.37890	0.02177	0.13887	0.14968	0.69143
WH_QUES	0.33493	0.38904	-0.00394	0.16201	0.07097	0.09828	0.13752	0.40173
N_NOM	-0.38657	-0.32713	0.25260	-0.03543	0.21669	0.05516	-0.07981	-0.43092
N_VBG	-0.22527	-0.33620	0.09815	-0.07722	0.09114	0.00234	-0.07189	-0.29698
N	-0.48304	-0.47180	-0.11790	-0.48899	-0.10784	-0.15288	-0.19017	-0.74585
AGLS_PSV	-0.47067	-0.36544	0.11165	-0.09702	0.15988	-0.08748	-0.12146	-0.47198
BY_PASV	-0.37119	-0.31556	-0.00652	-0.15700	0.06424	-0.15590	-0.09715	-0.37646
BE_STATE	0.49263	0.54448	0.15683	0.35205	0.10691	0.14367	0.06830	0.62005
EX_THERE	0.16055	0.26530	0.11435	0.09062	0.07232	0.00553	0.10640	0.19279
TH_CL	0.00794	0.19606	0.26711	0.17304	0.18261	0.16176	0.25632	0.22514
ADJ_CL	-0.01060	0.02649	0.21637	0.01727	0.18087	0.09292	-0.02620	0.00161
WH_CL	0.26296	0.18692	0.06385	0.23714	0.01510	0.14123	0.23231	0.42957
INF	0.09755	-0.05127	-0.01173	0.29473	0.30720	0.33962	0.12793	0.12233
CL_VBG	-0.19033	-0.26249	-0.17412	-0.08142	-0.06599	-0.07090	0.01657	-0.06823
CL_VBN	-0.21391	-0.15178	0.03640	-0.00686	0.00874	-0.01875	-0.11536	-0.15880
WHIZ_VBN	-0.43386	-0.34909	0.07078	-0.24403	-0.01603	-0.17578	-0.21305	-0.50619
WHIZ_VBG	-0.34451	-0.30183	-0.03889	-0.24909	-0.03930	-0.08917	-0.12917	-0.43588
THTREL_S	0.13268	0.05245	0.15671	0.10787	-0.00267	0.12097	-0.06681	0.05565
THTREL_O	-0.02340	0.07819	0.22008	0.04959	0.12564	0.15332	0.08852	0.02105
REL_SUBJ	-0.15707	-0.11638	0.13652	-0.03991	0.02186	0.00979	-0.12329	-0.20493
REL_OBJ	-0.24656	-0.19278	0.19602	-0.06560	0.11652	0.03637	-0.12651	-0.24928
REL_PIPE	-0.22382	-0.18180	0.17651	-0.07496	0.11899	-0.04765	-0.12395	-0.24902
SENT_REL	0.30418	0.34523	0.04672	0.14946	0.08290	0.08758	0.11953	0.38937
SUB_COS	0.42918	0.47500	0.06576	0.32543	0.03843	0.10677	0.07959	0.49441
SUB_CON	0.05952	-0.11554	0.01176	0.01015	-0.00644	0.01277	-0.01128	0.01378
SUB_CND	0.30470	0.31765	0.05102	0.45647	0.32156	0.32875	0.05456	0.38781
SUB_OTHR	-0.13370	-0.19531	0.11675	-0.00861	0.11080	0.03109	-0.07128	-0.11377
PREP	-0.50803	-0.46622	0.20729	-0.34250	-0.01624	-0.21265	-0.25720	-0.67237
ADJ_ATTR	-0.31658	-0.47044	0.11614	-0.22580	0.05086	-0.20704	-0.31672	-0.60171
ADJ_PRED	0.12317	0.03263	0.02584	0.30765	0.17465	0.19578	0.01024	0.20714
ADVS	0.59629	0.48692	-0.05915	0.27194	0.02210	0.00549	-0.01160	0.57979
TYPETOKN	-0.26820	-0.42774	-0.22333	-0.27931	-0.07657	-0.14511	-0.09496	-0.41191
WRDLNGTH	-0.47515	-0.48025	0.12367	-0.31773	0.04219	-0.13655	-0.19088	-0.68072
CONJNCTS	-0.19812	-0.21308	0.31151	0.06220	0.22828	0.04520	-0.16925	-0.20807
DOWNTONE	-0.03897	-0.09642	0.13254	0.04145	0.00803	-0.07373	-0.14442	-0.11483
GEN_HDG	0.45953	0.43194	-0.06813	0.25767	-0.02768	0.06081	-0.01023	0.46880
AMPLIFR	0.46886	0.52874	0.06716	0.20622	-0.02134	0.02719	-0.03838	0.46075
GEN_EMPH	1.00000	0.47967	0.00381	0.32722	-0.00011	0.09513	0.03162	0.60666
PRTCLE	0.47967	1.00000	0.06227	0.30994	0.02610	0.11495	0.04200	0.54772
DEM	0.00381	0.06227	1.00000	0.09587	0.09166	0.07442	-0.02252	0.00822
POS_MOD	0.32722	0.30994	0.09587	1.00000	0.23832	0.24790	0.01170	0.43201
NEC_MOD	-0.00011	0.02610	0.09166	0.23832	1.00000	0.19705	-0.01481	0.05020
PRD_MOD	0.09513	0.11495	0.07442	0.24790	0.19705	1.00000	0.13078	0.14512
PUB_VB	0.03162	0.04200	-0.02252	0.01170	-0.01481	0.13078	1.00000	0.16664
PRV_VB	0.60666	0.54772	0.00822	0.43201	0.05020	0.14512	0.16664	1.00000
SUA_VB	-0.18655	-0.11537	0.01398	0.07187	0.22736	0.15878	0.06481	-0.17673
SEEM	0.10076	-0.04890	0.07031	0.11208	0.04199	-0.05930	-0.00489	0.07268
CONTRAC	0.65036	0.72691	-0.04073	0.34393	-0.01857	0.05174	0.08660	0.77719
THAT_DEL	0.59535	0.58640	-0.08929	0.36289	0.00086	0.13937	0.26178	0.79705
FINLPREP	0.32777	0.43395	0.11805	0.12876	-0.04857	0.00044	0.01403	0.35842
SPL_INF	0.00793	-0.02394	-0.06527	-0.02375	0.02090	0.01547	-0.03177	0.06575
SPL_AUX	-0.07705	-0.14788	0.11868	0.25280	0.32069	0.20223	-0.00166	-0.07715
P_AND	-0.26962	-0.42612	-0.10110	-0.21977	-0.01752	-0.13084	-0.12330	-0.41032
O_AND	0.39887	0.42526	0.05906	0.20338	-0.05181	0.00341	0.10676	0.42576
SYNTHNEG	-0.10635	-0.16288	0.02528	0.00973	0.08726	0.01842	0.15059	-0.06197
NOT_NEG	0.57009	0.55157	-0.04508	0.39818	0.13131	0.18040	0.22879	0.74710

	SUA_VB	SEEM	CONTRAC	THAT_DEL	FINLPREP	SPL_INF	SPL_AUX	P_AND
PASTTNSE	-0.09767	0.03733	0.07162	0.15968	0.01620	-0.03914	-0.07418	-0.12138
PERFECTS	-0.09035	0.05795	0.22584	0.20932	0.01360	0.10029	0.15357	-0.12812
PRES	-0.06883	-0.00408	0.73228	0.64584	0.38137	0.08171	-0.01256	-0.35569
PL_ADV	-0.07080	-0.01308	-0.09693	-0.15507	0.00068	-0.00186	-0.08823	0.01021
TM_ADV	-0.12561	-0.04100	0.26306	0.14620	0.21747	0.08781	-0.11512	-0.25447
PRO1	-0.12319	-0.04479	0.71809	0.66963	0.39486	0.07311	-0.09936	-0.38114
PRO2	-0.14871	-0.04053	0.78950	0.70122	0.35019	0.04007	-0.13630	-0.39155
PRO3	-0.10397	0.08981	0.15458	0.21105	0.02595	0.00225	-0.00993	-0.12814
IT	-0.14103	0.04008	0.69432	0.56910	0.34546	-0.02783	-0.10258	-0.37876
PDEM	-0.15583	-0.06919	0.70670	0.58955	0.57438	-0.00557	-0.14036	-0.46896
PANY	-0.01137	0.03240	0.55695	0.52159	0.31640	-0.00099	-0.07481	-0.32003
PRO_DO	-0.04416	0.03249	0.71694	0.65689	0.39112	0.00057	-0.08455	-0.37624
WH_QUES	-0.11445	-0.06158	0.40299	0.42177	0.31576	-0.01753	-0.16498	-0.22611
N_NOM	0.26985	0.03998	-0.51898	-0.45604	-0.29929	-0.05368	0.18878	0.30522
N_VBG	0.26818	0.00788	-0.41476	-0.32020	-0.24537	-0.04767	0.15763	0.30452
N	0.07973	-0.14403	-0.62905	-0.59845	-0.37139	0.01861	-0.04923	0.41172
AGLS_PSV	0.20656	-0.04468	-0.55108	-0.47393	-0.31985	-0.05926	0.24998	0.27357
BY_PASV	0.07315	-0.04795	-0.39708	-0.34769	-0.26903	-0.03049	0.09257	0.23256
BE_STATE	-0.13007	0.00940	0.63155	0.55711	0.40777	0.09936	-0.03576	-0.38136
EX_THERE	-0.05069	0.04293	0.25305	0.17683	0.25784	-0.05530	-0.10178	-0.15916
TH_CL	0.09720	0.07650	0.03943	0.05366	0.13017	0.01063	0.14095	-0.25930
ADJ_CL	0.02029	0.06302	-0.03612	-0.06320	-0.00911	0.06161	0.14227	-0.06546
WH_CL	-0.01055	-0.00524	0.32786	0.33187	0.15948	0.01835	-0.01948	-0.11810
INF	0.31460	0.12019	-0.05114	0.05872	-0.08231	0.03383	0.30278	-0.00505
CL_VBG	0.02830	0.04054	-0.15134	-0.13853	-0.06955	-0.02688	-0.04974	0.09670
CL_VBN	0.05978	-0.02011	-0.20153	-0.16403	-0.11597	-0.01358	0.03529	0.15562
WHIZ_VBN	0.16040	-0.07407	-0.45852	-0.45484	-0.28888	-0.03734	0.00257	0.32971
WHIZ_VBG	0.04152	-0.04505	-0.42530	-0.37422	-0.13691	-0.04148	-0.04706	0.30000
THTREL_S	0.00383	-0.01812	0.08596	0.00139	0.23360	-0.02255	-0.03616	-0.05240
THTREL_O	0.14251	0.02650	-0.04886	-0.04618	0.14386	0.00777	0.08935	-0.09140
REL_SUBJ	0.07739	0.00945	-0.33063	-0.25942	-0.09512	-0.04877	0.07698	0.13646
REL_OBJ	0.09584	0.09197	-0.34271	-0.31410	-0.08667	-0.01161	0.13822	0.25514
REL_PIPE	0.10852	0.08597	-0.31589	-0.26732	-0.06591	0.01126	0.10045	0.25508
SENT_REL	-0.11157	-0.00870	0.44966	0.43533	0.30842	-0.01301	-0.05347	-0.21662
SUB_COS	-0.08148	-0.07372	0.53200	0.50057	0.33734	0.05135	0.00219	-0.30005
SUB_CON	-0.04411	0.16331	-0.08817	-0.00240	-0.06075	-0.02796	0.09270	0.03133
SUB_CND	0.12185	0.02771	0.38010	0.32138	0.25376	0.01099	0.15055	-0.30978
SUB_OTHR	0.08461	0.01149	-0.21384	-0.15608	0.00404	0.19895	0.10846	0.11242
PREP	0.12092	-0.01100	-0.67803	-0.66118	-0.23232	-0.05126	0.01359	0.40050
ADJ_ATTR	0.04153	0.07107	-0.62477	-0.60001	-0.40593	-0.03090	0.13521	0.47516
ADJ_PRED	0.02407	0.03776	0.14549	0.14098	-0.03818	0.07528	0.13455	-0.04946
ADVS	-0.20627	0.09233	0.65949	0.51491	0.37069	0.04261	0.05225	-0.43608
TYPETOKN	-0.09282	0.03883	-0.43388	-0.39615	-0.37300	-0.01000	0.05792	0.34294
WRDLNGTH	0.15476	0.02360	-0.70681	-0.65680	-0.42115	-0.06409	0.13586	0.46940
CONJNCTS	0.22174	0.11387	-0.31360	-0.30526	-0.09238	-0.03327	0.21466	0.10549
DOWNTONE	-0.01014	0.05067	-0.12730	-0.15256	-0.12516	-0.05573	0.16732	0.04331
GEN_HDG	-0.14535	0.05308	0.53865	0.44288	0.28939	-0.02199	-0.04495	-0.23766
AMPLIFR	-0.15336	-0.07247	0.54840	0.42739	0.37977	0.02332	-0.10280	-0.36789
GEN_EMPH	-0.18655	0.10076	0.65036	0.59535	0.32777	0.00793	-0.07705	-0.26962
PRTCLE	-0.11537	-0.04890	0.72691	0.58640	0.43395	-0.02394	-0.14788	-0.42612
DEM	0.01398	0.07031	-0.04073	-0.08929	0.11805	-0.06527	0.11868	-0.10110
POS_MOD	0.07187	0.11208	0.34393	0.36289	0.12876	-0.02375	0.25280	-0.21977
NEC_MOD	0.22736	0.04199	-0.01857	0.00086	-0.04857	0.02090	0.32069	-0.01752
PRD_MOD	0.15878	-0.05930	0.05174	0.13937	0.00044	0.01547	0.20223	-0.13084
PUB_VB	0.06481	-0.00489	0.08660	0.26178	0.01403	-0.03177	-0.00166	-0.12330
PRV_VB	-0.17673	0.07268	0.77719	0.79705	0.35842	0.06575	-0.07715	-0.41032
SUA_VB	1.00000	-0.01395	-0.20596	-0.14127	-0.15252	-0.04193	0.18164	0.06597
SEEM	-0.01395	1.00000	-0.07776	0.00654	-0.08947	-0.03351	0.12310	0.00839
CONTRAC	-0.20596	-0.07776	1.00000	0.77361	0.48698	0.00379	-0.21629	-0.48526
THAT_DEL	-0.14127	0.00654	0.77361	1.00000	0.34155	0.12230	-0.15599	-0.34255
FINLPREP	-0.15252	-0.08947	0.48698	0.34155	1.00000	-0.01664	-0.22983	-0.43124
SPL_INF	-0.04193	-0.03351	0.00379	0.12230	-0.01664	1.00000	0.00997	0.13046
SPL_AUX	0.18164	0.12310	-0.21629	-0.15599	-0.22983	0.00997	1.00000	0.06516
P_AND	0.06597	0.00839	-0.48526	-0.34255	-0.43124	0.13046	0.06516	1.00000
O_AND	-0.17453	-0.09534	0.50220	0.42907	0.45475	0.06267	-0.11115	-0.36167
SYNTHNEG	0.09404	0.02395	-0.14128	-0.14513	-0.12623	-0.04757	0.15068	0.01893
NOT_NEG	-0.06461	0.03565	0.77665	0.70543	0.35257	0.00391	0.03232	-0.43728

	O_AND	SYNTHNEG	NOT_NEG
PASTTNSE	0.14402	0.23031	0.16515
PERFECTS	0.09914	0.20833	0.24730
PRES	0.34629	-0.16484	0.62933
PL_ADV	-0.06129	0.01178	-0.22265
TM_ADV	0.21315	-0.04100	0.11472
PRO1	0.57964	-0.08553	0.59457
PRO2	0.40155	-0.11496	0.67825
PRO3	0.09991	0.23635	0.30780
IT	0.34821	-0.04182	0.59400
PDEM	0.46526	-0.17931	0.56545
PANY	0.33914	-0.00139	0.55855
PRO_DO	0.35708	-0.07831	0.73304
WH_QUES	0.30159	-0.04402	0.34282
N_NOM	-0.38073	-0.04479	-0.42409
N_VBG	-0.34427	0.04640	-0.34022
N	-0.34560	-0.03729	-0.68202
AGLS_PSV	-0.37278	-0.01418	-0.46781
BY_PASV	-0.29791	-0.10676	-0.39302
BE_STATE	0.39080	0.04504	0.62309
EX_THERE	0.20908	0.17278	0.19554
TH_CL	0.17397	0.07682	0.21415
ADJ_CL	-0.03598	0.07913	0.01284
WH_CL	0.23637	0.13862	0.37251
INF	-0.07334	0.09331	0.14087
CL_VBG	-0.23061	0.17171	-0.11266
CL_VBN	-0.17587	-0.09841	-0.18271
WHIZ_VBN	-0.32174	-0.07945	-0.50385
WHIZ_VBG	-0.26704	-0.02437	-0.41836
THTREL_S	0.04528	0.04249	0.03339
THTREL_O	-0.01211	0.10740	0.07045
REL_SUBJ	-0.07730	0.02142	-0.27593
REL_OBJ	-0.13562	0.00312	-0.26092
REL_PIPE	-0.20455	-0.01463	-0.25755
SENT_REL	0.32551	-0.12890	0.33185
SUB_COS	0.49205	-0.12807	0.49227
SUB_CON	-0.08851	-0.04264	-0.02521
SUB_CND	0.19057	0.01148	0.46208
SUB_OTHR	-0.13886	-0.04703	-0.15676
PREP	-0.44177	-0.07248	-0.67072
ADJ_ATTR	-0.42407	-0.01622	-0.59850
ADJ_PRED	-0.02639	0.08028	0.22773
ADVS	0.43039	0.02020	0.60358
TYPETOKN	-0.36203	0.10228	-0.37274
WRDLNGTH	-0.49800	-0.03846	-0.64892
CONJNCTS	-0.24764	-0.07156	-0.22872
DOWNTONE	-0.07314	0.06105	-0.08420
GEN_HDG	0.32827	-0.08401	0.40539
AMPLIFR	0.49339	-0.12154	0.41316
GEN_EMPH	0.39887	-0.10635	0.57009
PRTCLE	0.42526	-0.16288	0.55157
DEM	0.05906	0.02528	-0.04508
POS_MOD	0.20338	0.00973	0.39818
NEC_MOD	-0.05181	0.08726	0.13131
PRD_MOD	0.00341	0.01842	0.18040
PUB_VB	0.10676	0.15059	0.22879
PRV_VB	0.42576	-0.06197	0.74710
SUA_VB	-0.17453	0.09404	-0.06461
SEEM	-0.09534	0.02395	0.03565
CONTRAC	0.50220	-0.14128	0.77665
THAT_DEL	0.42907	-0.14513	0.70543
FINLPREP	0.45475	-0.12623	0.35257
SPL_INF	0.06267	-0.04757	0.00391
SPL_AUX	-0.11115	0.15068	0.03232
P_AND	-0.36167	0.01893	-0.43728
O_AND	1.00000	-0.07699	0.31301
SYNTHNEG	-0.07699	1.00000	0.01277
NOT_NEG	0.31301	0.01277	1.00000

References

Aijmer, Karin. 1984. *Sort of* and *kind of* in English conversation. *Studia Linguistica* 38:118–28.

1985. *Just.* In *Papers on language and literature presented to Alvar Ellegard and Erik Frykman*, ed. by S. Backman and G. Kjellmer, pp. 1–10. Gothenburg Studies in English 60.

1986. Why is *actually* so popular in spoken English? In *English in speech and writing: a symposium*, ed. by G. Tottie and I. Bäcklund, pp. 119–30. Studia Anglistica Upsaliensia 60. Stockholm: Almqvist and Wiksell.

Akinnaso, F. Niyi. 1982. On the differences between spoken and written language. *Language and Speech* 25:97–125.

Altenberg, Bengt. 1984. Causal linking in spoken and written English. *Studia Linguistica* 38:20–69.

1986. Contrastive linking in spoken and written English. In *English in speech and writing: a symposium*, ed. by G. Tottie and I. Bäcklund, pp. 13–40. Studia Anglistica Upsaliensia 60. Stockholm: Almqvist and Wiksell.

Aronoff, Mark. 1985. Orthography and linguistic theory. *Language* 61:28–72.

Bäcklund, Ingegerd. 1984. *Conjunction-headed abbreviated clauses in English.* Studia Anglistica Upsaliensia 50. Stockholm: Almqvist and Wiksell.

1986. Beat until stiff: conjunction-headed abbreviated clauses in spoken and written English. In *English in speech and writing: a symposium*, ed. by G. Tottie and I. Bäcklund, pp. 41–56. Studia Anglistica Upsaliensia 60. Stockholm: Almqvist and Wiksell.

Basso, K.H. 1974. The ethnography of writing. In *Explorations in the ethnography of speaking*, ed. by R. Bauman and J. Sherzer, pp. 425–32. Cambridge: Cambridge University Press.

Beaman, Karen. 1984. Coordination and subordination revisited: syntactic complexity in spoken and written narrative discourse. In *Coherence in spoken and written discourse*, ed. by Deborah Tannen, pp. 45–80. Norwood, N.J.: Ablex.

Bernstein, Basil. 1970. *Class, codes, and control.* Volume 1: *Theoretical studies towards a sociology of language.* London: Routledge & Kegan Paul.

Besnier, Niko. 1986a. Spoken and written registers in a restricted-literacy setting. Unpublished Ph.D. dissertation, University of Southern California.

1986b. Register as a sociolinguistic unit: defining formality. In *Social and cognitive perspectives on language*, ed. by J. Connor-Linton, C.J. Hall and M. McGinnis, pp. 25–63. Southern California Occasional Papers in Linguistics 11. Los Angeles: University of Southern California.

Biber, Douglas. 1984. A model of textual relations within the written and spoken modes. Unpublished Ph.D. dissertation, University of Southern California.

1985. Investigating macroscopic textual variation through multi-feature/multi-dimensional analyses. *Linguistics* 23:337–60.

1986a. Spoken and written textual dimensions in English: resolving the contradictory findings. *Language* 62:384–414.

1986b. On the investigation of spoken/written differences. *Studia Linguistica* 40:1–21.

1987. A textual comparison of British and American writing. *American Speech* 62:99–119.

Forthcoming. A typology of English texts. *Linguistics.*

Biber, Douglas, and Edward Finegan. 1986. An initial typology of English text types. In *Corpus linguistics II*, ed. by Jan Aarts and Willem Meijs, pp. 19–46. Amsterdam: Rodopi.

1988a. Adverbial stance types in English. *Discourse Processes* 11:1–34.

1988b. Drift in three English genres from the 18th to the 20th centuries: a multidimensional approach. In *Corpus linguistics, hard and soft*, ed. by Merja Kyto, Ossi Ihalainen, and Matti Rissanen, pp. 83–101. Amsterdam: Rodopi.

1988c. Historical drift in three English genres. Paper presented at GURT '88, Georgetown. [Forthcoming in conference proceedings, ed. by Thomas J. Walsh. Washington, D.C.: Georgetown University Press.]

Forthcoming. Styles of stance in English: lexical and grammatical marking of evidentiality and affect. *Text* (special issue on *The pragmatics of affect*, ed. by Elinor Ochs).

Blankenship, Jane. 1962. A linguistic analysis of oral and written style. *Quarterly Journal of Speech* 48:419–22.

1974. The influence of mode, submode, and speaker predilection on style. *Speech Monographs* 41:85–118.

Blass, Thomas, and Aron W. Siegman. 1975. A psycholinguistic comparison of speech, dictation, and writing. *Language and Speech* 18:20–33.

Bloomfield, Leonard. 1933. *Language.* New York: Holt, Rinehart and Winston.

Brainerd, Barron. 1972. An exploratory study of pronouns and articles as indices of genre in English. *Language and Style* 5:239–59.

Brown, Gillian, and George Yule. 1983. *Discourse analysis.* Cambridge: Cambridge University Press.

Brown, Penelope, and Colin Fraser. 1979. Speech as a marker of situation. In *Social markers in speech*, ed. by Klaus R. Scherer and Howard Giles, pp. 33–62. Cambridge: Cambridge University Press.

Carroll, John B. 1960. Vectors of prose style. In *Style in language*, ed. by Thomas A. Sebeok, pp. 283–92. Cambridge, Mass.: MIT Press.

Cayer, Roger L., and Renee K. Sacks. 1979. Oral and written discourse of basic writers: similarities and differences. *Research in the Teaching of English* 13:121–8.

Chafe, Wallace L. 1982. Integration and involvement in speaking, writing, and oral literature. In *Spoken and written language: exploring orality and literacy*, ed. by D. Tannen, pp. 35–54. Norwood, N.J.: Ablex.

1984a. How people use adverbial clauses. In *Proceedings of the tenth annual meeting of the Berkeley Linguistics Society*, ed. by Claudia Brugman and Monica Macaulay, pp. 437–49. Berkeley: Berkeley Linguistics Society.

1984b. Speaking, writing, and prescriptivism. In *Meaning, form, and use in context: linguistic applications*, ed. by D. Schiffrin, pp. 95–103. GURT '84. Washington, D.C.: Georgetown University Press.

1985. Linguistic differences produced by differences between speaking and writing. In *Literature, language, and learning: the nature and consequences of reading and writing*, ed. by D.R. Olson, N. Torrance, and A. Hildyard, pp. 105–23. Cambridge: Cambridge University Press.

Chafe, Wallace L., and Jane Danielewicz. Forthcoming. Properties of spoken and written language. In *Comprehending oral and written language*, ed. by Rosalind Horowitz and S.J. Samuels. New York: Academic Press.

Coates, Jennifer. 1983. *The semantics of the modal auxiliaries*. London: Croom Helm.

Connor-Linton, Jeff, Christopher J. Hall, and Mary McGinnis (eds.). 1986. *Social and cognitive perspectives on language*. Southern California Occasional Papers in Linguistics 11. Los Angeles: University of Southern California.

Cook-Gumperz, Jenny, and John J. Gumperz. 1981. From oral to written culture: the transition to literacy. In *Variation in writing*, ed. by M. F. Whiteman, pp. 89–109. Hillsdale, N.J.: Erlbaum.

DeVito, Joseph A. 1966. Psychogrammatical factors in oral and written discourse by skilled communicators. *Speech Monographs* 33:73–6.

1967. Levels of abstraction in spoken and written language. *Journal of Communication* 17:354–61.

Dillon, George. 1981. *Constructing texts*. Bloomington, Ind.: Indiana University Press.

Drieman, G.H.J. 1962. Differences between written and spoken language. *Acta Psychologica* 20:36–57; 78–100.

Dubuisson, Colette, Louisette Emirkanian, and David Sankoff. 1983. *The development of syntactic complexity in narrative, informative and argumentative discourse*. CRMA–1170, Centre de Recherche de Mathématiques Appliquées, Université de Montréal.

Duranti, Alessandro. 1985. Sociocultural dimensions of discourse. In *Handbook of discourse analysis*, vol. 1, ed. by Teun van Dijk, pp. 193–230. New York: Academic Press.

Eisenstein, Elizabeth L. 1985. On the printing press as an agent of change. In

Literacy, language, and learning: the nature and consequences of reading and writing, ed. by D.R. Olson, N. Torrance, and A. Hildyard, pp. 19–33. Cambridge: Cambridge University Press.

Elsness, J. 1984. *That* or zero? A look at the choice of object clause connective in a corpus of American English. *English Studies* 65:519–33.

Erwin-Tripp, Susan. 1972. On sociolinguistic rules: alternation and co-occurrence. In *Directions in sociolinguistics*, ed. by John J. Gumperz and Dell Hymes, pp. 213–50. New York: Holt, Rinehart and Winston.

Farhady, Hossein. 1983. On the plausibility of the unitary language proficiency factor. In *Issues in language testing research*, ed. by J. W. Oller, pp. 11–28. Rowley, Mass.: Newbury House.

Farrell, Thomas. 1977. Literacy, the basics, and all that jazz. *College English* 38:443–59.

Feigenbaum, Irwin. 1978. The use of the perfect in an academic setting: a study of types and frequencies. Unpublished Ph.D. dissertation: University of Wisconsin–Milwaukee.

Ferguson, Charles A. 1959. Diglossia. *Word* 15:325–40.

1977. Baby talk as a simplified register. In *Talking to children*, ed. by C.E. Snow and C.A. Ferguson, pp. 209–33. Cambridge: Cambridge University Press.

1983. Sports announcer talk: syntactic aspects of register variation. *Language in Society* 12:153–72.

Fillmore, Charles J. 1981. Pragmatics and the description of discourse. In *Radical pragmatics*, ed. by Peter Cole, pp. 143–66. New York: Academic Press.

Finegan, Edward. 1980. *Attitudes toward English usage: the history of a war of words.* New York: Teachers College Press.

1982. Form and function in testament language. In *Linguistics and the professions*, ed. by Robert J. Di Pietro, pp. 113–20. Norwood, N.J.: Ablex.

1987. On the linguistic forms of prestige. In *The legacy of language*, ed. by Phillip C. Boardman, pp. 146–61. Reno: University of Nevada Press.

Finegan, Edward and Douglas Biber. 1986a. Toward a unified model of sociolinguistic prestige. In *Diversity and diachrony*, ed. by David Sankoff, pp. 391–8. Amsterdam: John Benjamins.

1986b. Two dimensions of linguistic complexity in English. In *Social and cognitive perspectives on language*, ed. by J. Connor-Linton, C.J. Hall, and M. McGinnis, pp. 1–24. Southern California Occasional Papers in Linguistics 11. Los Angeles: University of Southern California.

Fishman, Joshua. 1972. The sociology of language. In *Language and social context*, ed. by Pier Paolo Giglioli, pp. 45–58. New York: Penguin Books.

Ford, Cecilia E., and Sandra A. Thompson. 1986. Conditionals in discourse: a text-based study from English. In *On conditionals*, ed. by E. C. Traugott, A. T. Meulen, J. S. Reilly, and C. A. Ferguson, pp. 353–72. Cambridge: Cambridge University Press.

Francis, W. Nelson, and Henry Kucera. 1982. *Frequency analysis of English usage: lexicon and grammar.* Boston: Houghton Mifflin.

Frawley, William. 1982. Universal grammar and composition: relativization, complementation, and quantification. In *Linguistics and literacy,* ed. by William Frawley, pp. 65–90. New York: Plenum Press.

Frederiksen, Carl H., and Joseph F. Dominic (eds.). 1981. *Writing: the nature, development, and teaching of written communication.* Volume 2: *Writing: process, development and communication.* Hillsdale, N.J.: Lawrence Erlbaum Associates.

Gibson, James W., C.R. Gruner, R.J. Kibler, and F.J. Kelly. 1966. A quantitative examination of differences and similarities in written and spoken messages. *Speech Monographs* 33:444–51.

Golub, L.S. 1969. Linguistic structures in students' oral and written discourse. *Research in the Teaching of English* 3:70–85.

Goody, Jack (ed.). 1968. *Literacy in traditional societies.* Cambridge: Cambridge University Press.

　　1977. *The domestication of the savage mind.* Cambridge: Cambridge University Press.

Goody, Jack, and I.P. Watt. 1963. The consequences of literacy. *Comparative Studies in History and Society* 5:304–45.

Gorsuch, Richard L. 1983. *Factor analysis,* 2nd edition. Hillsdale, N.J.: Lawrence Erlbaum Associates.

Grabe, William P. 1984a. Towards defining expository prose within a theory of text construction. Unpublished Ph.D. dissertation, Department of Linguistics, University of Southern California.

　　1984b. Written discourse analysis. *Annual Review of Applied Linguistics* 5:101–23.

Grabe, William P., and Douglas Biber. 1987. Freshman student writing and the contrastive rhetoric hypothesis. Paper presented at SLRF 7, University of Southern California.

Green, Georgia M., and Jerry L. Morgan. 1981. Writing ability as a function of the appreciation of differences between oral and written communication. In *Writing: the nature, development, and teaching of written communication,* vol. 2, ed. by C.H. Frederiksen and J.F. Dominic, pp. 177–88. Hillsdale, N.J.: Lawrence Erlbaum Associates.

Greenfield, P.M. 1972. Oral or written language: the consequence for cognitive development in Africa, the United States and England. *Language and Speech* 15:169–78.

Gumperz, John J., Hannah Kaltman, and Mary Catherine O'Connor. 1984. Cohesion in spoken and written discourse. In *Coherence in spoken and written discourse,* ed. by Deborah Tannen, pp. 3–20. Norwood, N.J.: Ablex.

Hall, Robert A. 1964. *Introductory linguistics.* Philadelphia: Chilton Books.

Halliday, Michael A.K. 1968. The users and uses of language. In *Readings in the sociology of language,* ed. by Joshua F. Fishman, pp. 139–69. The Hague: Mouton.

1978. *Language as social semiotic: the social interpretation of language and meaning*. London: Edward Arnold.

1979. Differences between spoken and written language: some implications for literacy teaching. In *Communication through reading: Proceedings of the 4th Australian Reading Conference*, vol. 2, ed. by Glenda Page, John Elkins, and Barrie O'Connor, pp. 37–52. Adelaide, S.A.: Australian Reading Association.

Halliday, Michael A.K., and Ruqaiya Hasan. 1976. *Cohesion in English*. London: Longman.

Halpern, Jeanne W. 1984. Differences between speaking and writing and their implications for teaching. *College Composition and Communication* 35:345–57.

Harris, Mary M. 1977. Oral and written syntax attainment of second graders. *Research in the Teaching of English* 11:117–32.

Havelock, Eric A. 1963. *Preface to Plato*. Cambridge, Mass.: Harvard University Press.

Heath, Shirley Brice. 1982a. Protean shapes in literacy events: ever-shifting oral and literate traditions. In *Spoken and written language: exploring orality and literacy*, ed. by D. Tannen, pp. 91–117. Norwood, N.J.: Ablex.

1982b. What no bedtime story means: narrative skills at home and school. *Language in Society* 11:49–76.

1983. *Ways with words*. Cambridge: Cambridge University Press.

Hermeren, Lars. 1986. Modalities in spoken and written English: an inventory of forms. In *English in speech and writing: a symposium*, ed. by G. Tottie and I. Bäcklund, pp. 57–92. Studia Anglistica Upsaliensia 60. Stockholm: Almqvist and Wiksell.

Hillocks, George. 1986. *Research on written composition*. Urbana, Ill.: ERIC Clearinghouse on Reading and Communication Skills.

Hinofotis, Frances B. 1983. The structure of oral communication in an educational environment: a comparison of factor analytic rotational procedures. In *Issues in language testing research*, ed. by J.W. Oller, pp. 170–87. Rowley, Mass.: Newbury House.

Holmes, Janet. 1984. Hedging your bets and sitting on the fence: some evidence for hedges as support structures. *Te Reo* 27:47–62.

Horowitz, Milton W., and John B. Newman. 1964. Spoken and written expression: an experimental analysis. *Journal of Abnormal and Social Psychology* 68:640–7.

Householder, Fred W. 1964. *Adjectives before 'that'-clauses in English*. Bloomington, Ind.: Indiana University Linguistics Club.

1971. *Linguistic speculations*. Cambridge: Cambridge University Press.

Hu, Zhuang-Lin. 1984. Differences in mode. *Journal of Pragmatics* 8:595–606.

Hymes, Dell H. 1972. On communicative competence. In *Sociolinguistics*, ed. by J.B. Pride and Janet Holmes, pp. 269–93. Baltimore: Penguin Books.

1974. *Foundations in sociolinguistics*. Philadelphia: University of Pennsylvania Press.

Irvine, Judith. 1984/1979. Formality and informality in communicative events. In *Language in use: readings in sociolinguistics*, ed. by John Baugh and Joel Sherzer, pp. 211–28. Englewood Cliffs, N.J.: Prentice-Hall.

Janda, Richard D. 1985. Note-taking as a simplified register. *Discourse Processes* 8:437–54.

Johansson, Stig (ed.). 1982. *Computer corpora in English language research.* Bergen: Norwegian Computing Centre for the Humanities.

Johansson, Stig, Geoffrey N. Leech, and Helen Goodluck. 1978. *Manual of information to accompany the Lancaster–Oslo/Bergen Corpus of British English, for use with digital computers.* Department of English, University of Oslo.

Kay, Paul. 1977. Language evolution and speech style. In *Sociocultural dimensions of language change*, ed. by Ben G. Blount and Mary Sanches, pp. 21–33. New York: Academic Press.

Kochman, Thomas. 1981. *Black and white styles in conflict.* Chicago: University of Chicago Press.

Kroch, Anthony S. 1978. Toward a theory of social dialect variation. *Language in Society* 7:17–36.

Kroch, Anthony S., and Donald M. Hindle. 1982. A quantitative study of the syntax of speech and writing. Final Report to the National Institute of Education.

Kroch, Anthony S., and C. Small. 1978. Grammatical ideology and its effect on speech. In *Linguistic variation: models and methods*, ed. by David Sankoff, pp. 45–55. New York: Academic Press.

Kroll, Barbara. 1977. Ways communicators encode propositions in spoken and written English: a look at subordination and coordination. In *Discourse across time and space (SCOPIL no. 5)*, ed. by Elinor O. Keenan and Tina Bennett, pp. 69–108. Los Angeles: University of Southern California.

Kurzon, Dennis. 1985. Signposts for the reader: a corpus-based study of text deixis. *Text* 5:187–200.

Labov, William. 1972/1969. The logic of nonstandard English. In *Language and social context*, ed. by Paolo Giglioli, pp. 179–215. New York: Penguin Books.

  1972. *Sociolinguistic patterns.* Philadelphia: University of Pennsylvania Press.

  1984. Intensity. In *Meaning, form, and use in context: linguistic applications*, ed. by D. Schiffrin, pp. 43–70. GURT '84. Washington, D.C.: Georgetown University Press.

Lakoff, Robin. 1982a. Some of my favorite writers are literate: the mingling of oral and literate strategies in written communication. In *Spoken and written language: exploring orality and literacy*, ed. by D. Tannen, pp. 239–60. Norwood, N.J.: Ablex.

  1982b. Persuasive discourse and ordinary conversation, with examples from advertising. In *Analyzing discourse: text and talk*, ed. by Deborah Tannen, pp. 25–42. Georgetown: Georgetown University Press.

Liggett, Sarah. 1984. The relationship between speaking and writing: an annotated bibliography. *College Composition and Communication* 35:334–44.

Marckworth, Mary L. and William J. Baker. 1974. A discriminant function analysis of co-variation of a number of syntactic devices in five prose genres. *American Journal of Computational Linguistics, Microfiche 11*.

McClure, Erica, and Esther Geva. 1983. The development of the cohesive use of adversative conjunctions in discourse. *Discourse Processes* 6:411–32.

Michaels, Sarah, and James Collins. 1984. Oral discourse styles: classroom interaction and the acquisition of literacy. In *Coherence in spoken and written discourse*, ed. by Deborah Tannen, pp. 219–44. Norwood, N.J.: Ablex.

Nystrand, Martin (ed.). 1982. *What writers know: the language, process, and structure of written discourse*. New York: Academic Press.

Ochs, Elinor. 1979. Planned and unplanned discourse. In *Discourse and syntax*, ed. by Talmy Givón, pp. 51–80. New York: Academic Press.

O'Donnell, Roy C. 1974. Syntactic differences between speech and writing. *American Speech* 49:102–10.

O'Donnell, Roy C., W.J. Griffin, and R.C. Norris. 1967. A transformational analysis of oral and written grammatical structures in the language of children in grades three, five, and seven. *Journal of Educational Research* 61:36–9.

Oller, John W. (ed.). 1983. *Issues in language testing research*. Rowley, Mass.: Newbury House.

Olson, David R. 1977. From utterance to text: the bias of language in speech and writing. *Harvard Educational Review* 47:257–81.

Olson, David R., and Nancy Torrance. 1981. Learning to meet the requirements of written text: language development in the school years. In *Writing: the nature, development, and teaching of written communication*, vol. 2, ed. by C.H. Frederiksen and J.F. Dominic, pp. 235–55. Hillsdale, N.J.: Lawrence Erlbaum Associates.

Olson, David R., Nancy Torrance, and Angela Hildyard (eds.). 1985. *Literacy, language, and learning: the nature and consequences of reading and writing*. Cambridge: Cambridge University Press.

Ong, Walter J. 1982. *Orality and literacy: the technologizing of the word*. New York: Methuen.

Osgood, Charles E. 1960. Some effects of motivation on style of encoding. In *Style in language*, ed. by Thomas A. Sebeok, pp. 293–306. Cambridge, Mass.: MIT Press.

Pellegrino, M.L. Morra, and A.A. Scopesi. 1978. Oral and written language in children: syntactical development of descriptive language. *International Journal of Psycholinguistics* 5:5–19.

Perera, Katharine. 1986. Language acquisition and writing. In *Language acquisition*, ed. by P. Fletcher and M. Garman, pp. 494–518. Cambridge: Cambridge University Press.

Philips, Susan U. 1983. *The invisible culture: communication in classroom and community on the Warm Springs Indian Reservation*. New York: Longman.

Poole, Millicent E. 1973. A comparison of the factorial structure of written coding patterns for a middle-class and a working-class group. *Language and Speech* 16:93–109.

1979. Social class, sex and linguistic coding. *Language and Speech* 22:49–67.

1983. Socioeconomic status and written language. In *The psychology of written language: developmental and educational perspectives*, ed. by Margaret Martlew, pp. 335–76. New York: John Wiley.

Poole, Millicent E., and T.W. Field. 1976. A comparison of oral and written code elaboration. *Language and Speech* 19:305–11.

Postal, Paul. 1966. Review of M.W. Dixon, *Linguistic science and logic*. *Language* 43:84–93.

Preston, Joan M., and R.C. Gardner. 1967. Dimensions of oral and written fluency. *Journal of Verbal Learning and Verbal Behavior* 6:936–45.

Price, Gayle B., and Richard L. Graves. 1980. Sex differences in syntax and usage in oral and written language. *Research in the Teaching of English* 14:147–53.

Prince, Ellen F. 1981. Toward a taxonomy of given-new information. In *Radical pragmatics*, ed. by Peter Cole, pp. 223–55. New York: Academic Press.

Quirk, Randolph, Sidney Greenbaum, Geoffrey Leech, and Jan Svartvik. 1985. *A comprehensive grammar of the English language*. London: Longman.

Rader, Margaret. 1982. Context in written language: the case of imaginative fiction. In *Spoken and written language: exploring orality and literacy*, ed. by D. Tannen, pp. 185–98. Norwood, N.J.: Ablex.

Redeker, Gisela. 1984. On differences between spoken and written language. *Discourse Processes* 7:43–55.

Rubin, Andee. 1980. A theoretical taxonomy of the differences between oral and written language. In *Theoretical issues in reading comprehension: perspectives from cognitive psychology, linguistics, artificial intelligence, and education*, ed. by Rand J. Spiro, Bertram C. Bruce, and William F. Brewer, pp. 411–38. Hillsdale, N.J.: Lawrence Erlbaum Associates.

Sahlin, Elisabeth. 1979. '*Some*' and '*any*' in spoken and written English. Studia Anglistica Upsaliensia 38. Stockholm: Almqvist and Wiksell.

Sapir, Edward. 1921. *Language*. New York: Harcourt Brace and World.

de Saussure, F. 1916/1959. *Course in general linguistics* (translated by Wade Baskin). New York: Philosophical Library.

Schafer, John C. 1981. The linguistic analysis of spoken and written texts. In *Exploring speaking–writing relationships: connections and contrasts*, ed. by Barry M. Kroll and Roberta J. Vann, pp. 1–31. Urbana, Ill.: National Council of Teachers of English.

Schiffrin, Deborah. 1981. Tense variation in narrative. *Language* 57:45–62.

1982. Discourse markers: semantic resource for the construction of conversation. Unpublished Ph.D. dissertation, University of Pennsylvania.

(ed.). 1984a. *Meaning, form, and use in context: linguistic applications*. GURT '84. Washington, D.C.: Georgetown University Press.

1984b. Jewish argument as sociability. *Language in Society* 13:311–35.

1985a. Conversational coherence: the role of *well*. *Language* 61:640–67.

1985b. Multiple constraints on discourse options: a quantitative analysis of causal sequences. *Discourse Processes* 8:281–303.

Schourup, Lawrence C. 1985. *Common discourse particles in English conversation.* New York: Garland.

Scribner, Sylvia, and Michael Cole. 1981. *The psychology of literacy.* Cambridge, Mass.: Harvard University Press.

Shopen, Timothy. 1985. *Language typology and syntactic description.* Volume 2: *Complex constructions.* Cambridge: Cambridge University Press.

Smith, Frank. 1982. *Writing and the writer.* New York: Holt, Rinehart, and Winston.

Smith, Raoul, and William J. Frawley. 1983. Conjunctive cohesion in four English genres. *Text* 3:347–74.

Stenström, Anna-Brita. 1986. What does *really* really do? Strategies in speech and writing. In *English in speech and writing: a symposium*, ed. by G. Tottie and I. Bäcklund, pp. 149–64. Studia Anglistica Upsaliensia 60. Stockholm: Almqvist and Wiksell.

Street, Brian V. 1984. *Literacy in theory and practice.* Cambridge: Cambridge University Press.

Stubbs, Michael. 1980. *Language and literacy: the sociolinguistics of reading and writing.* London: Routledge and Kegan Paul.

1982. Written language and society: some particular cases and general observations. In *What writers know: the language, process, and structure of written discourse*, ed. by M. Nystrand, pp. 31–55. New York: Academic Press.

Svartvik, Jan, and Randolph Quirk (eds.). *A corpus of English conversation.* Lund: CWK Gleerup.

Tannen, Deborah. 1982a. Oral and literate strategies in spoken and written narratives. *Language* 58:1–21.

1982b. The oral/literate continuum in discourse. In *Spoken and written language: exploring orality and literacy*, ed. by D. Tannen, pp. 1–16. Norwood, N.J.: Ablex.

1982c. The myth of orality and literacy. In *Linguistics and literacy*, ed. by William Frawley, pp. 37–50. New York: Plenum Press.

(ed.). 1982d. *Spoken and written language: exploring orality and literacy.* Norwood, N.J.: Ablex.

1985. Relative focus on involvement in oral and written discourse. In *Literacy, language, and learning: the nature and consequences of reading and writing*, ed. by D.R. Olson, N. Torrance, and A. Hildyard, pp. 124–47. Cambridge: Cambridge University Press.

Thompson, Sandra A. 1982. The passive in English: a discourse perspective. Unpublished ms.

1983. Grammar and discourse: the English detached participial clause. In *Discourse perspectives on syntax*, ed. by Flora Klein-Andreu, pp. 43–65. New York: Academic Press.

1984. 'Subordination' in formal and informal discourse. In *Meaning, form, and use in context: linguistic applications*, ed. by D. Schiffrin, pp. 85–94. GURT '84. Washington, D.C.: Georgetown University Press.

1985. Grammar and written discourse: initial vs final purpose clauses in English. *Text* 5:55–84.

Thompson, Sandra A., and Robert E. Longacre. 1985. Adverbial clauses. In *Language typology and syntactic description*, vol. 2, ed. by T. Shopen, pp. 171–233. Cambridge: Cambridge University Press.

Tomlin, Russell S. 1985. Foreground–background information and the syntax of subordination. *Text* 5:85–122.

Tottie, Gunnel. 1981. Negation and discourse strategy in spoken and written English. In *Variation omnibus*, ed. by H. Cedergren and D. Sankoff, pp. 271–84. Edmonton, Alberta: Linguistic Research.

1982. Where do negative sentences come from? *Studia Linguistica* 36:88–105.

1983a. *Much about 'not' and 'nothing': a study of the variation between analytic and synthetic negation in contemporary American English.* Lund: CWK Gleerup.

1983b. The missing link? Or, why is there twice as much negation in spoken English as in written English? (Proceedings from the Second Scandinavian Symposium on Syntactic Variation, ed. by S. Jacobson). *Stockholm Studies in English* 62:67–74.

1984. Is there an adverbial in this text? (And if so, what is it doing there?) In *Proceedings from the Second Nordic Conference for English Studies*, ed. by Hakan Ringbom and Matti Rissanen, pp. 299–315. Abo, Norway: Abo Akademi Foundation.

1985. The negation of epistemic necessity in present-day British and American English. *English World-Wide* 6:87–116.

1986. The importance of being adverbial: focusing and contingency adverbials in spoken and written English. In *English in speech and writing: a symposium*, ed. by G. Tottie and I. Bäcklund, pp. 93–118. Studia Anglistica Upsaliensia 60. Stockholm: Almqvist and Wiksell.

Tottie, Gunnel, Bengt Altenberg, and Lars Hermeren. 1983. *English in speech and writing* (ETOS Report 1). Lund: Engelska Institutionen.

Tottie, Gunnel, and Gerd Övergaard. 1984. The author's *would*: a feature of American English. *Studia Linguistica* 38:148–65.

Tottie, Gunnel, and Ingegerd Bäcklund (eds.). 1986. *English in speech and writing: a symposium.* Studia Anglistica Upsaliensia 60. Stockholm: Almqvist and Wiksell.

Vachek, Josef. 1973. *Written language: general problems and problems of English.* The Hague: Mouton.

1979. Some remarks on the stylistics of written language. In *Function and context in linguistic analysis*, ed. by D.J. Allerton, Edward Carney, and David Holdcroft, pp. 206–15. Cambridge: Cambridge University Press.

Vygotsky, L.S. 1962/1934. *Thought and language.* Cambridge, Mass.: MIT Press.

Weber, Elizabeth G. 1985. From feelings to knowledge: verbs of cognition. Paper presented at NWAVE XIV, Georgetown.

Weiner, E. Judith, and William Labov. 1983. Constraints on the agentless passive. *Journal of Linguistics* 19:29–58.

Wells, Gordon. 1985. Preschool literacy-related activities and success in school. In *Literacy, language, and learning: the nature and consequences of reading and writing*, ed. by D.R. Olson, N. Torrance and A. Hildyard, pp. 229–54. Cambridge: Cambridge University Press.

Wells, Rulon. 1960. Nominal and verbal style. In *Style in language*, ed. by Thomas A. Sebeok, pp. 213–20. Cambridge, Mass: MIT Press.

Widdowson, David. 1979. The process and purpose of reading. In *Explorations in applied linguistics*, ed. by David Widdowson, pp. 173–81. New York: Oxford University Press.

Williams, Joseph M. 1980. Non-linguistic linguistics and the teaching of style. *Language and Style* 13:24–40.

Winter, Eugene. 1982. *Towards a contextual grammar of English: the clause and its place in the definition of sentence.* London: George Allen and Unwin.

Young, George M. 1985. The development of logic and focus in children's writing. *Language and Speech* 28:115–27.

Zipf, G.K. 1949. *Human behavior and the principle of least effort.* Cambridge, Mass: Addison-Wesley.

Index

abstractness, 47, 50, 112–13, 119, 151ff, 227, 228
  cf. detachment
academic lectures – *see* speeches
academic prose
  as typical writing, 37, 44–6, 161–2
  compared to official documents, 178
  frequencies of all linguistic features, 255
  linguistic and functional characteristics, 57–8, 152–3
  relations among sub-genres, 182–3, 185–90, 192–5
  situational characteristics, 38–42, 44–6, 70–1
  sub-genres, 68–9
  variation within, 171–80, 202–3
adjectives, 50–1, 104, 109, 111–12, 114, 139–41, 237–8
adverbial clauses – *see* subordination
adverbs
  place adverbials, 105, 110, 147, 224
  time adverbials, 110, 147, 224
  general adverbs, 50, 110, 114, 237–8
affect, 105, 106, 107, 114, 131ff
  cf. stance
Akinnaso, 48, 51, 53
algorithms – *see* computer programs
Altenberg, 236, 240
amplifiers, 106, 240
argumentative discourse, 111, 148–51
attitudes, expression of – *see* stance

be as main verb, 106, 229
Beaman, 50, 51, 53, 54, 229–30, 231, 232, 234
Besnier, 53, 205–6
Biber (1986) model of variation, 56–8
  comparison of dimensions to present model, 115–20
  comparison of computer programs to present analysis, 212–13
  comparison of linguistic features to present analysis, 221

biographies
  frequencies of all linguistic features, 253
Blankenship, 49, 50, 51
broadcasts
  frequencies of all linguistic features, 267
  linguistic and functional characteristics, 57–8, 134–5, 138–41, 145–7, 151
  multi-dimensional characterization, 164–9
  relations among sub-genres, 183–4, 185–90, 196–7
  situational characteristics, 71
  sub-genres, 68–9
  variation within, 171–80
Brown and Fraser, 21, 28–9, 34, 227

Carroll, 61–2
causative adverbial clauses – *see* subordination
Chafe, 21, 33, 42, 43–4, 48, 104, 108, 113, 224, 225, 226, 227, 237, 238, 240, 241, 242, 243, 244, 245
complement clauses – *see* subordination
complexity, 47–8, 49, 50, 229
  discourse, 202
composition research, 203–4
computer programs for grammatical analysis, 211–21
  algorithms for individual features, 221–45
  evaluation of, 217, 220
  grammatical categories used in, 214
  notation for algorithms, 222–3
  overview, 211–13
  resolution of grammatical ambiguities, 215–17
  sample output, 218–19
computerized text corpora, 65–6, 208–10
  Brown corpus, 66
  LOB corpus, 66
  London–Lund corpus, 66

293